IMAGINING BLACK AMERICA

IMAGINING BLACK AMERICA

★ ★ ★

Michael Wayne

Yale UNIVERSITY PRESS • *New Haven and London*

Published with assistance from the income of
the Frederick John Kingsbury Memorial Fund,
and from the foundation established in memory of James
Wesley Cooper of the class of 1865, Yale College.

Yale University Press books may be purchased in quantity
for educational, business, or promotional use. For
information, please e-mail sales.press@yale.edu (U.S. office)
or sales@yaleup.co.uk (U.K. office).

Printed in the United States of America.

Library of Congress Cataloging-in-Publication Data

Wayne, Michael, 1947–
Imagining Black America / Michael Wayne.
pages cm
Includes bibliographical references and index.
ISBN 978-0-300-19781-5 (hardback)
1. African Americans—Race identity—History. 2. Race
awareness—United States—History. 3. Race—Philosophy.
4. United States—Race relations—History. I. Title.
E185.625.W39 2014
305.896'073–dc23   2013033551

A catalogue record for this book is available from the
British Library.
This paper meets the requirements of ANSI/NISO
Z39.48-1992 (Permanence of Paper).

10 9 8 7 6 5 4 3 2 1

*To the students in HIS408Y and HIS476H
and to the memory of Claire Clarke*

Contents

A Personal Introduction

This is a study about nation and race in the making of identity. Or to be precise: a study about nation and race in the making of the *ascribed public identity* and the *self-identity* of Americans of African descent. And to be more precise still: a study about nation and race in the making of the *ascribed public identity* and the *self-identity* of Americans with *greater or lesser degrees* of African descent. It is based, overwhelmingly, on investigations by other scholars. But the course I chart is an independent one, designed to invite new ways of thinking about the meaning of race in the American past, and in the American present as well. If the questions I ask and the connections I draw at times lead me away from well-marked paths of scholarly debate, that may be because my background is rather unusual for someone writing on the black experience in the United States.

I was born and raised in Toronto, Canada. There were no black children in the overwhelmingly Jewish neighborhood where my family lived and none in the elementary school or high school I attended. So far as I can recall, I only ever encountered one person of African ancestry during the early years of my life, a woman from the West Indies who did the cleaning in my grandmother's apartment. My grandmother, born in eastern Europe and reflecting the all-too-common prejudices of her generation and social set, referred to the woman by the demeaning term "the schwartze."

I did have one occasion to see large numbers of black Americans during these impressionable years, though at a distance. It was when I was eleven or twelve. My father, one half of the celebrated Canadian comedy team of Wayne and Shuster, had begun to make regular appearances on the *Ed Sullivan Show.* On rare weekends—very special weekends for my brothers and me—my mother would take us down to New York so we could see the show, which aired live on Sunday nights. Ordinarily we traveled by plane, but on one occasion she decided to treat us with a trip on an overnight train. Two memories from that train ride have remained with me through the years. The first is waking up, looking out the window, and finding that we were racing along beside the Hudson River. The second, and much more important for where I am heading here, is coming into what I now realize was Harlem and passing block upon block of black men, women, and children. I had a few friends from the United States in those days, boys and girls from Buffalo, Cleveland, Cincinnati, and Detroit who, like me, spent their summer holidays at Camp Arowhon in northern Ontario. But their grandparents, like mine, were Jewish immigrants from eastern Europe. I didn't think of them, my friends, as real Americans. To me, the black people I saw from the window of the train, now, they were *real* Americans. How my pre-teen self arrived at that conclusion I can't say. Like most boys my age, I was preoccupied with sports, so maybe it was because many of the baseball stars in the 1950s—many stars of "America's game"—were black: Jackie Robinson, Willie Mays, Roy Campanella, Don Newcombe.[1]

In 1965, I entered the University of Toronto. Two years later I transferred to Amherst College in Massachusetts, arriving at the very end of the summer of 1967, marked by its explosion of what were then called "urban race riots." The following April, just weeks before my twenty-first birthday, Martin Luther King, Jr. was assassinated. On the evening of that fateful day, I joined other Amherst students, and, linked arm-in-arm, we marched to the center of town singing "We Shall Overcome." When we reached the village green, we found students from the University of Massachusetts already there, as well as some local residents. Two or three people stepped forward to make impromptu speeches. Then, suddenly, a young black man I did not recognize emerged from the crowd and shouted that all the whites should "Go home!" "You killed him!" he screamed. "You killed him!" Shortly after that, the gathering broke up.

It was the early days of Black Power. Black students at the college had recently taken to eating by themselves in the dining hall. In the following months they would demand creation of a Black Studies program and a black culture center. It was widely taken for granted on the campus, as across the United States, that there existed a profound divide between whites and blacks, perhaps an unbridgeable divide. And me, I was bewildered. The black students, the white students, they seemed so alike to me. They seemed so *American*. So different from Canadians.

That was almost half a century ago. Since then, through all my years of researching, writing, and teaching the history of the United States, I have never found reason to think that black Americans are somehow less truly, less completely, American than white Americans. Quite the contrary, in the pages that follow I will argue that black Americans are *quintessential* Americans: that their presence as slaves at the founding of the nation gave definition to the ideals advanced by the Founding Fathers, and that no element of the population has had more reason to look forward to—and to commit itself to bringing about—the day when those ideals would be fully realized. But then, no other Americans have known what it means to come "up from slavery."[2]

★

Call my Amherst experience the first entry point into the development of this book. The second goes back to my days as a graduate student at Yale. My dissertation, written under C. Vann Woodward, distinguished historian of the American South, was a study of the planting elite of the Natchez district during the Civil War and Reconstruction. When I began my research, I thought most of my time would be devoted to tracing the planters' struggles to hold on to their land, and to their power. I discovered, instead, that the single most significant challenge they faced was adjusting to the changed status of their black laborers. Because the planters believed that people of different races had different inherent attributes, it took them considerable time fully to accept that the freed slaves would respond to market incentives in the same way as white laborers. During those years, freedmen and freedwomen were able to exploit the uncertainty of their former owners, and the shortage of labor, not only to improve their material circumstances but also to win a measure of autonomy unimaginable under the old regime.[3]

Subsequently, questions about racial ideology moved to the forefront of my intellectual horizon. And when I began teaching, I decided to offer a seminar on the history of black-white relations in the United States. It was the early 1980s, a time when scientists were turning out sophisticated studies demonstrating that conventional racial categories effectively have no meaning in biological terms. I decided it would be a good idea to assign students some of the more accessible literature on population genetics at the beginning of the semester. During the weeks that followed, I would occasionally ask them to consider how the scientific findings might require us to look at the history of American race relations with new eyes.

I had been offering the seminar for just a year or two when the historians Michael Johnson and James Roark published a groundbreaking biographical study that proved especially valuable for the kind of discussion I wanted to foster. *Black Masters* charts the life of a remarkable man named William Ellison, born a slave in antebellum South Carolina and trained to be a mechanic by his owner (who was probably either his father or half-brother). Allowed to buy his freedom at the age of twenty-five, he quickly gained a reputation as a skilled ginwright, enjoying so much success that he eventually earned enough money to acquire a plantation. And to acquire slaves, more than sixty in total. It appears that whenever he wanted to raise capital to expand his operations, he resorted to the sale of young girls. In time he was admitted to two associations in Charleston that restricted membership to the tiny fraction of individuals of mixed European and African ancestry who lived in much more comfortable circumstances than the great majority of white Southerners. And to protect the social standing of his family, he saw to it that his children married within that very select social circle.[4]

I took separate but related lessons from the scientific literature and the story of William Ellison. First, from the scientific literature: it is imperative to resist the widely held assumption that races are natural—permanent or near-permanent—divisions of humanity. Second, from the story of William Ellison: it should not be assumed that different groups of Americans with African ancestry have always (or ever) perceived the boundaries and defining characteristics of their racial community in the same way. Those lessons informed my teaching over the following decades and they have shaped the questions about race and identity that I ask in this book.

They have also dictated the racial terminology I use throughout the text, and that requires an explanation involving a bit of foreshadowing. When African slaves were first brought to the British colonies, they were called "Negroes." When slaves had sexual relations with British and Irish colonists, their children were called "mulattoes." Gradually the color-coded noun "Negroes" came to be used as an umbrella term covering all persons with African ancestry. But through the colonial era and for more than a century after the founding of the United States, the assumption persisted that there was an important distinction—a "racial" distinction—between "mulattoes" and people of pure African descent. During those years, individuals whose appearance suggested that they belonged to the latter group—to the population of pure African ancestry—were commonly referred to as "blacks."[5] By the first decades of the twentieth century, a clear majority of Americans with African ancestry also had some European ancestry, and the implementation of the notorious "one-drop rule" effectively declared that in the eyes of the state, "blacks" and "mulattoes" represented a single racial category. "Negroes" remained the preferred term for identifying men, women, and children assigned to that category—preferred by the state but also preferred by most individuals of African descent themselves. In view of this history of racial classification, in Part 2, which covers the almost two centuries from the founding of the nation to the dawn of the Civil Rights Era, I too use the term "Negroes" to refer to Americans whose family tree is known to include one or more Africans. It would be misleading to call such people "blacks" since, again, the noun had a meaning different in those days than it would come to have in the 1960s. In the remaining chapters, covering the past half century, I drop the term "Negroes" in favor of "blacks" in recognition of the change in attitude that took place during the Civil Rights Era regarding what was a respectful form of address.[6]

A WORD ABOUT RACE

To begin with, some basic biology. Human beings share fully 99.5 percent of our DNA. In other words, the individual differences between us—in height and weight, in skin color, in hair texture—are shaped by a mere 0.5 percent of our genetic material. In 1972, the evolutionary geneticist Richard Lewontin examined data on blood groups and proteins to determine how that 0.5 percent was distributed across populations. He looked at local entities such as tribes; at races, as they were commonly defined at the time; and at groups intermediate between the two. He found that, on average, a mere 6 percent of all genetic variation could be apportioned to race. By contrast, 85 percent of the variation existed within the smallest of the three groups (tribes and so forth). "That means," he, Steven Rose, and Leon Kamin explained in a later work, "that the genetic variation between one Spaniard and another, or between one Masai and another, is 85 percent of all human genetic variation. . . . If everyone on earth became extinct except for the Kikuyu of East Africa, about 85 percent of all human variability would still be present in the reconstituted species." For more than two centuries, most scientists had believed that race was a real—a natural—biological division of humanity (even if they had never agreed on the boundaries for, or total number of, racial categories). Lewontin's landmark article signaled that a radical change in thinking was under way.[1]

During the 1980s, advances in technology allowed researchers to extend their investigations beyond blood groups and proteins to DNA itself. The new generation of studies, while producing statistics that differed marginally from those derived by Lewontin, almost without exception confirmed his fundamental conclusion: even local populations of relatively modest size contain an overwhelming majority of human genetic diversity. Conventional racial categories explain very little.[2]

In 1994, Luigi Luca Cavalli-Sforza, Paolo Menozzi, and Alberto Piazza completed a fourteen-year-long analysis of what was by then extensive research on genetic variation. Their justly acclaimed *The History and Geography of Human Genes* sought to map the contours of human evolution and migration by linking the genetic evidence to findings in physical anthropology, archeology, historical demography, and, especially, linguistics. They concluded that because humankind has been in existence for a comparatively short period of time, because migration has been a constant feature of our history, and because a great many individuals have (whether willingly or not) taken sexual partners from outside their local populations, conditions have not existed for the development of large divisions of humanity with fundamentally different genetic profiles. Physical traits change gradually across the face of the globe. "The classification into races has proved to be a futile exercise. . . . Whatever genetic boundaries may have developed . . . there probably never were any sharp ones, or if there were, they were blurred by later movements."[3]

Today the great majority of biologists and anthropologists would agree that past attempts to order humanity according to racial divisions have grossly exaggerated the meaning of a small number of visible characteristics (skin color, hair, facial features). In 1998 the executive board of the American Anthropological Association issued a "Statement on Race" that expresses the prevailing opinion:

> In the United States both scholars and the general public have been conditioned to viewing human races as natural and separate divisions within the human species based on visible physical differences. With the vast expansion of scientific knowledge in this century, however, it has become clear that human populations are not unambiguous, clearly demarcated, biologically distinct groups. . . . In neighboring populations there is much overlapping of genes and their phenotypic (physical) expressions. Throughout history whenever different groups have come into contact, they have interbred. The continued sharing of genetic materials has maintained all of humankind as a single species. Physical variations in any given trait tend to occur gradually rather than abruptly over geographic areas. And because physical traits are inherited independently of one another, knowing the range of one trait does not predict the presence of others. For example, skin color varies largely from light in the temperate areas in the

north to dark in the tropical areas in the south; its intensity is not related to nose shape or hair texture. Dark skin may be associated with frizzy or kinky hair or curly or wavy or straight hair, all of which are found among different indigenous peoples in tropical regions. These facts render any attempt to establish lines of division among biological populations both arbitrary and subjective.[4]

One other thing, and this is of particular relevance for the pages that follow: as numerous studies have now demonstrated, there is far greater genetic diversity within Africa than across the rest of the planet. That diversity finds expression in striking differences between African populations in stature, facial features, and, notably, skin color. Under the circumstances, any claims that there exists a single "black race" cannot be taken seriously.[5]

PART 1 • COLONIAL ORIGINS

★ ★ ★

1 • Birth of a Race

If "black" is a term devoid of biological meaning, then how are we to understand race? Scholars in recent decades have labeled it a "myth," a "fiction," an "invention," an "illusion," a "delusion," a "chimera," and, sardonically, a "four-letter word." Most commonly, though, they refer to it as a "social construct." Indeed, it has become almost obligatory for anyone writing on the history of American race relations to include a statement acknowledging that racial categories are shaped by social context, above all the distribution of power and privilege in society. Logically, then, we should expect racial classification to be unstable, subject to change over time as social conditions change. Too often, however, historians fall into the trap of treating races as if they are fixed—as if, in other words, they are, indeed, biological divisions of humanity. Consider the following passage from Eric Foner's acclaimed textbook *Give Me Liberty! An American History:* "In 1619, the first twenty blacks arrived in Virginia on a Dutch vessel." The perhaps not immediately obvious question we need to ask is: In what sense were the individuals Foner refers to "blacks"?[1]

There are two surviving references to them in records from the period. John Smith commented in his *Generall Historie of Virginia:* "About the last of August came in a Dutch man of warre that sold us twenty Negars." And John Rolfe wrote to a friend: "About the latter end of August, a Dutch man of Warr of the burden of a 160 tunnes arrived at Point-Comfort, the Commandors name Capt Jope, his Pilott for the West Indies one Mr Marmaduke an Englishmen. They met wth the Trier in the West Indyes, and determined to hold consort ship hitherward, but in their passage lost one the other. He brought not any thing but 20. and odd Negroes, wch the Governor and Cape Marchant bought for

victualle (whereof he was in greate need as he pretended) at the best and easiest rate they could."[2]

Leaving aside for a moment the question of what Smith and Rolfe meant
by the term "Negro," let's address the issue of how the "20. and odd" individuals identified themselves. Thanks to some inspired sleuthing by the historian
Engel Sluiter, we can now say something about the circumstances that brought
them to Virginia. They were originally part of a consignment of slaves bound
for Vera Cruz from Angola aboard the Portuguese ship *São João Bautista*. English pirates intercepted the vessel near the coast of Mexico and carried off
most of its slave cargo. Later, likely by prior agreement, they met up with a
man-of-war from the Netherlands and turned over an undetermined number
of the hijacked slaves. It was this Dutch ship that finally transported the "20.
and odd Negroes" to Virginia.[3]

Additional detective work by John Thornton has provided us with further
information: probably most if not all of the captives were victims of a major military campaign in 1618–19 mounted by the Portuguese against the Kingdom of
Ndongo. The enslavement operation was actually carried out by the Imbangala,
a fearsome "quasi-religious" African "cult." While it is ordinarily quite difficult
to determine how men and women swept up in the slave trade identified themselves, Thornton is able, in this case, to offer informed speculation: "People in
seventeenth century Ndongo had primary political loyalties connected to local
territories, called xi in Kimbundu, which were ruled by the sobas. Within the
area of the 1618–1619 campaigns, people in the royal districts considered themselves 'people of the court' (thus serving the king as a soba) . . . and subjects of
Ndongo, whereas those living farther away might have taken their loyalty to
the soba as equally important as their loyalty to the king. . . . [Residents of the
area] also had a larger and vaguer identity as those who spoke Kimbundu . . .
Kimbundu speakers [referred to themselves] as the 'Ambundu people.'"[4]

In other words, the individuals who ended up in Virginia may have identified
themselves with a ruler or a political unit or a geographical region or, given what
Thornton has to say about language, a cultural or perhaps ethnic group. Common sense suggests that they also identified with their immediate or extended
families. But there is no suggestion that they defined themselves by reference to
the color of their skin, that they thought of themselves as "Negroes," as "blacks."[5]

Of course, they still faced the trauma of the Middle Passage. They likely
spent weeks, or perhaps months, together in a slave pen in Luanda. Afterward,
there would have been extended time aboard the *São João Bautista*, first off the
coast of Africa while the crew added to its stock of provisions, and finally dur-

ing the transatlantic crossing. Then they fell into the hands of the pirates. No doubt their many trials caused them to wonder about the relevance of their traditional attachments. This might well have been a period when they began to ask whether skin color carried some significance they had not previously recognized. Still, the Imbangala, who subdued them, were physically much like themselves. And Portuguese captains customarily sought to reduce the likelihood of shipboard rebellion by privileging particular slaves. So there is little likelihood that the "20. and odd Negroes" would have suddenly concluded that skin color was the central determinant of identity. If Michael Gomez is correct, the principal result of the "shared experience in suffering" that slaves endured during the transatlantic crossing was the formation of close bonds between shipmates. But close bonds between shipmates do not equate to race consciousness. Some of the enslaved men who stepped on shore at James-town in 1619 may have been ancestors of blacks. But they were not blacks themselves. To impose an identity on them that they would have rejected is, at the very least, anachronistic.[6]

Yes, race is a social construct. But as these last comments should make clear, it is something more than that as well. The process of race formation does not take place mechanistically. A given labor system, a given demography, does not automatically give rise to a particular set of racial beliefs. Human imagination plays a mediating role. Races have to be imagined into existence. And racial identity has to be imagined as well—and constantly reimagined, as circumstances change over time. After all, races too are "imagined communities," to borrow the term Benedict Anderson has so usefully applied to nations.[7]

★

No work has had more influence in shaping how historians understand the origins of American race consciousness than *White over Black: American Attitudes toward the Negro, 1550–1812*, by Winthrop Jordan. It is, as many reviewers have proclaimed, a magisterial piece of scholarship. But the book, published in 1968, was a product of thinking about race that is now outdated. When he wrote it, Jordan believed that race was a real biological category. In an appendix entitled "Note on the Concept of Race," he observed, "Human groups which differ markedly in appearance also differ genetically. One of the most important recent breakthroughs has been the concept of *race* as a group of individuals sharing a common gene pool." He even referred to races as "incipient species," although he acknowledged that circumstances allowing human speciation to take place were unlikely ever to come into existence.[8]

This understanding of race clearly influenced the way in which Jordan struc-
tured his famous work. While he was well aware that cultural factors significantly influenced how the English perceived the peoples they encountered on
the coast of Africa, he chose to begin by looking at what he called "the most
arresting characteristic" of the Africans, their skin color. He continued: "Long
before they found that some men were black, Englishmen found in the idea of
blackness a way of expressing some of their most ingrained values. No other
color except white conveyed so much emotional impact. As described by the
Oxford English Dictionary, the meaning of black before the sixteenth century
included 'Deeply stained with dirt; soiled, dirty, foul. . . . Having dark or deadly
purposes, malignant; pertaining to or involving death, deadly; baneful, disas-
trous, sinister. . . . Foul, iniquitous, atrocious, horrible, wicked. . . . Indicating
disgrace, censure, liability to punishment, etc.'"[9]

It was a provocative opening suggesting that when the first English colonists arrived in North America, they believed that personal attributes and human
worth could be deduced from skin color. It helped spawn a massive literature
dealing with the issue of whether the color associations drawn by the English
represented a new direction in the history of Western thought. This has been
a very fruitful line of inquiry, but the assumption Jordan made about the underlying biological reality of race has had unfortunate consequences for our
understanding of black Americans as an imagined community. By representing race as something that was discovered rather than invented, he has given
a significant measure of legitimacy to the view that the early colonists looked
on all individuals with African ancestry as members of a fundamental, and
distinct, division of humanity identifiable by skin color. There are, however,
good reasons to think otherwise.[10]

Consider, for example, the meaning that seventeenth-century colonists attached to "Negro." On the face of it, this term, borrowed from the Spanish,
would seem to establish the primacy of color as the determinant of group
identity. But as James Sweet has pointed out, on the Iberian Peninsula "Negro"
connoted slave status as well as dark skin. Indeed, he notes, "the Portuguese
utilized the term 'Negro' to imply slave status, regardless of skin color." It is
true that English colonists on the Chesapeake limited "Negro" to Africans and
the descendants of Africans. But for much of the seventeenth century they
seem to have used it principally as a synonym for slaves. For example, a Virginia law from 1639 required "all persons except negroes to be provided with
arms and amunition [sic]." The clear intent of the law was to ensure that every
free man, Africans included, was prepared to defend the colony in the event of

an Indian attack. It was only during the eighteenth century that the House of Burgesses barred all people of African ancestry from owning weapons. But most telling are two phrases that appeared regularly in the statutes of Maryland and, to a somewhat lesser extent, Virginia: "Negroes and other slaves" and "Negroes or other slaves." Here are two examples. In September 1664, the Assembly in Maryland passed "An Act Concerning Negroes & other Slaves." "Bee itt Enacted," the statute read, "that all Negroes or other slaues already within the Prouince And all Negroes and other slaues to bee hereafter imported into the Prouince shall serue Durante Vita." A Virginia law of 1692 entitled "An act for the more speedy prosecution of slaves committing Capitall Crimes" carried the following preamble: "Whereas a speedy prosecution of negroes and other slaves for capital offences is absolutely necessary . . ."[11]

Now, there were free people of African descent in the colonies at the time, as lawmakers were well aware. Some small number may have arrived as indentured servants, but the great majority were either slaves who had been granted or allowed to purchase their freedom, or children or grandchildren of former slaves. They did not operate under legal disabilities during most of the seventeenth century. Masters who freed slaves in their wills seem to have expected that they would become "regular members of the free community." And as a number of scholars have shown, skin color was apparently rarely a factor in court decisions.[12]

Two centuries later, in the decades leading up to the Civil War, apologists for slavery in the South would argue that anyone with African ancestry was by nature suited for bondage. But in the seventeenth century, the phrase "Negroes and other slaves" did not signify that black skin was considered the outward expression of a servile nature. It was simply an acknowledgment that an overwhelming majority of slaves were, in fact, people of African descent. Almost certainly, when John Rolfe wrote to a friend that a Dutch captain had sold "20. and odd Negroes" in Jamestown, the main information he wanted to convey was that there were now slave laborers in the colony. Their physical appearance was intriguing no doubt, but not of primary interest. In the first decades of settlement in the Chesapeake, biology—or, to be more accurate, skin color—was not considered destiny.[13]

★

Religion, on the other hand, *was* destiny. Or more properly in the case of the slaves, irreligion. What made Africans suitable for slavery in the minds of colonists was not their supposed inherent nature, but their heathenism. Africa was, as far as the English could see, a continent empty of religion, ignorant of God and His precepts. Logically, then, someone with black skin was very likely a heathen. And heathens were deserving of enslavement.[14]

In the first decades of settlement, some slaves were able to gain freedom by demonstrating that they had been baptized. To protect their property interests, planters in Virginia in 1667, and Maryland in 1671, secured the passage of legislation stipulating that any slave who took instruction in Christianity and received the sacraments would remain a slave. Not all slaveowners were reassured, however. In 1704 and again in 1715, the Maryland Assembly felt compelled to pass laws reiterating the principle set down in 1671. "Many people," the statutes noted, "have neglected to baptize their Negroes or Suffer them to be baptized on a vain Apprehension that Negroes by receiving the Sacrament of Baptism are manumitted and sett free."[15] Nor, for that matter, did slaves themselves believe that the question had necessarily been settled. As late as the 1690s, individual bondsmen were still bringing forward petitions requesting freedom on the grounds that they had been baptized. Furthermore, in the 1730s a rumor spread among slaves in a corner of Virginia that local authorities were ignoring orders from Parliament to free all Christians. This rumor led to "a widespread, narrowly averted revolt."[16]

There is general agreement among historians that colonists found the presumed godlessness of Africans their most troubling characteristic. Winthrop Jordan himself stated that "for Englishmen settling in America, the specific religious difference [between Christian and heathen] was initially of greater importance than color." But Jordan and others have failed to appreciate the degree to which, as Colin Kidd has recently and very skillfully demonstrated, theological dictates undercut the development of race consciousness. Scripture was the ultimate authority. And Scripture taught that all human beings, no matter how divergent their bodily characteristics, traced their ancestry back to Noah. To suggest that the physical distinctions between Africans and English had some profound meaning, Kidd points out, "was to risk courting accusations of heresy."[17]

During the first decades of settlement through the 1660s, the legislatures of Virginia and Maryland brought forward few statutes explicitly directed at individuals of African descent. Those they did enact reveal no notable antipathy or fear. Historians who believe that racism, or at least something approximating it, arrived in the colonies with the earliest settlers explain this apparent discrepancy by arguing that "Negroes" were too few to warrant the attention of the authorities. But an element of the population even less numerically significant provoked panic among Chesapeake legislators. These "vnreasonable and turbulent sort of people," the Virginia House of Burgesses declared in 1660, "do dayly gather together vnto them vnlaw'll Assemblies and congregations of people teaching and publishing, lies, miracles, false visions, prophecies and doctrines, which have influence vpon the comunities of men both ecclesiasticall and civil endeavouring and attemping thereby to destroy religion, lawes, comunities and all bonds of civil societie, leaving it arbitrarie to everie vaine and vitious person whether men shall be safe, lawes established, offenders punished, and Governours rule." The individuals referred to did not have dark skin, nor, indeed, did they differ whatsoever in physical appearance from the members of the House of Burgesses. On the contrary, the Quakers were English and self-proclaimed Christians. But they preached egalitarianism and questioned the authority of the Anglican hierarchy, and so, in the eyes of colonial lawmakers, they were "unreasonable" and "turbulent." The legislature introduced heavy fines for any ship's captain who transported members of the Society of Friends to Virginia and ordered Quakers already in the colony taken into custody and deported.[18]

The alarm provoked by the Quakers highlights the extent to which religion (or, depending on the point of view of the observer, heresy or irreligion) was the principal determinant of social identity in the seventeenth-century Chesapeake. By one hundred years later, race—measured by outward appearance rather than professed inner conviction—had assumed that role. That leads us to one of the central questions in American colonial history: What brought about this change in colonial perceptions?

The answer most commonly offered is that it was simply a matter of demography. Once large numbers of Africans, so alien in appearance and culture, began to arrive in the Chesapeake, colonists reacted with alarm. This argument, based largely on inference—racism became manifest at the same time as the African population grew dramatically—is open to serious criticism. While Africans and their descendants may have numbered only a few thousand in the Chesapeake prior to 1700, their cultural adaptability was well known. In 1698, Francis Nicholson, governor of Maryland, informed the Board of Trade that "the major part of the Negros speak English." Over time, the historian Lorena Walsh notes, some of the enslaved "added to their store of wisdom an understanding of European workers' customary rights." Slaves who petitioned for their freedom "often demonstrated an astute knowledge of local legal process and English common law." Hugh Jones, a Virginia clergyman, claimed in 1724 that slaves born in the colony "talk good English and affect our language, habits, and customs." And by that time, a majority of the slaves in Virginia were native-born.[19]

Then there is the evidence provided by other British colonies, in the Caribbean. Despite having a much higher proportion of slaves in their populations, Barbados and Jamaica accorded free people of African descent many opportunities denied them on the mainland after the seventeenth century. I made the point earlier: a given labor system, a given demography does not automatically produce a particular set of racial beliefs. Human imagination plays a mediating role. And in the case of the Chesapeake, those individuals most advantageously placed to shape public perceptions belonged to the planting elite.[20]

★

To understand the actions and motivations of the planters, it is best to begin with the labor force and its changing character over time. During the seventeenth century, the great majority of laborers on the farms and plantations of Maryland and Virginia were indentured servants. Most were poor, many desperately so. In principle, they had come voluntarily, sacrificing their freedom for a specified number of years in return for transportation to North America and the promise of food, shelter, and clothing. Over time, however, the servant population came to include convicted criminals from England, Scottish prisoners of war, vagrant adolescents rounded up by magistrates, and "hapless men, women, and especially children kidnapped and spirited on board Chesapeake-bound ships by overzealous merchants and their henchman."[21]

While this diverse selection of what one merchant called the "scruffe and scumme" of British society—which was joined, beginning in the 1660s, by large numbers of impoverished Irish—may have fulfilled the labor needs of the planters, it also introduced what contemporaries regarded as a dangerous element into the colonies. And here I am not just referring to the convicts. As Edmund Morgan has shown, the English poor generally had a miserable reputation. They were said to be "vicious, idle, dissolute," addicted to "Laziness, Drunkenness, Debauches, and almost every Kind of Vice." Commentators in England proposed various forms of "involuntary servitude" to deal with the problem of the poor, with a small number even championing slavery itself. "The contempt that lay behind these proposals," Morgan observes, "is not easy to distinguish from the kind of contempt that today we call racism." And it crossed the Atlantic with the earliest colonists.[22]

Planters in the Chesapeake treated indentured servants little differently than they treated slaves. They subjected them to vicious beatings, abused them sexu-

ally, sometimes even murdered them. In 1662, the House of Burgesses complained that "the barbarous usage of some servants by cruell masters bring soe
much scandal and infamy to the country in generall, that people who would
willingly adventure themselves hither, are through feare thereof diverted."
Planters bought and sold servants, even gambled them away. In 1625 a ship's
captain objected that "Servants were sold here upp and downe like horses."
Potential buyers tested their arms and legs, looked in their mouths to check
their teeth.[23]

Under the circumstances, it is hardly surprising that servants frequently
engaged in acts of resistance. They malingered, destroyed equipment, ran away,
sometimes even assaulted masters and overseers. Early in the seventeenth
century opportunities existed for individuals who worked off their indentures
to acquire a modest stake in the society, perhaps accumulate substantial property. Even those who did not own land were able to vote in elections, fill minor
offices, and serve on juries. But by the 1660s, material prospects for freedmen
were declining. Consequently, they could frequently be found encouraging
servants to steal hogs, or helping them to run away. In 1670 the House of Burgesses responded by restricting the vote to "ffreeholders and housekeepers";
other men, the legislators claimed, had "little interest in the country."[24]

Servants formed alliances with slaves from the early days of settlement. It
was common for servants and slaves "to run away together, steal hogs together,
get drunk together." They also committed acts of violence together. Former
servants testified in memorials to their close bonds with slaves. James Revel,
one of the convicts sent to Virginia in the 1660s, recorded his feelings in a
poem. It included the following verse:

> At length, it pleased God I sick did fall
> But I no favour could receive at all,
> For I was Forced to work while I could stand,
> Or hold the hoe within my feeble hands.
> Much hardships then in deed I did endure.
> No dog was ever nursed so I'm sure
> More pity the poor Negroe slaves bestowed
> Than my inhuman brutal master showed.[25]

The most noteworthy instance of servants, slaves, and freedmen uniting
against planters came in 1676 during Bacon's Rebellion in Virginia, when a
conflict with Indians turned into something resembling class war. Thomas

Grantham, who negotiated with the rebels on behalf of Governor Berkeley, has left us the following evidence:

> I went to Colonel West's house about three miles farther, which was their Cheife Garrison and Magazine; I there mett about foure hundred English and Negroes in Armes, who were much dissatisfied at the Surrender of the Point, saying I had betray'd them, and thereupon some were for shooting mee, and others were for cutting mee to peeces. I told them I would willingly surrender myselfe to them, till they were satisfied from his Majestie, and did ingage to the Negroes and Servants, that they were all pardoned and freed from their Slavery: and with fair promises and Rundletts of Brandy, I pacified them, giving them severall Noates under my hand, that what I did was by the Order of His Majestie and the Governor. . . . Most of them I persuaded to goe to their Homes . . . except about Eight Negroes and Twenty English which would not deliver their Armes.[26]

★

During the first decades of settlement, planters in the Chesapeake relied largely on repression to control their laborers. But demographic changes opened up the possibility of a different strategy. In the 1660s, the supply of available indentured servants began to decline, their price to rise. By twenty years later planters were importing Africans in large numbers. Still they did so with some reluctance, fearful that more slaves would mean greater danger of insurrection.[27]

In Virginia, the House of Burgesses responded with a series of legislative measures, brought forward over the course of several decades, that were intended to fracture the united front of slaves and servants. The lawmakers denied slaves the right to hold property. They granted county officials the authority to dismember runaway slaves. And most notably, they outlawed manumission, "except for some meritorious services, to be judged and allowed by the governor, and council." At the same time, they significantly improved the lives and prospects of servants. They allowed them to bring complaints about ill treatment before justices of the peace. They required masters to provide for servants who because of illness were "of little or no use." And they directed masters to give those men and women who had completed their indentures the resources necessary to make a hopeful beginning as free members of the colony.[28]

There was, of course, another way of dividing potential rebels. Skin color had carried meaning in the seventeenth century, if principally because of its assumed links to religious identity. The efforts of the Anglican Church to win converts and the willingness of at least some slaves to accept Christianity served to weaken those links. But the possibility was open for planters to make physical appearance itself a prerequisite of privilege. And in a series of laws during the first decades of the eighteenth century, the House of Burgesses took away from "any Negro, mulatto, or Indian" the right to appear as a witness in court, the right to acquire "Christian white" servants, the right to bear arms, the right to vote, the right to hold any office, "ecclesiasticall, civill, or military, or be in any place of public trust or power."[29]

But the commitment of planters to dividing society on the basis of physical characteristics was never unqualified. For one thing, they were ambivalent about suggesting to recently freed indentured servants of English or perhaps even Irish origin that they were equal in worth to the wealthiest and most respected members of the community. Moreover, in a society divided along color lines, free men, women, and children of African ancestry stood as evidence that the link between physical appearance and legal status was arbitrary and artificial. And to the extent that free people identified with slaves, they became potential—and potentially very dangerous—rebels.

It is understandable, then, that the planters were halting and at times inconsistent in their efforts to promote race consciousness. Maryland did not follow Virginia in banning manumission, nor did it pass equally extensive measures restricting the legal rights of free people of African descent. And as Kathleen Brown has pointed out, even Virginia planters "seemed unable to develop a consistent legal approach to the problem of free black people in a slave society, a difficulty that stemmed from their ambivalence about free men as both potential rebels against white society and potential pillars of free communities. Lawmakers sporadically restricted free Afro-Virginians' liberties, inadvertently encouraging the racial collectivity they feared. These periodic crackdowns were followed by intervals of seeming improvement in the racial climate, during which free men gained special privileges that distinguished them from their enslaved counterparts."[30]

Then there was the question of how to classify the children produced by sexual relations between "Negroes" and colonists. The contrary approaches initially taken by the legislatures of Maryland and Virginia underscore just how much experimentation was involved in the early construction of race. The House of Burgesses dictated in 1662 that "all children borne in this country shalbe held bond or free only according to the condition of the mother." A mere two years later, the Maryland Assembly mandated that "all Children born of any Negro or other slaue shall be Slaues as their ffathers were." The authorities in both colonies did in time embrace the view that marriage between "Negroes" and "whites" was contrary to the will of God. In 1691, the House of Burgesses notoriously called for "prevention of that abominable mixture and spurious issue" that would result from unions across the color line. And during the eighteenth century, legislators in Maryland and Virginia confined "mulattoes" and "Negroes" to the same degraded social caste even while treating them as distinct biological entities. But this only begged the question of who, exactly, was a "mulatto"? It was a matter that the House of Burgesses attempted to address in 1705, but as the legal historian Thomas Morris has noted, the answer the lawmakers provided sounds "odd" today: a mulatto was defined as "the child of an Indian" or the "child, grand child, or great grand child, of a Negro." By the end of the century a rather different definition was in the statute books: a mulatto was anyone with "one-fourth part or more of Negro blood." That only illuminates the uncertainty that planters exhibited about how a society founded on race should properly be designed.[31]

The behavior of Maryland legislators is even more indicative in that regard. A law in 1715 prohibited the marriage of whites "to any Negro whatsoever, or Mulatto Slave." It said nothing, however, about marriage between whites and free mulattoes. Another law, two years later, attempted to address the apparent oversight, but did so in a way that promised to undermine the presumptive link between physical appearance and social place: "If any Free Negro, or Mulatto, intermarry with any White Woman, or if any White Man shall intermarry with any Negro, or Mulatto Woman, such Negro or Mulatto shall become a Slave during Life, excepting Mulattoes born of White Women, who for such Intermarriage shall only become Servants for Seven Years."[32]

★

Planters would be the principal beneficiaries of a society divided along color lines. It is tempting, then, to conclude that the actions they took during the late seventeenth and eighteenth centuries were based on a clear understanding of how the future would unfold. That is a temptation we should resist, however. As Gordon Wood has observed: "Because historians write history looking backward, sometimes over centuries, they often tend to assume that what happened had to have happened the way it did. Consequently, they tend to ignore that people had to choose among different possible actions, just as we do in the present. . . . It is often healthy to be reminded of the uncertainty and

lack of inevitability in the way many events in the past took place."[33] Much of
the legislation that helped create black America was quite clearly ad hoc, probably hastily drafted, part of an ongoing effort by planters to secure order and
the continued productivity of the plantation system. To point out that their
actions had long-term consequences is not to claim that the planters anticipated all the consequences nor that they necessarily would have approved of
them in every respect.[34]

Nor, for that matter, is it to suggest that the planters alone brought black
America into being. They were the dominant element in society, and had the
resources, both political and social, to exercise significant influence over public
opinion. But their power was not absolute, and in any event, they themselves
were never entirely clear on the appropriate architecture for a society based on
race. Inevitably, then, others came to play a role. Those others would include
less privileged men and women who at one time would have identified themselves as "English" or "Christian" but by the eighteenth century had become
"white." They would also include Native Americans. But races being imagined
communities, inevitably the story of how Africans became "Negroes" must
give prime attention to the Africans themselves and to their descendants.[35]

Scholars have written extensively and often with great insight on the degree
to which the cultures and traditions of African peoples survived the transatlantic crossing. But no one has seriously addressed the question of when individuals of African ancestry began to identify themselves as "Negroes" and
"mulattoes" and what meaning they may have attached to those terms. To
be sure, the direct evidence is limited. My goal here, then, must inevitably be
modest: to initiate a conversation. I take as my methodological starting point
a seminal article by Ira Berlin in the *American Historical Review* some years
ago. Berlin argued that historians concerned with the development of American slavery needed to give more attention to considerations of time and space.
He himself did not address the question of race consciousness among men
and women of African ancestry, but his approach offers the best opportunity
for coming up with sound inferences on the subject.[36]

Through most of the seventeenth century, Africans and their descendants
represented only a small fraction of Chesapeake society, about 3 percent in
1650, rising to 15 percent in 1690. In addition, they were distributed widely
among the English population. During those years, Lorena Walsh contends,
"pressures for accommodation to the predominant language and culture were
especially strong." Presumably Africans would have been very attentive to English views about the significance of physical characteristics. But, as we have

seen, it was professed religious belief rather than skin color that served as the principal determinant of public identity during the better part of the seventeenth century. At the same time, the willingness of disaffected indentured servants and freedmen to form alliances with slaves sent the message that neither physical appearance nor religious affiliation should be of overriding consequence to exploited laborers.[37]

By the time planters began to introduce legislation drawing a color line in the late seventeenth century, African slaves were flooding into the Chesapeake; as many as 100,000 arrived between 1690 and 1770. In addition, by the second decade of the eighteenth century, the slave population had started to grow by natural increase. Slaves more and more lived separate lives, away from the influence of indentured servants and freedmen. Here a second demographic factor was presumably important: the distribution of native-born (creole) and African-born among the slave population. Despite the massive importation of Africans, 40 percent of the slaves in the Chesapeake in 1730 were creoles, a proportion that would rise to 80 percent by mid-century. Newly arrived Africans "struggled on a number of fronts, but especially to communicate and to comprehend their new lives. The immediate urge was to seek out members of their own ethnic groups or someone who spoke their native language. Those who were unable to do so spent years in silence before they were able to converse fluently in a creole language." Friction between Africans and creoles has been well documented. Many creoles saw Africans as backward, while Africans lamented that creoles were ignorant of traditional ways. Charles Ball, who escaped from slavery, famously wrote that his African-born grandfather "always expressed great contempt for his fellow slaves, they being as he said, a mean and vulgar race, quite beneath his rank, and the dignity of his former station."[38]

Still, tension tended to decrease in frequency and significance as the proportion of Africans in the slave population declined during the eighteenth century. If we assume that Africans were predisposed to reject skin color as the defining characteristic of identity, while creoles, called "Negroes" by their owners from birth, were inclined to accept that racial designation but give it a different, more favorable meaning than the one intended by planters, then the general tendency would have been for slaves to develop race consciousness gradually over time, with geographic variations according to the rapidity of growth in local creole populations. The process must have been painful. We can only imagine the anguish a slave woman born in West Africa must have felt when she first heard a son or grandson refer to himself as a "Negro," the term used by the planter who held them both as property.[39]

Of course, not all people of African ancestry were slaves. Although Virginia enacted a law in 1691 requiring anyone freeing a slave to secure his or her transportation out of the colony, and another, in 1748, outlawing manumission altogether, the number of free Negroes and mulattoes continued to grow by natural means. Meanwhile, Maryland never formally prohibited manumission. The massive importation of African slaves did reduce the proportion of those who were free (more than six thousand individuals at the time of the Revolution) to a small fraction of the total Chesapeake population. But as Kathleen Brown has observed, "It was not the size of the freed population . . . that made it significant. Rather, it was the anomaly of its existence in a society increasingly committed to racial slavery."[40]

Free people of African ancestry and slaves were often related and, especially during the seventeenth century, could be found working alongside each other. They also traded in stolen goods. In 1736, the governor of Virginia, William Gooch, asked the House of Burgesses "to fix a perpetual Brand" on free Negroes and mulattoes because "they adhere to and favour [sic] the slaves." No doubt the legislation dividing the society along color lines further served to tie slave and free together.[41] Still, planters were of a divided mind about how to treat free people of African ancestry. And an element of the free population made up largely of mulattoes was able to exploit the situation to create something of a separate existence. They "clustered in towns like Williamsburg and Norfolk and along the Tidewater's numerous rivers." They also worked assiduously to win the favor of influential planters. A tiny fraction did exceptionally well. Edward Nicken was wealthier than half the white residents of Lancaster County, Virginia, when he died in 1735. John Rawlinson, a shoemaker, owned eight houses in Williamsburg. Most notable was Benjamin Banneker of Maryland, who became an astronomer, clockmaker, mathematician, and author and was on friendly terms with prominent figures in Revolutionary society. After his death in 1806, an attorney recalled that he "exercised in his life the rights of a free man in holding real property, in voting at elections, and being allowed and permitted to give evidence in courts of justice in cases in which free white citizens were concerned." Presumably James Madison was thinking of just such unrepresentative individuals when he claimed that, once given his liberty, "a freedman immediately loses all attachment and sympathies with his former fellow slaves."[42]

Those free men and women who isolated themselves and enjoyed a relatively comfortable existence no doubt had some predisposition to embrace ideas that would privilege their unique status. Had they been similar in physical appearance to the slave population, presumably they would have disputed that skin color was a meaningful indicator of social rank. But, as indicated earlier, most of them were mulattoes. According to Joel Williamson, on the eve of the Revolution 80 percent of free individuals with African ancestry also had European ancestry. So while laws in the Chesapeake placed "mulattoes" and "Negroes" in the same social caste, free people of mixed African and European descent had some reason to insist on drawing distinctions.[43]

Then again, many slaves also had mixed ancestry, being products of sexual relations between indentured servants and slaves or, increasingly over time, planters and slaves. Under the circumstances, the conception of race that the comparatively privileged minority of light-skinned free men and women adopted could not have been based entirely on physical characteristics. Perhaps they told themselves that their ancestors, whether European or African, were different than—superior to—the ancestors of light-skinned slaves.[44] In his research for *White over Black,* Winthrop Jordan found the documentary record almost silent on the self-perception of mulattoes. Yet he did come across one reference, in a 1735 issue of the *South-Carolina Gazette,* that is suggestive:

> It is observed concerning the Generation of Molattoes, that they are seldom well belov'd either by the Whites or the Blacks. Their Approach towards Whiteness makes them look back with some kind of Scorn upon the Colour they seem to have left, while the Negroes, who do not think them better than themselves, return their Contempt with Interest; And the Whites, who respect them no Whit the more for the nearer Affinity in Colour, are apt to regard their Behaviour as too bold and assuming and bordering upon Impudence. As they are next to Negroes, and but just above 'em, they are terribly afraid of being thought Negroes, and therefore avoid as much as possible their Company or Commerce; and Whitefolks are as little fond of the Company of Molattoes.[45]

One final point. The development of the cotton economy in the early nineteenth century would cause a massive shift of Chesapeake slaves to the south and west. During the colonial period, however, the slave trade took place mostly within localities. Many creoles never left the neighborhood where they were born. The communities they formed, which extended across a limited range of plantations and farms, were narrowly circumscribed in space. It is an open question what the terms "Negro" and "mulatto" may have meant to illiterate men and women who, during their lifetimes, encountered only those people who lived in, or passed through, their immediate surroundings. Could they conceive of race in the broad terms of later centuries? Consider the following scenario. A creole slave, dark-skinned, lives on a plantation in a corner of Virginia where the only people of African descent she has ever known are slaves who dress, speak, and look much like herself. A man arrives whose physical appearance suggests he has mixed European and African ancestry. He is free, a well-to-do artisan from Williamsburg. His clothing suggests dignity, even refinement; his manner and speech mimic the manner and speech of the slave's owner. Can we say with any confidence that the slave would regard the visitor as part of her "imagined community"? And the artisan from Williamsburg. Is there reason to believe that he would feel a meaningful sense of community with the slave?[46]

PART 2 • FROM THE REVOLUTION TO THE DAWN OF THE CIVIL RIGHTS ERA

★ ★ ★

2 • On Immigration, Citizenship, and Being "Not-Black"

The United States was the first nation in human history conceived in white supremacy. The delegates who gathered in Philadelphia in 1787 to write the Constitution did not recognize Native Americans as candidates for citizenship. And one of the first pieces of legislation enacted during George Washington's first term as president was a law providing, in part, that "any alien, being a free white person, who shall have resided within the limits and under the jurisdiction of the United States for the term of two years, may be admitted to become a citizen thereof." This stipulation, which effectively restricted naturalization to "white" immigrants, was passed by Congress with no debate. It remained the law of the land until 1952.[1]

For the better part of two centuries, white privilege was a defining element of American national identity. Of course, the "white race" is every bit as much an imagined division of humanity as the "black race." Consider how Benjamin Franklin marked its boundaries in 1751: "The Number of purely white People in the World is proportionably very small. All Africa is black or tawny. Asia chiefly tawny. America (exclusive of the new Comers) wholly so. And in Europe, the Spaniards, Italians, French, Russians and Swedes, are generally of what we call a swarthy Complexion; as are the Germans also, the Saxons only excepted, who with the English, make the principal Body of White People on the Face of the Earth. I could wish their Numbers were increased." Asked to determine whether Syrian immigrants were eligible for naturalization, different courts ruled that, yes, they were white and therefore eligible for naturalization—this was in 1909, 1910, and 1915—and no, they were not white and so ineligible for naturalization—this in 1913 and 1914. Indians from the subcontinent were, according to various judges, not white in 1909, white in 1910 and 1913, not white in 1917, white in 1920, and not white in 1923.[2]

The diverse histories of Native Americans and of immigrants are intricately connected to the imagining of black America. From the Revolution to the dawning of the Civil Rights Era, slavery—and the memory of slavery as read into the physical characteristics of the descendants of slaves—played a formative role in the construction and reconstruction, of "white" America and exerted significant influence over the opportunities available to those Americans judged ineligible for membership in the white race.

★

In recent years, scholars have devoted considerable attention to the historical construction of "whiteness" in the United States. The literature produced has opened new windows onto American identity, although a debate over whether various European immigrant groups "became" white after a process of acculturation or were white "on arrival" has, arguably, turned into something of a distracting sideshow. If we confine ourselves to the question of political rights or standing before the courts, the evidence appears to be clear. As Eric Foner has pointed out: "No Irish migrants were barred from naturalization as nonwhite. All European immigrants were allowed to vote in states that restricted the suffrage to whites (or, if they were disenfranchised, it was because of failure to meet property or literacy tests, not racial ones). Miscegenation laws were never enforced so as to prevent marriages between Irish Americans and persons of English background, or between Scandinavian and Jewish Americans."[3]

Still, Irish Catholics in the nineteenth century, and Russian Jews, Sicilians, and Slavs in the early twentieth century, did suffer hateful attacks and were victims of harassment and, at times, discriminatory legislation. Matthew Jacobson has demonstrated how Americans effectively resolved this seeming contradiction. They told themselves that there were a multitude of white races, hierarchically arranged. Members of certain of those races were hard-working, possessed of the qualities necessary for self-government; others were "beaten men from beaten races" with "none of the ideas and aptitudes which . . . belong to those who are descended from the tribes that met under the oak trees of old Germany to make laws and choose chieftains." The story of European immigration to the United States between the Revolution and the dawn of the Civil Rights Era is at heart the story of how, to borrow Ian Haney López's useful double negative, "not not-white" immigrants established that they were suitable candidates for assimilation and eventually overcame opposition from native-born Americans to win the right to enter the white mainstream.[4]

The emblematic example is the Irish. Between 1820 and 1860, approximately 1,700,000 Irish Catholics arrived in the United States. Most came after 1845, fleeing the Potato Famine that was killing off an estimated one million of their countrymen. They settled mainly in New York, Boston, and other urban centers of the Northeast, finding jobs at near starvation wages in the factories of the emerging industrial economy and making ramshackle homes in congested ghettos notorious for their violence, crime, and disease.[5]

The conspicuous presence of the Irish immigrants produced anxiety among native-born Protestant Americans. Scurrilous pamphlets circulated, allegedly disclosing the nefarious deeds committed by agents of the Catholic Church. The most notorious, *The Awful Disclosures of Maria Monk,* purported to document wild sex orgies involving priests and nuns at a convent in Montreal. Mob action against Irish Catholics was commonplace. In the summer of 1844 alone, Philadelphia was embroiled in a series of riots that targeted the Irish community and left at least twenty dead.[6]

Irish Catholics were said to be lazy and slaves to their passions. Indeed, they were often compared to slaves. They were dependent, nativists charged; they lacked the attributes expected of citizens in a republic. The height of the backlash against them came in 1854 with the establishment of the American, or Know-Nothing, Party. The Know-Nothings advocated severe restrictions on immigration and limitations on the rights of the foreign-born. The success of the party in elections in the Northeast revealed, one observer claimed, "a deep seated feeling in favor of human freedom and also a fine determination that hereafter none but Americans shall rule America."[7]

But the Know-Nothing Party proved short-lived. And its principal opponents, the Democrats, helped usher Irish Catholics into the white mainstream. In return for votes, Democrat leaders fought back the demands of nativists and, no less important, provided the Irish with social assistance and jobs. The advancement for Irish Catholic immigrants was sufficiently marked that fifty years later their children and grandchildren were active in the movement to exclude "white" immigrants from southern and eastern Europe. The *Dictionary of Races or Peoples* produced by the Dillingham Commission, established by Congress in 1907 to study the national origins and social consequences of American immigration, effectively acknowledged the remarkable racial redefinition that had taken place. It classified the Irish as Anglo-Saxon rather than Celt. "Like the English," it stated, "the Irish came to the United States speaking

our own language and imbued with sympathy for our ideals and our democratic institutions."[8]

★

The 1848 Treaty of Guadalupe Hidalgo, which ended the Mexican War, increased the territory of the United States by about half a million square miles. It
also, not incidentally, added an estimated 75,000 to 100,000 Spanish-speaking
Mexicans to the American population, granting "all the rights of citizens" to
any individuals who chose to remain one year after the treaty came into effect.
Given the existing racial restriction on the naturalization of immigrants, this
was an implicit acknowledgment that the officials who had negotiated the
treaty viewed Mexicans as "whites." The California Constitutional Convention
reaffirmed this assessment the following year when it limited the vote to "White
male citizens of the United States and every White male citizen of Mexico,
who shall have elected to become a citizen of the United States."[9]

The apparent intentions of lawmakers notwithstanding, Americans of European ancestry who settled in California after the Treaty of Guadalupe Hidalgo
did not regard all their Mexican neighbors through the lens of whiteness.
Writes Tomás Almaguer, "Those [Mexicans] whose class position and osten-
sible European ancestry placed them at the top of the hierarchy during the
Mexican period, the 'gente de razon', were reluctantly viewed as 'white' by
Anglo Americans. The dark complexioned, mestizo population (the 'greasers'
or *gente sin razon*—literally 'people without reason'), on the other hand, were
viewed as 'nonwhite' and not significantly different from pureblood, Indian
'savages' in the state." In fact, the California legislature enacted discriminatory
legislation directed specifically against the *gente sin razón*, including a va-
grancy law widely referred to as the "Greaser Act."[10]

As for the *gente de razón*, the arrival of eastern business interests in California led to a rapid reversal of their fortunes. In an attempt to protect their social
standing, they "sometimes undertook to Europeanize or 'whiten' themselves,
accenting a Spanish line of descent, to distinguish themselves from mestizos,
people of mixed Spanish and Indian backgrounds." But they were denied the
opportunity to participate in the benefits of the gold rush, and by the late nineteenth century, giant corporations such as the Southern Pacific Railroad had
swallowed up much of their land. In New Mexico and Texas as well, American
businessmen used political connections to wrest property and economic influence from the old elite.[11]

Deeply affecting how Hispanic Americans were perceived by other members of society was the ongoing, if uneven, arrival of migrant laborers from south of the border. Between 1900 and 1930 approximately one million Mexicans entered the United States, nearly half a million in the 1920s alone. The migrants came to find jobs as unskilled workers in factories and as field hands on vast corporate fruit and vegetable farms, chasing wages that, while low by American standards, might be ten times higher than what was available in Mexico.[12]

While the arrival of natives from the ancestral homeland provided opportunities for cultural renewal in Hispanic American communities, it also gave rise to anxiety. Mexicans and Mexican Americans often competed for the same low-paying jobs. And there was the danger, it seemed to many Hispanic Americans, that the influx of poor, largely illiterate workers would mislead the population at large into believing that everyone of Mexican ancestry was deficient in the values and qualities associated with American "whiteness." To set themselves apart from the migrant workers, some Mexican Americans, especially individuals belonging to the middle class, began to refer to themselves as "Latin Americans" or "Spanish Americans." During the 1920s, civic organizations promoting the interests of Hispanic Americans appeared in a number of Texas cities. They publicly championed assimilation and excluded those who were not American citizens from their membership. Writes David Gutiérrez, "While members of these new organizations continued to profess respect for Mexico and for their Mexican cultural heritage, they insisted that the best way to advance in American society was to convince other Americans that they too were loyal, upstanding American citizens. In keeping with these beliefs the new Mexican American organizations carefully cultivated what they considered to be an appropriate American public image by conducting their proceedings in English, by prominently displaying the American flag in their ceremonies, stationery, and official iconography, by singing such songs as 'America' at their gatherings, and by opening their meetings with a recitation of the 'George Washington Prayer.'"[13]

Foremost among these organizations was the League of United Latin American Citizens (LULAC), founded in Corpus Christi in February 1929. LULAC members pledged to promote the "best and purest" form of Americanism and to educate their children in the rights and responsibilities of American citizenship. They pointedly stressed their inclusion in the white race, implicitly representing themselves as founding members of the republic. "As a matter of absolute record," commented the LULAC News in 1932, "it was the Latin American who first braved and tamed the Texas wilderness. They were the first white race to inhabit this vast empire of ours."[14]

Such efforts proved largely unavailing, however. White Americans stubbornly refused to distinguish between Mexican Americans and Mexican immigrants. Former Texas congressman James L. Slayden wrote in 1921, "In Texas, the word 'Mexican' is used to indicate the race, not a citizen or subject of the country. There are probably 250,000 Mexicans in Texas who were born in the state but they are 'Mexicans' . . . though they may have five generations of American ancestors." Twenty years later, the president general of LULAC, George Sánchez, referred to Mexican Americans as "an orphan people." "'Mexican' has become a term of opprobrium," he lamented, "applied indiscriminately to citizen and alien alike, and associated with discriminatory practices in wage scales and employment procedures, in education, in the exercise of civil rights and the like."[15]

As Sánchez observed, Mexican Americans were not only looked on as aliens, they were also treated as aliens. During the Great Depression, a Mexican immigrant in Hick's Camp, California, reported the following incident: A Hispanic veteran "was proudly taking two American girls to a dance one evening and at the door of the dance he was turned away and told Mexicans were not admitted. The veteran produced his citizenship papers and then was told that he wasn't an American just because he had American citizenship papers—he was still a Mexican." Another veteran reported how he was denied work at a construction site: "The supervisors come out and tell the people that are waiting to get a job to line up on one side, all the white people, and on the other side the ones that are not. Because I am of dark complexion I stay with the people of my race and of course, do not get hired because the supervisor has the order to hire only the 'white people' and that is what he does."[16]

Mae Ngai refers to Americans such as these veterans as "alien citizens." They "are American citizens by virtue of their birth in the United States but . . . are presumed to be foreign by the mainstream of American culture and, at times, by the state." A particularly telling instance can be found in newspaper coverage of the highly publicized Sleepy Lagoon murder in 1942. After the body of a young man named José Díaz was discovered at the Sleepy Lagoon reservoir in southeast Los Angeles—Díaz was born in Mexico but raised in the United States—police rounded up several hundred members of the Eastside gang for interrogation. Subsequently twenty-two were brought to trial on the charge of murder. Although all were American-born and citizens of the United States, the *Los Angeles Times* and *Los Angeles Examiner* repeatedly referred to the accused as "Mexican youths." In the end, twelve were convicted of homicide and five of assault.[17]

ing a Gentlemen's Agreement in which the Japanese government agreed to stop issuing passports to laborers. In 1924, the Johnson-Reed Act, which prohibited the entry of "aliens ineligible to citizenship," effectively shut off immigration from the island nation.[22]

While some individuals who had established residence in the United States, or were descendents of immigrants who had established residence, chose to return, or emigrate, to China or Japan during the years when exclusion was in effect, the number of people with Chinese ancestry in the United States remained largely stable during the first half of the twentieth century, while the population with Japanese ancestry grew over the same period of time. The 1940 census recorded 77,504 members of the Chinese "race," just over half of whom were born in the United States, and 125,947 members of the Japanese "race," almost two-thirds of whom were American-born.[23]

Many Asian immigrants and their children and grandchildren engaged in a campaign to secure assimilation. A noteworthy, if extreme, example is represented by the case of *Ozawa v. United States,* which appeared before the U.S. Supreme Court in 1922. Takao Ozawa had come to the United States as a child, in 1894. He attended high school and university in California, then in 1906 moved to Honolulu, where he married and worked for an American company. In terms of culture and conviction, he assured the Court, he was thoroughly American. But he also claimed that although the Japanese had mixed with the "Mongolian" and "Malay" races, "their dominant strains are 'white persons,' speaking an Aryan tongue and having Caucasian root stock." That, explained Ozawa, was why "the uncovered part of the [Japanese] body [is] white." It also explained why the Japanese exhibited a "mental alertness, a quality of mind in which they differ from other Asiatics and resemble the Europeans and the inhabitants of North America, above the Mexican line." Perhaps needless to say, his argument was rejected by the Court.[24]

With no real possibility of validating claims to whiteness, American-born men and women of Asian ancestry sought to win acceptance by openly embracing American culture and values. Xiao-Huang Yin has found that Chinese American autobiographies written during the exclusion era reveal a "strong quest for a place in American life." He adds: "Because the experience of U.S.-born Chinese was governed by a profound compulsion to be accepted in American society, their struggle to enter the mainstream world and their quest for a place in American life became the dominant themes of their autobiographical works and fictionalized life stories. These themes are expressed in terms of conflicts between the cultural values of East and West, the divergent views on interracial marriages held by their parents and themselves, the generation gap, the pursuit of the American dream, the imperative to assert their American-ness, and their anxiety to demonstrate patriotism as a 'loyal minority' on the eve of America's entry into World War II." The professionals and businessmen who established the Japanese American Citizens League in 1929 "believed that the best way for them to prove their worthiness in the eyes of European-Americans was to be totally loyal to American ideals."[25]

Overwhelmingly, however, such efforts had limited influence on public opinion. Secretary of Labor James Davis told representatives of the Union of American Hebrew Congregations in 1922, "It is not only evident to truly American people but even to these Orientals themselves that they will never become assimilated into a united American Republic. They are not of us. Their economic and moral standards are those of a thousand years ago." This assertion, just two years before the Johnson-Reed Act imposed strict limits on immigration from Eastern Europe, only underscores the fact that Jews, while considered alien in so many respects, nonetheless possessed the single attri-bute that held open the possibility of future assimilation: a claim to "white-ness." A July 1924 editorial in the *Los Angeles Times* stated that the Japanese should be made to understand that the government adopted a policy of exclu-sion "not because America deems them inferior, but because it finds them unassimilable." As Mae Ngai observes, during the 1950s, after the exclusion laws had been repealed, Asian Americans remained "subject to enormous cultural denial by the mainstream of American society, which regarded 'Asian' and 'American citizen' as mutually exclusive concepts." The assumed inherent contradiction was well captured in testimony from a Chinese American citi-zen in 1931: "I speak fluent English, and have an American mind. I feel that I am more American than Chinese. I am an American citizen by birth, having the title for all rights, but they treat me as if I were a foreigner." Indeed, in the American mind, Asian Americans *were* foreigners.[26]

Nothing better demonstrates the precarious nature of the situation in which alien citizens found themselves than the internment of Japanese Americans during World War II. In January 1942, the entire Congressional delegation from California, Oregon, and Washington petitioned President Roosevelt "to remove all persons of Japanese lineage . . . alien and citizens alike" from the West Coast. In a report to the Army's chief of staff, General John L. DeWitt, commanding general of the Western Defense Command, laid out the logic of the proposed action: "In the war in which we are now engaged racial affinities are not severed by migration. The Japanese race is an enemy race and while many second and third generation Japanese born on United States soil possessed of United States citizenship have become 'Americanized,' the racial strains are undiluted. To conclude otherwise is to expect that children born of white parents on Japanese soil sever all racial affinity and become loyal Japanese subjects, ready to fight and, if necessary, to die for Japan in a war against the nation of their parents."[27]

Roosevelt signed an executive order on February 19, 1942, authorizing the army to remove all individuals of Japanese descent from the Pacific Coast and place them in internment facilities. In total, 120,000 individuals, two-thirds of them citizens, were forced from their homes and placed in "relocation centers" on lands in the desert-like Western interior. "Given no more than a week to sell, store, or otherwise dispose of their property, people sold their possessions at great loss. Each family was told to take bedding and linen, toilet articles, clothes, kitchen utensils, and whatever other personal effects they could hand carry. Nothing else was allowed, and people could not even send packages to themselves through the mail."[28]

Washington finally revoked the internment policy in December 1944. Still, as of the following summer, 44,000 individuals remained in the relocation centers, uncertain where to go, and fearful of what awaited them. In the end, they were "forcibly pushed back into a society that did not want them. . . . Those who still owned property found their homes dilapidated and vandalized, their farms, orchards, and vineyards choked with weeds, their personal belongings stolen or destroyed."[29]

★

The Fourteenth Amendment, ratified in 1868, conferred citizenship on "all persons born or naturalized in the United States." It left in place, however, the exception made for Native Americans at the time the Constitution was drafted. In 1884, the Supreme Court confirmed that Indians—even Indians who wished to abandon their tribal allegiances—were ineligible for citizenship.

Under the Constitution of the United States as originally established, "Indians not taxed" were excluded from the persons according to whose numbers representatives and direct taxes were apportioned among the several states, and Congress had and exercised the power to regulate commerce with the Indian tribes, and the members thereof, whether within or without the boundaries of one of the states of the Union. The Indian tribes, being within the territorial limits of the United States, were not, strictly speaking, foreign states, but they were alien nations, distinct political communities, with whom the United States might and habitually did deal as they thought fit, either through treaties made by the President and Senate or through acts of Congress in the ordinary forms of legislation. The members of those tribes owed immediate allegiance to their several tribes, and were not part of the people of the United States.[30]

How to treat members of these "alien nations" was a major preoccupation from the earliest days of the republic through the nineteenth century. Here there was a profound disjunction between the views of policymakers in Washington and those of settlers on the frontier. Leading policymakers considered Native Americans suitable candidates for assimilation. Settlers, by contrast, demanded their removal or, if necessary, extermination.

George Washington's secretary of war, Henry Knox, was the most influential spokesman on Indian affairs in the early years of the new republic. Bringing civilization to Indians "would be an operation of complicated difficulty," he conceded to the president in 1789. "But to deny that under a course of favorable circumstances it could not be accomplished is to suppose the human character under the influence of such stubborn habits as to be incapable of melioration or change—a supposition entirely contradicted by the progress of society from the barbarous ages to its present degree of perfection." It would be "a happy commencement of the business," he continued, if it were possible "to introduce among the Indian tribes a love for exclusive property. . . . Missionaries of excellent moral character should be appointed to reside in their nation, who should be well supplied with all the implements of husbandry and the necessary stock for a farm." It is not the case, he assured Native Americans in Ohio who had taken up arms against the government, that the president wished to deprive them of their lands. On the contrary, "we should be greatly gratified with the opportunity of imparting to you all the blessings of civilized life, of teaching you to cultivate corn, to raise oxen, sheep and other domestic animals; to build comfortable houses; so as ever to dwell upon the land."[31]

As president, Thomas Jefferson committed himself to the same course of action. "Let me entreat you," he told a delegation of Indians who came to Washington in 1808, "on the lands now given you to begin to give every man a farm, let him enclose it, cultivate it, build a warm house on it, and when he dies let it belong to his wife and children after him. Nothing is so easy as to learn to cultivate the earth; all your women understand it, and to make it easier, we are always ready to teach you how to make plows, hoes, and necessary utensils. If the men will take the labor of the other away from the women, they will learn to spin and weave and clothe their families." But to Jefferson, that would be only the first step—the first step toward not merely assimilation but amalgamation: "When once you have property, you will want laws and magistrates to protect your property and person. . . . You will find that our laws are good for this purpose; you will wish to live under them, you will unite yourselves with us, join in our great counsels and form one people with us, and we shall all be Americans; you will mix with us by marriage, your blood will run in our veins, and will spread with us over this great continent."[32] Nor was this just empty rhetoric designed to appease a distrustful audience. Jefferson wrote to Benjamin Hawkins, his agent among the Creeks, "The ultimate point of rest and happiness for them is to let our settlements and theirs meet and blend together, to intermix, and become one people. Incorporating themselves with us as citizens of the United States, this is what the natural progress of things will of course, bring on, and it will be better to promote than retard it."[33]

Before the War of 1812, Congress did little in practical terms to bring about Indian assimilation beyond paying the salaries of agents assigned to various tribes and giving gifts to native leaders. But the Civilization Fund Act of 1819 authorized $10,000 a year for the purpose of "providing against the further decline and final extinction of the Indian tribes, adjoining the frontier settlements of the United States, and for introducing among them the habits and arts of civilization." By then, however, indeed by some years earlier, settlers on the frontier had concluded that native peoples had to be removed, not transformed. Congress had repeatedly introduced into legislation and treaties provisions designed to ensure that those Indians who made good faith efforts to adopt civilized ways would be treated with respect and have their property protected. But conflict on the frontier inevitably meant that the military had to choose whether to defend Indians or white settlers. The outcome was never seriously in doubt. Bernard Sheehan summarizes: "The frontier could not be controlled. Threats to use the courts or to send in troops, instructions to agents to clear the native lands [of settlers], all came to nothing. Even granting the Indian the right to kill the settlers' cattle or drive the animals out of the tribal territory did not stop the avalanche of intruders. Tribal leaders petitioned the government, appealed to state authorities and to the intruders themselves, and attempted to curb the belligerence of their own younger tribesmen. Nothing helped; the white man kept coming."[34]

Indian removal can properly be seen as a compromise between settlers and Washington. Relocating native peoples beyond the Mississippi would eliminate them as competitors for land. But it would also, federal officials told themselves, allow the civilizing process to continue, albeit at a distant remove. Indeed, many policymakers were prepared to claim that isolating the Indians would create a safer and more secure environment for teaching them the values and skills necessary for assimilation into the American mainstream. By the 1820s removal had gained legitimacy within Washington as a "permanent" solution to the "Indian problem."[35]

The main difficulty in dispossessing the Indians, reported John Calhoun, James Monroe's secretary of war, in February 1824, "arises from the progress of the Cherokees in civilization. They are now, within the limits of Georgia, about fifteen thousand, and increasing in equal proportion with the whites; all cultivators, with a representative government, judicial courts, Lancaster schools, and permanent property." He might have added that the Cherokee, and the four other so-called "Civilized Tribes," had copied the whites in acquiring slaves to work their farms and plantations. The problem posed was obvious: how could the government justify removing peoples who had seemingly taken the promises of Knox, Jefferson, and many other officials at face value, who had believed that they would be allowed to "unite yourselves with us, join in our great counsels and form one people with us, and we shall all be Americans"?[36]

The story of the Cherokee removal is as well known as it is tragic. Georgia and Alabama introduced legislation designed to weaken and, ultimately, eliminate native property rights. Then in 1830, Congress, under Andrew Jackson's prodding, passed the Indian Removal Act. This legislation gave the president authority to negotiate a land exchange: Native Americans would get territory across the Mississippi "that the United States will forever secure and guaranty to them, and their heirs or successors." In return, they would relinquish their landholdings in the East. The movement of Indians across the country "should be voluntary," Jackson told the Congress, "for it would be as cruel as unjust to compel the aborigines to abandon the graves of their fathers and seek a home in a distant land." But when the elected leaders of the Cherokee Nation declined to give up title to their territory, he had his officials negotiate a treaty with a more pliant minority faction within the tribe. The resulting agreement called for the Cherokee to cede their territory to Georgia in return for $5 million and a tract of land west of the Mississippi. When most of the tribal members refused to honor the treaty, Jackson sent an army of seven thousand to remove them at bayonet point. Their subsequent journey to the new "Indian Territory" during the brutal winter of 1838–39—a journey aptly named the "Trail of Tears"—resulted in the death of one-quarter of the 18,000 men, women, and children forcibly driven from their homes.[37]

By the 1840s, most Native Americans were living beyond the Mississippi River. Officials had imagined that they were at too distant a remove to represent a barrier to white settlement. But after the Civil War, farmers and ranchers flooded into the Great Plains and the Southwest. Between 1870 and 1880 the population west of the Mississippi grew by more than 50 percent, from 7 million to over 11 million.[38] For settlers, the trajectory of history was clear. A statement in 1870 by the Big Horn Association of Cheyenne, Wyoming, stated the position bluntly:

> The rich and beautiful valleys of Wyoming are destined for the occupancy and sustenance of the Anglo-Saxon race. The wealth that for untold ages has lain hidden beneath the snow-capped summits of our mountains has been placed there by Providence to reward the brave spirits whose lot it is to compose the advance-guard of civilization. The Indians must stand aside or be overwhelmed by the ever advancing and ever increasing tide of emigration. The destiny of the aborigines is written in characters not to be mistaken. The same inscrutable Arbiter that decreed the downfall of Rome has pronounced the doom of extinction upon the red men of America.[39]

Some years earlier the anthropologist Lewis Henry Morgan had complained that the slogan "The destiny of the Indian is extermination" had become "a general theme for school-boy declamation." The carnage of the Plains Wars speaks to the cold seriousness of the mantra.[40]

But during the late nineteenth century, federal officials still believed that assimilation represented a viable alternative to extermination. Or, rather, they continued to maintain that cultural obliteration, with Indians turning into carbon copies of white Americans, represented the one acceptable means of extermination. In the first years after the Civil War, Ulysses S. Grant adopted what became known as the Peace Policy. Since they could no longer be pushed farther west, native peoples were now to be rounded up on reservations. "On these reservations," claimed Columbus Delano, Grant's secretary of the interior,

> they can be taught as fast as possible, the arts of agriculture, and such pursuits as are incident to civilization, through the aid of the Christian

organizations of the country now engaged in this work, cooperating with the Federal Government. Their intellectual, moral, and religious culture can be prosecuted, and thus it is hoped that humanity and kindness may take the place of barbarity and cruelty. . . . [It] is the further aim of the policy to establish schools, and through the instrumentality of the Christian organizations, acting in harmony with the Government, as fast as possible, to build churches and organize Sabbath schools, whereby these savages may be taught a better way of life than they have heretofore pursued, and be made to understand and appreciate the comforts and benefits of a Christian civilization, and thus be prepared ultimately to assume the duties and privileges of citizenship.[41]

To ensure that the project was carried through to a successful completion, agents of the federal government were given absolute authority on the reservations.

But soon thereafter, officials decided that the reservation system was poorly suited for furthering the goal of assimilation. If anything, segregation served to help native peoples preserve their distinctive ways of life. Because they created "a cultural barricade," Frederick Hoxie has observed, "the tribes considered their reservations to be their most important possessions." Officials in Washington concluded that the reservations were perpetuating the very values and customs they were intended to eradicate. "The reservation system," commented Commissioner of Indian Affairs Thomas J. Morgan in 1889, "is an anachronism which has no place in our modern civilization."[42]

The solution, champions of assimilation argued, was two-fold: educate Indian boys and girls in ways that would prepare them for life in white America, and partition property held communally by native peoples into individual landholdings. Morgan articulated the optimistic expectations for education when he addressed a conference on the subject in upstate New York:

When we speak of the education of the Indians, we mean that comprehensive system of training and instruction which will convert them into American citizens, put within their reach the blessings which the rest of us enjoy, and enable them to compete successfully with the white man on his own ground and with his own methods. Education is to be the medium through which the rising generation of Indians are to be brought into fraternal and harmonious relationship with their white fellow-citizens, and with them enjoy the sweets of refined homes, the delight of social intercourse, the emoluments of commerce and trade, the advantages of travel, together with the pleasures that come from literature, science, and philosophy, and the solace and stimulus afforded by a true religion.[43]

Between 1879 and 1894 Congress increased appropriations for native schools from $75,000 to over $2 million. Instruction passed from the hands of evangelical missionaries to trained professionals, with a superintendent of Indian education overseeing the program.[44]

By the end of the century, schools could be found on every reservation in the United States. But the greatest fanfare was reserved for, and the greatest hopes inspired by, a series of boarding schools established off the reservations. The first of these schools, and the one that served as a model for those to follow, was the Carlisle Indian School in Pennsylvania, founded in 1879 by Captain Richard Pratt. Pratt, a former army officer who had served in campaigns against the Plains Indians, believed passionately in the cause of assimilation. He argued in an address delivered in 1892, "A great general has said that the only good Indian is a dead one, and that high sanction of his destruction has been an enormous factor in promoting Indian massacres. In a sense, I agree with the sentiment, but only in this: that all the Indian there is in the race should be dead. Kill the Indian in him, and save the man."[45]

Killing the Indian, figuratively speaking, meant above all removing children from the purportedly debilitating cultural environment of the reservations. According to this view, boys and girls had to be placed in boarding schools like Carlisle, where they would be given common American names and would not be allowed to dress in native clothing, wear their hair in traditional styles, or speak their native languages. Where possible they were to be boarded with Christian families. Said Pratt:

We make our greatest mistake in feeding our civilization to the Indians instead of feeding the Indians to our civilization. America has different customs and civilizations from Germany. What would be the result of an attempt to plant American customs and civilization among the Germans in Germany, demanding that they shall become thoroughly American before we admit them to the country? Now, what we have all along attempted to do for and with the Indians is just exactly that, and nothing else. We invite the Germans to come into our country and communities, and share our customs, our civilization, to be of it; and the result is immediate success. Why not try it on the Indians? Why not invite them into experiences in our communities? Why always invite and compel them to remain a people unto themselves?[46]

The experiment did not, however, prove successful. By the first decade of the twentieth century, many government officials were complaining about the academic deficiencies of native children. By the second decade of the century, policymakers were no longer claiming that schools like Carlisle would produce Indians ready to enter American society on an equal footing with whites.[47]

The new land policy produced equally disappointing results. The General Allotment Act of 1887, or Dawes Act as it is commonly known, promised to replace the purportedly stultifying communal values of native peoples with the dynamic promise of American individualism. Treaties calling for the partition of tribal lands into individual landholdings dated back to the 1830s. While they had not appreciably changed the face of Indian culture, enthusiasm for the new legislation, which extended land allotment to all tribes living on reservations and made it compulsory, was high.[48]

Under provisions of the Dawes Act, each head of a family was to receive 160 acres; each single person over eighteen years of age, 80 acres; each orphan child under eighteen, 80 acres; and every other single person under eighteen, 40 acres. In addition, the secretary of the interior was given the authority to negotiate with individual tribes for the purchase of any surplus lands "on such terms and conditions as shall be considered just and equitable between the United States and said tribe of Indians." And "every Indian born within the territorial limits of the United States to whom allotments shall have been made under the provisions of this act, or under any law or treaty, and every Indian born within the territorial limits of the United States who has voluntarily taken up, within said limits, his residence separate and apart from any tribe of Indians therein, and has adopted the habits of civilized life, is hereby declared to be a citizen of the United States, and is entitled to all the rights, privileges, and immunities of such citizens." The purpose of the act, Philip Deloria has noted, was "to turn Indian people into Jeffersonian farmers by breaking up communal landholdings and allotting parcels to individual owners." The government would sell the surplus lands to white homesteaders who, it was assumed, would serve as "neighborly role models."[49]

After passage of the Dawes Act, federal agents drew up "tribal rolls" in which they registered individuals according to established American notions of the nuclear family. This represented a first step toward breaking down the traditional Indian sense of obligation to wider communities—bands, clans, tribes.

Still, the Dawes Act hardly produced its promised result. Rather than facilitate the introduction of Indians into the American mainstream, its main consequence was simply to expedite the continued rapid transfer of land to white settlers. What had begun as a campaign to raise Indians to equality with whites and pave the way for their assimilation into the mainstream became "a campaign to integrate native resources into the American economy." Of the original 138 million acres covered by the act, more than 60 percent was disposed of through sales of surplus lands, while allotments sold by individual Indian landowners totaled another 20 percent. And that does not take into consideration the acres that Indians chose to lease to whites.[50]

In 1934, Congress replaced the Dawes Act with the Indian Reorganization Act (IRA), or, as it is often called, the Indian New Deal. The IRA ended the allotment system, allowed tribes to recover some of the surplus lands that had been sold, and restored elements of self-government on the reservations. But the vision of Indian assimilation did not die, at least not in the minds of some government officials. During the 1950s, the Bureau of Indian Affairs attempted to break the hold of tribal communities by transplanting native peoples from reservations to urban centers. The relocation "helped create inter-Indian communities in almost every major city in the United States."[51]

★

For more than a century and a half after the writing of the Constitution, policymakers and westward-moving settlers sought to eliminate Indians from the United States. If the preferred means in Washington was cultural obliteration and the preferred means of settlers was removal and extermination, the end was effectively the same. There was no place in the white republic for descendents of the original colonizers of the land. While many white Americans had no difficulty contemplating this turning of the historical page, there were others for whom it produced genuine feelings of sadness. They comforted themselves with the thought that Indians were fulfilling their providential destiny "to vanish in the face of a superior race." "By a law of nature," wrote Supreme Court Justice Joseph Story in 1828, "they seem destined to a slow, but sure extinction. Everywhere, at the approach of the white man, they fade away. We hear the rustling of their footsteps, like that of the withered leaves of autumn, and they are gone for ever. They pass mournfully by us, and they return no more."[52]

"The nostalgia and pity aroused by the dying race," Robert Berkhofer has written, "produced the best romantic sentiments and gave that sense of fleeing

time beloved of romantic sensibilities. The tragedy of the dying Indian, especially as portrayed by the last living member of the tribe, became a staple of
American literature. . . . It made its mark on world literature through James
Fenimore Cooper's *The Last of the Mohicans* (1826), and inspired George Catlin
to do his famed portraits of noble Indians on the plains and prairies before it
was too late to capture on canvas a dying race. In short, whether Indians were
portrayed as bad or as good, they were in romantic eyes a poetical people whose
activities took place in a sublime landscape and whose fate aroused sentiment." Catlin gave expression to such feelings in his writings as well as his
paintings: "Nature has no where presented more beautiful and lovely scenes,
than those of the vast prairies of the West; and of man and beast, no nobler
specimens than those who inhabit them—the Indian and the buffalo—joint
and original tenants of the soil, and fugitives together from the approach of
civilized man; they have fled to the great plains of the West, and there, under an
equal doom, they have taken up their last abode, where their race will expire,
and their bones will bleach together."[53]

Still, despite the fact that they were destined to disappear as a race, or, more
accurately, *because* they were destined to disappear, Indians could be accorded
a celebrated place in the historic construction of American identity. "Now that
he and his kind were gone, vanished according to the same destiny that pledged
dominion of the continent to the ascendant nation," writes Alan Trachtenberg,
"Indians could and should be hailed as forefathers and -mothers of us all."
After they had been dispossessed of all the lands that white settlers desired,
after they ceased to be a real presence in the life of most Americans, their
imagined past as noble, if metaphoric, ancestors could be embraced. It was in
1913 that the government introduced the famous Indian-head nickel (with a
buffalo on the reverse side) "representing the new symbolic role of Indians as
First Americans."[54]

In early 1916, Secretary of the Interior Franklin K. Lane inducted 150 Indians into American citizenship on the Yankton Sioux reservation in South Dakota. The ceremony for one of the Indians began this way:

"Joseph T. Cook, what was your Indian name?"
   "Tunkansapa," answered the Indian.
   "Tunkansapa, I hand you a bow and arrow. Take this bow and shoot the
arrow."
   The Indian did so.

"Tunkansapa, you have shot your last arrow. That means you are no longer to live the life of an Indian. You are from this day forward to live the life of the white man. But you may keep that arrow. It will be to you a symbol of your noble race and of the pride you may feel that you come from the first of all Americans."[55]

★

As Orlando Patterson has noted, the devotion to freedom in Western civilization "was generated from the experience of slavery. People came to value freedom, to construct it as a powerful shared vision of life, as a result of their experience of, and response to slavery." Edmund Morgan has applied the same insight to the specific case of Revolutionary Virginia: "The presence of men and women who were, in law at least, almost totally subject to the will of other men gave to those in control of them an immediate experience of what it could mean to be at the mercy of a tyrant. Virginians may have had a special appreciation of the freedom dear to republicans, because they saw every day what life without it could be like."[56]

That slavery could exist in a land whose founding document proclaimed that "all men are created equal" and that identified "liberty" and "the pursuit of happiness" as "inalienable rights" was, on the face of it, absurd. But the century leading up to the Revolution had witnessed the invention of race as a fundamental division of humanity. This was a transformative moment in the history of Western thought. The purported inequality between races not only provided a rationale for slavery; it also fostered the impression that the equality English republican tradition associated with freedom existed exclusively within the "white" race. Slavery was the pedestal on which American national self-identity was erected in the late eighteenth century—a self-identity that fused liberty, equality, and white supremacy.[57]

The formative role that people of African descent played in the shaping of American self-identity became a central element in the "positive good" defense of slavery adopted by Southerners in the decades leading up to the Civil War. In a speech directed at his Northern counterparts in the Senate in 1858, James Hammond of South Carolina charged: "Your whole hireling class of manual laborers and 'operatives,' as you call them, are essentially slaves." Yet "you are brothers of one blood. They are your equals in natural endowment of intellect, and they feel galled by their degradation." By contrast, "We do not think that whites should be slaves either by law or necessity. Our slaves are black, of

another and inferior race. The status in which we have placed them is an elevation. They are elevated from the condition in which God first created them, by
being made our slaves."[58]

As David Roediger has shown, wage laborers in the North rejected the
charge that they themselves were "essentially slaves" while affirming the interpretation of freedom articulated by Hammond and other apologists for the
slaveholding regime. "White workers," he notes, "could, and did, define and
accept their class positions by fashioning identities as 'not slaves' and as 'not
Blacks.'" Indeed, the abolition of slavery in the North following the Revolution
did not signify a fundamental abandonment of the presumed connection between freedom, equality, and whiteness. The many discriminatory laws passed
by Northern states, and the widespread antagonism to abolitionists, demonstrate that Southern slaves remained the negative point of reference defining
American identity for the great majority of Northerners. Support for the Republican Party in the years leading up to the Civil War was based overwhelmingly on the desire to keep slavery out of the western territories, not to ensure
its destruction in the South—to protect white freedom, not extend freedom to
Americans of African descent.[59]

In principle, the destruction of slavery, along with the passage of the Fourteenth and Fifteenth Amendments, established preconditions for a transformation in thinking about the meaning of race and national identity. But in the
South, the legacy of slavery, compounded no doubt by the enduring memory
of military defeat and occupation, left whites effectively in a state of denial.
The story of developments following Reconstruction is too familiar to need
elaboration here: disfranchisement, the proliferation of segregation laws, increasingly stringent anti-miscegenation legislation, lynchings. White Southerners continued to define their identity by reference to black Americans long
past the day when slavery ended. Wrote Ralph Ellison in 1963, "Southern whites
cannot walk, talk, sing, conceive of laws or justice, think of sex, love, the family
or freedom without responding to the presence of Negroes."[60]

Had the former slaves and their descendants remained overwhelmingly a
Southern population in the century following the Civil War, perhaps their presence in the consciousness of Americans elsewhere would have diminished.
But the disruption of immigration from Europe during World War I opened
up jobs in Northern industry that had previously been denied to people of
African descent. Approximately 500,000 black Southerners migrated north
between 1916 and 1919, nearly one million more the following decade. In the
1940s, economic opportunities created by World War II and its aftermath would

draw another two million north. The great majority both early and late settled in cities. Not incidentally (nor coincidentally), it was in the cities where most immigrant communities were located.[61]

Those who claimed the role of spokesmen for the black population sought political advantage by drawing attention to the purportedly deficient qualities of immigrants. In his famous speech at the Cotton States and International Exposition in Atlanta in 1895, Booker T. Washington promised white Americans, "We shall stand by you with a devotion that no foreigner can approach, ready to lay down our lives, if need be, in defence of yours, interlacing our industrial, commercial, civil, and religious life with yours in a way that shall make the interests of both races one." The *Chicago Defender* reminded whites in 1918 that, unlike immigrants from southern and eastern Europe, Negroes "need no Americanization."[62]

Slavs, Russian Jews, Greeks, and Italians discovered before long, however, as had Irish Catholics decades earlier, that not only was "Americanization" available to everyone of European ancestry, but a necessary first step was establishing social distance from, and demonstrating disrespect for, Negroes. In the summer of 1918, George Schuyler, "proudly dressed in the uniform of the United States Army," stopped at the train station in Philadelphia to get his boots shined. "The bootblack, a recent immigrant from Greece, refused in a loud voice to serve 'a nigger.'" Forty years later, local newspapers in the Calumet Park neighborhood of Chicago boasted that "it was Southern and Eastern Europeans who really built this country while Negroes were 'swinging in trees,' 'eating each other.'" A century earlier, Irish immigrants had gone to the polls in New York City shouting "Down with Nagurs!" and "Let them go back to Africa, where they belong."[63]

Immigrant communities were prominent in the making and perpetuation of black urban ghettos. Chicago provides an instructive example. After World War I, Wentworth Avenue served as a boundary separating Irish and black neighborhoods. Langston Hughes recalled his first visit to Chicago in his autobiography: "I went out walking alone to see what the city looked like. I wandered too far outside the Negro district, over beyond Wentworth, and was set upon and beaten by a group of white boys, who said they didn't allow niggers in that neighborhood. I came home with both eyes blacked and a swollen jaw." The next summer Chicago was embroiled in the worst urban race riot the nation had yet witnessed. In almost a week of fighting, twenty-three Negroes lost their lives and more than five hundred were injured. Hundreds of black families were left homeless when rioters torched their homes.[64]

After World War II the Irish were again involved in rioting in Chicago, this time to keep Negroes out of Englewood. Meanwhile, Slavs, Czechs, and Poles resorted to violence to bar them from Cicero and Trumbull Park. Walter White, executive secretary of the NAACP, claimed that he had never encountered as much "implacable hatred" in the South as he had in Cicero. "It was appalling to see and listen to those who were but recently the targets of hate and deprivations, who, beneficiaries of American opportunity, were as virulent as any Mississippian in their willingness to deny a place to live to a member of a race that had preceded them to America by many generations."[65]

It is unlikely that the Poles, Slavs, and Czechs saw the cruel irony so evident to White. European immigrants learned quickly that by sublimating their ethnic differences and publicly asserting racial kinship with the Founding Fathers, they could lay claim to the "inalienable rights" reserved for white citizens. Oakwood, a neighborhood on Detroit's far southwest side, was home to many Poles, Hungarians, and Italians in the years during and after World War II. Homeowners seeking to keep Negroes out of the community referred to themselves as "we the white people" when addressing public officials and insisted that the Constitution conferred on them, as one contemporary noted, "a vested, exclusive, and permanent 'right' to certain districts."[66]

★

Alien citizens were constantly reminded of the costs of being "not-white." But they learned quickly enough the compensation for being "not-black." So it was that, during the second decade of the twentieth century, when white farmers in central Texas were seeking allies in their fight against high rents, low wages, and poor living conditions, they turned to Mexican American sharecroppers and tenant farmers, not to Negroes. "Over time," Neil Foley writes, "Mexicans came to locate themselves in the ethnoracial middle ground between Anglo Americans and African Americans, not white enough to claim equality with Anglos and yet, in many cases, white enough to escape the worst features of the Jim Crow South." The influential League of United Latin American Citizens "emphasized the importance of maintaining the color line between its members and African Americans and urged members not to associate with Negroes. Mexican Americans objected strenuously to being labeled as 'colored' and to being forced to share facilities with African Americans." LULAC expelled one of its members for marrying a black woman; Mexican American families shunned the couple.[67]

In the 1870s, some plantation owners in the Mississippi Delta recruited male laborers from China, thinking to replace their recently freed slaves. Before long, however, many of the Chinese abandoned the cotton fields to set up grocery stores. In terms of segregation laws, they were initially treated as Negroes. They lived in black communities and some married black women. By the early 1920s, however, affluent merchants of Chinese ancestry were bringing petitions before the courts seeking the right to send their children to white schools. When their applications were denied, "the close-knit Chinese American community mobilized to demonstrate through their adoption of white social norms and etiquette that they should not be treated as if they were black—that is, to change the de facto racial definition of 'Chinese.'" Social pressure was brought to bear on men to abandon black wives; those who refused to do so faced ostracism, as did their children. In time, Chinese American men attained a measure of the upward mobility they sought. They were allowed to move their families into white residential neighborhoods and their children attended white schools.[68]

In the early years of the twentieth century, Negroes imagined that the West Coast offered a refuge from the discriminatory practices of the South. The social scientist Charles S. Johnson, speaking about Los Angeles, commented: "The focusing of racial interest upon the Oriental has in large measure overlooked the Negro, and the city accordingly, has been regarded by them, from a distance, as desirable and likely to yield for them important opportunities for living and earning a living." But Japanese immigrants in Los Angeles, like the Chinese in Mississippi, learned soon enough that demonstrating disdain for Negroes offered social advantages. Apparently at least some Japanese restaurants refused to admit black customers, leading the Los Angeles Times to observe, "The little brown Jap serves notice that the negro is no brother of his."[69]

The level of hostility toward both Japanese immigrants and Negroes was high during the 1920s and 1930s, producing "a measure of solidarity" between the two groups. And of course, Japanese Americans suffered the singular and abyssal pain of internment during World War II. Which makes it all that much more noteworthy that, in the very midst of the war, Gunnar Myrdal offered the following judgment: "Among the groups commonly considered unassimilable, the Negro people is by far the largest. The Negroes do not, like the Japanese and the Chinese, have a politically organized nation and an accepted culture of their own outside of America to fall back upon. Unlike the Oriental, there attaches to the Negro an historical memory of slavery and inferiority."[70]

★

In early colonial Virginia and Maryland, lawmakers often treated Africans and Native Americans as a single social entity. But then, in those days, some Indians were slaves. By the time of the founding of the United States, prominent public figures had concluded that Indians were candidates for assimilation. And even if settlers thought otherwise, through the nineteenth century there was a stark contrast between popular perceptions of Indians and of Negroes. Black men could not, Gary Gerstle notes, "play the role of the proud savage foe" because, in the minds of whites, "Africans were already a bowed and conquered people when they arrived, forced to obey their masters' every command."[71]

During the early twentieth century, racial theorists such as Madison Grant and Lothrop Stoddard invariably ranked Indians higher than Negroes on the scale of human intelligence. As evidence, they cited what they took to be the contrasting political and social histories of the two races in ancient times. In *The Rising Tide of Color,* Stoddard wrote, "there can be no doubt that the Indian is superior to the negro. The negro, even when quickened by foreign influences, never built up anything approaching a real civilization; whereas the Indian, though entirely sundered from the rest of mankind, evolved genuine polities and cultures." "The much praised dignity, independence, and virile manhood of Indians," Alan Trachtenberg has pointed out, "were often cited as a rebuke against the so-called inferiority of African Americans."[72]

★

Slavery defined the contours of, and gave substance to, American liberty and equality. And the memory of slavery—its constant manifestation in the deprivation of people of African descent—continued to shape racial identities in the United States for a century beyond Emancipation. Oklahoma, despite its tortured history of conflict between Indians and white settlers, produced a constitution in 1907 that included the following clarification: "Wherever in this Constitution and laws of this state, the word or words, 'colored' or 'colored race,' 'negro,' or 'negro race,' are used, the same shall be construed to apply to all persons of African descent. The term 'white race' shall include all other persons." The president of the union of railway clerks, based in Chicago, was asked in 1919 whether Mexicans were white and therefore eligible for membership. "They are certainly considered white, as is the American Indian," he replied. The provision of the constitution defining qualifications for membership "has always been construed as simply to debar the Negro or those who have African blood in their veins." During World War II, future U.S. senator Daniel Inouye later recalled, young Japanese American men who had been released from the internment camps and inducted into the army were told when they arrived in the South for training that "we would be considered as white people," and were not to use the facilities marked "colored."[73]

The United States was conceived in liberty. It was conceived in white supremacy as well. While both concepts had origins in Western thought, the specific meaning attached to liberty at the time of the Revolution, and to white supremacy, was largely determined by the presence of 500,000 slaves of African descent, one-fifth of the population. As Nikhil Singh has observed, "Blacks presented the anomaly of an exclusion that was at once foundational and located within the polity." The slaves of the Revolutionary generation, it might be said, shared paternity with the Founding Fathers in the birth of the nation, or rather in the birth of America's national identity.[74]

3 • The Negro, "Incarnation of America"

From the founding of the United States to the dawn of the Civil Rights Era, Americans of African ancestry lived in a nation committed to white supremacy. It was a nation, as well, in which those citizens and immigrants who could not claim the benefits conferred by "whiteness" were at least able to gain certain privileges and a measure of protection by asserting their social distance from those whose skin color marked them as slaves or the descendants of slaves. Under the circumstances, it is more than noteworthy that during those years—a span of almost two centuries—black Americans time and again, and in diverse ways, demonstrated their commitment to the United States. Not, of course, to its racial ideology, to its institutionalization of white racial privilege. And not, with the notable exceptions of Abraham Lincoln and Franklin Roosevelt, to its leaders. No, the commitment made by black Americans was to the ideals of freedom and equality set out in the Declaration of Independence, to its promise of democracy. Through the logic of their own deprivation, individuals of African descent became the most forward looking of all Americans.

★

On January 15, 1817, three thousand residents of Philadelphia packed into the Bethel African Methodist Church. They were there to offer their collective response to the founding, a month earlier, of the Society for the Colonization of the Free People of Color in the United States (better known by the name it later adopted, the American Colonization Society). At the inauguration of the new organization, Henry Clay had asked: "Can there be a nobler cause than that which, whilst it proposes to rid our country of a useless and pernicious, if not dangerous portion of its population, contemplates the spreading of the

arts of civilized life, and the possible redemption from ignorance and barbarism of a benighted quarter of the globe?"[1] The Negroes of Philadelphia gave
their answer resoundingly in the preamble to a series of resolutions passed
unanimously at the January 15 event:

> WHEREAS, Our ancestors (not of choice) were the first successful cultiva-
> tors of the wilds of America, we their descendants feel ourselves entitled
> to participate in the blessings of her luxuriant soil, which their blood and
> sweat manured; and that any measure or system of measures, having
> a tendency to banish us from her bosom, would not only be cruel, but
> in direct violation of those principles which have been the boast of this
> republic.

Responding directly to Clay, the document continued,

> We view with deep abhorrence, the unmerited stigma attempted to be
> cast upon the reputation of the free people of color, by the promoters of
> this measure, "that they are a dangerous and useless part of the commu-
> nity," when in the state of disfranchisement in which they live, in the
> hour of danger they ceased to remember their wrongs, and rallied around
> the standard of their country.[2]

"The standard of *their* country." The sentiments expressed in Philadelphia
were echoed by Negroes from Boston down into the South.[3]

To be sure, during the first years following the Revolution, some Negroes
had argued that emigration to Africa was preferable to life in the new nation.
The African Society of Providence sent an emissary in 1795 to explore the
possibility of settlement in the British colony of Sierra Leone. The founding
document for the Free African Union Society of Newport, Rhode Island, the
first mutual aid society in the United States established by and for people of
African descent, expressed the "earnest desire" on the part of the membership
for "returning to Africa." "*Returning* to Africa" could have had either literal or
metaphorical meaning since the slave trade did not formally come to an end
until 1808. Still, the widespread use of the adjective "African" in the names of
churches and societies during the early years of the republic demonstrates
that many American-born Negroes must have felt a strong sense of connected-
ness to the continent of their ancestral homelands.[4]

Then again, it tells us something that in 1795 a free husband and wife of

African descent living in Virginia chose to name their newborn daughter "America." And it tells us much more that Negroes protested heatedly against their exclusion from the state militias. We are "the descendants of Revolution sires, and Revolution mothers," argued William Watkins of Massachusetts, "the descendants of those, who, in those times that tried men's souls, counted not their lives dear unto them, but their blood flowed freely in defense of their country; they fought, they bled, they conquered—aye, they died, that we might live as free men. . . . Our fathers were not able-bodied white male citizens; but they were able enough to face British cannon in 1776 and 1812."[5]

Then came the formation of the American Colonization Society. Such support as had existed among free Negroes for emigration to Africa collapsed almost immediately. The few who agreed to go to the ACS colony of Liberia faced vitriol. In his famous antislavery *Appeal* in 1829, David Walker lashed out: "Those who are ignorant enough to go to Africa, the coloured people ought to be glad to have them go, for if they are ignorant enough to let the whites *fool* them off to Africa, they would be no small injury to us if they reside in this country." Antagonism to the "meaning, methods, and motives of the American Colonization Society," the historian Leonard Sweet has argued, "did more to generate black solidarity and engender a sense of identity among the black community than any other single issue in the first half of the nineteenth century." Declared Peter Williams, the pastor at St. Philip's Episcopal Church in New York on July 4, 1930:

> We are natives of this country, we ask only to be treated as well as foreigners. Not a few of our fathers suffered and bled to purchase its independence; we ask only to be treated as well as those who fought against it. We have toiled to cultivate it, and to raise it to its present prosperous condition; we ask only to share equal privileges with those who come from distant lands to enjoy the fruits of our labour. Let these moderate requests be granted, and we need not go to Africa nor anywhere else, to be improved and happy. We cannot but doubt the purity of the motives of those persons who deny us these requests and would send us to Africa to gain what they might give us at home.[6]

When whites increasingly pressed for colonization following the Nat Turner Rebellion, the new National Negro Convention movement called for removal of "the title of African" from "institutions, the marbles of their churches, and etc." The African Methodist Episcopal Church was the most prominent organization to resist, but it was unrepresentative. "'African' was literally effaced from the dedicatory plaques and escutcheons of hundreds of churches, schools, and benevolent societies." "Since colonial days," observes James Campbell, "'African' had remained the accepted term of address for black people in North America. For some at least, it was a term of great pride, as the various 'African' institutions chartered in the late-eighteenth and early-nineteenth centuries attested. But by the early 1830s, many black leaders had concluded that the term was an unaffordable luxury, that in calling themselves Africans they lent credence to colonizationists' claims that they rightly 'belonged' in Africa rather than the United States."[7]

The growing sectional tensions after the Mexican War and the passage of the Fugitive Slave Act in 1850 led some free Negroes to entertain the overtures of the American Colonization Society. Between 1848 and 1860, no fewer than 649 black Northerners sailed for Africa under ACS sponsorship, two and a half times as many as had emigrated during the previous thirty years. Still, when Negroes tried to organize emigration schemes of their own before the Civil War, they showed as much interest in Canada, Central America, and Haiti as Africa. That, James Meriwether has suggested, "reflected at least in part ongoing fears by free blacks that identifying too strongly with Africa would undermine the quest for freedom and for full citizenship." But emigration schemes, whether directed south, north, or across the Atlantic, gained little support even in the moments of greatest pessimism about the future. "The truth is, dear madam," Frederick Douglass wrote Harriet Beecher Stowe in March 1853, during the heart of the sectional crisis, "we are *here,* and here we are likely to remain. Individuals emigrate—nations never. We have grown up with this republic, and I see nothing in her character, or even in the character of the American people as yet, which compels the belief that we must leave the United States."[8]

★

In 1859 Martin Delany purchased land in Liberia, intending to establish a settlement there. During the Civil War, however, he began to hope that the United States might yet extend the promise of freedom and equality to all its people. He recruited troops and received a commission as the first black major in the Union Army. Later he served in the Freedmen's Bureau and went to work for the Republican Party in South Carolina. But by a decade after the war, he had grown disillusioned. Repudiating the possibility of a meaningful "Reconstruction," he directed his energies to assisting those Negroes who wished to emigrate to Liberia. At the same time he wrote *Principia of Ethnology: The Origin of Races and Color,* an attempt to trace the history and present circumstances of the black race. The two exercises—assisting emigration to Africa and writing on race—were related, because he believed that history demonstrated both the backwardness of Africans and American Negroes' responsibility to bring about their—the Africans'—elevation on the scale of humanity.

> Untrammeled in its native purity, the race is a noble one, and worthy to emulate the noble and Anglo-Saxon, now at the top round of the ladder of moral and intellectual grandeur in the progress of civilization. . . . With an abiding trust in God our Heavenly King, we shall boldly advance, singing the sweet songs of redemption, in the regeneration of our race and restoration of our father-land from the gloom and darkness of superstition and ignorance, to the glorious light of a more than pristine brightness— the light of the highest godly civilization.[9]

He famously called for "Africa for the African race, and black men to rule them" and insisted that the "regeneration of the African race can only be effected by its own efforts, the efforts of its own self." But believing as he did in the superiority of Western civilization, he was calling, as James Campbell has aptly phrased it, for "a kind of racial trusteeship" by black Americans.[10]

The most noteworthy proponent of emigration to Africa in the last decades of the nineteenth century was Henry McNeal Turner, a bishop in the African Methodist Episcopal Church. Like Martin Delany, he became involved in Republican politics during Reconstruction—in Turner's case in Georgia—but ultimately he too grew disillusioned and called for abandonment of the United States. He attacked the "Negro dirt-eaters" and "scullions" who chose "extermination" in the American South rather than freedom and independence in Africa. But like Delany, he took it as a given that Africans were backward, requiring uplift by black Americans, who apparently had benefited from their immersion in American values and beliefs. Turner and Delany were key figures in the creation of the Liberian Exodus Company, which in 1878 funded the passage of 206 men, women, and children from Charleston to Liberia. Turner consecrated the voyage, saying that black Americans had been called by God to "take back the culture, education and religion acquired here." Other proponents of emigration such as Alexander Crummell and Henry Highland Garnet also saw themselves engaged in "a kind of civilizing mission." Crummell believed that slavery was "part of God's providential design for Africa as well as punishment for her heathenism. Through slavery, God paradoxically blessed Africans in America with democracy and Christianity."[11]

The majority of black Americans in the last decades of the nineteenth century did not identify with Africa as an ancestral homeland. It is no coincidence that the most outspoken opponent of emigration, Frederick Douglass, was also the most respected black public figure of his generation. He made his perspective clear in a speech at the Metropolitan A.M.E. Church in Washington on January 9, 1894:

> Now I hold that the American Negro owes no more to the Negroes in Africa than he owes to the Negroes in America. There are millions of needy people over there, but there are also millions of needy people over here as well, and the millions in America need intelligent men of their own number to help them, as much as intelligent men are needed in Africa to help her people. . . . The native land of the American Negro is America. His bones, his muscles, his sinews, are all American. His ancestors for two hundred and seventy years have lived and labored and died, on American soil, and millions of his posterity have inherited Caucasian blood. . . . I object to the colonization scheme, because it tends to weaken the Negro's hold on one country, while it can give him no rational hope of another. Its tendency is to make him despondent and doubtful, where he should feel assured and confident. It forces upon him the idea that he is forever doomed to be a stranger and a sojourner in the land of his birth, and that he has no permanent abiding place here.[12]

For all the disagreements that Douglass had with advocates of emigration, he did share their perceptions of Africa, and they shared his fundamental commitment to American values. Douglass agreed with Turner and Delany that Africa was plagued by irreligion; he often drew sharp distinctions between "the splendors of Europe" and "the wilds of Africa." Meanwhile, Turner and Delany imagined remaking Africa in the image of America. Like most proponents of emigration, they dreamed of building "modern, civilized, powerful nations where black people could create their own wealth and rule themselves. They imagined a society patterned on the West—its schools, railroads, factories, and religion—without the racism, inequality, and oppression." They believed, as well, in the fundamental principles that underlay the American political order. A protégé of Bishop Turner, Reverend Anthony Stanford, organized the Liberian Exodus Arkansas Colony, which settled about seven hundred black

Americans in Africa at the end of the nineteenth century. The charter of the organization began: "We hold these truths to be self-evident, that all men are created equal; that they are endowed by their creator with certain inalienable rights; that among these are life, liberty, and the pursuit of happiness."[13]

★

Three figures came to dominate black American public life during the thirty years following the death of Frederick Douglass in 1895. Booker T. Washington, W. E. B. Du Bois, and Marcus Garvey could hardly have been more different from each other in background or in the images they projected to whites. Yet each of the three men, in his own way, testified to the commitment among Americans of African descent to the United States—not only to the principles celebrated in its founding documents, but also to the underlying capitalist foundation on which the nation was built, a foundation that historically had tolerated, if not produced, social relations at odds with those principles.

The devotion of Booker T. Washington to American values hardly needs elaboration. It was manifest in the school he established in Tuskegee and in his autobiography *Up from Slavery*, published in 1901. He preached the virtues of thrift and self-help and crafted his image as the exemplary self-made man. As his biographer Louis Harlan explains, "He presented himself simply but without false modesty as possessing all the virtues extolled by Cotton Mather, Poor Richard, and Ralph Waldo Emerson, and his life as a string of anecdotes illustrating these traits." Meanwhile, his material success and elevated social standing effectively identified him to contemporaries as "the Horatio Alger myth in black."[14]

Washington actively worked behind the scenes to subvert the discriminatory apparatus of the Southern legal system that he appeared to accept in speeches before white audiences. But his goal was hardly to subvert the character of the capitalist order in which the discriminatory apparatus operated. As Wilson Jeremiah Moses has observed, "Washington, like most progressive liberals, was committed to promoting fundamental changes in American race relations, but like most conservatives, he believed that these changes must occur naturally within the framework of evolving corporate capitalism." In 1910, the sociologist Robert E. Park traveled across the Atlantic with Washington to investigate the lives of the European poor. Park later commented privately, "When he [Washington] was abroad he was not interested in the common people as I thought he would be. They were just foreigners. He was an American and thought everything in America surpassed anything in Europe."[15]

Marcus Garvey read *Up from Slavery* when he was living in London. It prompted him to ask (or so he later claimed), "'Where is the black man's government?' 'Where is his King and his kingdom?' 'Where is his President, his country, and his ambassador, his army, his navy, his men of big affairs?' I could not find them, and then I declared, 'I will help to make them.'" In 1914, after he had returned from England to Jamaica and created the Universal Negro Improvement Association (UNIA), Garvey corresponded with Washington, sending him promotional literature for the organization and a copy of his newspaper, *The Negro World*. The two men never met, however. Washington died in late 1915, just months before Garvey came to the United States.[16]

Some scholars have argued that Washington had a significant influence on the development of black nationalism in America. But observers at the time hardly saw Garvey as Washington's natural heir. For one thing, unlike Washington, whose father was white, Garvey was contemptuous of Negroes with European ancestry. Beyond that, where Washington argued that Negroes were largely responsible for their own struggles, Garvey charged: "For over three hundred years the white man has been our oppressor, and he naturally is not going to liberate us to the higher freedom—the truer liberty—the truer Democracy. We have to liberate ourselves."[17]

But seemingly the most noteworthy difference between the two men lay in the simple fact that Washington was above all concerned with securing the future for Negroes in America while Garvey concentrated his attention on the development of Africa. Not that Washington was indifferent to conditions in colonial regimes. In the latter part of his career he sent Tuskegee students to work in Africa, he collaborated with Robert E. Park to expose the horrors in the Belgian Congo, and, in 1912, he hosted an International Conference on the Negro at Tuskegee. But if Louis Harlan is right, a prime concern of such efforts was "to demonstrate the impracticality of American black emigration to a colonialized Africa as a solution to racial problems in the United States."[18]

Garvey, by contrast, saw Africa as the continent of destiny for Negroes. In 1920, in one of the more flamboyant acts in a flamboyant career, he had himself elected provisional president of Africa at a mass rally for the UNIA in Madison Square Garden. Not that he championed an exodus of Negroes from the United States. UNIA official William Sherrill explained in 1922, "The UNIA is not a 'Back to Africa' movement, it is a movement to redeem Africa. The Negro in America has had a better opportunity than any other Negro." Garvey himself said, just eight months after he first arrived in Harlem, "Industrially, financially, educationally, and socially, the Negroes of both hemispheres have to defer to the American brother, the fellow who has revolutionized history in race development." Like Martin Delany, Henry McNeal Turner, and other nineteenth-century spokesmen for colonization, Garvey saw Africa as the land where Negroes would finally realize the promise of the American way of life, a promise they all cherished in the ideal.[19]

"Be it known to all men that whereas all men are created equal and entitled to the rights of life, liberty and the pursuit of happiness . . . " begins the preamble to the Declaration of the Negro Peoples of the World, drafted and adopted at the same UNIA convention in New York where Garvey assumed the title "Provisional President of Africa." The document then goes on to attack taxation without representation as "unjust and tyrannous"; to endorse democracy, freedom of the press, and free speech; and to "declare for the freedom of religious worship." "If black men have to die in Africa or anywhere else," wrote Garvey at the time of the Peace Conference in Paris following World War I, "then they might as well die for the best of things, and that is liberty, true freedom and true democracy."[20]

But Garvey was not only a champion (in rhetoric at least) of Western political ideals. "If native Africans," he wrote, "are unable to appreciate the value of their own country from the standard of western civilization, then it is for us, their brothers to take to them the knowledge and information that they need to develop the country for the common good." And the form development must take? "Capitalism is necessary to the progress of the world, and those who unreasonably or wantonly oppose or fight against it are enemies to human development." "If the oil of Africa is good for Rockefeller's interest; if iron ore is good for the Carnegie Trust; then surely these minerals are good for us," he wrote. "Why should we allow Wall Street and the capitalist group of America and other countries to exploit our country when they refuse to give us a fair chance in the countries of our adoption? Why should Africa not give to the world its black Rockefeller, Rothschild and Henry Ford? Now is the opportunity. Now is the chance for every Negro to make every effort toward a commercial, industrial standard that will make us comparable with the successful businessmen of other races."[21] Whatever differences in style and language divided Garvey and Washington, whatever differences they had in their imaginings about Africa and the future for Negroes in the United States, they shared a fundamental faith in American values.

W. E. B. Du Bois was an outspoken opponent of both men. His public criticism of Garvey even descended to vicious personal attacks: "Marcus Garvey is, without doubt, the most dangerous enemy of the Negro race in America and in the world. He is either a lunatic or a traitor." But during the first quarter of the twentieth century, Du Bois was not yet the committed radical he would become later in life. As Judith Stein has observed, Du Bois and Garvey each in his own way "sought to replicate the latest achievements of the modern world. They probed beneath the rhetoric of racism but not of capitalism. . . . Rejecting the political control of an alien race, they did not question the cultural values that instructed that race." Indeed, Du Bois had kind words for both Washington and Garvey, at least when discussing their economic programs. On Washington: "So far as Mr. Washington preaches Thrift, Patience, and Industrial Training for the masses, we must hold up his hands and strive with him, rejoicing in his honors and glorying in the strength of this Joshua called of God and of man to lead the headless host." On Garvey: "He has worthy industrial and commercial schemes. . . . His dreams of Negro industry, commerce and the ultimate freedom of Africa are feasible."[22]

To be sure, even in the early years of the twentieth century, Du Bois expressed qualms about American capitalism—or at least materialism—that are not evident in the pronouncements of either Washington or Garvey. And in a number of his early writings, Du Bois identified himself as a socialist. Not, however, a socialist in the sense Marx would have understood the term. He saw no basis for an alliance of workers across color lines: "Theoretically we are a part of the world proletariat in the sense that we are mainly an exploited class of cheap laborers; but practically we are not a part of the white proletariat and are not recognized by that proletariat to any great extent. We are the victims of their physical oppression, social ostracism, economic exclusion and personal hatred; and when in self defense we seek sheer subsistence we are howled down as 'scabs.'" The triumph of Bolshevism in Russia and the advance of communist political organizations in Europe filled him with foreboding rather than expectation. As he wrote in July 1921: "The editor of *The Crisis* considers himself a Socialist but he does not believe that German State Socialism or the dictatorship of the proletariat are perfect panaceas. He believes with most thinking men that the present method of creating, controlling and distributing wealth is desperately wrong; that there must come and is coming a social control of wealth; but he does not know just what form that control is going to take, and he is not prepared to dogmatize with Marx or Lenin."[23]

In those days the mission he prescribed for Americans of African descent was less to overturn capitalism than to make it more humane. Indeed, he suggested that Negroes were uniquely qualified for the job. Just a month before he refused "to dogmatize with Marx or Lenin," he wrote with evident hopefulness about the movement to create a bank in Harlem:

> The Negro bank is eventually going to bring into cooperation and concentration the resources of fifty or sixty other Negro banks in the United States, and this aggregation of capital is going to be used to break the power of white capital in enslaving and exploiting the darker world. Whether this is a program of socialism or capitalism does not concern us. It is the only program that means salvation to the Negro race. The main danger and the central question of the capitalistic development through which the Negro-American group is forced to go is the question of the ultimate control of the capital which they must raise and use. If this capital is going to be controlled by a few men for their own benefit, then we are destined to suffer from our own capitalists exactly what we are suffering from white capitalists today. And while this is not a pleasant prospect, it is certainly no worse than the present actuality. If, on the other hand, because of our more democratic organization and our widespread inter-class sympathy we can introduce a more democratic control, taking advantage of what the white world is itself doing to introduce industrial democracy, then we may not only escape our present economic slavery but even guide and lead a distrait economic world.[24]

"Du Bois," notes Tommie Shelby, "viewed the world-historical mission of African Americans to be the perfecting of the ideals of American democracy."[25]

★

By the 1930s Du Bois had begun the intellectual odyssey that would lead him to Marxism and, ultimately, membership in the Communist Party. But, then, the Great Depression created conditions that arguably should have led many black Americans to question the capitalist underpinnings of the nation. As Harvard Sitkoff points out, "The depression dealt a staggering blow to blacks. It magnified all their traditional economic liabilities. It created newer and harsher ones. No group could less afford the precipitous decline that followed the stock market crash of 1929. None suffered more from it." Indeed, the great majority of Negroes experienced "extreme privation and the concomitant ravages of malnutrition, disease, overcrowding, and family disintegration." Over 40 percent of black men in Harlem could not find work. The situation was much the same in Philadelphia, Chicago, and Detroit. In Atlanta, whites formed an organization called the Black Shirts. Its slogan was "No Jobs for Niggers until Every White Man Has a Job." "At no time in the history of the Negro since slavery," concluded T. Arnold Hill of the Urban League, "has his economic and social outlook seemed so discouraging."[26]

In the aftermath of World War I and into the 1920s, a small number of black activists had embraced socialism. The African Blood Brotherhood was a secret organization of "militant black-nationalist Marxists" founded by Cyril Briggs, an immigrant to Harlem from the island of Nevis. Another recent arrival to Harlem from the West Indies, Hubert Harrison, created the Liberty League and championed a New Negro Manhood movement, both of which combined black nationalism and opposition to capitalism. In 1917, A. Philip Randolph and Chandler Owen launched *The Messenger*, a journal dedicated both to socialism and to black liberation.[27]

Still, Marxist ideology attracted few black followers in the 1920s. Part of the reason had to do with the blinkered position adopted by the leadership of the Socialist Party. "What the Negro wants and needs," claimed Norman Thomas, "is what the white worker wants and needs; neither more nor less." In 1928, the Communist International (Comintern), hoping to take advantage of the spirit of black nationalism inspired by Marcus Garvey, proclaimed the right of self-determination for Negroes in the black belt. But "regardless of our efforts and the large sums of money spent on that sort of propaganda," admitted a Jewish organizer, "we made very little headway among the Negro masses."[28] Made little headway until, that is, the trial of the "Scottsboro Boys."

In March of 1931, nine black boys ranging in ages from twelve or thirteen to nineteen were pulled by a posse from a Memphis-bound freight train in northern Alabama and charged with the rape of two white women. In a matter of days, they were put on trial in the town of Scottsboro, Alabama, and convicted. Eight of the nine received death sentences. Communist organizations, seeing an opportunity to raise their profile among Negroes, launched demonstrations across the United States. And the International Labor Defense (ILD), effectively the legal arm of the American Communist Party, stepped in to take responsibility for mounting appeals in the state courts of Alabama and, later, the federal courts. Over the next four years, the ILD won two groundbreaking victories before the U.S. Supreme Court, getting one conviction overturned because the legal counsel provided had clearly been inadequate, and a second overturned because Alabama had historically excluded Negroes from jury service.[29]

The efforts of the ILD on behalf of the Scottsboro Boys gained communist spokesmen access to black social organizations and churches across the country. Muting their attacks on capitalism, the communists concentrated on developing strategies to help Negroes survive the Depression. In Chicago, "the Communists began a vigorous program of organization in the Black Belt, forming neighborhood Unemployed Councils to demand adequate relief. It was these councils that led the fight against evictions, and hundreds of non-Communists followed their lead." What happened in Chicago happened, in one form or another, in other cities in the North, and in the South. Hosea Hudson, an Alabama steelworker who rose to prominence in the Communist Party, remembered: "The main thing that attracted people [to the Party] was unemployed relief. That was the main thing we talked about in the units. Unemployed relief didn't just mean food. It meant getting some coal, it also meant paying the rent, cause a lot of people couldn't pay the rent, and the landlords would be threatening to put them outdoors. We'd get us a postcard, get the landlord's name, go to writing down, demanding not to put the people out the room." Party activists launched an interracial unemployed council in Winston-Salem. Recalled union organizer Robert Black: "They would go down to city hall or to the county commissioners and put pressure on them to appeal for government help. My mother along with a few others were able to get some food and clothes, a ton of coal or a load of wood every now and then, and sometimes six or eight dollars to help pay the rent. Now it was nothing but just the roughest food, pinto beans and fatback meat, but it was something to keep you from starving."[30]

The decision by the Comintern in 1935 to sanction cooperation between party members and other organizations dedicated to fighting fascism—the plan of action known as the Popular Front—only furthered the tendency of party spokesmen to downplay Marxist rhetoric. Before long, American communists were openly seeking alliances with liberals. Still, the communists took much more aggressive steps than liberals to combat racism and promote equality across the color line. When the party expelled a white member for segregating guests at a social function, the *Chicago Defender* ran an editorial under the heading "Why We Can't Hate Reds": "How, under such circumstances, can we go to war with the Communist Party? Is there any other political, religious, or civic organization that would go to such lengths to prove itself not unfriendly to us?" The editor of the *Oklahoma Black Dispatch*, himself a member of the NAACP board of directors, praised the communists for denouncing "Jim Crow, segregation and anti-marriage laws, yes, everything which has hitherto separated the black and white here in America." Duke Ellington agreed to provide entertainment for a party-sponsored dance at Harlem's Rockland Palace in

March 1931. "More than one thousand black and white activists showed up for the affair. In between dancing to Ellington, they sang the Internationale, watched an interracial dance troupe, and listened to speeches by Party leaders."[31]

But if the communists were able to capture the hearts of many Negroes, they were notably unsuccessful in capturing minds. While Harlem intellectuals represented something of an exception, "the dominant voices in upper-crust African-American political culture—Walter White, James Weldon Johnson, A. Philip Randolph—were, by and large, staunchly anticommunist." The Communist Party reported a black membership of more than 1,400 in 1934. By 1939 the number had risen to 5,005. But scholars agree that officials inflated enrollment figures and, in any case, most black members did not participate actively in party affairs and many abandoned their affiliation after only a few months. At the height of the Depression, the great majority of Negroes chose to place their faith not in the Communists but in the existing American political system. Or rather, quite improbably they chose to place their faith in the head of a party that historically had been dominated by its Southern wing—a party that in the South had brought in legalized segregation and disfranchisement. In the election of 1936, the Democratic candidate for president, Franklin Roosevelt, captured 81 percent of the vote in Harlem, 75 percent in black neighborhoods in Pittsburgh, 69 percent in black neighborhoods in Philadelphia, and 66 percent in black neighborhoods in Detroit. The figures far exceeded the percentage of the popular vote he picked up nationwide. Four years later he once again secured a massive majority of the black vote. Of course, few Negroes in the South were able to cast a ballot during the Depression years. But the evidence suggests that here, too, Roosevelt was immensely popular.[32]

Historians have identified a number of factors that explain support for the president in black communities. His wife, Eleanor, formed close friendships with prominent black leaders such as Walter White and Mary McLeod Bethune, brought forward their concerns within the administration, and became a public spokesperson for civil rights. She also helped Negroes secure government appointments. By the middle of 1935, there were about forty-five men and women of African descent holding down positions in New Deal agencies or cabinet departments. These officials began to meet and plot strategy about how best to take advantage of the new activist role of government. The "Black Cabinet," as it came to be known, helped Negroes get government jobs, fought discriminatory practices, and directed individuals through the maze of New Deal agencies. Above all, it kept the news media focused on issues of concern to the black population.[33]

But the single most important reason Negroes supported Roosevelt was his determination to improve the material conditions of all Americans who were victims of the Depression, regardless of race. Nancy Weiss, whose *Farewell to the Party of Lincoln* remains the best guide to black political allegiances during the 1930s, makes the point concisely: "The transcendence of economic over racial concerns during the Depression, indeed the close congruence of race and class for blacks, made it possible for the Democratic party to win black voters by the simple fact of not excluding them from the economic benefits that it brought to suffering Americans generally. To be sure, the New Deal's excursions into racial symbolism helped appreciably to cement the bond, but the essential political tie was forged in the cauldron of economic distress."[34]

By 1941 there were more than 150,000 Negroes employed in the federal government. Nearly a quarter of a million learned to read and write under programs offered by the Works Progress Administration (WPA—renamed the Work Projects Administration in 1939); tens of thousands received the training necessary to become skilled workers. Black musicians, writers, artists, and performers received funding from the Federal Music Project, the Federal Art Project, the Federal Writers' Project, and the Federal Theatre Project. By 1939 the WPA was providing basic earnings for a million Negroes. "The millions of dollars spent by the WPA in African American communities," writes Harvard Sitkoff, "meant survival, when even that had been previously in doubt. After 1936 the proportion of black WPA workers varied from 15 to 20 percent. In many cities the percentage of blacks in the WPA ran as high as three to five times their percentage in the population, a testament both to the acute effect of the depression on blacks and to the readiness of the New Deal to come to their rescue. . . . The Work Projects Administration, in fact, provided an economic floor for the whole black community in the 1930s, rivaling both agriculture and domestic service as the chief source of income for blacks."[35]

Yet for all that Roosevelt did to improve the material conditions of many Negroes during the Depression, he hardly made a meaningful effort to eliminate racial injustice. The legislation he introduced to address the economic crisis after he first took office in 1933—the first New Deal—allowed, and to some degree even fostered, discrimination. The Civilian Conservation Corps (CCC) was created to provide work for unemployed young men, but although over half the population of Mississippi was black, fewer than 2 percent of CCC positions in the state went to Negroes. According to the Agricultural Adjustment Act, federal grants were to be divided equitably between Southern planters and their tenants. But local committees determined the distribution of funds and not a single black planter or tenant received a committee appointment. Discrimination was rampant in the Tennessee Valley Authority. And after passage of the National Recovery Act (NRA), which required companies to give the same wages to all workers, employers fired previously underpaid black laborers and handed their jobs to whites. The situation was so bad that black critics came to refer to the NRA as the "Negro Removal Act" or "Negroes Robbed Again." A conference in Washington organized by black leaders in May 1935 concluded that "black labor finds itself comparatively in a worse position than it occupied at the beginning of the depression" and that "the will of those who have kept the Negroes in economic disfranchisement has been permitted to prevail, and the government has looked on in silence and at times with approval. Consequently, the Negro worker has good reason to feel that his government has betrayed him under the New Deal."[36]

It is true that beginning in 1935, the Roosevelt administration made serious, if halting, efforts to prevent discrimination in the implementation of its programs, especially in the North. Harry Hopkins, in particular, won praise from black leaders for his efforts at the WPA. But the summary that Sitkoff provides of the situation faced by Negroes at the end of the New Deal highlights how limited the actions of the administration were in rewriting the racial script in America:

Little had changed in the concrete aspects of life for most blacks. They remained a submerged caste, commonly discriminated against by industry, the labor movement, and government at all levels. Blacks continued to be mired in the ranks of menials, sharecroppers, unskilled laborers, and domestics. They were twice as likely to be unemployed as whites and earned only half the income of whites when they could find work. The advances made in educational opportunities, infant and maternal mortality rates, and occupational mobility served mainly to heighten black awareness of the disparities between African Americans and whites that still existed. Blacks in the North overwhelmingly lived in ghettos that had turned into slums. In the South, where a majority of blacks endured, white supremacy and segregation remained the rule. The bulk of African Americans could not vote. None could go to school with whites. All had to ride in the back of the bus. Every public toilet and drinking fountain in the region had signs lettered "White Only" or "Colored." In the heart of the nation's capital, blacks could not attend a movie, stay at a hotel, or buy a cup of coffee.[37]

And then there is the fact that throughout his time in office, Roosevelt steadfastly resisted pressure to endorse anti-lynching legislation. During a meeting with Walter White, head of the NAACP, the president justified his inaction this way: "I've got to get legislation passed by Congress to save America. The Southerners by reason of the seniority rule in Congress are chairmen or occupy strategic places on most of the Senate and House committees. If I come out for the anti-lynching bill now, they will block every bill I ask Congress to pass to keep America from collapsing. I just can't take that risk." The same logic explains why he did so little to combat racial discrimination in the implementation of New Deal programs in the South.[38]

On the basis of this evidence, it would be easy to conclude that Negroes must have supported Roosevelt provisionally and just to the extent that they gained material benefits from the legislation he introduced. But in fact, as Nancy Weiss has observed, they not only voted for Roosevelt, "they idolized him." More than a few black parents named their children after the president. "They hung his picture—often a full-page campaign photograph cut out of a newspaper—beside that of Christ or Lincoln on the walls of their homes." Wrote a woman from Texas: "It seem lak we got a unseen Eye watchin' an' studyin' our troubles an' lookin' after 'em . . . I feel lak he's jes' another Moses God has done sent to head His chillun . . . I'se restin' easy cause I know he's got his han' on de throttle an' his eye on de rail." A South Carolina man told a WPA interviewer: "I think Mr. Lincoln was raised up by de Lord, just like Moses, to free a 'culiar people. I think Mr. Roosevelt is de Joshua dat come after him."[39]

How to explain this adulation for a president who was accepting of segregation and disfranchisement, who tolerated a substantial measure of discrimination against Negroes in relief programs, and who failed to offer even minimal endorsement to anti-lynching legislation? It was, it seems, because Negroes assumed—or rather, convinced themselves—that he shared their own "emancipatory vision." The obituary for Roosevelt in the *Norfolk Journal and Guide* makes the point: He did "more than any other," the writer concluded, "to make our emancipation real, to lift us from the depths of second-class citizenship, to make us free and equal men in a nation pledged to democracy in fact as well as in theory." The assessment, of course, was faulty. But it speaks to the fundamental commitment that the vast majority of Negroes felt toward America, to what they believed it represented, and how much they conceived of themselves as a vital part of the imagined community that was the United States.[40]

In the end that was why the communists, for all their grassroots activism and genuine racial egalitarianism, had little chance of winning converts beyond an unrepresentative element of Harlem intellectuals. Their emancipatory vision of international revolution and the destruction of capitalism was not the vision of the great majority of American blacks. James W. Ford clearly recognized the problem. In his acceptance speech as the vice-presidential candidate for the Communist Party in 1936—the first black man ever to be placed on a presidential ticket—he invoked John Brown, Frederick Douglass, and Abraham Lincoln. "We Communists, Negro and white," Ford proclaimed, "will carry out what they dreamed of."[41]

★

In 1916, while war raged in Europe, A. Philip Randolph organized a campaign to persuade Harlem Negroes not to enlist in the National Guard. When the United States finally joined the Allies in the quest "to make the world safe for democracy," he gave speeches encouraging Negroes to resist conscription and devote their martial energies to battling discrimination at home, "to make America unsafe for hypocrisy." In 1940, by contrast, when a second war engulfed Europe, Randolph, then president of the Brotherhood of Sleeping Car Porters, became an active member of the Committee to Defend America by Aiding the Allies. Then, once the United States had entered the conflict, he founded the March on Washington Movement to put pressure on the Roosevelt administration to ensure just treatment for Negroes in the war effort. The different positions taken at different times by Randolph illustrate the diverse reactions by people of African descent when the nation faced a call to arms and sought the unquestioning support of all its citizens—reactions that included resistance, compliance, and compliance with conditions. But within that range of responses there was a common theme: the principles on which America was founded were principles worth fighting for. At issue was the location of the battlefields.[42]

Black men fought in the Revolutionary War and in all major American conflicts of the nineteenth century with the exception of the war with Mexico. By far their most noteworthy contribution came in the Civil War, when an estimated 180,000 Negroes served in the Union Army. The discrimination black soldiers faced on a daily basis—they were paid less than white soldiers and denied the opportunity to serve as officers—inevitably provoked debates in Northern black communities over whether military service would advance or retard the quest for a meaningful freedom. Frederick Douglass presented his own view at a speech in Philadelphia in June 1863. Its message would echo for a century:

> I am content with nothing for the black man short of equal and exact justice. The only question I have, and the point on which I differ from those who refuse to enlist, is whether the colored man is more likely to obtain justice and equality, while refusing to assist in putting down this tremendous rebellion, than he would be if he should promptly, generously, and earnestly give his hand and heart to the salvation of the country in this its day of calamity and peril. Nothing can be more plain, nothing more certain, than that the speediest and best possible way open to us to manhood, is that we enter this service. . . . Once let the black man get upon his person the brass letters U. S., let him get an eagle on his button, and a musket on his shoulder, and bullets in his pocket; and there is no power on the earth, or under the earth, which can deny that he has earned the right of citizenship in the United States. . . . Slavery can be abolished by white men; but liberty so won for the black man, while it may leave him an object of pity, can never make him an object of respect.[43]

Needless to say, service in the Civil War did not win Negroes justice and equality, and whatever respect they gained was insufficient to prevent the Southern states from taking away the vote guaranteed to black men by the Fifteenth Amendment and from introducing segregation laws. And so when the United States went to war against Spain in 1898, debate once again arose in black communities over the appropriate response. An editorial in the *Iowa State Bystander* captured the view of those opposing black participation in combat: "The American white man's rule in dealing with the American Negro . . . in times of peace and prosperity [relegates] him to the rear, deprives him of his rights as an American citizen, cuts off his opportunities of existence, outrages colored women, burns down his home over his wife and children." Still, Negroes "rallied to the flag on the wave of the patriotic upsurge." "The black man," claimed Booker T. Washington in pressing for participation in the war effort, was "an American through and through." An American, he meant, in contrast to recent immigrants from southern and eastern Europe. Black allegiances were unalloyed; there are, he said, "no hyphenates among us." Washington frequently claimed with apparent sincerity that "in slavery and freedom, we have always been loyal to the Stars and Stripes."[44]

Once again military service did not bring the anticipated rewards. The South expanded its apparatus of segregation, and political leaders in Washington turned to Social Darwinist conceptions of racial hierarchy to justify imperialist adventures abroad. It should hardly come as a surprise, then, that the American decision to enter World War I in 1917 was met with a certain amount of cynicism in black neighborhoods, and not just from socialists such as A. Philip Randolph. The Boardola Brothers, who performed with washboards in Philadelphia, sang a song that went:

> I don't think I want to go.
> The white folks makes the law.
> Let white folks fight the war.[45]

Still, most historians have been struck by the support that Negroes gave to the war effort. Young men rushed to enlist, even though in the early days most were turned away. Later, after conscription was instituted, Negroes showed little inclination to try and avoid service. A newspaper editor in Kansas observed, "It is generally acknowledged that on the whole the Negroes of the United States have responded more universally and cheerfully to the call of the Government than the white man. When called under the selective service draft they have rarely asked for exemption." Ida B. Wells remembered, "Every church in town had military services urging the boys to go to war and every congregation had done its bit by organizing nurse training classes, by meeting trains with cigarettes and sweets to give to our boys who were passing through, by patriotic demonstrations, by Liberty Loan drives, by every sort of means which could fire the hearts of our young men to offer their lives if need be in defense of this government." By the end of the war, 2.3 million Negroes had registered for the draft, with approximately 370,000 serving in the armed forces. Negroes purchased more than $250 million worth of Liberty Bonds and thrift stamps.[46]

There were moments during the war when the obvious contradiction between the struggle for democracy in Europe and the discrimination and political deprivation they suffered at home led people of African descent to vent feelings of bitterness. After the East Saint Louis riot during the summer of 1917 in which more than forty black men, women, and children were killed and thousands left homeless, the Negro Fellowship League called for a meeting in Chicago. Ida B. Wells recalled: "I presided at that meeting and suggested to the audience that while we were waiting for our speakers, they might sing 'America' or the 'Star-Spangled Banner' if they wished, but nobody wished to do so." And W. E. B. Du Bois was roundly criticized for his famous "Close Ranks" editorial in *The Crisis* in which he urged his readers: "Let us not hesitate. Let us while this war lasts forget our special grievances. And close our ranks shoulder to shoulder with our white fellow citizens and the allied nations that are fighting for democracy."[47]

But resentment about the betrayal of American ideals at home did not translate into disillusionment with the ideals themselves. At a conference in Washington in June 1917, leaders from a variety of black organizations met to discuss the appropriate attitude for Negroes to adopt in wartime. "Despite the unfortunate record of England, of Belgium, and of our own land in dealing with colored peoples," the resolutions passed at the conference stated,

> we earnestly believe that the greatest hope for ultimate democracy, with no adventitious barriers of race and color, lies on the side of the Allies, with whom our country has become companion in arms. . . . We, therefore, earnestly urge our colored fellow citizens to join heartily in this fight for eventual world liberty; we urge them to enlist in the army; to join in the pressing work of providing food supplies; to labor in all ways by hand and thought in increasing the efficiency of our country. We urge this despite our deep sympathy with the reasonable and deep-seated feeling of revolt among Negroes at the persistent insult and discrimination to which they are subject and will be subject even when they do their patriotic duty. Let us, however, never forget that this country belongs to us even more than to those who lynch, disfranchise, and segregate.[48]

Indeed, the great majority of people of African descent believed that service in the war represented a grand opportunity. It sparked "hopes and ambitions," observed the influential educator Kelly Miller, that Negroes would become full participants "in the fruition of that democracy" they had been "called upon to sustain and perpetuate." When the government failed to establish an officers' training camp for Negroes, Howard University organized the Central Committee of Negro College Men, a protest group that came to represent students at several black colleges. After the War Department agreed to set up a black officers' training camp, the committee issued a press release declaring "the race is on trial": "Just think how serious the situation is. Peal the tocsin; stand by the race. If we fail, our enemies will dub us COWARDS for all time; and we can never win our rightful place. But if we succeed—then eternal success."[49]

Dedicated military service did not, however, bring "eternal" or even temporary "success." The summer of 1919, just months after the war ended, was marked by the worst racial violence Americans had yet experienced. There were more than seventy reported lynchings and twenty-five race riots. While the most publicized riot took place in Chicago, the most horrific violence was in Phillips County, Arkansas, where whites massacred as many as several hundred Negroes after local sharecroppers began to organize in an attempt to win better terms from their landlords. Wrote James Weldon Johnson: "The Red Summer of 1919 broke in a fury. The colored people throughout the country were disheartened and dismayed. The great majority had trustingly felt that, because they had cheerfully done their bit in the war, conditions for them would be better. The reverse seemed to be true."[50]

Memories of the Red Summer and the difficult years that followed produced cynicism among some Negroes when Europe descended into war once again in 1939. George Schuyler scoffed, "So far as the colored peoples of the earth are concerned . . . it is a tossup between the 'democracies and the dictatorships.' . . . What is there to choose between the rule of the British in Africa and the rule of the Germans in Austria." Editorialized *The Crisis:* "*The Crisis* is sorry for brutality, blood, and death among the peoples of Europe, just as we were sorry for China and Ethiopia. But the hysterical cries of the preachers of democracy for Europe leave us cold. We want democracy in Alabama and Arkansas, in Mississippi and Michigan, in the District of Columbia—*in the Senate of the United States.*" A resolution adopted by the National Negro Congress and entered in the *Congressional Record* in April 1940 urged black men to refuse to fight for democracy abroad while discrimination and segregation were still characteristic features of life at home. There were even scattered pockets of sympathy for the Japanese after the attack on Pearl Harbor. One man told an NAACP field secretary that while "I don't want them to quite win," he did hope the Japanese "dish out to these white people all they can dish out to them."[51]

Much more representative, however, was an editorial in the *California Eagle,* a black newspaper in Los Angeles: "We must defend this democracy, for it is the child of our blood and suffering. Despite their disheartening shortcomings, their instances of savagery and hypocrisy, America's people are the freest in the world." Another editorial, this one from *The Crisis* in January 1942, reveals how loyalty was refracted through the lived experiences of blacks:

> *The Crisis* would emphasize with all its strength that now is the time not to be silent about the breaches of democracy here in our own land. Now is the time to speak out, not in disloyalty, but in the truest patriotism, the

patriotism with an eye—now that the die is cast—single to the peace which must be won. Of course, between the declaration of war and the making of a just peace there lies the grim necessity of winning the conflict. To this task the Negro American quickly pledged his fullest support. Be it said once more that black Americans are loyal Americans; but let there be no mistake about the loyalty. It is loyalty to the democratic ideal as enunciated by America and by our British ally; it is not loyalty to many of the practices which have been—and are still—in vogue here and in the British empire.[52]

As during World War I, that loyalty found expression in many forms. In the aftermath of Pearl Harbor, black men swarmed to recruitment offices, offering their services in much greater numbers and with much greater enthusiasm than the military had anticipated: "Because the army did not have a sufficient number of segregated training centers and because it felt too great a proportion of black GIs would demoralize the white majority, it began turning blacks away from enlistment centers." Still, Negroes responded to this rejection more frequently with persistence than with disillusionment. "I am one of the Negro citizens who is awfully proud that I am an American," wrote a man who had been rebuffed when he went to enlist in Dallas. He was, he said, "ready to contribute my share whatever it is for the defence of my country. . . . I speak the sentiment of a number of my race . . . [who] certainly want an opportunity for training that we may be better able to defend America with you."[53]

Within a matter of months, the pressing need to increase the size of the military led the army to abandon its practice of excluding Negroes. By the end of the war almost a million black men and women would serve in the armed forces. In addition, Negroes volunteered as nurse's aides and drivers in motor corps and filled other vital jobs in the Red Cross. Only certain black-nationalist organizations—the Nation of Islam most prominent among them—counseled draft evasion. "To the majority of their fellow black Americans and the integrationist press," claims Neil Wynn, "these people were no more than 'foolish fanatics,' 'crackpots and starry-eyed cultists,' or members of 'obscure religious sects.'"[54]

On the home front, many Negroes took part in volunteer activities to help the war effort, among them such notable figures as A. Philip Randolph, Father Divine, Paul Robeson, Joe Louis, Hattie McDaniel, and W. E. B. Du Bois. In addition, as in World War I, black men and women organized rallies to sell war bonds in schools, churches, and community centers. Concludes Gary Gerstle,

Negroes "demonstrated as much patriotic ardor as any other group in the population."[55]

It is important to keep in mind, however, that Negroes' "patriotic ardor" was not for the United States as it existed at the time. Their loyalty, to repeat the telling phrase by *The Crisis*, was to "the democratic ideal as enunciated by America." Despite that ideal, the military remained segregated. Discrimination against, and abuse of, black soldiers was widespread. And racial violence recurrently broke out on the home front. Even so, as during World War I, the great majority of Negroes believed that military service offered a means to overcome the historic pattern of racial injustice. When the 369th, a black regiment of the National Guard, was called to active duty, the editor of *Opportunity* wrote, "No one knows now what will be the ultimate disposition of the 369th, but we do know—that with a fair chance it will be a shining example of the loyalty of the American Negro to his country."[56]

Yet black involvement in World War II was different from black involvement in World War I. Negroes now argued that the battle to secure democracy must be carried forward on two fronts, at home as well as abroad. The origin of the famous Double V campaign traces back to a letter from a black cafeteria worker in Wichita, Kansas, to the *Pittsburgh Courier* just a month after the attack on Pearl Harbor:

> Like all true Americans, my greatest desire at this time . . . is for a complete victory over the forces of evil which threaten our existence today. Behind that desire is also a desire to serve this, my country, in the most advantageous way.
>
> Most of our leaders are suggesting that we sacrifice every other ambition to the paramount one, victory. With this I agree; but I also wonder if another victory could not be achieved at the same time. . . .
>
> Being an American of dark complexion . . . these questions flash through my mind: "Should I sacrifice my life to live half American?" "Will things be better for the next generation in the peace to follow?" "Would it be demanding too much to demand full citizenship rights in exchange for the sacrificing of my life?" "Is the kind of America I know worth defending?" "Will America be a true and pure democracy after this war?" "Will colored Americans suffer still the indignities that have been heaped upon them in the past?" . . .
>
> I suggest that while we keep defense and victory in the foreground that we don't lose sight of our fight for true democracy at home.

The V for victory sign is being displayed prominently in all so-called democratic countries which are fighting for victory over aggression, slavery, and tyranny. If this V sign means that to those now engaged in this great conflict, then let we colored Americans adopt the double VV for a double victory. The first V for victory over our enemies from without, the second V for victory over our enemies from within. For surely those who perpetuate these ugly prejudices here are seeking to destroy our democratic form of government just as surely as the Axis forces.[57]

Two weeks later the *Courier* inaugurated its Double V campaign. By mid-July the paper had recruited 200,000 Double V members. Other publications echoed the call for combat on two fronts. The editor of the *New York Age* warned in June 1942: "The Negro can less afford to keep silent at this time than at any time in his history. For the record shows that we only get what we are willing to fight and die for. At the same time we are fighting to repel an invading foe, we must insist that our neighbors here at home realize and recognize us as and give us all the rights and privileges of Americans too." Polls showed that this sentiment was widespread among the black population.[58]

The Double V campaign should not be taken as evidence that black commitment to the United States was more contingent than in previous wars. Rather it represented a recognition, on the basis of past experience, that military service in and of itself would not be enough to secure people of African descent the rights that they had historically been denied. And so Negroes committed themselves to continuing the battle for justice at home even during wartime. But underlying that battle—sustaining it—was the sense that America and the ideals that made America worth dying for belonged as truly to them as they did to whites. Gary Gerstle has found this sentiment in letters that black men wrote to Roosevelt, to Secretary of War Henry Stimson, and to other government officials, requesting nothing more than the right to serve. Such letters, he writes, "reveal how deeply many African American youth felt their Americanness and how committed they were to making their country's civic nationalist tradition the dominant one in social and political life."[59]

★

Given the injustice they faced from 1787 to the dawn of the Civil Rights Era, the conspicuous patriotism of black Americans might seem perplexing. Many historians have devoted a considerable portion of their professional lives to

tracking down evidence of resistance by Negroes, whether overt or surrepti-
tious. They have discovered that, in the great majority of cases, such resistance
was directed not to overturning the existing order but to securing its promised
benefits. Even many followers of black nationalists such as Martin Delany
and Marcus Garvey—to whites, the very contradiction of what it meant to be
"American"—operated, to use Gunnar Myrdal's memorable phrase, "under the
spell of the great national suggestion." "The direction of Black Nationalism in
the nineteenth century, which manifested itself in black separatism, black solidarity, and black consciousness," Leonard Sweet has written, "was not towards
exclusion from America but inclusion into American society. Black leaders
were Americans, that they knew, but to secure that status they had to separate
themselves from white Americans and assert themselves as black Americans.
Black separatism, therefore, was often the means of concretizing an identity as
Americans and an image of America which recognized no racial distinctions."
To which Waldo Martin, Jr. has added, "The basic frame of reference and outlook of black nationalism have been quintessentially American."[60]

There has been a perhaps understandable tendency in some circles to at-
tribute this quintessential Americanism to the legacy of white domination, to
the efforts of Negroes to win acceptance by remaking themselves in the image
of whites. But while the social and cultural power exercised by white elites
undoubtedly influenced the beliefs held by less privileged members of society,
Negroes came to their commitment to the United States and its professed
ideals through the logic of their own very distinctive historical experience. As
noted in Chapter 2, it has become an accepted truth among historians that the
Virginia statesmen who crafted the foundational documents of the nation
"had a special appreciation of the freedom dear to republicans" because they
themselves lived among slaves—because they saw every day what life would
be like without freedom. But no one had a greater "appreciation" of the benefits of freedom than the slaves themselves. As a slave who escaped to Canada
expressed it: "A man who has been in slavery knows, and no one else can
know, the yearnings to be free." No one had a more compelling reason than
the slaves and their descendants for embracing the concept of natural rights
embodied in the Declaration of Independence. No one had more to gain from
the implementation of a truly inclusive democracy.[61]

Over the decades, black Americans witnessed the arrival of a multitude of
immigrant groups from Europe—most notably, Irish Catholics before the Civil
War, and Italians, Slavs, Russian Jews following it—groups that were, after

two or three generations, able to claim most of the benefits available to native-born white Protestants. They witnessed as well the progressive tendency of alien citizens—Hispanic Americans, Asian Americans—to win, if incompletely, a measure of protection and social acceptance by establishing their distance from people of African descent. And they saw Native Americans slaughtered and confined to reservations, then, in the end, offered "whiteness" and celebrated as ancestors of the nation itself.

To all this, Negroes responded with a single indisputable fact. Unlike any other racial group—and, remember, this was a society that believed race existed as a real, a biological, division of humanity—unlike any other racial group, their life *within* the nation coincided with the life *of* the nation. Most of the original inhabitants of the land, Native Americans, had been pushed beyond the boundaries of settlement by 1787. And on the eve of the Civil Rights Era, the white race was dominated numerically by individuals whose ancestors had arrived after 1840. It was with understandable bitterness that a black man, embroiled in a dispute with European immigrants over public housing in Detroit during World War II, lamented: "The Negro was a part of this country before the ancestors of these people ever heard of America." Twenty years later James Baldwin asserted in *The Fire Next Time,* "It is entirely unacceptable that I should have no voice in the political affairs of my own country, for I am not a ward of America; I am one of the first Americans to arrive on these shores."[62]

The Civil War had brought emancipation, but emancipation within the extremely tight limits dictated by white supremacist assumptions about American society. Negroes quickly came to appreciate, in a way most other Americans have not acknowledged until recently, that realizing the principles articulated in the Declaration of Independence depended on extending its inalienable rights to the descendants of the very slaves whose bondage was so crucial in conferring meaning on the concept of American liberty in the first place. Listen to the words of Booker T. Washington before a July 1903 meeting of the National Afro-American Council, in Louisville, Kentucky:

There should be meted out equal justice to the black man and the white man whether it relates to citizenship, the protection of property, the right to labor, or the protection of human life. Whenever the nation forgets, or is tempted to forget, this basic principle, the whole fabric of government for both the white and the black man is weakened and threatened with destruction.[63]

W. E. B. Du Bois in *The Gift of Black Folk,* 1924:

It was the black man that raised a vision of democracy in America such
as neither Americans nor Europeans conceived in the eighteenth century, and such as they have not even accepted in the twentieth century;
and yet a conception which every clear sighted man knows is true and
inevitable.[64]

James Weldon Johnson in the *Chicago Defender,* 1925:

The Negro . . . is striving for the basic principles upon which the American democracy was built. If those principles are allowed to rot and wither
away, if they perish, then American democracy must fail.[65]

Roy Wilkins, speaking at the Cooper Union in 1959:

Abridgment or denial of the freedoms of Negro citizens constitutes a
threat to the freedoms of white Americans. The best hope of mankind to
achieve liberty and human dignity is our own America, founded upon the
immortal proposition that 'all men are created equal, that they are endowed by their Creator with certain unalienable Rights, that among these
are Life, Liberty and the pursuit of Happiness.'[66]

But perhaps no leader gave more eloquent testimony to black belief in
American exceptionalism—and to the role Negroes had in defining that exceptionalism—than A. Philip Randolph, speaking at the opening ceremonies of
the Sesquicentennial Exposition in Philadelphia on May 31, 1926:

One hundred and fifty years ago, the Founding Fathers gave eloquent
expression in one of the world's immortal documents, the Declaration of
Independence, to a formula which may serve as the solvent key to our
perplexing problems. This formula reads: We hold these truths to be self-
evident; that all men are created equal, that they are endowed by their
Creator with certain inalienable rights; that among these are life, liberty
and the pursuit of happiness. That to secure these rights, governments are
instituted among men, deriving their just powers from the consent of the
governed. To Aframericans, the embodiment of this formula of practical,

righteous idealism into the warp and woof of American life, its laws, its customs, its institutions, its practices, its traditions, in politics, in industry, in education and religion, is a consummation devoutly to be wished; for no people on God's green earth have suffered as poignantly as the Negro peoples of the world, on account of the failure of the world to achieve higher reaches of humanity. Thus, no group of people in America can have a greater and more genuine concern in the commemoration and perpetuation of the spirit of the Declaration of Independence on this Sesqui-Centenary than the Negro. But if there are those, either because of ignorance or malice who would challenge the right of Aframericans to share in the glories and achievements of our country, my answer is that of all the Americans, the Negro is, doubtless, the most typically American. He is the incarnation of America.[67]

4 • Color and Class

During the colonial period, authorities identified "mulattoes" and "Negroes" as members of separate biological categories but legislated them into a single social caste. The belief that mulattoes represented a distinct biological community continued to find expression in government records through the nineteenth century and into the early decades of the twentieth century. In every census but one between 1840 and 1920, enumerators were under instructions to enter the race of each individual and to distinguish between "mulattoes" and "blacks." It was not until 1930 that the U.S. Census Bureau adopted the "one-drop-rule": "A person of mixed white and Negro blood should be returned as a Negro, no matter how small the percentage of Negro blood." Here the bureau was evidently lagging behind popular opinion. A South Carolina man commented in 1876, "They call everybody a negro that is as black as the ace of spades or as white as snow, if they think he is a negro or know that he has negro blood in his veins."[1]

Census categories hardly reflected the complicated attitude toward color distinctions on the "black" side of the one-drop line, however. In the 1940s, the sociologist Charles H. Parrish, Jr. interviewed approximately four hundred individuals of African descent living in Louisville. He discovered that they used a wide range of different terms to describe skin color, among them "half-white," "yaller," "high yellow," "fair," "bright," "light," "red-bone," "light brown," "teasing brown," "medium brown," "brown," "brownskin," "dark brown," "chocolate brown," "dark," "rusty black," "ink spot," "blue black," and "tar baby." Such terminology revealed an acute sensitivity among Negroes to color distinctions—color distinctions that had no meaning in the eyes of the state. But adjectives like "high yellow" and "chocolate brown" were more than just judgments on physical appearance. They were judgments on physical appearance refracted through the prisms of class, region, and gender. And they had profound implications for how different groups of Americans with African ancestry imagined the boundaries of their racial community.[2]

★

It is significant that, notwithstanding the early legislating of people of varying degrees of African ancestry into a single social caste, planters in the antebellum South showed a deep interest in differences between the skin tones of slaves. The historian Walter Johnson offers this description of the slave market in New Orleans:

> As the slaves were paraded before them, slave buyers began by reading the slaves' skin color, groping their way from visible sign to invisible essence. No doubt buyers were seeing skin color when they described a slave as "a Negro or griff boy," "a griff colored boy," "dark Griff color," or "not black nor Mulatto, but what I believe is usually called a griff color, that is a Brownish Black or a bright Mulatto." But in describing the blurred spectrum they saw before them, buyers used descriptive language that was infused with the reassuring certitude of race. The words they used attempted to stabilize the restless hybridity, the infinite variety of mixture that was visible all over the South, into measurable degrees of black and white. They suggested that slaves' skin color could be read as a sign of a deeper set of racial qualities.[3]

Buyers seeking to acquire an artisan looked for men of a lighter shade, believing such individuals had the intelligence and self-discipline necessary to master a craft. Light-skinned females were assumed to have the domestic qualities sought in household servants. Such attitudes help explain why mulattoes were disproportionately represented among servants and craftsmen on Southern plantations. So does the predisposition of certain planters to privilege slave offspring they fathered.[4]

Artisans on the plantations received a variety of advantages. They were generally given better clothes and food than field hands, had a measure of control over how and at what pace they did their work, and often had the opportunity to go to town. Cooks and maids, too, received better clothing and food and, because of the close relations they had with their owners' families, could hope, with some reason, that their children would not be put up for sale. Intimacy with whites often came at a price—planters and their wives would commonly take out their frustrations on the nearest slave at hand. But domestic servants and artisans prized the material benefits they received. And the tendency of some planters to see that domestic and skilled work remained within certain slave families effectively made those benefits heritable, at least on particular estates.[5]

Since planters generally assigned mulattoes to the roles of house servants and artisans and encouraged a "pride of caste," it should not come as a surprise that substantial evidence exists of mutual suspicion and animosity between field hands and more privileged slaves—evidence of what might loosely be called a blending of color and class consciousness. "There is, in the Southern states," wrote the escaped slave William Wells Brown, "a great amount of prejudice against colour amongst the negroes themselves. The nearer the negro or mulatto approaches to the white, the more he seems to feel his superiority over those of a darker hue." In his novel *Clotel*, first published in Britain in 1853, Brown included the following scene:

> "Dat reminds me," said Currer, "dat Dorcas Simpson is gwine to git married." "Who to, I want to know?" inquired Peter. "To one of Mr. Darby's fieldhands," answered Currer. "I should tink dat dat girl would not trow herself away in dat manner," said Sally. "She good enough looking to get a house servant, and not to put up wid a fiel' nigger," continued she. "Yes," said Sam, "dat's a wery sensible remark of yours, Miss Sally. I admire your judgment very much, I assure you. Dah's plenty of susceptible and well-dressed house servants dat a gal of her looks can get, wid out taken up wid dem common darkies." "Is de man black or mulatto?" inquired one of the company. "He's nearly white," replied Currer. "Well den, dat's some exchuse for her," remarked Sam; "for I don't like to see dis malgemation of blacks and mulattoes, no how," continued Sam. "If I had my rights I would be a mulatto too, for my mother was almost as light-coloured as Miss Sally," said he. Although Sam was one of the blackest men living, he nevertheless contended that his mother was a mulatto, and no one was more prejudiced against the blacks than he.[6]

Still, the lines between skin color and assigned roles were never clearly drawn on most plantations. Dark-complexioned women served as cooks, light-complexioned men worked the ploughs. House servants and artisans would be sent to labor alongside field hands during the planting season and at harvest time. And all members of the slave force would typically join together for the occasional holiday that the growing season (and their masters) allowed. Of course, what above all united the most dark-complexioned of field hands and house servants who might have passed for white was their shared vulnerability. They were, all of them, even the most privileged, human property. Color prejudice within the slave population repeatedly gave way before the need for community. Yet the evidence of such prejudice is noteworthy. It suggests that without the soldering effect of slavery, light-skinned artisans and dark-skinned field hands might have found themselves on different imagined racial trajectories.[7]

★

Not all people of African descent in the antebellum South were held in bondage. At the time of the first U.S. Census, in 1790, those who were free numbered fewer than 33,000 among a total black and mulatto population of more than 680,000. But the natural rights philosophy invoked to justify the American Revolution led a minority of Southern slaveholders to free some or all of their slaves. Manumission declined rapidly after the first decade of the nineteenth century due to "harsh laws, judicial obstructions, and hostile public opinion," but the free population continued to grow through natural means; by 1860 it numbered more than 260,000.[8]

The great majority of free Negroes lived in the Upper South. They were, for the most part, rural laborers who eked out a marginal existence working on farms and plantations, frequently alongside slaves—slaves who, in some instances, were their own relatives. The free people of African ancestry in the Lower South, who numbered fewer than 37,000 in 1860, tended to be found in urban centers. The great majority of them, too, suffered from material deprivation. And free Negro men and women in both sections of the South were victims of racial oppression. Indeed, as the Civil War approached, state legislatures introduced ever more draconian measures narrowing the differences between the lives of free Negroes and the lives of slaves. It is hardly surprising, then, that many free blacks and mulattoes formed close and mutually supportive relations with slaves.[9]

Still, a small fraction of the free Negro population earned enough income to acquire property. And in certain cities, some mulatto craftsmen were able to succeed to the extent that they could imagine themselves part of a community separate from those, both slave and free, with whom they visibly shared African ancestry. Many of these artisans were the children of planters or were descended from the children of planters. And all of them benefited from the presumption among influential whites that light-skinned craftsmen were more intelligent and trustworthy than their dark-complexioned competitors—indeed, more intelligent and trustworthy than many white workingmen. Members of the planting elite afforded them protection, ensured that they were spared much of the humiliation and abuse suffered on a daily basis by the great majority of free blacks and mulattoes.[10]

In 1858, Cyprian Clamorgan, a free mulatto, published a collective biography entitled *The Colored Aristocracy of St. Louis*. By "colored aristocracy," Clamorgan explained, he meant "those who move in a certain circle; who, by means of wealth, education, or natural ability, form a peculiar class—the elite of the colored race." "Wealth makes the man, the want of it the fellow," Mrs. Pelagie Nash, owner of nearly an entire city block, assured Clamorgan. "It was her great ambition," she added, "to have her daughter marry a man as nearly white as possible."[11]

The most coveted form of wealth in the South was slaves. While for many free blacks and mulattoes purchasing a slave was simply a means of rescuing a family member from bondage, most commonly for the elite it was, as for whites, an investment. And their comments about, and behavior toward, the men, women, and children they owned revealed no hint that they saw themselves as members of the same imagined community. As noted earlier, it appears that William Ellison, a wealthy ginwright and planter in South Carolina who on the eve of the Civil War owned more than sixty slaves, made it a practice to sell young girls when he was seeking money to expand his operations. Andrew Durnford, who had a Louisiana plantation with seventy-five slaves, was forever complaining about the incompetence of his "rascally Negroes."[12]

"Like the white aristocracy they idealized," Ira Berlin has written, the mulatto elite "had a flair for high living. They lived in fine houses, rode in elegant carriages, and wore fashionable clothes." William Johnson, a barber in Natchez, Mississippi, furnished his home with expensive furniture and carpets. He bred racehorses, gave his daughters music lessons, subscribed to the *Saturday Evening Post*, owned the collected works of Shakespeare, and socialized with prominent planters (even if never on equal terms). In 1853, Frederick Olmsted witnessed the following scene in Richmond, Virginia:

In what I suppose to be the fashionable streets, there were many more well-dressed and highly-dressed coloured people than white; and among this dark gentry the finest French cloths, embroidered waistcoats, patent-leather shoes, resplendent brooches, silk hats, kid gloves, and eau de mille fleurs, were quite common. Nor was the fairer, or rather the softer sex, at all left in the shade of this splendour. Many of the coloured ladies were dressed not only expensively, but with good taste and effect, after the latest Parisian mode. Some of them were very attractive in appearance, and would have produced a decided sensation in any European drawing-room. Their walk and carriage were more often stylish and graceful. Nearly a fourth part seemed to me to have lost all African peculiarity of feature, and to have acquired, in place of it, a good deal of that voluptuousness of expression which characterizes many of the women of the South of Europe.[13]

Such free mulattoes, a Baltimore minister observed, looked "upwards, not downwards . . . constantly seeking, and acquiring too, the privileges of whites." They were at pains to ensure that their children married within their select social circle, which was defined by both wealth and light complexion. And they congregated in separate, exclusive churches and formed their own social organizations to strengthen—and to display before the public—the bonds that united them. An applicant for membership in the Friendly Moralist Society of Charleston had to provide testimony from three existing members that he was "a bona fide free brown man, over the age of eighteen, of moral character, and of good standing in the community."[14]

There were successful free blacks in the South, although they were far fewer in number than the mulatto elite. Members of the two groups typically knew each other and had business dealings. By and large they lived separate lives, however, and only very rarely did they intermarry. As for those free men and women—dark-skinned or light-skinned—below the ranks of the well-to-do, the "colored aristocracy" looked down on them and frequently referred to them with contempt. William Johnson complained in his diary about "darky parties" in Natchez attended by slaves and the less reputable element of the local free black and mulatto population. On one occasion, particularly annoyed with his apprentice, he wrote, "Bill Nix is up to this day a pure, pure Negro at heart and in action." The racial slur was not incidental. The elite viewed their own light skin as a significant marker of their superior breeding. But there were many mulatto slaves as well, and many poor mulatto free men and women, so it could hardly serve as the only such marker. Their success in accumulating wealth and approximating the lifestyle of respectable whites then became the public expression of their distinctiveness. They frequently dismissed other free men and women of African descent by reference to racial terminology—"darky," "black," "pure Negro," "nigger"— as a way of signaling to others but above all to themselves that they represented a racial category separate from other individuals of African descent. In personal communications they defined the elite social circle to which they belonged by the restrictive term "our people." The son of the Louisiana planter Andrew Durnford wrote his godfather with enthusiasm about the possibility of repatriating freed slaves to Africa, to "the land of *their* father race, the land of *their* fathers."[15]

In June of 1848, Michael Eggart, the incoming vice president of the Friendly Moralist Society in Charleston, gave a speech before the organization in which he described the elite as living on a "middle ground" between "the prejudice of the white man" and the "deeper hate of our more sable brethren." Prevailing scientific theory held that mulattoes were weak, doomed to extinction. But such was false belief, Eggart assured his audience. "Ours is gods [*sic*] own image. In our nostrils is his breath." Michael Johnson and James Roark have adeptly summarized the racial perceptions of the mulatto elite in the Old South: "Scrupulous observance of the distinction between brown and black allowed free mulattoes to make the middle ground visible, to reproduce in all the activities of daily life their separateness from blacks. Free mulattoes' racial rituals represented their attempts to shape social reality to their sense of themselves as an intermediate class, to give repeated public demonstrations that their social niche had clear racial boundaries and that their racial niche had equally crisp social limits. Free mulattoes' discrimination against blacks was their way of staking claim to the middle ground."[16]

★

The Reconstruction Acts, passed in 1867, just over a year after the Thirteenth Amendment ended slavery, conferred the vote on men of African ancestry in the states of the former Confederacy. Representatives of the free mulatto elite were obvious candidates for leadership roles in the Republican Party because they were educated and because they had connections with influential whites, material resources, and some knowledge of the operations of the political system. Still, their ability to shape the political agenda would depend not only on the deals they were able to negotiate with white Republicans but also on how successful they were in gaining and retaining the confidence of those many voters who had been slaves on the farms and plantations of the South before the war.[17]

South Carolina, where men of African ancestry represented a substantial majority of the electorate and where Negro politicians wielded the greatest influence, serves as an instructive case study. No black or mulatto was elected to the South Carolina governorship nor did any secure a U.S. Senate seat; at no time was there more than one man of African ancestry on the three-member state supreme court. Throughout Reconstruction, however, Negroes comprised a substantial majority in the state house and, from 1874 to 1877, a majority in the state senate. And for all or part of the period of Republican rule, a black or mulatto occupied the posts of secretary of state, lieutenant governor, secretary of the treasury, speaker of the house, and president pro tempore of the senate. While a clear majority of the men who acquired office were former slaves, members of the antebellum free mulatto elite took control of key positions in the legislature and in the party infrastructure.[18]

Some years ago, Thomas Holt examined the voting records of the men of African descent who had been elected to state and federal offices. He discovered that legislators of all backgrounds were united in their commitment to protect the civil and political rights that Washington had extended, and to break down racial barriers. They showed broad support for democratic reforms, for funding public education, and for expanding social services. Holt also discovered, however, that members of the antebellum mulatto elite tended to be conservative on economic issues. Determined to protect their own privileged position, they were unwilling to support the kind of radical labor legislation or land reform championed by spokesmen for plantation laborers.[19]

Republican rule in the South was short-lived—nine years in South Carolina but only two or three years in most states. And by the end of the first decade of the twentieth century, Democratic legislatures throughout the former Confederacy and in Oklahoma had contrived elaborate means to deny the vote to the overwhelming majority of black men. Disenfranchisement effectively ended the need for the mulatto elite to curry favor with plantation laborers and unskilled workers. At the same time, however, the Southern legislatures, and some municipal governments as well, enacted segregation laws that subjected all people of African descent—light-skinned and dark-skinned, wealthy and poor, former free men and women, former slaves—to the same legal proscriptions. Members of the elite were shocked, outraged. When the Virginia legislature took up discussion of a segregation law in 1900, one of their spokesmen objected that there were "thousands of Negroes . . . as refined in their ways and as pure in their lives as are the blue blood aristocracy of the South." People of his background, he asserted, found the "indecent, unclean and boisterous Negro as repugnant" as did the "most refined white man or woman" and had "no communication" with him "save as he comes into contact with him in his daily work."[20]

The introduction of Jim Crow legislation occurred almost simultaneously with the triumph of the "one-drop" rule in the South. All people of African descent, including those with European ancestors, were now, in law as well as in the popular perceptions of whites, a single biological entity, a single "people." But here, ironically, disenfranchisement created an opportunity for the elite to exercise a measure of political influence without regard to the concerns or aspirations of others on the "black" side of the one-drop line. As Karen Ferguson explains, writing here specifically about developments in Atlanta: "Beginning with Jim Crow's effective disenfranchisement of African Americans at the turn of the century, black politics were limited to brokerage by a tiny group of literate spokespeople who negotiated on behalf of the black community with white elites. This group's stranglehold on influence with the outer wheel meant that its particular ideology and program for liberation began to represent all African Americans to the outer wheel with little or no accountability to the rest of the black community and with disregard to or dismissal of other strategies for freedom." During the 1930s, the Negro elite of Atlanta supported New Deal housing initiatives intended to reshape the residential geography of the city. The reforms, when implemented, did significantly improve the housing available to members of the middle class. In the process, however, many poor Negroes were uprooted from their homes and saw their neighborhoods destroyed.[21]

★

Of the almost 4.5 million people of African descent living in the United States on the eve of the Civil War, only about 230,000 lived in the free states, mainly in urban centers. Here too, as in the South, an elite had emerged. It was composed of skilled laborers, tradesmen, and a very small number of professionals, almost all of whom were employed by whites or had whites as clients. Not incidentally, the members of this class were, with few exceptions, light-complexioned. Well-to-do Northern whites, like Southern planters, preferred to deal with mulattoes, "feeling that their closer proximity to Caucasian features also made them more intelligent and physically attractive." While discriminatory legislation publicly consigned all people of African ancestry to a single social category, the material advantages available to men and women of mixed European and African ancestry at times translated into a sense of entitlement. "I mourn over the aristocracy that prevails among our colored brethren," the abolitionist Sarah Grimké wrote to Theodore Weld in 1837. "I cherished the hope that suffering had humbled them and prepared them to perform a glorious part in the reformation of our country, but the more I mingle with them the fainter are my hopes. They have as much caste among themselves as we have and despise the poor as much I fear as their pale brethren."[22]

For more than a generation after the end of the Civil War, the social circumstances and self-perception of the mulatto elite remained largely unchanged. Families continued to depend on the patronage of whites, continued to insist that their color and material well-being signified their superiority over other Americans of African descent. This situation produced two tendencies that were in tension with each other. On the one hand, members of the elite were inclined to separate themselves both geographically and socially from those who did not enjoy their material and physiological advantages. Like the free mulatto aristocracy of the antebellum South, they married within their exclusive social set, congregated in restrictive churches, and found recreation in their own social organizations. Commented the respected journalist Ray Stannard Baker in 1908, "In some Northern cities some of the ablest Negroes will have nothing to do with the masses of their own people." Well-to-do light-skinned men and women, much like the privileged free mulattoes of the antebellum South, represented themselves as a distinct racial group. When the sociologist and writer John Daniels interviewed members of the elite in Boston in the early twentieth century, one man urged him, "When you write of the Negroes in Boston tell about us who are neither Negroes or whites, but an ambiguous something-between;—a people not yet known or named. While our sympathies tend to unite us with the Negroes and their destiny, all our aspirations lead us toward the whites."[23]

By the late nineteenth century, however, most whites had become blind to, or were refusing to acknowledge, distinctions among people of African descent. Many members of the Negro elite, like their counterparts in the South, concluded it was in their interest to position themselves as "brokers" between the races. John Daniels again: "The elite's natural endowments, education, and conditions of life tend to divide them from the mass of the Negroes, and in fact, most of them have comparatively little close association with the Negro rank and file. . . . They tend to keep within a small social circle of their own kind, while at the same time cultivating affiliation with whites. Nevertheless, they are wont to assume before the public the position of understanding intimately the conditions and needs of the Negro race, and of being its best accredited representatives."[24]

Two developments, one beginning at the end of the nineteenth century, the second during World War I, altered the dynamic of class status and color consciousness in northern cities. The first was the emergence of inner-city ghettos; the second was the Great Migration, during which millions of people of African descent left the poverty and the social and political repression of the South for the seeming promise of the North.

There had been little residential segregation in Northern cities through much of the nineteenth century. Of necessity, most individuals had lived within walking distance of their businesses or places of employment. But the harnessing of electric power late in the century and the subsequent construction of streetcar and subway systems allowed the emergence of neighborhoods with distinct ethnic, religious, and racial boundaries. At the same time, the hardening of the one-drop rule and the arrival of millions of immigrants from southern and eastern Europe whose claims to "whiteness" demanded separating themselves from people of African ancestry resulted in almost all Negroes, poor and well-to-do alike, being restricted to ghettos. George Cleveland Hall, a doctor, personal friend of Booker T. Washington, and, later, one of the founders of the Chicago Urban League, complained in 1904: "Those of the race who are desirous of improving their general condition are prevented to a great extent by being compelled to live with those of their color who are shiftless, dissolute and immoral. . . . Prejudice of landlords and agents render it almost impossible for [a Negro] to take up his residence in a more select quarter of the city . . . no matter . . . how much cultivation and refinement he may possess."[25]

The concentration of blacks and mulattoes in neighborhoods many blocks long and wide did create a potential market for enterprising Negro businessmen and aspiring professionals. But members of the old elite had placed great weight on their close relations with whites and believed deeply in the cause of integration; most were not predisposed to recognize the economic opportunities represented by a captive audience of ghetto residents. Indeed, they despaired that residential segregation "would force their social life inward toward the black community, rather than outward as they hoped." And so it was that a new set of entrepreneurs emerged to serve and supply what historians refer to as the "institutional ghetto": stores, churches, hospitals, schools, restaurants, recreational facilities. Not incidentally, these men and women tended to be less well educated than the old elite and to have darker complexions.[26]

The Great Migration, however, proved a complicating development. Suddenly Northern cities were flooded with blacks and mulattoes who had different tastes in food and music, different clothing, different ways of speaking, different forms of religious expression. Although many of the earliest migrants had spent some time in Southern towns and were financially better off than the mass of plantation laborers, Northern Negroes interpreted their distinctive culture as evidence of backwardness, even depravity. Elites in New York commonly referred to the migrants as a "hoodlum element," while their counterparts in Cincinnati formed the National Negro Reform League and Criminal Elimination Society, whose stated purpose was to help "the better class of Negroes" distinguish themselves from the "bad citizens" (meaning the newcomers). One Chicago professional who sold his home and moved fifteen blocks in an attempt to separate himself from the migrants complained, "They creep along slowly like a disease."[27]

Arguably it was novelists who most powerfully captured how assumptions about the class status of the migrants, readings of their character, and even assessments of their skin color shaped the mentality of Northern blacks and mulattoes. Here are two examples. First, Wallace Thurman in *The Blacker the Berry.* The passage details the regional prejudice of his protagonist, Emma Lou Brown, born and raised in Boise, Idaho:

All her life she had heard talk of the "right sort of people," and of "the people who really mattered," and from these phrases she had formed a mental image of those to whom they applied. Hazel Mason most certainly could not be included in either of these categories. Hazel was just a vulgar little nigger from down South. It was her kind, who, when they came North, made it hard for the colored people already resident there. It was her kind who knew nothing of the social niceties or the polite conversations. In her own home they had been used only to coarse work and coarser manners. And they had been forbidden the chance to have intimate contact in schools and in public with white people from whom they might absorb some semblance of culture. When they did come North and get a chance to go to white schools, white theatres, and white libraries, they were too unused to them to appreciate what they were getting, and could be expected to continue their old way of life in an environment where such a way was decidedly out of place.[28]

And from *Invisible Man* by Ralph Ellison. The eponymous narrator has just dropped a package in a garbage can in Harlem. A light-complexioned woman standing on the stoop of one of the nearby houses shouts at him to take away his trash: "We keep our place clean and respectable and we don't want you field niggers coming up from the South and ruining things."[29]

As the two passages suggest, it was commonplace for Northern Negroes to blame the migrants for what they perceived to be a significant increase in white hostility during the early decades of the twentieth century. The old elite in particular "came to glorify the premigration era as a time of racial harmony and goodwill." But even the emerging middle class of businessmen, professionals, and shopkeepers, though they depended on the patronage of newcomers, feared that their own chances for social acceptance within the broader society would be undermined by association with people whose outward appearance—their physical features, their clothes, their public behavior—presumptively marked them as unworthy. Not surprisingly, then, organizations that represented the new institutional ghetto sought to inculcate in the migrants appropriate values and forms of self-presentation. "Keep your mouth shut, please!" advised the *Chicago Defender.* "There is entirely too much loud talking on the street cars among our newcomers." An Urban League pamphlet in the same city urged the migrants to pledge: "I WILL REFRAIN from wearing dust caps, bungalow aprons, house clothing and bedroom shoes out of doors."[30]

In time the old elite came to align itself with the rising class of entrepreneurs and professionals, an increasing number of whom were themselves Southern migrants. The light-skinned children of successful nineteenth-century tradesmen whose elevated social rank rested on fulfilling the needs of wealthy whites married lawyers, doctors, and businessmen who grew prosperous serving an exclusively ghetto clientele. The "amalgamation and transformation" of the elite took place gradually, but it was effectively complete by the time of the Great Depression. And so wealth and privilege remained disproportionately accorded to those with conspicuous evidence of European ancestry. "Concentrated in Strivers Row . . . were the dowagers of Harlem's society," recalled Congressman Adam Clayton Powell, Jr. "These queenly, sometimes portly, and nearly always light-skinned Czarinas presided over the Harlem upper class. Their protocol was more rigid than that of the Court of St. James. There was an open door for all who were light-skinned and for most of those of the professional group. The entire pattern of society was white. Social functions were particularly successful if one or more of the guests were white. If invited Harlemites brought with them their dark-skinned friends, they were shunned and sometimes pointedly asked to leave."[31]

Or consider testimony collected by the sociologists St. Clair Drake and Horace Cayton, Jr. for *Black Metropolis,* their influential study of Chicago's Bronzeville neighborhood during the 1940s. Complained one woman they interviewed, "We always had a lot of trouble with the darker women in clubs. We found them disagreeable—you had to be careful of every move you made. So we organized a club that we could enjoy. We went places and enjoyed a lot of opportunities we wouldn't have if we had had a darker group with us. I found that darker people don't know how to mix amiable." Another woman claimed she liked dark-skinned people "in their places . . . I mean I like them, but not around me. Their place is with the rest of the dark-skinned folks." And a third woman: "I have no ill-feeling for the 'less fortunate,' but I don't care to entertain them outside of closed doors. I really feel embarrassed when people see me with black persons. I do have a friend who is quite dark. I love her and really forget that she is black until we start outdoors. I never go very far with her, though."[32]

★

The problem for the elite women of Chicago and, indeed, for all privileged light-complexioned people of African ancestry, was that the white arbiters of mainstream beliefs relegated them to the same social category as the dark-skinned and lower-class people they scorned. It scarcely mattered where they themselves marked the boundaries of their imagined community. Under the circumstances, many members of the elite, both Northern and Southern, concluded that to validate their own claims to equality with whites they would have to uplift the black masses. And so the "aristocrats of color," or "best people" as they liked to refer to themselves, created a variety of organizations devoted to promoting what they thought of as sacrosanct American values— middle-class values—sobriety, hard work, thrift, chastity.[33]

To many members of the elite, the prospect of engaging with men and women of the "baser classes" was frightening. Henry H. Proctor, who graduated from Yale Divinity School in the late nineteenth century and became minister of First Congregational Church in Atlanta, recognized that his "upper class" parishioners worried about being "dragged down by contact with the lower." Nonetheless, at a conference on "Negro City Life" in 1897, he urged the elite to visit the homes of the underprivileged. Remember, he said, "the immaculate swan comes unspotted from the vilest sewer." And to the possible objection that the poor would "presume upon our social reserve," he responded, "There is not the least danger in the plainest people mistaking our kindly interest as an invitation to our private social functions. The plain people have wonderfully keen instincts." Then he concluded with a warning: "You can not elevate society by lifting from the top; you must put the jackscrews under the mudsills of society."[34]

Putting "the jackscrews under the mudsills of society" did not, for the vast majority of members of the elite, mean helping the "plain people" find their collective voice and it certainly did not mean encouraging them to pursue their class interests. Rather it meant, as Alexander Crummell, minister of the prestigious St. Luke's Protestant Episcopal Church in Washington, explained, shaping their "opinions and habits," guiding them to adopt the kind of "respectable" behavior thought necessary to win approval from mainstream white society. It meant, as Kevin Gaines has observed, pushing them to embrace "bourgeois morality, patriarchal authority, and a culture of self-improvement." What young people needed to do, one member of the Cleveland elite wrote, was "devote more of their time to literary societies, musical clubs, debating societies and sewing circles . . . and less to pool playing, dancing, and playing and other virtue-robbing pleasures." "The politics of uplift was deeply condescending," acknowledges Thomas Sugrue, "but also hopeful that the poor and working classes could be redeemed through the charitable efforts and good example of their betters."[35]

"The poor and working classes," however, often bridled at what they took to be the presumption of the mulatto elite. "Proletarian Negroes," observed Wallace Thurman in 1929, "are as suspicious of their more sophisticated brethren as they are of white men, and resent as keenly their intrusions into their social world." Her mother, the singer and actress Ethel Waters remembered, "always despised 'dictys,' which is the name my people have for those who look down on others and consider themselves superior to plebeian folk." The comedian and civil rights activist Dick Gregory recalled his first high school prom in Saint Louis. Though from a very poor background, he was a track star and managed to get a date with a girl from a prominent family. When the dance ended and it was time to leave,

> there were hundreds of them out there, all the cats who couldn't make it, the guys who couldn't get dates, whose processed hair was too long, whose pants rode down too far on their hips. The line ran for blocks, mean-looking guys just waiting. We went down the steps, and one of them knocked the doctor's son's hat off. When he reached down to pick it up, he got kicked right in the face. Then the fight started. I took my little

group back inside. From the window, I could see the mess of pink and blue formal gowns, rust-colored pegged suits, black and white tuxes, and greasy jackets boiling around together like a pot of beans and fatback. Society was paying its dues.[36]

Certain journalists had a reputation for excoriating the "upper class." W. Calvin Chase, editor and publisher of the *Washington Bee,* carried out a decades-long war against "would-be whites." Even more influential was John Edward Bruce, born a slave on a plantation in Maryland a few years before the Civil War. Bruce found work at the *New York Times* in the 1870s and a decade later was producing a regular column under the byline "Bruce Grit" for the *Gazette* of Cleveland and the *New York Age.* Eventually his readership would extend beyond the United States to the Caribbean, Europe, and Africa. Dark-skinned himself, he repeatedly savaged the elite for the pride—the self-satisfaction—they took in their light complexion, as well as their "Injun hair" and "aristocratic insteps." It was the "pin-headed dudes and dudines" of the upper class, he insisted, who had first introduced, and now perpetuated, class distinctions based on color among Americans of African ancestry.[37]

The charge that the elite were driven by a desire to be white—were "would-be whites," to borrow Calvin Chase's phrase—was voiced by many of their critics. "Dictys," Ethel Waters assured the writer and patron of the Harlem Renaissance Carl Van Vechten, "tried to be as much like white people as possible." In his short story "The Morning, This Evening, So Soon," published in 1948, James Baldwin included the following scene: Louisa, black and from Alabama, has come to Paris to visit her expatriate brother. She falls into a conversation with her Swedish sister-in-law. "'Language is experience and language is power,' says Louisa, after regretting that she does not know any of the African dialects. 'That's what I keep trying to tell those dicty bastards down South. They get their own experience into the language, we'll have a great language. But, no, they all want to talk like white folks. . . . You know some of them folks are ashamed of Mahalia Jackson? Ashamed of her, one of the greatest singers alive! They think she's common.'"[38]

Critics of the elite read meaning into skin color as well as behavior. A black state senator in South Carolina posed this question about his light-complexioned counterparts during Reconstruction: "To what race do they belong? . . . I know that my ancestors trod the burning sands of Africa, but why should men in whose veins run a great preponderance of white blood seek to specially ally themselves with the black man, prate of 'our race,' when they are simply mongrels?" Lena Horne was born into privilege in the Bedford-Stuyvesant district of Brooklyn in 1917. Her parents divorced when she was just three and two years later she was taken to Macon, Georgia, by her actress mother and placed in a boarding school. Blacks in Macon called her "a little yellow bastard." "To some Negroes," she commented ruefully years later, "light color is far from being a status symbol; in fact it's quite the opposite. It is evidence that your lineage has been corrupted by the white people." St. Clair Drake and Horace Cayton, Jr. found that "the few Negroes light enough to pass for white" in Chicago were "liable to obscene taunts about the way they acquired their light blood." The mulatto elite, John Edward Bruce—"Bruce Grit"—asserted, were but "the illegitimate progeny of the vicious white men of the South." "Yellow don't have no race," a dark-skinned boy in the rural South told the sociologist Charles S. Johnson in 1941. "They can't be white and they ain't black either."[39]

Marcus Garvey took this line of thinking to what can only be called its logical conclusion. "Some of us in America, the West Indies and Africa," he wrote,

> believe that the nearer we approach the white man in color the greater our social standing and privilege and that we should build up an "aristocracy" based upon caste of color and not achievement in race. It is well known, although no one is honest enough to admit it, that we have been, for the past thirty years at least, but more so now than ever, grading ourselves for social honor and distinction on the basis of color. . . . There is a subtle and underhand propaganda fostered by a few men of color in America, the West Indies and Africa to destroy the self-respect and pride of the Negro race by building up what is commonly known as a "blue vein" aristocracy and to foster same as the social and moral standard of the race.

The solution seemed self-evident:

> I believe in a pure black race just as how all self-respecting whites believe in a pure white race, as far as that can be. I am conscious of the fact that slavery brought upon us the curse of many colors within the Negro race, but there is no reason why we of ourselves should perpetuate the evil; hence instead of encouraging a wholesale bastardy in the race, we feel we should now set out to create a race type and standard of our own which could not, in the future, be stigmatized by bastardy, but could be recognized and respected as the true race type anteceding even our own time.[40]

★

As Marcus Garvey recognized, by the twentieth century the great majority of individuals designated "Negro" under the one-drop rule were of mixed African and European ancestry. Ralph Linton, a leading American anthropologist, speculated in 1947 that the figure might be as high as 90 percent. Not that sex across the color line was widespread during the first half of the twentieth century. Most states had anti-miscegenation laws and there were strict social taboos as well. No, the "steady infiltration of white blood into the Negro group," to use Linton's words, was due to mulattoes intermixing with men and women of pure African descent—"internal miscegenation," scientists of the day called it.[41]

But intermixing did not lead to a decline in color consciousness. Many observers during the first half of the twentieth century commented on the keen eye that individuals of African descent brought to distinctions in skin tones. In a review of the hit Broadway musical *Shuffle Along*—this was in 1921—the Jamaican-born novelist and poet Claude McKay observed, "As whites have their blonde and brunette, so do the blacks have their chocolate, chocolate-to-the-bone, brown, low-brown, teasing-brown, high-brown, yellow, high-yellow, and so on." In an editorial for *Opportunity* published in October 1925—it had the provocative title "The Vanishing Mulatto"—Charles S. Johnson wrote: "Mixed bloods, they are suspended between two races—mulattoes, quadroons, musters, mustafinas, cabres, griffies, zambis, quatravis, tresalvis, coyotes, saltaras, albarassados, cambusos—neither black nor white."[42]

Color was believed to be not only a signifier of class and class aspirations, but also an indicator of how an individual understood the boundaries of his or her racial community. The singer Etta James, who grew up in South Central Los Angeles, remembered, "I caught hell from brothers and sisters thinking I was too light. . . . I lived on a block where almost everyone was dark-skinned, and I'd hear shit like, 'Jamesetta thinks she's better than everyone. Just who does this yellow nigger think she is?'" She won acceptance only after her neighbors heard her "raspy voice sounding like I came from way 'cross [Waycross] Georgia. They saw I wasn't putting on airs."[43]

Color consciousness was particularly evident in choice of sexual partners, although as will become apparent in a moment, here men and women were not entirely operating on the same assumptions. "When Negroes show preferences or draw invidious distinctions on the basis of skin-color," Drake and Cayton observed, "Bronzeville calls them 'partial to color.' And 'partial to color' always means 'partial to *less* color'—to light color. The outstanding example of partiality to color is seen in men's choices of female associates. It is commonly charged that successful Negro men of all colors tend to select very light-brown and fair women. One cynical man summed up the situation by declaring that 'no man, irrespective of how dark or light he is, wants a dark woman.'"[44]

George Schuyler parodied this attitude in his wicked satire *Black No More*. Max Disher and Bunny Brown are at a nightclub in Harlem:

The two had in common a weakness rather prevalent among Aframerican bucks: they preferred yellow women. Both swore there were three things essential to the happiness of a colored gentleman: yellow money, yellow women and yellow taxis. They had little difficulty in getting the first and none at all in getting the third but the yellow women they found flighty and fickle. It was so hard to hold them. They were so sought after that one almost required a million dollars to keep them out of the clutches of one's rivals.

"No more yallah gals for me!" Max announced with finality, sipping his drink. "I'll grab a black gal first."

"Say not so!" exclaimed Bunny, strengthening his drink from his huge silver flask. "You ain't thinkin' o' dealin' in coal, are you?"

"Well," argued his partner, "it might change my luck. You can trust a black gal; she'll stick to you."

"How do you know? You ain't never had one. Ever' gal I ever seen you with looked like an ofay."[45]

Critics accused men who were "partial to color" of having an unspoken yearning for white women. And it is possible to find scattered evidence to support this charge. A song from the nineteenth century goes,

> She got to be white, Jack—
> 'Cause white is right
> Both day and night!
> She got to be old and white,
> 'Cause if she's old
> She's been white longer!
> She got to be big and white,
> 'Cause if she's big

> She's much more white!
> But listen, Jack—
> If she just can't be white
> Then let her be real light brown![46]

Still, few members of the "colored aristocracy" aspired to marry white women—or at least aspired to marry the class of white women who might be available to them. Men who did marry across the one-drop line were typically vilified for it. After Frederick Douglass took a white woman for his second wife, Booker T. Washington noted, "His own race especially condemned him, and the notion seemed to be quite general that he had made the most serious mistake of his life." A dispatch published in a black-owned newspaper ranted: "Fred Douglass has married a red-head white girl. . . . Goodbye, black blood in that family. We have no further use for him. His picture hangs in our parlor, we will hang it in the stables."[47]

Men of African ancestry sought light-skinned sexual partners not, in the great majority of cases, because of some unacknowledged yearning to enter the white world but, quite the contrary, because of the advantages a light-skinned partner brought on the "black" side of the one-drop line. Or, put another way, there were severe social costs to choosing a partner whose skin tone was read as a sign of low status, even deficient values. The "near white" principal at J. Saunders Redding's high school in Wilmington, Delaware, warned the future scholar to end his friendship with the very dark-complexioned girl who worked as her servant: "Let her alone! Or she'll trap you to marry her. And what would you look like married to a girl like that. No friends, no future. You might as well be dead!" "Mule on de Mount," the best known of all "Negro work songs," includes the following lyrics:

> I don't want no coal-black woman for my regular
> I don't want no coal-black woman for my regular,
> She's too low-down, Lawd, Lawd, she's too low-down.[48]

Gwendolyn Brooks captured the limited romantic opportunities—the tragically limited romantic opportunities—open to dark-complexioned girls in "The Ballad of Chocolate Mabbie":

> It was Mabbie without the grammar school gates.
> And Mabbie was all of seven.

And Mabbie was cut from a chocolate bar.
And Mabbie thought life was heaven.

The grammar school gates were the pearly gates,
For Willie Boone went to school.
When she sat by him in history class
Was only her eyes were cool.

It was Mabbie without the grammar school gates
Waiting for Willie Boone.
Half hour after the closing bell!
He would surely be coming soon.

Oh, warm is the waiting for joys, my dears!
And it cannot be too long.
Oh, pity the little poor chocolate lips
That carry the bubble of song!

Out came the saucily bold Willie Boone.
It was woe for our Mabbie now.
He wore like a jewel a lemon-hued lynx
With sand-waves loving her brow.

It was Mabbie alone by the grammar school gates.
Yet chocolate companions had she:
Mabbie on Mabbie with hush in the heart.
Mabbie on Mabbie to be.[49]

Studies in both the rural South and the urban North during the 1940s found that, while dark-complexioned women were looked on with scorn, most men—the fictional Max Disher notwithstanding—expressed reluctance to enter into a relationship with someone whose skin color approximated white—who was "yellow" or "yaller," to cite the terms commonly applied. All the same, it cannot be considered surprising that many dark-skinned women took extraordinary measures to try to lighten their complexions. During the nineteenth century some resorted to arsenic wafers or lye. One mother submerged her daughter daily in a tub of bleach. The earliest commercial skin lighteners had attractive packaging and fancy names, but were made, most of them, from chalk and grease.

By the period between the two world wars, companies had developed ointments and powders that did to a degree lighten one's complexion, but the preparations typically had unwanted side effects, leaving the skin dry, even blotchy. Still, the products proved profitable for their manufacturers, a result of clever marketing and the desperate dreams of many dark-skinned women. Newspapers ran weekly advertisements for items such as Palmer's High Brown Face Powder ("The original and best face powder for dark skin—smooth as velvet") and Ford's Royal White Skin Lotion ("Makes the skin look whiter as it is put on"). In a magazine advertisement from the 1920s for a solution called Ro-Zol, a wealthy couple is shown at a table covered with a starched white linen cloth, sipping tea from fine china cups. The woman, who is several shades lighter than the man, is admiring herself in a small mirror. The ad reads: "Ro-Zol was the first preparation made expressly for bleaching. . . . It is received by the pigment and combines and harmonizes to produce a remarkably satisfactory, youthful, wholesome and *whitened* complexion." Or consider this arresting advertisement with its not-at-all subtle allusion to the slave past, its invocation of race pride, and its promise of the American Dream: "Lighten your dark skin. Race men and women, protect your future by using Black & White Ointment. Be attractive. Throw off the chains that have held you back from the prosperity that rightly belongs to you."[50]

Wallace Thurman satirized the obsession that many dark-skinned women had with skin lighteners in a scene from *The Blacker the Berry*. Emma Lou is getting ready to head off to a dance hall: "Before putting on her dress she stood in front of her mirror for over an hour, fixing her face, drenching it with a peroxide solution, plastering it with a mudpack, massaging it with a bleaching ointment, and then, as a final touch, using much vanishing cream and powder. She even ate an arsenic wafer. The only visible effect of all this on her complexion was to give it an ugly purple tinge, but Emma Lou was certain that it made her skin look less dark."[51]

While surveys conducted during the first half of the twentieth century appear to suggest that the two sexes read color differences in much the same way, in fact, dark skin carried far more social costs for a woman than for a man. Once again from *The Blacker the Berry*:

Not that [Emma Lou] minded being black, being a Negro necessitated having a colored skin, but she did mind being too black. She couldn't understand why such should be the case, couldn't comprehend the cruelty of the natal attenders who had allowed her to be dipped, as it were, in indigo ink when there were so many more pleasing colors on nature's palette. . . . She should have been a boy, then color of skin wouldn't have mattered so much, for wasn't her mother always saying that a black boy could get along, but that a black girl would never know anything but sorrow and disappointment?[52]

Indeed, some women expressed a clear preference for dark-skinned sexual partners. In 1915 and 1916, female workers in Auburn, Alabama, sang:

> Ain't crazy 'bout no high yellows, worried about no brown,
> Come to picking my choice, gimme
> The blackest man in town.

And the following verse was popular among blueswomen:

> Going to find me a black man
>   somewhere in this town
> Black man will stay by you
>   when your brown skin throws you down.[53]

Etta James remembered how, in the 1950s, she and Bobby Lopas—his father provided the buses when she was on tour—would stand outside the nightclub doors and "look over the fine brothers, one by one, as they came stepping on in. We'd carry on and gossip and share secrets of the heart. I'd tell him how I liked dark-skinned men. I didn't have anything against white boys, but I was turned on by coal-black brothers. Bobby wanted to know why. Couldn't say for sure, but I know it's sexual. Maybe forbidden fruit. Maybe the grass is greener on the other side. Not that light-skinned boys don't interest me. But my heat's turned up—back then and even now—by superdark complexions. Other light-skinned women have told me the same thing, so I think it's opposites attracting."[54]

Beyond framing "coal-black" male bodies as "forbidden fruit"—and the term uncomfortably invokes the sexualized imagery of lynch victims in Billie Holiday's haunting rendition of "Strange Fruit"—women had practical reasons for looking favorably at dark-complexioned men. For one thing, as already noted, many men preferred to be seen with, and wished to marry, women lighter than themselves. For women, especially those who had skin that was a deep brown or darker, the pool of potential partners was correspondingly limited. But arguably more important was the role that women played within their families. The pattern of American individualism directed men to pursue upward mobility through material accumulation. Women, by contrast, carried the primary responsibility for preserving culture and inculcating values. It was principally mothers who passed on to children—in their stories, in their songs, in their food preparation, in their counsel—what it meant to be a "Negro." And for at least some women, finding a partner with features that conspicuously evoked African origins was an important means of ensuring cultural continuity. Wallace Thurman captured this attitude in an aside about the mother of light-skinned Gwendolyn in *The Blacker the Berry:* "So afraid was she that her daughter would develop a 'pink' complex that she willingly discouraged her associating with light people and persistently encouraged her to choose her friends among the darker elements of the race. And she insisted that Gwendolyn must marry a dark brown man so that her children would be real Negroes."[55]

★

Skin color was not the only physical characteristic read for meaning. Complained one commentator in an April 1859 essay for *Anglo-African Magazine:* "Flat noses must be pinched up. Kinky hair must be subjected to a straightening process—oiled, and pulled, twisted up, tied down, sleeked over and pressed under, or cut off so short that it can't curl. . . . Thick lips are puckered up." More than a century later, Elaine Brown remembered her days as a schoolgirl in Philadelphia: "Everyone had always known that dark-skinned colored girls with 'bad,' or kinky, hair were ugly. . . . We derided girls who had short 'nappy' hair, or thick 'liver' lips, or protruding, high behinds. Or skin 'so black it's blue.' I did not want to get back. Despite that I was, like most girls on York Street, a few shades 'too dark,' I had 'good' hair and white facial features. I was really not like the other colored girls. My mother had told me that."[56]

During the nineteenth century, Negro women engaged in a variety of practices to straighten "nappy" hair: "Some used a 'mammy-leg' cap—the leg of a woman's stocking pulled over greased hair. When it was removed, hours later, the hair was flatter, but the cap worked only so well, and humid weather quickly made the hair go back to its natural state." Commercial hair-straightening preparations made their way to market even before skin lighteners. An advertisement for Ford's Hair Pomade promised: "Makes harsh kinky hair softer, more pliable, easier to comb, and put up in any style the length will permit." Mainstream publications including *The Crisis* and *Opportunity* as well as A. Philip Randolph's socialist *The Messenger* routinely carried advertisements for hair straighteners. So, contrary to popular impression, did Marcus Garvey's *The Negro World*, although, granted, only when the Universal Negro Improvement Association was experiencing financial difficulties.[57]

The person most closely associated in the public mind with hair straightening during the early decades of the twentieth century was Madam C. J. Walker. Born Sarah Breedlove to former slaves in Louisiana shortly after the Civil War, she was orphaned at a young age. Eventually she made her way to Saint Louis where she first learned about the hair care industry. A brilliant entrepreneur, within a few years she had adapted European-style hot combs for use by women of African descent, was marketing a hair ointment of her own creation, had built a factory in Indianapolis, and had opened schools where "hair culturists" were taught her "scientific scalp treatment." A true rags-to-riches story in the classic American tradition, Walker, at the time of her death in 1919, was living in a thirty-four-room mansion on a 4.5-acre estate along the Hudson River, less than twenty miles from Manhattan.[58]

For men no less than women, straight hair conferred significant social advantages. Consider this scene from Charles W. Chesnutt's novel *The House behind the Cedars:* "Mis' Molly's impression of Wain was favorable. His complexion was of a light brown—not quite so fair as Mis' Molly would have preferred; but any deficiency in this regard, or in the matter of the stranger's features, which, while not unpleasing, leaned toward the broad mulatto type, was more than compensated in her eyes by very straight black hair, and, as soon appeared, a great facility of complimentary speech."[59]

Examples of men who devoted attention to their hair are not confined to the elite. Richard Berry, who in 1955 wrote the rock-and-roll classic "Louie, Louie," wore his hair in a conk. "Conk," Etta James explains, "was the goop you bought at the drugstore or the liquor store to paste your hair down. Some of the cats— the lighter-skinned guys—wore their hair in what we called water waves, which weren't as sticky or pasty as conks. 'Do's' were a whole 'nother deal, and involved pressing and burning and God knows what else. These were the haircuts of the times, and we girls took notice."[60]

Not long after he moved to Boston—this was during his hustling days— Malcolm X also had his hair conked. Reflecting back on that period in his life from the perspective of the 1960s, he commented bitterly, "This was my first really big step toward self-degradation. . . . I had joined the multitude of Negro men and women in America who are brain washed into believing that the black people are 'inferior'—and white people 'superior'—that they will even violate and mutilate their God-created bodies to try to look 'pretty' by white standards." But here, as Lawrence Levine has argued, Malcolm was misreading his own personal history and, indeed, the history of black Americans in general. "Conking" dates back to the early twentieth century when a barber in New York produced a hair preparation called "Kink-No-More." "Whatever the original motives for conking," Levine writes, "and certainly white standards may have played a prominent role, by the time young Malcolm did it in the 1940s it had become an in-group phenomenon among certain strata of blacks and it is clear from the evidence of his own autobiography that, whatever he thought of his motives later, at the time his standard of reference was a black peer group not the white world."[61]

The charge that Madam C. J. Walker developed her system of hair treatment in thrall to white standards of beauty can be answered in much the same way. After the *Indianapolis Recorder* referred to her as the "de-kink queen," she responded, "Right now let me correct the erroneous impression by some that I claim to straighten hair. I deplore such impression because I have always held myself out as a hair culturist." Her purpose, she insisted, was to ensure that women of African descent had healthy, attractive hair. "I have absolute faith in my mission. I want the masses of my people to take a greater pride in their appearance and to give their hair proper attention. I dare say that in the next ten years it will be a rare thing to see a kinky head of hair and it will not be straight either." What she was offering, observes her great-great-granddaughter A'Lelia Bundles, was "her vision of an evolving beauty aesthetic for black women."[62]

That the beliefs and values—the prejudices as well—of powerful and wealthy whites influenced the social practices of less privileged members of society presumably goes without saying. But it would be a mistake to conclude that, therefore, the popularity of "the Walker System" or of Ro-Zol skin cream represented a determination on the part of people of African descent to mimic whites, much less a desire to be white. From the Civil War to the dawn of the Civil Rights Era, most members of the "colored aristocracy" were seeking to protect the positions they had acquired as the privileged members of a subordinate caste. And those below the ranks of the elite recognized that light skin and straight hair carried social advantages and, possibly, would open the door to material opportunities, again within the confines of the subordinate caste. Ralph Ellison captured the prevailing frame of reference in a sardonic scene from *Invisible Man*. Here the narrator is reflecting on the president of the Tuskegee-like college in the South where he is enrolled as a student: "He was the example of everything I hoped to be: Influential with wealthy men all over the country; consulted in matters concerning the race; a leader of his people; the possessor of not one, but two Cadillacs, a good salary and a soft, good-looking and creamy-complexioned wife."[63]

★

From the Revolution—indeed from some decades earlier—to the dawn of the Civil Rights Era, white men with the power to determine the laws of the land and white men and women with the dominant voice in shaping public consciousness dictated that mulattoes and blacks belonged to a single social caste. The triumph of the one-drop rule in the decades following the emancipation of the slaves helped ensure that the boundaries of that caste would be seen as natural, biological. But a social hierarchy emerged within the caste, one shaped by the predisposition of both Southern and Northern elites to give preferential treatment to individuals with visible evidence of European ancestry. Preferential treatment led to material advantage for mulattoes. And in this way material advantage within the caste came to be associated with light skin and straight hair.

For those men and women of African ancestry who did particularly well within the limited opportunities available to them, there were two logical paths for self-imagining. On the one hand, they could define themselves as the natural leaders of the caste. On the other, they could seek as far as possible to represent themselves as a distinct people—distinct by virtue of their European ancestry, their wealth, and what one historian has called their "genteel performance."[64] Context determined which path was more heavily traveled at any given time and in any particular place.

In the South, it was during the antebellum period that circumstances contrived most powerfully to foster a sense among privileged mulattoes that they represented a separate division of humanity. The vast majority of people of African ancestry were slaves. And among those who were free, only a select few mulattoes enjoyed the patronage and protection of the planting elite—patronage and protection that allowed them a comfortable existence, not excepting the opportunity to acquire slaves themselves, and allowed them, as well, largely to escape the worst forms of abuse at the hands of lower-class whites. Despite laws proscribing all blacks and mulattoes, such privileged men and women had obvious reasons for excluding others of African ancestry from their imagined community.

Then, however, came the Thirteenth Amendment, emancipating the slaves, and the decision by the Republican government in Washington to grant the vote to all men, regardless of race. At once the social distance between the elite and other members of the black and mulatto caste was reduced, if more in principle than fact. Then, beginning in the late nineteenth century, segregation laws provided a sledgehammer-like leveling. That the plaintiff in *Plessy v. Ferguson* was a very light-complexioned man allied with prominent mulatto professionals and artisans only made the implications of the "separate but equal" decision that much more clear.[65]

In the North, the view among the mulatto elite that they represented a separate community exerted its strongest appeal before the emergence of urban ghettos. Through much of the nineteenth century the most successful people of African ancestry were skilled urban laborers who worked for whites, or tradesmen who served a white clientele. Despite the existence of laws segregating schools and public places, such individuals did not have much to do with the vast majority of Negroes who were domestic servants or unskilled laborers. The development of the ghetto brought about dramatic changes. Members of the light-skinned elite lost many of their white clients and benefactors and were forced to live among other people of African ancestry, including, after the beginning of the Great Migration, the children and grandchildren of Southern slaves. In time their own children married into the rising class of entrepreneurs who depended on inner-city residents for their livelihood.

In both North and South, the triumph of the one-drop rule made it substantially more difficult for wealthy light-skinned men and women to imagine their racial community in narrowly circumscribed terms. During the first half of the twentieth century such men and women increasingly took on the role of spokespersons for all Americans of African descent. Inevitably, their wealth and superior education provoked resentment among those who were less privileged. But it was resentment often mixed with some envy and even pride. And their comparatively light complexion and straight or straightened hair—along, again, with their education and wealth—allowed them political access to white men and women with power. This too could give rise to resentment. But to the extent that they used such access to benefit all people on the black side of the one-drop line, they won respect. What they did not do was give voice to the class-specific interests of ordinary working people. As a result, the caste they purported to represent remained divided—divided along class lines shaded by skin color.

PART 3 • BEYOND CIVIL RIGHTS

★ ★ ★

5 • The Civil Rights Movement

To Americans who have come of age since the 1950s, it is more recognizable than the Gettysburg Address. Its cadences, its poetic invocations, are as familiar as its inspiring message.

I have a dream,

proclaimed Martin Luther King, Jr.

It is a dream deeply rooted in the American dream. I have a dream that one day this nation will rise up and live out the true meaning of its creed: "We hold these truths to be self-evident: that all men are created equal."

And moments later:

I have a dream that my four little children will one day live in a nation where they will not be judged by the color of their skin but by the content of their character.

Then the stirring appeal:

Let freedom ring!

And the promise:

And when this happens, when we allow freedom to ring, when we let it ring from every village and every hamlet, from every state and every city, we will be able to speed up that day when all of God's children, black men and white men, Jews and Gentiles, Protestants and Catholics, will be able to join hands and sing in the words of the old Negro spiritual, "Free at last! Free at last! Thank God Almighty, we are free at last![1]

★

Nineteen years before the March on Washington, at the young age of fifteen, Martin Luther King, Jr. delivered an address entitled "The Negro and the Constitution" at a Baptist church in Dublin, Georgia. The occasion was a public speaking contest for high school students sponsored by a black fraternal organization.

"America gave its full pledge of freedom seventy-five years ago," King said. "Slavery has been a strange paradox in a nation founded on the principles that all men are created free and equal. Finally after tumult and war, the nation took a new stand—freedom for all people. The new order was backed by amendments to the national constitution making it the fundamental law that thenceforth there should be no discrimination anywhere in the 'land of the free' on account of race, color or previous condition of servitude.

"Black America still wears chain," he continued. But now there was reason for hope. "The spirit of Lincoln still lives . . . America experiences a new birth of freedom in her sons and daughters; she incarnates the spirit of her martyred chief." The task now was to "cast down the last barrier to perfect freedom."[2]

In the years ahead, King would repeatedly claim spiritual kinship with Lincoln. And both he and Lincoln, he would maintain, were asking no more than that the nation live up to the ideals professed at its creation. In his famous "Letter from the Birmingham Jail," he argued that the thousands of men and women who had taken part in sit-ins across the South were "bringing our nation back to those great wells of democracy which were dug deep by the founding fathers in their formulation of the Constitution and the Declaration of Independence." If, as defenders of segregation charged, he was an extremist, then surely Jefferson was an extremist for penning the words—the "majestic words"—"We hold these truths to be self-evident, that all men are created equal."[3]

The same theme resonated in his speech at the March on Washington: "In a sense we have come to our nation's capital to cash a check. When the architects of our republic wrote the magnificent words of the Constitution and the Declaration of Independence, they were signing a promissory note to which every American was to fall heir. This note was a promise that all men, yes, black men as well as white men, would be guaranteed the unalienable rights of life, liberty, and the pursuit of happiness."[4]

The truth is, however, King was offering a vision distinctly at odds with the freedom imagined by the author of the Declaration of Independence, and even by the author of the Emancipation Proclamation. Jefferson and Lincoln and the other men who shaped the political order of the republic during the nearly two centuries before the Civil Rights Era believed in white supremacy with as much conviction as they believed in freedom and democracy. Or, to put it another way, they believed that whites alone had the attributes required to build and sustain a free and democratic society. It is not incidental that both Jefferson and Lincoln advocated colonizing slaves, once freed, beyond the boundaries of the nation.[5]

There were Americans in the nineteenth century and in the first half of the twentieth century who genuinely anticipated King's claim that freedom must be colorblind. One hundred years before the March on Washington, with the nation in the midst of a bloody civil war, Frederick Douglass stood at the pulpit of the Church of the Puritans in New York City and declared: "The Negro and the nation are to rise or fall, be killed or cured, saved or lost together. Save the Negro and you save the nation, destroy the Negro and you destroy the nation, and to save both you must have but one great law of Liberty, Equality and Fraternity for all Americans without respect to color." And Douglass again, thirty years later, in 1893: Greeted with verbal assaults by whites as he began to read a prepared speech at the Chicago World's Fair, he threw down his notes and shouted: "There is no Negro problem. The problem is whether the American people have loyalty enough, honor enough, patriotism enough, to live up to their own Constitution."[6]

The visionaries who preceded King were overwhelmingly men and women like Douglass, individuals of African descent who had themselves known slavery or had personally experienced how imperfect was the freedom that emancipation had conferred. Among their number we must count every slave who looked at his or her owner and thought, "Why in a nation dedicated to liberty and equality, am I held as a piece of property?" We must count every woman who asked, "Why in a nation dedicated to liberty and equality must I sit at the back of a bus?" Every serviceman who asked, "Why in a nation dedicated to liberty and equality must I serve in a segregated unit under white officers?" Every businessman who asked, "Why in a nation dedicated to liberty and equality am I barred from buying a home in the suburbs?" The Civil Rights Movement posed a fundamental question for the nation: Who were the true patriots? Those who sought to preserve the historic link between white privilege and freedom or those who would destroy that link?

To the vast majority of Southern whites of the 1950s and 1960s, laws separating the races and limiting the franchise were self-evidently necessary to ensure democracy and underwrite their own claims to freedom and equality. And so when the campaign was put in motion to end segregation, they mounted "massive resistance"—in the state legislatures, in county courthouses, on the steps of public schools, along city avenues and dusty back roads. Spokespersons for the Civil Rights Movement and spokespersons for the White Citizens' Council both claimed lineage from the Founding Fathers, and both claimed to be representing the "true" meaning of the Declaration of Independence. Perhaps the racial divide was most dramatically—and most poignantly—illustrated at the funeral for Medgar Evers. The casket bearing the slain civil rights leader was draped with the Stars and Stripes. As the procession streamed quietly, peacefully along the streets of Jackson, Mississippi, policemen angrily wrenched from the hands of the mourners dressed in their Sunday best, including the hands of young children, the small American flags they proudly carried.[7]

A generation earlier such scenes—and, indeed, scenes of much greater brutality—would have received little notice outside the South. But the arrival of the television in American homes meant that they now were widely disseminated, and frequently within a matter of hours. White liberals in the North flooded the White House and Congress with calls for federal intervention. But of even more consequence, the images became ammunition for the Soviet Union in the Cold War. Washington, in its effort to secure client states in Africa and Southeast Asia, was exporting the message that the West stood for freedom and democracy, communism represented totalitarianism and repression. But how to convince the leaders of, say, a newly independent Ghana that America offered the best hope for realizing their national aspirations when evidence was circulating of dogs savaging young children of African descent on the streets of Birmingham?[8]

Meanwhile, in the minds of Southern whites, the civil rights activists were themselves the advance guard of communism. "The actions of African-Americans were so novel, so fearful, so unthinkable," Jason Sokol has observed, "that many believed civil rights protests had to be the work of outside influences—namely the Communist Party." Even Hodding Carter, the thoughtful editor of the *Delta Democrat-Times* in Greenville, Mississippi—a man sufficiently liberal in his judgments that Southern politicians routinely referred to him as "nigger-loving"—even he suggested, in 1965, that the Southern Christian Leadership Conference was "slipping out of [Martin Luther King's] grasp and into the hands of militants under communist influence."[9]

Participants in the Civil Rights Movement repeatedly found themselves pressed to answer questions about their loyalty. In response, they argued—argued relentlessly—that victory in the Cold War was itself dependent on extending to black Americans those rights that had historically been reserved for whites. Wrote Roy Wilkins in *The Crisis* in 1951:

> As the world's most powerful democratic nation, America is engaged in a cold war with Soviet Russia, the nation of godless communism, dedicated not only to that way of life within its borders, for its own people, but to evil conspiracies to spread communism abroad, to bring nations toppling, and hundreds of millions of men beneath its slave banner. While armed preparedness and strength are necessary in this cold war in the defense against Trojan horse tactics, treachery, proselyting [sic], false propaganda, and diplomatic double-talk, armed force alone will not assure the military victory. Nor will our massed billions in money, nor our fantastically productive economy. No, the ultimate and final decisive victory will be attained, and secured, through the full employment of the spiritual forces which undergird the democratic political ideal. This ideal is embodied in that portion of the Declaration of Independence which reads: "We hold these truths to be self-evident, that all men are created equal, that they are endowed by their Creator with certain inalienable rights, that among these are Life, Liberty, and the Pursuit of Happiness." . . . Our Negro citizens have made their position clear. . . . They believe that the survival of the American democratic system in the present global conflict of ideologies, depends on the strength it can muster from the minds, hearts, and spiritual convictions of all its people. It cannot muster the necessary strength if one-tenth of its people are second- or third-class citizens.[10]

At a press conference six years later, in the fall of 1957, fifteen-year-old Terrence Roberts spoke about the mob violence that he and other members of the Little Rock Nine had faced just weeks earlier when they integrated Central High School: "I would like to say that I know that Communists enjoy taking advantage of situations such as these to twist the minds of peoples of the world, but I'm thankful that in America their actions are being foiled by the efforts of many democratic-minded citizens."[11]

★

On June 4, 1965, just two months before enactment of the Voting Rights Act, President Lyndon Johnson addressed graduating students and their families at Howard University's commencement ceremony:

> In far too many ways American Negroes have been another nation: deprived of freedom, crippled by hatred, the doors of opportunity closed to hope. In our time change has come to this Nation, too. The American Negro, acting with impressive restraint, has peacefully protested and marched, entered the courtrooms and the seats of government, demanding a justice that has long been denied. The voice of the Negro was the call to action. But it is a tribute to America that, once aroused, the courts and the Congress, the President and most of the people, have been the allies of progress. Thus we have seen the high court of the country declare that discrimination based on race was repugnant to the Constitution, and therefore void. We have seen in 1957, and 1960, and again in 1964, the first civil rights legislation in this Nation in almost an entire century. As majority leader of the United States Senate, I helped to guide two of these bills through the Senate. And, as your President, I was proud to sign the third. And now very soon we will have the fourth—a new law guaranteeing every American the right to vote. No act of my entire administration will give me greater satisfaction than the day when my signature makes this bill, too, the law of this land. The voting rights bill will be the latest, and among the most important, in a long series of victories. But this victory—as Winston Churchill said of another triumph for freedom—"is not the end. It is not even the beginning of the end. But it is, perhaps, the end of the beginning." That beginning is freedom; and the barriers to that freedom are tumbling down. Freedom is the right to share, share fully and equally, in American society—to vote, to hold a job, to enter a public place, to go to school. It is the right to be treated in every part of our national life as a person equal in dignity and promise to all others.

"But," Johnson continued, "freedom is not enough."

> You do not wipe away the scars of centuries by saying: Now you are free to go where you want, and do as you desire, and choose the leaders you please. You do not take a person who, for years, has been hobbled by chains

and liberate him, bring him up to the starting line of a race and then say, "You are free to compete with all the others," and still justly believe that you have been completely fair. Thus it is not enough just to open the gates of opportunity. All our citizens must have the ability to walk through those gates. This is the next and the more profound stage of the battle for civil rights. We seek not just freedom but opportunity. We seek not just legal equity but human ability, not just equality as a right and a theory but equality as a fact and equality as a result. For the task is to give 20 million Negroes the same chance as every other American to learn and grow, to work and share in society, to develop their abilities—physical, mental and spiritual, and to pursue their individual happiness.

The president went on to announce a White House conference "of scholars, and experts, and outstanding Negro leaders—men of both races—and officials of Government at every level."

This White House conference's theme and title will be "To Fulfill These Rights." Its object will be to help the American Negro fulfill the rights which, after the long time of injustice, he is finally about to secure. To move beyond opportunity to achievement. To shatter forever not only the barriers of law and public practice, but the walls which bound the condition of many by the color of his skin. To dissolve, as best we can, the antique enmities of the heart which diminish the holder, divide the great democracy, and do wrong—great wrong—to the children of God. And I pledge you tonight that this will be a chief goal of my administration, and of my program next year, and in the years to come. And I hope, and I pray, and I believe, it will be a part of the program of all America. For what is justice? It is to fulfill the fair expectations of man. Thus, American justice is a very special thing. For, from the first, this has been a land of towering expectations. It was to be a nation where each man could be ruled by the common consent of all—enshrined in law, given life by institutions, guided by men themselves subject to its rule. And all—all of every station and origin—would be touched equally in obligation and in liberty. Beyond the law lay the land. It was a rich land, glowing with more abundant promise than man had ever seen. Here, unlike any place yet known, all were to share the harvest. And beyond this was the dignity of man. Each could become whatever his qualities of mind and spirit would permit— to strive, to seek, and, if he could, to find his happiness. This is American justice. We have pursued it faithfully to the edge of our imperfections, and we have failed to find it for the American Negro. So, it is the glorious opportunity of this generation to end the one huge wrong of the American Nation and, in so doing, to find America for ourselves, with the same immense thrill of discovery which gripped those who first began to realize that here, at last, was a home for freedom.[12]

In the years beyond 1965, increasing numbers of Americans would come to hold the view expressed by Johnson at Howard: that for the better part of two centuries the United States had failed to live up to the ideals set down in its founding documents. Martin Luther King, Jr.—or at least the Martin Luther King, Jr. of the "I Have a Dream Speech"—has become, to borrow Taylor Branch's felicitous phrase, "a new founding father," with a national holiday and a memorial on the Mall in Washington. In this "mythic" role, Nikhil Singh has observed, King allows Americans "not only to celebrate their progress into a more inclusive and tolerant people, but also to tell themselves that this is who they always were."[13]

Countless studies during the past thirty years have demonstrated how thoroughly the nation has woven antiracism into the fabric of American freedom. In survey after survey, a substantial majority of Americans reaffirm the belief that individuals must be judged by the "content of their character," not "the color of their skin." They express support for integration in schools, integration in public facilities, integration in housing. They even testify to their acceptance of marriage across the color line. Of course, the argument can be made that some individuals hide their true opinions, tell pollsters what they believe their neighbors think they should say. But that, after all, is the point. As the legal scholar Richard Thompson Ford has written: "The civil rights reform of the 1960s codified a remarkable transformation in social attitudes and norms. In less than a generation, racial bias was demoted from legally enforced common sense to legally prohibited nonsense. Racism became unlawful, immoral, and, perhaps more important, déclassé."[14]

Evidence of the persistence of racial discrimination in hiring, the ongoing poverty in inner-city neighborhoods, and the appalling rate of incarceration of young black men can easily lead to cynicism about what this change in public outlook actually signifies. But we would commit a grave mistake if we were to conclude that therefore the Civil Rights Movement must have been of limited historical significance. As the following chapters will make clear, in opening up unparalleled opportunities for a select element of the black population, the

Movement created just the kind of dramatic social change that was bound to produce challenges to entrenched racial meanings.

Beyond that, it matters a great deal that American society has come to acknowledge (even if more often tacitly than explicitly) that for the better part of two centuries the nation failed to live up to the promise of its ideals. The actress Ellen Holly recalled that, growing up in New York during the 1930s and 1940s,

> I was desperate to love my country, and so I struggled to piece together some coherent and patriotic view of America based on all that I knew. The Constitution, the Bill of Rights, and the Declaration of Independence were all luminous with ideas and language that caught my imagination. On the basis of those transcendent documents, therefore, I was able to construct an America of intention, a country to be honored for what it wanted rather than for what it was. And so I went, from decade to decade, until the sixties and the gift from God for which I had so endlessly prayed—a cue to love my country not out of duty, but out of passion: the Civil Rights Movement.[15]

That passion brought Holly, along with several hundred thousand other Americans, to the National Mall in Washington on August 28, 1963, where she heard Martin Luther King, Jr. deliver his "fabled" speech.

> I . . . brought back from that spectacular day the button celebrating the occasion. The little American flag we were given I will always love without ambivalence and will always keep with me to my grave.[16]

6 · Black Power

In August 1965, just five days after Lyndon Johnson signed the Voting Rights Act into law, rioting exploded in Watts, a Los Angeles ghetto with a population of 250,000. It was the first of nearly three hundred urban "race riots" and disturbances that shook America over the course of four summers. An estimated 500,000 blacks participated in the burning and looting. By the end of 1968, no fewer than 250 had lost their lives, more than eight thousand had been wounded, and about fifty thousand had been arrested.[1]

The riots occurred at a time of profound change in the public face of the campaign for black "freedom." If this change had a single defining moment, it came in Greenwood, Mississippi, in June of 1966. Some background: James Meredith, the man who had integrated the University of Mississippi, began a solo walk from Memphis to Jackson with the goal of encouraging blacks to exercise their constitutional right to vote. Not long after he set off, he was shot by a white sniper, badly wounded, and hospitalized. Determined not to let an act of violence subvert his message, civil rights leaders descended on Mississippi to complete the march. It was, reported *Newsweek,* "the biggest parade since Selma." Among the participants were Martin Luther King, Jr. and Stokely Carmichael, the newly elected leader of the Student Nonviolent Coordinating Committee (SNCC). Although the two men had cordial relations, they were of very different temperaments and, by this time, held profoundly different views about the direction the movement should be taking. Carmichael, increasingly dubious of the benefits to be gained by working with whites, had begun a philosophical journey that would lead him to black nationalism and, eventually, self-imposed exile in Africa.[2] On this occasion, in Greenwood, after he had spent some hours in jail, he made his way to a local park and, before a crowd of several hundred, delivered the remarks that would instantly thrust him into the national spotlight and ensure him a prominent place in history books:

> This is the twenty-seventh time that I've been arrested. I ain't going to jail no more. The only way we gonna stop them white men from whuppin' us is to take over. What we gonna start sayin' now is "Black Power!"[3]

The crowd shouted back, "Black Power!" Carmichael repeated the phrase, and so began a call and response that carried on for several minutes in a crescendo of enthusiasm. "The day's events," Peniel Joseph has observed, "had turned the assembly into a kind of an outdoor church meeting with Carmichael starring in the role of country preacher."[4]

"Black power" became the watchword of the struggle for freedom in the following years. It was a period that witnessed the emergence of new radical organizations, an unprecedented display of political engagement, and diverse expressions of cultural assertiveness. Important developments without question, but as important as they were, they did not stop the vast majority of black men and women from dreaming in traditional American imagery. Nor, for that matter, did they put an end to those questions of color and class that, since the founding of the nation, had marked the boundaries of black America as contested terrain.

★

To whites, the urban riots were a revolutionary act, a declaration of war on America. And in an age of decolonization and with the Cold War raging, there were black militants who were more than happy to endorse that view. The best known of the new radical organizations was the Black Panther Party for Self-Defense, started in Oakland, California, by Huey P. Newton and Bobby Seale in the fall of 1966. It rose to national prominence two years later when Newton went on trial for the murder of an Oakland police officer. By 1970 the organization had chapters in thirty-five cities as well as England, France, and Canada. Male Panthers—and most Panthers were men younger than thirty—dressed in black leather jackets and powder blue shirts, wore berets and sunglasses, and carried high-powered rifles in public. Detachments of three or four Panthers would trail police, whom they routinely referred to as "pigs," and closely monitor their activities in black neighborhoods. Party chapters offered classes in firearm use and the manufacture of bombs, engaged in close order drills, and studied literature on guerrilla warfare. J. Edgar Hoover, head of the FBI, declared that the organization represented "the greatest threat to the internal security of the country."[5]

Panther leaders immersed themselves in the writings of Marx and Lenin, Frantz Fanon, and especially Mao Zedong. In December 1970, the party issued a set of "Resolutions and Declarations" in which it pledged "to end imperialism and distribute the wealth of the world to all the people of the world. We foresee a system of true communism where all people produce according to their abilities and all receive according to their needs." In reality, however, the Panthers were much less revolutionary than their pronouncements and public image suggested. The oft-cited Ten-Point Program written by Huey Newton was a curious mixture of revolutionary idealism, black nationalism, and Great Society liberalism. It demanded, surely with provocative intent, "the power to determine the destiny of our Black Community"; an exemption for blacks from military service; "freedom for all black men held in federal, state, county and city prisons and jails"; and "as our major political objective, a United Nations–supervised plebiscite to be held throughout the black colony in which only black colonial subjects will be allowed to participate for the purpose of determining the will of black people as to their national destiny." At the same time, however, the program called for something very much akin to Lyndon Johnson's War on Poverty: "full employment," "decent housing," and improved education. And as if to confound our expectations—but entirely in keeping with practices adopted by earlier generations of black radicals—Newton invoked Thomas Jefferson to justify the Panther demands:

When in the course of human events, it becomes necessary for one people to dissolve the political bands which have connected them with another, and to assume, among the powers of the earth, the separate and equal station to which the laws of nature and nature's God entitle them, a decent respect to the opinions of mankind requires that they should declare the causes which impel them to the separation. We hold these truths to be self evident, that all men are created equal; that they are endowed by their Creator with certain unalienable rights; that among these are life, liberty, and the pursuit of happiness. That, to secure these rights, governments are instituted among men, deriving their just powers from the consent of the governed; that, whenever any form of government becomes destructive of these ends, it is the right of the people to alter or to abolish it, and to institute a new government, laying its foundation on such principles, and organizing its powers in such form, as to them shall seem most likely to effect their safety and happiness.[6]

The Panthers helped inner-city residents to secure health care and legal representation. They also distributed groceries to people in need and, most famously, organized a breakfast program for schoolchildren. These services won them widespread popularity in poor black communities. It is also the case that many blacks, especially young men, took vicarious satisfaction in the "cool pose" the Panthers projected and in the Panthers' willingness, indeed determination, to challenge white authority. But the party never had a large membership. And it remained a force in American life for only a few years into the 1970s. One reason for its decline was the now well-known campaign of infiltration and subversion waged by the FBI. Another was infighting, sometimes violent, within the leadership. There was, however, a more fundamental problem, as Huey Newton acknowledged in his autobiography: "We were looked upon as an ad hoc military group, acting outside the community fabric and too radical to be a part of it." "Too radical to be part of it." Like other revolutionary organizations of the day and, indeed, of earlier times, the Panthers were asking people of African descent to abandon their historic dreams for America, and that was something the vast majority of blacks were entirely unprepared to do.[7]

As for the urban rioters, despite white fears, they were not agents of revolution. They were individuals who had celebrated the destruction of legalized segregation in the South, only to ask why Northern cities remained "invisibly divided by race." They were individuals who were finding that the factory work that had drawn their parents and grandparents North had disappeared and that those employers with jobs to fill routinely rejected applications from blacks, black men in particular. According to the Kerner Commission, set up by Lyndon Johnson to report on the urban upheaval, the typical rioter was a male between the ages of fifteen and twenty-four.

Although he had not, usually, graduated from high school, he was somewhat better educated than the average inner-city Negro, having at least attended high school for a time. Nevertheless, he was more likely to be working in a menial or low status job as an unskilled laborer. If he was employed, he was not working full time and his employment was frequently interrupted by periods of unemployment. He feels strongly that he deserves a better job and that he is barred from achieving it, not because of lack of training, ability, or ambition, but because of discrimination by employers. He rejects the white bigot's stereotype of the Negro as ignorant and shiftless.[8]

The Civil Rights Movement had both given young Northern blacks a sense of empowerment and heightened their anger at the legacy of injustice in their own communities.

Still, while the uprisings are routinely referred to as "race riots," it is important to recognize that not all people of African ancestry identified with the participants, let alone approved of their actions. When the rioters from Watts moved toward Compton, they faced a group of black and white homeowners armed with shotguns. The men had been organized by Leroy Conley, the black head of the local Business Men's Association. He recalled: "We were all working together. There wasn't any black or white." When Martin Luther King, Jr. visited Watts following the riot, he found "a growing disillusionment and resentment toward the Negro middle class and the leadership which it had produced. This ever-widening breach was a serious factor which led to a feeling on the part of the ghetto-imprisoned Negroes that they were alone in their struggle and had to resort to any method to gain attention to their plight."[9]

The Kerner Commission also found bitterness toward the well-to-do. Investigators in Newark recorded that more than half the rioters agreed with the statement "Negroes who make a lot of money are as bad as white people." Undoubtedly they were thinking of individuals like the parents of Lawrence Otis Graham. Just a boy at the time of the riots, he confessed years later:

What I now recall lacking . . . was any real sense of the anger and dissatisfaction that the rest of black America was expressing in the late 1960s and early 1970s. Martin Luther King had been shot, cities had been burned, Nixon and Agnew were in the White House, and yet we were learning how to ride horses, make leather belts, or commander a small yacht. In retrospect, it all seemed as if we were operating in a world that was separate from what we saw on TV news or in local newspapers. Of course parents would make vague remarks about "giving back to the community," "appreciating the struggle," or "advancing the black cause," but to suburban kids like me and my brother, the "community," the "struggle," and the "cause" were just terms we nodded at before we turned to the Jack and Jill kid next to us and politely said, "It's my turn to drive the boat."[10]

★

During the Great Depression of the 1930s most people living in black communities applauded the public stand the Communist Party took against racism and applauded as well its efforts to fight discrimination and provide needed services to the poor. Yet only a small fraction of the black population actually joined the party or embraced communist doctrines; the great majority chose instead to place their faith in the existing political structure, in particular in the benevolent intentions of President Franklin Roosevelt. We find an analogous situation during the Black Power era. Blacks in the inner cities cheered acts of resistance against white authority by radical organizations like the Black Panthers and were grateful for the material assistance such groups provided to those in need. But in the end most placed their faith in the existing political system. Not in the White House, however. The Republican Richard Nixon won office in 1968 by promising "law and order"—a not-at-all-veiled reference to the urban riots—and by exploiting fears of working-class whites. No, in the twenty years following passage of the Voting Rights Act, it was not the federal government that inspired hope among blacks but local black politicians, especially politicians in the cities.[11]

By 1970, blacks represented one out of every four residents in New York; one out of every three residents in Chicago, Philadelphia, and Cleveland; and four out of every ten residents in Detroit. In Newark, New Jersey, and in Gary, Indiana, blacks made up a majority of the population. The political possibilities became clear in 1967 when Carl Stokes was elected mayor in Cleveland by winning 95 percent of the black vote and 20 percent of the white vote. After that, the pattern was repeated in a growing number of major cities: in Detroit in 1973, Coleman Young became mayor while winning only 8 percent of the white vote. In that same year, Maynard Jackson swept to victory in Atlanta by capturing 95 percent of the black vote and 17 percent of the white vote. In Chicago in 1983, Harold Washington was elected with more than 99 percent of the black vote, but only 12 percent of the white vote. By the middle of the 1980s, "black-led and black-dominated administrations" governed thirteen cities with populations over 100,000.[12]

The newly elected mayors were able to rein in police departments with a reputation for brutality against blacks. They also introduced affirmative action in hiring and ensured that black-owned companies received a greater share of government contracts. The problems they confronted were daunting, however. Since the 1950s, factories had been abandoning Northern and Midwestern urban centers, carrying well-paying blue-collar jobs to the suburbs or the Sun Belt. This industrial exodus and the contemporaneous flight to the suburbs of middle-class whites and, by the 1980s, middle-class blacks, led to a serious decline in the urban tax base. Then, during the Reagan years, Washington dramatically slashed federal subsidies for municipal programs: programs designed to support mass transit, social services, public works, job training, education. In 1980, the federal government provided cities with 18 percent of their revenue. A decade later the figure was just 6 percent.[13]

Almost all black mayors sought to solve their financial problems by forging alliances with business interests and promoting development. Some did so with evident enthusiasm, a smaller number with resignation. Writes Thomas Sugrue,

> A new mall, a skyscraper, a convention center, or a stadium would serve as bricks-and-mortar (or glass-and-steel) evidence that a city was "on the move again." Growth politics entailed forging close relationships with business leaders and responding to their demands for tax abatements and other subsidies. It meant, for many mayors who had once been involved in grassroots protests, building alliances with business leaders who they had picketed just a few years earlier. Mayors faced real pressure to show results, particularly as cities competed with one another for high-profile development projects. Corporate leaders played on cities' fears that they would pick up and relocate. No mayor wanted to see the loss of a major corporate taxpayer on his or her watch.[14]

These developments are reminiscent of what happened in the South during Reconstruction. In one state after another, the Republicans rose to power in the aftermath of the Civil War by winning the votes of the vast majority of blacks and a small proportion of whites. With the regional tax base drastically weakened and with no financial assistance coming from Washington, governments placed their faith in development schemes. There is another similarity between the regimes that took power in the South during Reconstruction and black-led municipal governments in the latter part of the twentieth century. In both cases, those blacks who acquired political office came from much more privileged backgrounds than the voters who elected them. They were, on the whole, better educated and financially much more secure, and, not at all incidentally, they tended to be light-skinned. We can assume, I like to think, that all, or at the very least almost all, of the black men and women who became

mayors and council members in the 1970s and 1980s era were genuinely devoted to addressing the problems of inner-city residents. But their own relatively privileged circumstances left them more comfortable promoting development than progressive redistribution of city resources, more comfortable
seeking advice from corporate leaders than from representatives of the poor.[15]

As it happened, then, in cities during the latter part of the twentieth century
as in Southern states during Reconstruction, few benefits of economic development flowed down to those most in need. In an attempt to revitalize Philadelphia, Wilson Goode championed construction of new office towers, the
upscale Liberty Place Mall, and a convention center. But the tax breaks he offered developers and major corporations arguably redistributed scarce resources
away from the poor. And for all that Maynard Jackson did to ensure contracts
for black businessmen in Atlanta, he responded with massive firings when
unionized sanitation workers, most of whom were black and earning less than
seven thousand dollars a year, went on strike. Some years later, after Andrew
Young had succeeded Jackson as mayor, a member of the Fulton County Board
of Commissioners was asked what Jackson had done for poor blacks. "Not a
lot," he responded. "They were poor in 1973, they were poor eight years later
at the end of his term, and they're still poor." As the political scientist J. Phillip
Thompson has caustically observed: "It is far easier to address middle-class
demands for business contracts, for high-profile patronage appointments, or
for the removal of threatening elements from neighborhoods, such as homeless shelters, drug rehabilitation clinics, or public housing units, none of which
require additional revenue, than it is to meet poor constituents' demands for
jobs, affordable housing, and increased services."[16]

Inevitably, disillusionment set in among many struggling blacks whose votes
had been critical to the campaigns of black mayoral candidates and who had
celebrated each electoral victory with hope-filled enthusiasm. A poll carried out
by the *Atlanta Constitution* in May 1988 found that 37 percent of blacks with
less than a high-school education thought that conditions of life in the city
had deteriorated during Andrew Young's term in office. Even a mayor such as
Harold Washington, deeply committed to addressing the problems of inner-
city blacks, found it impossible to fulfill his constituents' expectations. He introduced a variety of creative proposals intended to benefit the poor in Chicago,
but, faced with a hostile council and needing to calm the fears of corporate
interests, he backed off from fighting for radical initiatives. Complained a minister, recalling those years: "We said [to Washington's people], 'We need jobs,
we got people with drug problems, we got people who need help, who need

housing.' What we got back, and I mean this is coming from black folk! We were told, 'We have to be careful because we can't be seen as the poor people's mayor.'"[17]

★

The cry "Black Power!" was as much an act of self-affirmation as it was a political demand. In the decade following passage of the Voting Rights Act, public demonstrations of black pride surged dramatically. "Say it loud, I'm black and I'm proud!" sang the "godfather of soul," James Brown. When interviewed by a representative of the Kerner Commission, a man who had participated in the Detroit riot asserted: "I was feeling proud, man, at the fact that I was a Negro. I felt like I was a first-class citizen." The phrase "Black is Beautiful" appeared on t-shirts, posters, buttons, bumper stickers.[18] But this open celebration of black pride coincided with, indeed to some extent provoked, what were by and large hidden battles—battles hidden from whites, anyway—over the defining essence of black identity and, implicitly, over where racial boundaries should properly be drawn.

Observed Henry Louis Gates, looking back from the end of the twentieth century:

> Somehow, in the late sixties, in the aftermath of the King assassination, what was held to be "authentically" black began to change. Ghetto culture was valorized; the "bourgeois" lifestyle that the old guard leaders of the civil rights establishment embodied was held to be too great a price to pay for our freedom, or at least to admit to. We wanted to be "real," to "be down with the people," to be successful, yes, but to appear to be "black" at the same time. And to be black was to be committed to a revolution of values, of mores and manners, of economic relationships. We were "a people." The best way to dramatize this kinship was to dress, walk, talk like a "brother."[19]

Brenda Payton, a student at Claremont College, recalled: "It wasn't cool to be a doctor's daughter in 1969. You know everybody was supposed to be the lumpen proletariat. And, of course, the kids at Claremont College were hardly lumpen proletariat. Everybody was trying to be blacker than or downer than and poorer than because that was how we at the time defined authentically black."[20]

As in earlier times, physical appearance was read as an outward expression of the inner self. Throwing away hair straighteners became an act of resistance.

Notes Maxine Leeds Craig, who has written on race and the politics of beauty, "The natural hairstyle, black pride, and a militant stance became part of a symbolic repertoire that could be claimed by African Americans who had no direct involvement in any movement."[21] What you did with your hair was a statement to others; it was a statement to yourself. Confesses the author Jill Nelson:

> In 1970, at the height of the fervor for black nationalism, after a lifetime of privilege and private schools, I became obsessed with having an Afro, that living, ever-growing symbol of blackness, of being down with it, whatever "it" was. My hair, long and closer to straight than nappy, and once considered "good" by Negroes, was now "bad" according to black folks. It refused to curl, kink, or do much of anything except look unruly. After months of anguish, a barber in Harlem suggested I wash my hair with Octagon, a rough laundry soap sold in bar form. I did, repeatedly. While my hair didn't exactly nap up, it curled tightly enough for me to have a passable fro, as long as I stayed in out of the rain, which caused it to straighten into a pixie cut. So there I was, strutting around with my semi-Afro, studiously garbling the English language because I thought that "real" black people didn't speak standard English, mouthing slogans from the Black Panther Party, and contemplating changing my name to Malika, or something else authentically black. I even had a boyfriend who lived in the projects, had an African name, and could hardly read. "He's bad, therefore I am," or so I thought in a perversion of prep-school Descartes.[22]

Hairstyles could be adapted to make the desired political statement. Not so color, and for that reason the mantra "Black is Beautiful" came to have special meaning for women with dark skin. The writer Marita Golden recalls how, when she was growing up in Washington, D.C., during the 1950s, her mother would shout out to her from the porch on summer days, "Come on in the house—it's too hot to be playing out there, I've told you don't play in the sun. You're going to have to get a light-skinned husband for the sake of your children as it is." But then came "the Black Consciousness Movement of the Sixties." It allowed her

> to free myself from the prison of my mother's judgment that my color was a crisis, my color was a tragedy, my color was something to overcome. . . . Brown to black girls had a brief moment in the sun. We won a

few beauty pageants, graced the pages of some of the major mainstream magazines. Brothers started calling us African queens and wrote poetry filled with militant, devoted protestations of love and loyalty (as long as we created a lot of little warriors to save the race). Even *Ebony* and *Jet* eased up on their deeply entrenched colorism and featured a few darker-skinned sisters with naturals on their pages. I felt for the first time in my life comfortable in my brown skin.[23]

A prominent businessman recalled, "There was a time in the 60s when I would actively seek out only tar black woman to date. No puke yellow black women or snow queens for me. Dark-skinned women were not only a way for me to confirm my blackness but also a way for me to rebel against my parents and their bourgeois ways."[24]

Still, as Golden comments with ironic intent, their "moment in the sun" was "brief" for girls and women with dark complexions. Notwithstanding the businessman-in-making who dated only "tar black" women, most black men continued to show a preference for light-skinned partners. Or, indeed, for white partners, who now, in the turbulent 1960s, were suddenly available in growing numbers to men who projected "black power." Complained one woman in a letter to the editor of the *Village Voice* in September 1968, "It really hurts and baffles me and many other black sisters to see our black brothers(?) coming down the streets in their African garbs with a white woman on their arms. . . . It certainly seems to many black sisters that the Movement is just another subterfuge to aid the Negro male in procuring a white woman. If this be so, then the black sisters don't need it, for surely we have suffered enough humiliation from both white and black men in America."[25]

While attending a dinner party in Washington, D.C., thirty years after the Black Power era, Marita Golden reflected on those often hopeful, at times painful, days:

The house is beautiful, the food attractive in presentation and delicious. The conversation is ironic, humorous, informed, shifting between Black bourgie erudition and comfortable lapses into Black slang. We are doctors, lawyers, journalists, actors, writers. Nibbling on my salad of arugula, roasted red peppers, spring onions, and mushrooms, eyeing the rack of lamb and the wild rice that sits in the center of the table, I look around and see what I have seen all evening. I am the only brown-skinned woman in the room. All the other wives or fiancées or dates are very light to nearly white. All evening I eat and close my mouth and open my ears. These successful, witty, articulate people whom I find amusing and quite interesting betray no sense of color privilege. Still, I close my mouth, for I am too full of wonder that not one of the brown to black men in the room could find a woman who looked like me to marry. This is what I see when I skim the pages of *Ebony* and *Jet,* when I watch BET: the dark-skinned male power elite and their light-skinned trophy wives. . . . This is the personal love equation I have seen all my life. Black Power and Black Consciousness didn't change it. Remembering those days I recall that even then the female icons of the movement, Civil Rights to Black Power, were light-skinned Angela Davis, Rosa Parks, Coretta Scott King, Kathleen Cleaver, and Elaine Brown, who headed the Black Panthers for a time. Righteous sisters. My sisters. But Fannie Lou Hamer was too black and too angry and too country to achieve the icon status her sacrifice and hard work should have earned her.[26]

Notwithstanding Golden's reference to the "dark-skinned male power elite," there is little evidence that the life chances of either men or women with dark complexions materially improved during the Black Power era. Quite the contrary: numerous studies have documented that whether we are talking about education, occupation, income, or status, the historic advantage enjoyed by those with light skin persisted through the 1960s to the end of the century and beyond. Jokes about dark skin remained a current of children's schoolyard banter:

You so black they marked you absent in night school.

You so black that your momma feed you buttermilk so you won't pee ink.

You so black you sweat tar.[27]

As for the Afro, while it did briefly acquire popularity beyond the apostles of Black Power—by 1970 easy-to-maintain Afro wigs were widely available, and flight attendants and even soldiers had won permission to have "natural" hairstyles—it surely tells us something that the woman most celebrated for her Afro was the light-skinned Angela Davis. Marita Golden again: "The light-skinned, straight- and 'good'-haired girls, who had in the face of the Afro despaired at the inability of their hair to kink up, learned and shared and traded the concoctions and the secret brews to give them the perfect high-riding Angela Davis 'fro. They then had it all. Light skin and keen features (which were never truly dethroned by dark skin and full features, no matter how loudly we shouted 'I'm Black and I'm Proud'), and they often had the biggest Afro in town."[28]

In any case, by the end of the 1970s, "natural" hairstyles had largely fallen out of favor. As Maxine Leeds Craig explains: "Industrial chemists created permanent straighteners that were somewhat milder than their home-brewed precursors. Cosmetic companies then euphemistically promoted these products as 'relaxers.' Black women in the 1970s flocked to drugstores to purchase the newly available chemical 'relaxers,' which produced the miracle of straightened hair that moved and could be washed. Straightened hair resumed its position as the dominant hair care practice for African American women, a status it has largely retained to this day." On one occasion in 1989, when she (Craig—then Maxine Leeds) was interviewing teenage girls in San Francisco about hairstyles and wanted to "liven up the discussion," she asked if their parents ever had Afros. "Immediate laughter broke out, and voices screamed 'yes,' as hands shot up to tell funny stories about the immense dimensions of the Afros their relatives once wore. Natural hair is no longer viewed as a political statement. It is seen either as a neutral choice or the mark of a woman who 'doesn't care about herself' or 'wants to be a boy.'"[29]

★

"Natural" hairstyles were just one expression of what was, during the 1960s, a new interest in, and attitude toward, Africa. Overwhelmingly, previous generations of black Americans had thought of the continent as backward, untouched by religion or civilization. Even individuals who promoted emigration—Henry McNeal Turner and Marcus Garvey, most notably—assumed that African peoples were in need of "redemption." It was the responsibility of black Americans to enlighten Africans about the spiritual benefits of Christianity, the material benefits of capitalist development, and the political benefits of democracy.

During the Black Power era, however, with movements for national independence surging across Africa, it seemed to many activists that lessons should be traveling in the other direction, westward across the Atlantic. They looked to Kwame Nkrumah, Patrice Lumumba, Jomo Kenyatta, and other African leaders for guidance and inspiration in the struggle for freedom. And many blacks now sought a personal link to Africa, the kind of connection with ancestors that Alex Haley appeared to achieve in his best-seller *Roots: The Saga of an Ameri-*

can Family. Suddenly black neighborhoods became staging areas for men in dashikis and women in kente cloth skirts and headscarves. Murals appeared on inner-city walls depicting lions and giraffes, young women pouring antelope milk from pitchers, proud Zulu warriors bearing spears. There was "soul food," largely created in the South but said to originate in Africa: barbecued ribs, sweet potato pie, gumbo, collard greens. And young black men and women rejected the identification "Negro," calling themselves "Afro-Americans."[30]

The most enduring developments took place in the field of education. Activists demanded that study of the African past be given priority in inner-city schools. Meanwhile, at universities, a new generation of scholars, most of them black, built African Studies programs that included courses on ancient Egypt and its influence on Western civilization; on medieval kingdoms such as Mali, Songhay, and Kongo; and on contemporary independence movements. It became commonplace to speak of American blacks as part of an "African diaspora."[31]

In this context, a new field of intellectual endeavor arose that sought to make Africa the cornerstone of black American identity. The two most influential proponents of "Afrocentrism" in the United States were and remain Maulana Karenga, who during the 1960s founded the radical group US and later was a professor at California State University, Long Beach; and Molefi Kete Asante, who in the 1980s created the first Ph.D. program in African American Studies, at Temple University.[32]

Asante explores the philosophical underpinnings of Afrocentric thought in his seminal work *Afrocentricity: The Theory of Social Change.* There exists, he asserts,

> an African Cultural System with numerous aspects in a transcontinental and trans-generational manner. The experiences of Africans in the United States, Costa Rica, Mexico, Jamaica, Haiti, Cuba, Puerto Rico, Barbados, Brazil, Venezuela, and other nations all conform to the main elements in the cultural system. . . . Unless they are off-center, mis-educated, de-centered, or culturally insane, most African people participate in the African Cultural System although it is modified according to specific histories and nations. In this way, we know that Yoruba, Asante, Wolof, Ewe, Igbo, Mandinka, Haitians, Guadelopeans [sic], and African-Americans possess values and beliefs derived from their own particular histories yet conforming to the African Cultural System.[33]

"Nija," Asante continues, "is the collective expression of the Afrocentric worldview which is grounded in the historical experience of African people." It "represents the inspired Afrocentric spirit found in the traditions of African-Americans, and the spiritual survival of an African essence in America. . . . Nija establishes a link to our own fundamental, primordial truths."[34]

There are, he acknowledges, people who contend that blacks in the United States and Africans "have nothing in common but the color of their skin." But "this is not merely error, it is nonsense. There exists an emotional, cultural, psychological connection between this people that span the oceans and the separate existence. It is in our immediate responses to the same phenomena, it is how we talk, how we greet, how we style, the essential elements of our habitual behavior. We are not African-Americans without Africanity; we are an African people, a new ethnic group to be sure, a composite of many ancient people, Asante, Efik, Serere, Touculur, Mande, Wolof, Angola, Hausa, Ibo, Yoruba, Dahomean, etc."[35]

Maulana Karenga is best known as the creator of Kwanzaa, celebrated from December 26 through January 1 "to affirm and restore our rootedness in African culture." His inspiration for the holiday was ancient African harvest festivals. The name itself, Kwanzaa, derives from the Swahili phrase "matunda ya kwanza," meaning "first fruits." "Kwanzaa provides African Americans with a kind of elegiac pastoralism," says the cultural critic Gerald Early, "a sense of ancient Africa as a paradise lost."[36]

For Karenga, the holiday is intended to serve above all as a vehicle for introducing blacks to an Afrocentric value system he calls the "Nguzo Saba," or "Seven Principles." Each day of Kwanzaa is devoted to celebration of one of the principles: Umoja (Unity), Kujichagulia (Self-Determination), Ujima (Collective Work and Responsibility), Ujamaa (Cooperative Economics), Nia (Purpose), Kuumba (Creativity), and Imani (Faith). The Nguzo Saba speak to "the importance of African communitarian values in general, which stress family, community and culture and . . . to the best of what it means to be African and human in the fullest sense."[37]

A number of scholars have offered incisive critiques of Afrocentrism, in particular its representation of the African past. At issue here is not the accuracy of Afrocentrism's claims but the extent of its influence: did the Black Power era produce a transformative moment after which a significant element of black Americans began to privilege their membership in the imagined community of Africans and descendants of Africans over their membership in the imagined community of Americans? As Asante explains, "Afrocentricity is a mode of thought and action in which the centrality of African interests, values, and perspectives predominate."[38]

In one very obvious and important way the values championed by Karenga and Asante would seem to contradict an essential element of the American Dream. The third principle of the Nguzo Saba is Ujima, "collective work and responsibility." As Karenga explains: "In opposition to alienation and isolation from others, fostered fear and hatred for political purposes, and a vulgar individualism at the expense of others, the principle of Ujima teaches us the necessary and compelling commitment to work together to conceive and build the good community, society and world we want and deserve to live in. And this means cooperatively repairing and renewing the world." Put into practice, Ujima presumably would require men and women of the black middle class to sacrifice their personal material advantage if it conflicted with the interests of the inner-city poor. To forgo moving to the suburbs, for example. To endorse higher property taxes. To support social housing in their own neighborhoods. As the criminologist William Oliver has stated: "Ujima encourages Black parents and adults to define maturity and manhood in terms of actions that contribute to the progress and development of Black people. And by definition, individualistic behavior is defined as a sign of immaturity and boyhood."[39]

Kwanzaa has captured the imagination of a great many black Americans, but there is little evidence that Karenga's holiday has led, as he hoped, to widespread acceptance of his Afrocentric value system or of an Afrocentric worldview. Indeed, according to Gerald Early, the very success of Kwanzaa merely illustrates how deeply blacks are invested in the American Dream:

> To be able to purchase [Kwanzaa products—for example, cookbooks, children's stories, mats, Unity Cups, candleholders] is an important sign of status for the black middle class. Indeed, such people would hardly be interested in the holiday if it remained a primitive practice, because it would lack the self-evident status of upward mobility they crave. And both the black middle class and the black working class are generally pleased to see Kwanzaa displays in bookstores and department stores, since these items are a sign that black tastes are being catered to, that blacks are being taken seriously as a market, that they have an economic presence that whites can't afford to ignore.[40]

Black commentators of diverse political opinions acknowledge the enduring commitment to individualism among black Americans, those on the right typically with approval, those on the left frequently with despair. Joseph Phillips: "Liberty in America is about empowering individuals to go as far as their dreams, talent, and hard work can carry them." And bell hooks: "The ethic of liberal individualism has so deeply permeated the psyches of black folks in America of all classes that we have little support for a political ethic of communalism that promotes the sharing of resources." In research for *Facing Up to the American Dream,* her award-winning study of black attitudes at the end of the twentieth century, Jennifer Hochschild found no evidence that "support for African-centered positions *instead* of the American dream" had increased since the 1960s.[41]

With that in mind, it is worth noting that although tourism to Africa has grown dramatically in recent years, the Black Power era produced no significant emigration movement. Few black Americans have chosen permanently to settle in the land of their African ancestors. And among those who have traveled to Africa, more than a few have reached the same conclusion as Henry Louis Gates: "The main thing I learned was how American I am." The *Washington Post* reporter Keith Richburg, who spent three years as a foreign correspondent in Africa, wrote:

> I am a stranger here, adrift. I see the people, but I cannot see what lies beyond their blank stares. I look like them, I can even alter my clothes to appear less "Western," but I cannot understand what it is like to be one of them. True, my ancestors came from this place, and these are my distant cousins. But a chasm has opened up, a chasm of four hundred years and ten thousand miles. Nothing in my own past, nothing in my upbringing, has instilled in me any sense of what it is like to be an African. Malcolm X said we black people in America are more African than American— "You're nothing but Africans"—but I don't feel it. I feel more lonely here than I have ever felt in America. In America, I may feel like an alien, but in Africa, I am an alien. But the loneliness is only part of this feeling that is gnawing away at me. There is more, something far deeper, something that I am ashamed to admit: I am terrified of Africa. I don't want to be from this place. In my darkest heart here on this pitch black African night, I am quietly celebrating the passage of my ancestor who made it out.[42]

In a survey taken of 759 blacks in 1991, only 15 percent said they wanted to be called "African American"; 72 percent preferred "black." A Chicago actor expressed what was a common view: "Talk to an African, they don't think of us as part of them. They say your ancestors may have come from Africa, but it's obvious that *you* haven't. I think it's kind of futile to define yourselves in terms of Africa." Or as Whoopi Goldberg expressed it with less delicacy: "Call me an asshole, call me a blowhard, but don't call me an African American. Please. It divides us, as a nation and as a people. . . . It diminishes everything I've accomplished and everything every other black person has accomplished on American soil. It means I'm not entitled to everything plain old regular Americans are entitled to."[43]

Still, it is important to recognize that, since the Civil Rights Era, Africa has come to occupy an important place in the hearts of many black Americans, especially members of the middle class. Not contemporary Africa with its poverty, AIDS, and ethnic and political strife, and certainly not colonial Africa. It is the Africa of their ancestors that animates the spirit of black Americans today, the possibility of reclaiming their "roots." The late-nineteenth and early twentieth-century goal of remaking Africa in the image of the West—the goal of Martin Delany, Henry McNeal Turner, and even Marcus Garvey—is absent from present conversations about the continent. Rather we find what the anthropologist John L. Jackson terms a "post-Afrocentric blackness": a form of self-identification that allows black Americans to cherish Africa as "an icon of heritage and history" but does not require that they include contemporary Africans or descendants of Africans in other lands as members of their imagined community.[44]

7 • Black Americans: A Changing Demographic

Social scientists commonly treat the black population of the United States, roughly 40 million in 2010, as a single unit for purposes of statistical analysis. And so we learn that "white families are typically five times as wealthy as black families." We learn that the unemployment rate has consistently been almost twice as high for blacks as for whites. That the median family income for blacks in 2007, at $42,000, was at least $21,000 less than the median family income for whites. That 34 percent of black children in 2007 lived in households below the poverty line compared with 14 percent of white children.[1]

Statistics like these would seem to suggest that, notwithstanding the election of a black president in 2008 and his reelection in 2012, the Civil Rights Era did not fundamentally address the historic deprivation of black Americans. Disadvantaged by law and custom for almost two centuries, they remain disadvantaged two generations after the elimination of discriminatory legislation, indeed two generations after the implementation of both public and private efforts purportedly designed to redress the injustices of the past. The problem with treating all people of African descent as a single, undifferentiated element of society is that doing so obscures critical demographic changes that have taken place over the past fifty years—changes affecting the structure and, potentially, the imagined boundaries of black America.[2]

★

Start with the elimination of legalized segregation and disfranchisement, the two institutional pillars for racism in the South. No step was more critical for undermining the regional dogma that white claims to liberty and equality depended on the continued subjugation of the descendants of slaves. While race prejudice can hardly be said to have vanished from a section of the country where seven states still celebrate "Confederate Memorial Day," it no longer drives significant numbers of blacks to dreams of flight. Quite the contrary, since the 1970s, many blacks have chosen to abandon urban centers in the North, Midwest, and even the West for the South. The five counties with the largest number of blacks in 2000—Cook in Illinois, Wayne in Michigan, Kings in New York, Philadelphia, and Los Angeles—each saw a drop in its black population between 2000 and 2010. Among the twenty-five counties with the biggest population increase, three-quarters were located in southern states. By 2010, almost 60 percent of American blacks lived in the South, the highest percentage since 1960. Some of the migrants were simply returning to family, their economic prospects obliterated by the disappearance of blue-collar jobs in the North. But many were young, middle-class adults drawn by emerging economic opportunities in their "ancestral homeland." They settled in new suburban communities rimming cities such as Charlotte, Houston, and especially Atlanta, which in the early years of the twenty-first century replaced Chicago as the metropolitan area with the second largest black population, after New York.[3]

★

In the decades following World War II, the federal government began to relax its restrictive immigration policies. In 1952, Congress abandoned the bar on Asian immigrants and finally, after 162 years, removed the stipulation that only "white" immigrants were eligible for naturalization. Then, thirteen years later, the Hart-Celler Act eliminated quotas based on national origins. Advocates for immigration reform linked their cause to the Civil Rights Movement. Breaking down barriers for aspiring immigrants was a logical consequence, they argued, of the freedom rides, the sit-ins, the marches in Birmingham, and other protests against racial discrimination.[4]

The Hart-Celler Act and subsequent legislation led to a surge in immigration from Asia and Mexico. Of particular interest here, however, are two additional groups of immigrants: people of African descent who have come to the United States from the West Indies, and migrants from Africa itself. The number of foreign-born among those enumerated as "black" in the census rose from 125,000 in 1960 to 816,000 in 1980 and more than tripled, to 2,815,000, between 1980 and 2005. Before 1980 about nine in ten of the immigrants were from the Caribbean, but newcomers from Africa increased over the following two decades to the point that they represented a majority of those arriving during the first years of the twenty-first century. More Africans have immigrated since 1990 than the total number forcibly transported across the Atlantic before Congress outlawed the international slave trade in 1807. Indeed, between 1990 and 2000 more Africans arrived annually—about 50,000 legal immigrants each year—than in any of the peak years of the Middle Passage. And the number who came illegally or overstayed their visas was likely at least four times as high.[5]

A majority of the West Indian immigrants of African descent are from Jamaica, Haiti, or Trinidad and Tobago. Ten nations have accounted for about 70 percent of the immigrants from Africa, with Nigeria and Ethiopia the two main countries of origin. A considerable majority of immigrants have taken up residence in metropolitan areas, with fully one-third settling in and around New York City. For the most part, the African-born and Caribbean newcomers have gravitated toward different cities, or when they locate in the same city, toward different neighborhoods. Immigrants from the West Indies are heavily concentrated along the East Coast, especially in and near New York, Miami, and Fort Lauderdale. Those from Africa tend to be more widely dispersed, scattered in cities spanning the continent, from Los Angeles to Lewiston, Maine, and including Minneapolis, Columbus, Dallas, and Philadelphia.[6]

There is conspicuous friction between both sets of immigrants and American blacks. Part of it is culturally based. Mary Andom, a young Eritrean woman, complained in an op-ed piece for the *Seattle Times* in 2003: "I don't know about 'chitlings' or 'grits.' I don't listen to soul music artists such as Marvin Gaye or Aretha Franklin. . . . I grew up eating *injera* and listening to *Tigrinya* music. . . . My parents maintained a strong cultural tie by passing on time-honored traditions. After school, I cook the traditional coffee, called boun, by hand for my mother. It is a tradition shared amongst mother and daughter." But of equal if not more importance is the perceived social distance between the immigrants and poor blacks of the inner cities. A significant proportion of the newcomers come from relatively privileged circumstances in their native lands. That largely explains why, as a group, they have a higher average household income than native-born blacks and a lower rate of unemployment.[7]

During the 1990s, the sociologist Mary C. Waters carried out a study of West Indian immigrants in New York City. She concluded:

> The immigrants did not regard having a strong racial identity as meaning that they identified with black Americans. In fact, most immigrants distanced themselves from black Americans and wanted other people to

know that they were not the same. They saw themselves as superior to black Americans, and they were disappointed and dismayed at the behaviors and characteristics they associated with black Americans. Although some adopted the term "American" as part of their identity, referring to themselves as Jamaican or West Indian American, they did not want to be seen as simply "black American" because for most of them assimilation to black America was downward mobility.[8]

Colin Powell, the former secretary of state and son of Jamaican immigrants, explains such attitudes in this way: "American blacks and West Indians . . . wound up on American soil under different conditions. My black ancestors may have been dragged to Jamaica in chains, but they were not dragged to the United States. Mom and Pop chose to emigrate to this country for the same reason that Italians, Irish, and Hungarians did, to seek better lives for themselves and their children. That is a far different emotional and psychological beginning than that of American blacks, whose ancestors were brought here in chains." To many black Americans, such comments are offensive. "[West Indian immigrants] honestly think they are better than American blacks," complained a young woman in New York. "I have heard a few of them even say so." African immigrants provoke even stronger reactions: "The worst thing is the Africans who come over here. You can't understand them. You don't know what they are saying. Gonna stand over here and act like they, I don't know what, like they are royalty, like they African queens. Africans want to be here in their African shit and act like they still in Africa."[9] Immigrants complain that black Americans yell at them to "go home." Black Americans complain that the immigrants are taking their jobs, that immigrant merchants exploit them.

A particularly sensitive issue for middle-class blacks is competition over access to college places for their children. Immigrants from Africa are, as a group, substantially better educated than black Americans or immigrants from the Caribbean—better educated, in fact, than Asian immigrants. Their children tend to do very well in high school and disproportionately benefit from affirmative action admission policies at prestigious institutions of higher learning. Claims *Washington Post* journalist Eugene Robinson, "Half or more of the black students entering elite universities such as Harvard, Princeton, and Duke these days are the sons and daughters of African immigrants." To black Americans this represents a perversion of affirmative action, which was introduced, they claim, "to redress the legacy of slavery and racial discrimination in the United States." The immigrants reply that since "their children live in the same troubled neighborhoods, attend the same failed schools, overcome language and cultural barriers, and still end up as their class valedictorians and win scholarships to attend exclusive universities, their achievements should not be marginalized or in any sense diminished with an asterisk—that black immigrant success should be celebrated as an example of how to climb out of dysfunctional surroundings and vault into the Mainstream and beyond."[10]

★

How the children of African and Caribbean immigrants negotiate their place in the American racial order—and, indeed, how the racial order will appear to future generations of immigrants—will no doubt depend on another development that has taken place since the Civil Rights Era: the transformation and rise of the black middle class. The roots of change trace back to the 1930s, when Franklin Roosevelt's New Deal tripled the number of black federal workers to almost 150,000—though, granted, most received only low-paying jobs. New public-sector opportunities arose during the 1940s and 1950s, especially in the postal service. But it was the implementation of Lyndon Johnson's "Great Society" programs that truly established government employment as a broadening avenue for black social mobility. The growth of public spending produced a massive expansion in the number of professional, managerial, and technical jobs available at the state and local, as well as the federal, levels. Largely as a result, the proportion of blacks employed in middle-class occupations more than doubled over the course of the 1960s, from 13 to 27 percent. By 1970, more than half of all black male college graduates and three-quarters of black female college graduates worked for the government.[11]

Public-sector employment continued to be a major factor in the expansion of the black middle class over the following decades. At the beginning of the twenty-first century, more than a third of black lawyers were employed in government departments, as were almost three in ten black scientists. But the Civil Rights Movement, by targeting discrimination in hiring, also created conditions for the advancement of black men and women in the private sector. Beginning in the 1970s, observes Thomas Sugrue,

> many employers began to reach out to minority workers out of fear of litigation. Some of the largest minority white-collar gains came in personnel offices that deal with state and federal agencies that enforce antidiscrimination laws. Many employers also began to create more diverse workforces when they realized that multicultural workplaces offered many competitive

advantages. In some firms, minorities have made gains in positions that required contact with minority customers or clients in Africa, Latin America, or the Caribbean. Others have hired minority executives in sales and marketing to reach lucrative ethnic niches in the market.[12]

Indeed, over time, companies have come to recognize that, precisely because of their historical outsider status, blacks can bring a fresh perspective to established business culture.[13]

The expansion of job opportunities has translated into significant financial gains for middle-class blacks. In 1967, only 26 percent of black households had an annual income of more than $35,000 in today's dollars. By 2005 that figure had risen to 46 percent. During the same period the percentage of black households earning more than $75,000 a year rose from 3 to 16 percent. One in ten black households currently earns more than $100,000 a year. If the black middle class were "a sovereign nation," writes Eugene Robinson, "it would have the seventeenth-largest economy in the world—bigger than that of Turkey, for example, or Saudi Arabia, or South Africa."[14]

★

The rise of the middle class has coincided with significant movement to the suburbs. In New York the proportion of the black population living in suburban communities rose from 7 percent to 17 percent between 1970 and 2000. A noteworthy increase, but it pales in comparison to suburban growth elsewhere during the same period: from 10 percent to 32 percent in Chicago; from 13 percent to 33 percent in Detroit; from 19 percent to 37 percent in Houston; from 13 percent to 51 percent in Cleveland. Most striking of all: by 2000, 83 percent of the black population of Washington, D.C., lived in suburbs, and 79 percent of the black population of Atlanta.[15]

The attractions of the suburbs for blacks are clear enough. Ghettos have historically suffered from overcrowded public schools with inadequate resources, haphazard public services, negligent policing, and limited recreation facilities. Dreams of escape have been endemic. For most of the twentieth century, however, suburbs were effectively off-limits to blacks. Then, beginning with the Fair Housing Act of 1968, the federal government took steps to outlaw discriminatory practices in the sale, renting, and financing of homes. Around the same time, popular opposition to residential integration began to decline. In 1963 the National Opinion Research Center at the University of Chicago asked whites whether they agreed with the statement "White people have a right to keep blacks out of their neighborhoods if they want to, and blacks should re-spect that right." Sixty percent responded, "Yes." By 1980 that figure had fallen to 34 percent, by 1996 to 13 percent. The election of black mayors temporarily raised hope among middle-class blacks that living conditions in the ghettos would improve. But once it became clear that black-run municipal govern-ments lacked the financial resources to produce far-reaching change, the exo-dus to the suburbs proceeded rapidly.[16]

The story of black migration to the suburbs is intricately linked to the story of the fight for civil rights. As early as 1952, Quaker activists spearheaded an attempt to integrate the Levittown development near Philadelphia. Their efforts would foreshadow the movement for open housing during the Civil Rights Era. Observes Thomas Sugrue: "The key was finding middle-class blacks with normative families. At the heart of the Levittown integration project was an unacknowledged but obvious class politics: Opening suburbia was not in-tended to provide new housing opportunities for the poor, it was intended to change the hearts and minds of white Americans." It was assumed that "any attempt to mix middle-class whites and poor blacks would fail miserably."[17]

Not much has changed since 1952. The doors to integrated neighborhoods are open mainly to the lawyers, doctors, business executives, professors, gov-ernment officials, athletes, and entertainers who make up what Michael Eric Dyson—a professor himself—has wryly labeled the "Afristocracy." Recent re-search has demonstrated that the higher up the social ladder, the more likely blacks are to have white neighbors. Not that blacks who move to suburbs are *seeking* white neighbors. While members of both races are committed to inte-gration, most middle-class blacks believe that a neighborhood is truly integrated when the population is half black, half white. For whites, "integrated" means about 80 percent white, 20 percent black. Given these perceptions, it should come as no surprise that many well-to-do blacks end up in suburbs with black majorities. Like Sherwood Park, Maryland, where 85 percent of the residents are black, 90 percent of the families are headed by college-educated professionals, and the median family income is well over $100,000. Or the wooded hills around Atlanta, where, notes Eugene Robinson, black professionals live on "sylvan tracts," "the relatively disadvantaged are marked by their puny entry-level BMWs and Benzes," and "cavernous McMansions line emerald-green golf courses."[18]

★

Needless to say, most middle-class blacks do not live on "sylvan tracts." Many have working-class origins. While some men achieved upward mobility by securing well-paying blue-collar jobs after World War II, particularly in the auto industry, few who did so were able to accumulate sufficient resources to ensure their own, let alone their children's, future. A recent study by the public policy research and advocacy organization Demos and the Institute for Assets and Social Policy at Brandeis University concluded that only one in four black middle-class families is financially secure; 68 percent have no net financial assets and live from paycheck to paycheck. More than a few of these families have joined the exodus from the inner cities. Typically, however, the homes they can afford are in racially segregated communities only blocks from the urban decay they are trying to escape. Here, notes the sociologist Mary Pattillo, they "must contend with the crime, dilapidated housing, and social disorder in the deteriorating poor neighborhoods that continue to grow in their direction."[19]

And as for those "poor neighborhoods," yes, conditions have indeed been deteriorating over the past decades. The percentage of black families living below the poverty line rose in the years following the Civil Rights Era, especially in cities of the North and Midwest devastated by the flight of industry. Between 1975 and 1992, the average income of the poorest one-fifth of black families in the United States declined by 33 percent. And this was at a time when the average income of the wealthiest one-fifth climbed by 23 percent, and the average income of the top 5 percent climbed by 35 percent. At the end of the twentieth century, income inequality was greater among blacks than among whites. And increasingly for many inner-city blacks, poverty has become an inescapable condition. Looking at the ten neighborhoods that have represented the historic core of Chicago's Black Belt, William Julius Wilson found that eight had rates of poverty exceeding 45 percent in 1990, including six with rates higher than 50 percent and three with rates that surpassed 60 percent. Twenty years earlier only two of these neighborhoods had poverty rates greater than 40 percent.[20]

Not at all incidentally, at the same time, during the final decades of the twentieth century, many cities with significant black populations fell victim to what the sociologists Douglas Massey and Nancy Denton have termed "hypersegregation," an extreme form of residential segregation. In 1980, sixteen metropolitan areas were hypersegregated for blacks. A decade later, that figure had risen to twenty-nine, where it remained in 2000. Among the cities in which blacks experienced hypersegregation at the turn of the century were Los Angeles, Chicago, Detroit, Cleveland, Milwaukee, and Buffalo, as well as smaller centers such as Dayton, Ohio; Gary, Indiana; and Flint, Michigan. Southern cities too: Atlanta, Houston, Miami, Birmingham, Baton Rouge, Memphis, and Mobile. This intensification of residential segregation is not entirely attributable to the growing isolation of the inner cities. But no factor is more important. And it is the black poor who suffer hypersegregation's most painful and enduring consequences.[21]

8 • The "Truly Disadvantaged"

At times of profound social change—following Emancipation, for example, or during the Great Migration—Americans of African descent have found themselves challenged to reimagine themselves: to reimagine the defining characteristics of their community, reimagine its boundaries. Since the Civil Rights Era, the distance between the upper echelons of the middle class and those inner-city residents the sociologist William Julius Wilson has called the "truly disadvantaged"—and here I mean both the social and geographic distance—has expanded dramatically. Looking more closely at these two extremes of the social hierarchy will help illuminate the questions that black Americans face as they reimagine themselves one more time, in an age some have wishfully called "post-racial." This chapter will deal with the poor of the inner cities, the next with the suburban elite.[1]

★

Let's begin with the physical decay and social pathology that so commonly frame discussions of ghetto life. In 1998, the sociologist Loïc Wacquant provided an evocative word picture of an inner-city neighborhood in Chicago:

The Chicago Housing Authority cannot even reckon just how many tenants it has. What with squatters, double-up families, illegal sublets and the "unattached" children and men who circulate between households, some projects house perhaps double the population officially recorded in the agency's books. Under the broken-down entrances denuded of light or vestibule, cliques of unemployed youth kill time "shooting the breeze," arguing and pushing each other about. The sound of rap music floats in

the air, its heady rhythms, as raucous as the street, filling the sparsely occupied parking lots at the foot of the buildings.

To the right, vacant lots strewn with refuse and detritus share blocks
with abandoned half-crumbled buildings. A hollowed-out gas station and
a former furniture shop of which only the walls remain testify to the life
that once inhabited the neighborhood. A smattering of food stores sport-
ing the sprightly logo of the Lotto and a profusion of liquor outlets, many
of them open 24 hours a day, compact brick cubes with narrow latticed
windows decorated with colorful pennants vaunting the latest sale on
six-packs of Colt 45, live catfish, and the special on Night Train (a cheap
rotgut that tastes worse than bromide) dot the area. The Jackson Park
train line of the "El" (elevated public transit system) passes alongside the
DuSable high school—christened by way of racial pride after the Haitian
explorer who "founded" the city—a massive Tudor-style structure built
like a fortress recently made famous across the country by its astronomi-
cal rate of student pregnancy, and stretches its rusty skeleton in the midst
of this bombed out landscape.

Not far away, a billboard stridently queries "Isn't It Time We Let Our
Children Live?" in large, fire-red, block letters that hardly stick out amidst
the lunar scenery. Another one exhorts: "Be Smart: Stay in School." And
a third one urges: "Save a Life: Tell On Your Neighborhood Drug Dealer."
An incongruous poster—probably a mishap in location by some advertising agency—displays an ivory-skinned, blonde little girl frowning on her
hospital bed: "She Needs Blood, Don't Forget to Give Some of Yours." The
Trinity Church of God on Garfield Boulevard closed down a little over two
years ago. Across the street, a Head Start center barricaded behind heavy
metal grates tries to brighten the block with blue frontage. A few blocks
going east, the remains of the former Michigan Theatre quietly rot away.
Rumor has it that it has been reconverted into a warehouse and dispatch
center by local drug merchants.[2]

Crack cocaine entered American cities during the 1980s and fired the rapid
expansion of the drug trade. A street hustler in Chicago told Wacquant, "The
killin' man, the drugs—see the drugs like a *epidemic* man. It came so *quick*. It
came so quick. It came so quick, it's like it was overnight, it's overnight thin';
like '*pow!*' [snap, snap], we here in space! You didn't even see it comin' but
it was *there*." Lamented one forty-six-year-old mother in Philadelphia, "[Drug
dealers and users] be all on the corner. They be sittin' in front of apartments

takin' the crack. . . . At nights they be roamin' up and down the streets, and they be droppin' the caps [used crack vials] all in front of your door. And when the kids out there playin,' you gotta like sweep 'em up."[3]

Competition within the drug market produced an explosion of violence. Drug dealers armed themselves and their supporting cast of gang members, many of them boys barely into their teens. That prompted others in the neighborhood to buy guns for protection. Inevitably, the weapons came to be used for settling disputes that had nothing to do with drugs. The results, for young men in particular, have been horrific. Homicide is the leading cause of death among black males between the ages of fifteen and twenty-four. Young black men are about twenty times more likely to die by violence than the population as a whole, and about ten times more likely than young white men. The writer Jim Myers, who lived only about a mile from the U.S. Capitol in the 1990s, reported that there were so many killings in his neighborhood "they were almost like community socials. Neighbors came out, greeted one another, shook hands, and shook their heads. I remember hearing one neighbor say to another, 'Hey, I didn't see you at last night's shooting.'"[4]

The psychological damage to children is terrible to contemplate. They grow up with nightmares, with frightening flashbacks to violent episodes they experienced or witnessed. In 1985 the journalist Alex Kotlowitz met two young brothers, Lafayette and Pharoah Rivers, who lived in the Henry Horner Homes, a public housing complex in Chicago where the sounds of gunfire were more familiar than bird songs. Kotlowitz asked Lafayette, who was then ten, what he wanted to be when he grew up. "If I grow up, I'd like to be a bus driver," Lafayette replied. *If* I grow up, not *when*. In 1993, the *Washington Post* ran an article under the headline "Getting Ready to Die Young; Children in Violent D.C. Neighborhoods Plan Their Own Funerals." "Children as young as 10," staff writer DeNeen Brown reported, "have told friends how they want to be buried, what they want to wear and what songs they want played at their funerals. Some young people dictate what they want their mourners to wear and say they want their funeral floral arrangements to spell out the names of their favorite brands of clothing."[5]

In all likelihood, most of the children interviewed for the article grew up in poverty and had, at best, only occasional contact with their fathers. More than 70 percent of inner-city children are born to unwed mothers, many of whom are barely in their teens. On average, a woman in the inner city becomes a grandmother at the age of thirty-seven. Poverty tends to be chronic for children in single-mother families in cases where the mother was either never married or was a teenager when she gave birth. And there are other tragic consequences. As Orlando Patterson has noted, children of adolescent mothers are "far more likely than other children to have lower intelligence and poorer academic performance, to drop out of school, and to suffer from 'social impairment (e.g. poor control of anger, feelings of inferiority, fearfulness, etc.) and mild behavior disorders.' Further, the sons of teenage mothers are more likely to be violent, to abuse drugs, and to engage in early sexual activity. Worst of all, the daughters are far more likely to become adolescent mothers themselves."[6]

★

The explosion of the drug trade with its attendant tragedies was a product of the economic transformation that took place in Northern cities during the decades following World War II. As factories migrated to the suburbs, to the Sun Belt, and, eventually, overseas in search of tax advantages and lower labor costs, those unskilled and semiskilled jobs that had seemed to offer blacks the promise of some financial security disappeared. New York lost 520,000 manufacturing jobs between 1967 and 1987; Chicago, 326,000; and Philadelphia, 160,000. Deindustrialization resulted in the exodus of banks from inner-city neighborhoods as well as the closure of many smaller enterprises dependent on sales to factory workers. In 1986, North Lawndale, on the West Side of Chicago, had a population of over 66,000, but just a single bank and one supermarket.[7]

In a truly colorblind society, blacks would have been no more disadvantaged than whites in adapting to changes in the labor market. And it is noteworthy that today there is little difference in the employment rate of white, black, and Hispanic college graduates. But the historic pattern of racial discrimination has translated into inferior schools in the inner cities. As a result, poor blacks, males in particular, typically enter the job market lacking the basic skills that would allow them to compete for places in the emerging post-industrial economy. Marian Wright Edelman, president of the Children's Defense Fund, has commented: "Too many poor black children begin school so far behind that they never catch up. Already burdened by health and nutrition deficiencies and little preschool preparation, they often attend schools that are generally ill-equipped to identify or remedy the developmental delays of children who need help. To compound this problem, schools with the highest percentages of minority, limited English proficient and low-income students are more likely to employ beginning teachers, teachers who are less educated, and those who teach subjects in which they are not certified or in which they did not major in college." Inner-city schools also have the highest teacher turnover rates in the nation and among the highest student-to-teacher ratios. It is not at all remarkable, then, that barely half of all black students graduate from high school on time. Or that black males are twice as likely as white males to be high-school dropouts. "Left at home without adult supervision if their parents work, some students simply hang out on street corners where they socialize with ex-offenders who are neither in school nor employed."[8]

In the days when heavy industry dominated the economy of Northern cities and sheer physical strength was the principal requirement for work, it was possible for many high-school dropouts to acquire a factory job. That has not been the case for several decades, however. As of 2004, fully 72 percent of black male high-school dropouts in their twenties were unemployed. Even graduates of inner-city high schools find they have limited job prospects. Officially joblessness among young black men who have never attended college stood at 30 percent in 2000, but the sociologist Bruce Western has shown that, if statisticians were to factor in the proportion of the population in prison or jail, that figure would rise to 42 percent. Those jobs that are available fall largely in the service sector, go disproportionately to women, and pay poorly. Not incidentally, dark-skinned blacks have a substantially harder time securing employment than blacks with light skin.[9]

Already at the dawn of the Civil Rights Era the Urban League was reporting that poor black men seeking work had a looming sense of "hopelessness." Commentators began to use the term "hard-core unemployed" to refer to the growing number of poorly educated young black men who had given up the search. By the 1980s—with deindustrialization continuing, with middle-class blacks starting to leave for the suburbs, with the federal government seemingly abandoning the cities, and with municipal governments financially incapable, if not unwilling, to address the needs of the poor—the drug trade emerged as an alternative source of income and employment. Explained an unemployed thirty-five-year-old man in Chicago: "And what am I doing now? I'm a cocaine dealer—'cause I can't get a decent-ass job. So, what other choices do I have? I have to feed my family. . . . Do I work? I work. See, don't . . . bring me that bullshit. I been working since I was fifteen years old. I had to work to take care of my mother and father and my sisters. See, so can't, can't nobody bring me that bullshit about I ain't looking for no job." People involved in the sale of drugs took to referring to what they did as "getting legal."[10]

A few dealers became rich, but they were the rare exceptions. For the most part, individuals in the drug trade overestimated how much money they would take in and underestimated their risks. Not much has changed since the 1980s. Typically, those selling crack earn about the legal minimum wage. Still, as the sociologist Elijah Anderson has observed, "Many youngsters dream of leading the drug dealer's life, or at least their highly glamorized conceptions of this life." Malcolm X explained the lure many years ago: "What makes the ghetto hustler yet more dangerous is his 'glamor' image to the school-dropout youth in the ghetto. These ghetto teen-agers see the hell caught by their parents struggling to get somewhere, or see that they have given up struggling in the prejudiced, intolerant white man's world. The ghetto teen-agers make up their own minds they would rather be like the hustlers whom they see dressed 'sharp' and flashing money and displaying no respect for anybody or anything." It is not, however, the illusions of teenagers that explain the rise and perpetuation of the drug trade, but the constant, and widespread, struggle of many inner-city residents to ward off hunger and homelessness. A thirty-three-year-old gang dealer admitted to investigators in 1991: "We all just tired of [dealing dope]. It's like you just don't know if you gonna be shot tomorrow. You could be in jail, shit they could kill your family. Who wants that shit? My family don't need it. When you're young, you just think about all the money you're going to make. Man, I see it in their eyes, these younger cats think they're going to be rich. But, it ain't like that. Only a few people making it like that, you dig? I got to get out, but the money helps, man, helps my family survive. It's about survival around here."[11]

★

Many commentators have noted the existence of an "oppositional culture" in the ghetto, particularly as expressed in the behavior of young black men. Anderson, perhaps the most influential interpreter of inner-city life, has identified an ongoing and passionate war between the values of "decent" families and the values of the "street," "decent" and "street" being terms commonly used by ghetto residents themselves. And a number of prominent blacks have publicly maligned the poor: for their alleged hostility toward education and work; for their alleged neglect of family; for their way of speaking, their way of dressing; even, as Bill Cosby sees it, for the names they give their children. It would be easy to conclude that inner cities are both in fact and metaphor war zones, fundamentally at odds with themselves, fundamentally at odds with America. Doing so, however, would underestimate the unity and strength often found in poor ghetto communities. And miss the degree to which inner-city residents demonstrate, by word and by action, a strong commitment to the values celebrated by middle-class Americans.[12]

Consider the description of an inner-city neighborhood in Chicago provided by the sociologist Sudhir Venkatesh. You might want to juxtapose it against the much more desolate picture of a similar neighborhood painted by Loïc Wacquant at the beginning of the chapter:

If one were to canvass the entrepreneurs in Maquis Park, a rich and busy portrait would emerge, contradicting the area's stark physical decimation. Beneath the closed storefronts, burned out buildings, potholed boulevards, and empty lots, there is an intricate, fertile web of exchange, tied together by people with tremendous human capital and craftsmanship. Electricians, mechanics, glassmakers and welders, accountants and lenders, carpenters and painters, sculptors, clothing designers, hairstylists and barbers, cooks, musicians, and entertainers. The list seems endless. In Maquis Park, these traders, brokers, and craftspeople move between socially legitimate and underground venues. Only a few are listed in the yellow pages, and only a few—such as Mandee Wilson, who runs "Mandee's Late Night" nightclub, and Ola Sanders, the proprietor of "Ola's Hair Salon"—can boast small businesses. But any resident of Maquis Park knows where to find these services. These entrepreneurs are foundations of the community, operating in a very different public sphere, exempt from yellow pages listings and business cards; they can be found in homes, on designated alleyways and street corners, and in bars and restaurants.

Whether one is starting or sustaining a business, "underground" institutions provide a backbone for all aspects of local enterprise, from loans and credit to advertisement. The cash economy abuts a world where trading and payment occur through verbal promises, in-kind payments, and barter. Laborers and entrepreneurs, including small business owners, general workers, equipment renters, and creditors, participate in highly intimate exchange networks, where personal connections and impersonal contractual exchanges coexist. In the ghetto, advertising and marketing, credit and capital acquisition, enforcement and regulation, and other aspects of commerce seem as easily conducted via informal channels and outside the government's eye as through legitimate venues where the state is arbiter and lawmaker.[13]

Here we see the functioning accommodation that helps ensure survival in the face of communal poverty: "The barber may rent his back room to a prostitute; the mechanic works out of an alley; the preacher gets donations from a gang leader; and everyone has a hand in keeping the streets tolerable and keeping the goods and services flowing."[14]

Local residents employed in mainstream jobs—most of whom belong to what we describe as the "working poor"—remain critical to the inner-city economy. At the beginning of the twenty-first century, 69 percent of families in central Harlem included at least one such worker. But that still leaves three in ten families dependent on the minimal assistance available from the state, contributions from friends, and, above all, work off the books. And the vicissitudes of life in the inner cities mean that many individuals find they have little choice but to move back and forth between the underground and mainstream economies. Reported a woman in Chicago: "Like if I don't have food, I have to make some extra money by turning a few tricks. I also do hair, babysitting, clean the landlord's house, laundry." A man may earn a few dollars by repairing cars down a back alley one day, selling drugs the next.[15]

Venkatesh gives a sense of the range of off-the-books possibilities in his description of thirteen women who live on a single block:

> Some sell legal goods and services like Eunice and receive their wages under the table. This work is underground, but it is licit. Two work as lunchroom cooks off the books at local elementary schools. Four work irregularly as nannies and babysitters—Marlene manages to find full-time jobs, but typically only part-time work is available. And two use their cars as "gypsy cabs," charging a few dollars to help local residents run errands. Some of these women also work as psychics, tax preparers, wedding consultants, and hairstylists. The remaining underground workers are in the illicit sectors. One is a local conduit for welfare recipients wishing to sell their food stamps to businesses for cash. Along with Bird, another neighbor, Cotton, is a prostitute. Unlike Bird, however, who came to prostitution from low-wage but legal service sector work (and plans to return someday), Cotton has not had work experience in the legal economy and has no desire to leave her street trade. Cotton says, "I'm fine where I am. My next job is taking care of my man, not serving no burgers or cleaning no toilets." Two women help traffic in narcotics—one "rents" her apartment to gang members and drug dealers as a place where they

can process and package cocaine and heroin, the other is a lookout for the local gang.[16]

None of this means that inner-city residents are indifferent to the social consequences of having children grow up in the shadow of drug deals. But any ethical dilemmas created by the sale of crack or sexual services are weighed against the needs of the individuals and households such activities help support, even the material needs of the larger community. And so residents work together to try to reduce the likelihood of conflict. Venkatesh speaks of the "moral pulse" of the underground economy, which dictates "codes of conduct, expectations of appropriate behavior, and patterns of conflict mediation." Residents of the inner cities develop methods to govern themselves, often under the leadership of local clergy. As the sociologist Katherine Newman, author of a seminal study on the working poor, describes:

> A code of honor regulates the relationships between denizens of the underground economy and the straight residents of inner-city neighborhoods: you don't deliberately harm people whom you've known a long time, unless they get tangled up in your business affairs. Innocent bystanders who have been neighbors or friends for a period of years are protected by these social ties. Respect for the elderly still holds some sway as a cultural practice, if the seniors are people who know your family and have some personal connection to you. For this reason, the working poor are careful to acknowledge troublemakers, to recognize their existence rather than ignore them or behave with total disdain toward them. Building this social relation, however perfunctory, is a protective act.[17]

There exists a "geography of illegal commerce." Drug dealers and prostitutes agree to stay away from certain residential blocks, gypsy cab drivers from certain parking lots. Efforts are taken to ensure that patches of parkland are safe for children.[18]

The code of conduct is only imperfectly observed. It could hardly be otherwise in neighborhoods where illegal activity, often accompanied by threats of violence, and indeed by violence itself, helps sustain the economic order. But its mere existence speaks to the powerful sense of community that unites so many of the disadvantaged. Consider the following testimony that Venkatesh recorded from some residents of Maquis Park:

A hustler: Don't you think it's strange, that the ones who ain't got nothing, not even a roof over their head, we're the ones who are caring for each other. We are the social vulnerables, the ones who really understand, I mean really understand, that you can't live alone, you always need somebody. . . . If you're rich, you always can buy a hotel, a friend. But, lot of us have nothing in our pockets. We have to know how to live with each other or else we couldn't get by. See, this is what you must understand about the ghetto, about this community.

A businessman: Yes, it's a desperate group out there that disrupts what we're doing, coming in here and begging or maybe stealing right outside our door. Stealing cars or bikes or robbing people, maybe selling drugs, they all make a buck and do what they have to. But these people are also our customers. That's what's hard about doing business here. You got people who you don't want around here, but who you depend on. And if you are committed to Maquis Park, you are always trying to help them, even though they may be hurting you in some ways. . . . Our business is never just about making money, it's about community relations at the same time.

A fifty-three-year-old woman who works off the books: You have to be part of the community, something bigger, see. I know my brother will always be there for me, just like I'm there for him right now, helping him out. But there are lots of folks out there [in Maquis Park] that help me too, and I help them. . . . Don't matter in some ways if it's the gang or the church. You just got to depend on people who been with you through thick and thin.

And another hustler: Write about how we make sure we all sleep at night safe, somewhere. That we share our food. Yeah, if you come around where I'm doing business, I'll get pissed at you. Yes sir. I'm protecting my livelihood. But at night, I may try and find you to make sure you ain't sleeping in the cold. Would you do that for the people you associate with?[19]

In any discussion of the ghetto as community, the role of gangs requires special comment. Gangs have long been a feature of inner-city life, but it was only with the dramatic escalation of the drug trade during the 1980s that they became significant players in the ghetto economy, that they became, to borrow a term from Venkatesh and the economist Steven D. Levitt, "corporate" entities. By any honest accounting, gang leaders have been deeply complicit in the rise of drug addiction in inner-city neighborhoods and in the terrible escalation of violence. But it is too infrequently acknowledged that among them can be found "Robin Hood types," individuals actively involved in trying to improve the circumstances of their impoverished neighbors. Such men help to ensure order in the community, organize dances and sports tournaments, arrange outings for children to amusement parks, distribute food and clothing, and help residents secure legal aid and medical care. They work with church agencies, community development corporations, and mainstream political organizations. When police officers in Chicago rummaged through the apartment of a murdered gang leader, they discovered an essay he had written to himself explaining his actions. He sold drugs, he said, to make it easier for the next generation of black children to become lawyers and doctors.[20]

★

While ghetto residents will on occasion confess to taking vicarious pleasure from the accomplishments of black professionals and businessmen, most are convinced that middle-class blacks do not truly understand their problems, and many can become positively cynical when prominent blacks claim to speak on their behalf. In 1991, a three-day National Conference on the Status of Black Males was held at the Omni Shoreham hotel in Washington. Among the distinguished scholars in attendance were the psychiatrist and social critic Alvin Poussaint and the historian John Hope Franklin. Virginia Governor Douglas Wilder opened the proceedings: "The hour has arrived for us to return to the unfinished business of the nation and make good on the promises of society."

While the conference was in session, *Washington Post* reporter Courtland Milloy set off toward the downtown to gauge the reaction of local blacks. At Logan Circle he came across several unemployed men, one of whom, Robert Brayboy, had been seriously injured a year earlier on a construction job. What did he think of the proceedings at the Shoreham? Milloy asked.

Brayboy shrugged. "Why would America want to save the men it's been trying to kill since slavery?"

Milloy explained that the organizers of the conference were themselves blacks—indeed, illustrious blacks.

"What do they know about me?" Brayboy shrugged again.

Another man, waving a bottle of wine, barked. "Those stiff suit necktied Negroes working for the white man. They won't give us a quarter on the street, now they want the white man to give them money so they can pretend to be helping their 'brothers.'"

A third man chimed in, "We hip to that trick."[21]

The divide between the upper ranks of the middle class and the disadvantaged is perhaps best revealed in the gentrification movement currently taking place in certain ghetto neighborhoods. Attracted by the relatively affordable price of what were once elegant old homes—the brownstones of Harlem serve as a good example—many upwardly mobile blacks have decided to relocate to inner cities. They are rarely greeted with open arms. "Poor people deserve Harlem," explained an unemployed man. "Not that it isn't nice to have good homes, and rich, like big homes and mansions and stuff, but Harlem belongs to us, to folks who are just regular. . . . Not big money and all that stuff. I'm barely making it. And most people I know is barely making it. That's what I'm talking about. Harlem is the place where you can not be ashamed and just feel proud." He understands an underlying truth expressed by the sociologist Monique Taylor: the material interests of the "black gentry" frequently define them "as class actors."[22]

In *Black on the Block* Mary Pattillo explores gentrification in North Kenwood and Oakland, adjoining neighborhoods on Chicago's South Side. In 1990, well over half of the resident families had incomes below the federal poverty line. During the following decade, however, with the arrival of black professionals and business executives, "the neighborhood's poverty rate declined precipitously, median family income more than doubled, the home ownership rate nearly doubled, and the cost of housing skyrocketed."[23]

To many local residents these changes foretold the end of their racial community. One public housing resident complained to Pattillo: "Well, the changes I see now, they tearing down all the buildings and they getting ready to build homes. You know how they say the white people moved all the way to the suburbs because they don't want to be around us. So now they building all these homes knowing damn well most of us cannot afford them. So they trying to get the white people back in. And that's the system." But it is not whites who have proved to be the agents of change in North Kenwood–Oakland; instead it is the black gentrifiers. They quickly gained control of community organizations and set about "translating their economic power into political voice." Part of their motivation was the widely applauded goal of reducing the crime rate, making streets safe. But in their role as "class actors" they also sought changes designed to protect and promote their privileged status. For instance, they pushed for a policy of "ability grouping" or "tracking" in the public schools, the underlying intention being to keep their children separate from the children of the poor. And they led a fight to demolish the existing public housing in the neighborhood while campaigning to see that future projects were located in other sections of the city. Complained one community organizer following a particularly contentious meeting over the question of replacement housing for the poor:

> They [the middle-class spokespersons] really looked at us like we were lower than dust. . . . It hurted me so bad because I never would think that our own people would feel that way. You know you look for different races to feel that way but not your own people. And I mean it was just something. I mean, it was just, I've never seen anything like it before in my life, not amongst our own people anyway. It was horrible. And I took my daughter with me because I told her, I said "I want you to understand and see for yourself exactly how your own people will treat you when it comes to certain things." And I told her, I say, "especially when they feel that they are above you." And I took her with me so she could see and hear things for herself.[24]

Class conflict extended to the use of public spaces, indeed to the very meaning of community. Drexel Boulevard had long been a place where men, women, and children gathered to talk, socialize, have barbecues. Loud music would echo into the night. The newly arrived middle-class homeowners sought to turn the street into a "passive decorative space with large flower arrangements and sculptures, and no walkways or benches." Many of them seemed to believe, Patillo observes, that there is "a slippery slope from loitering to assaults, from barbecues to theft. And when the worry is not about disorganization's links to serious crime, it is about the effects that indecorous acts may have on property values."[25]

At times language slips out that reveals the extent to which class differences can profoundly influence the boundaries of racial identification. Joe Baxter-Brown was born in Harlem but grew up in suburban Connecticut. Returning to Harlem years later as a married professional, he clearly did not think of his poorer neighbors as part of his imagined community: "You have to kick niggers off your front step because they're drinking beer. You go into your house, somebody is next door and blaring their radio so loud that you can hear it in Yankee Stadium, you know. Then you come outside, and folks look at you as if you're strange because you're home from work and would like a little peace and quiet. It's a pain to live in Harlem when you lead a life different from the life of your neighbors. When people don't have to be at work in the morning, they can stay up all night. When you have to get up in the morning, you don't want to hear that shit. You really don't." It is but a small step to a notorious standup routine by Chris Rock on the "civil war" between "black people" and "niggers."[26]

Still, most of the men and women who pioneered the gentrification movement at the end of the twentieth century expressed "a sense of race pride and duty," a desire to "model 'respectability.'" The problems of the ghetto, they suggested, repeating a line of argument advanced by middle-class reformers a century earlier, largely result from the "questionable values" of the poor. Inner-city residents lack the "individual initiative," "the sense of responsibility," "the work ethic" necessary to realize the promise of the American Dream. They rely on taxpayers to support them when they should be relying on themselves. Commented the black president of a business college: "I think there are differences in the work ethic of people, depending on where you find them value-wise and economically and socially. You can find middle-class blacks who would parallel white American values straight up and down the line, almost you'd find a value set that's interchangeable. What's happening, you're finding fewer of those people, because the abyss of unemployment and misery in the black community is so widespread that you're getting people now in this lower end and that creates such bizarre kinds of behavior that it breeds a different set of values, so you get these subcultural effects that just spews out all these bizarre range of things that happen."[27]

That the inner-city poor have their own distinct forms of cultural expression is beyond dispute. But that they have rejected the bedrock values celebrated by the middle class is, quite simply, false. Take the question of "work ethic." As Jennifer Hochschild found in research for *Facing Up to the American Dream*: "Many more black than white or Latina poor jobless mothers want regular work and are willing to work more than five days a week. The level of wages below which poor blacks will not accept a job is almost as low as immigrants' and much lower than comparably poor whites'. Jobless young black men are much more willing than comparable white men to accept unskilled jobs at low wages." The Urban Poverty and Family Life Study survey of poor neighborhoods in Chicago, conducted during the 1980s, found that "nearly all the respondents felt that plain hard work is either very important or somewhat important for getting ahead."[28]

As mentioned earlier, the great majority of inner-city families have at least one member who participates in the mainstream economy, overwhelmingly in poorly paying jobs with little possibility of advancement. "The nation's working poor do not need their values reengineered," concluded Katherine Newman after investigating teenagers and young adults holding down jobs at fast food restaurants in Harlem. "They do not need lessons about the dignity of work. Their everyday lives are proof enough that they share the values of their mainstream, middle-class counterparts. Indeed, it would be fair to say that they hold these values dearer because the intrinsic rewards of their employment are so much less than what the rest of us enjoy." She found that inner-city workers typically enter the labor force before they turn fifteen. "They go to work younger, take the jobs no one else wants, and work much harder as a consequence than their counterparts in the middle-class communities that we think of as emblems of the work ethic."[29]

Of course, many inner-city blacks find even menial jobs out of reach, or if they are able to secure work, soon realize that they are not earning enough to support themselves and their families. Which is why they often resort to work off the books. Sudhir Venkatesh describes the busy life of one of the women he came to know in Chicago:

> In the late seventies she began working full-time for her uncle's janitorial firm. She earned several hundred dollars per month under the table to supplement her welfare benefits. In 1991 she was caught by a government caseworker and became ineligible for public assistance income. She found a full-time minimum wage job at Drexel Cleaning, where she now works part-time—usually twenty to thirty hours per week, depending on availability. Each morning before leaving for work, she wakes at 5 a.m. to help her daughter make soul food, which is either purchased by customers at her door or delivered to customers by her children and grandchildren. (She pays a teacher $20 per week so that her grandchildren can leave school at lunchtime and assist with deliveries.) On occasion, [she] and her daughter cater weddings, baptisms, and other events.[30]

It is true that some inner-city residents, mainly teenagers and young adults (more often male than female), disdain the kind of menial labor that might be available in fast food restaurants. Many such individuals end up working for drug merchants. But their days are hardly less demanding than those of, say, cooks at a Burger King. The "social organization of the drug industry," William

Julius Wilson has observed, "is driven by discipline and a work ethic, however perverse." As a young dealer in Chicago put it quite simply: "It's work man, you go out there everyday and hustle."[31]

A corollary of the criticism that the inner-city poor are lazy is the claim that they have no qualms about living off taxpayers. Indeed, it is widely believed that many of them live very well off taxpayers. In his campaign for the Republican presidential nomination in 1976, Ronald Reagan made political capital out of the allegedly fraudulent activities of an unnamed woman on Chicago's South Side—a "welfare queen," as she came to be known—"whose tax-free income alone," he assured audiences, was "over $150,000." Here he was simply repeating the widespread view that the typical black mother in the ghetto was "content to sit around and collect welfare, shunning work and passing on her bad values to her offspring." As substantial research has shown, however, inner-city residents hold much the same attitude toward welfare as other Americans. The sociologist Kimberly Battle-Walters has produced a revealing study of the regulars at a beauty shop in a black working-class neighborhood in the South. Of the customers who had at one time or another relied on state assistance to help support their families, most saw their need for welfare as a sign of personal failure: "A welfare existence was not something that the women desired for themselves or their children." As for those who had never been on welfare, while they insisted it should "not be used for long-term purposes," they did acknowledge its indispensability in hard times. One woman gave expression to the dominant view: "I don't downgrade welfare for those ladies that need it. I would rather see them get a check, and some food stamps, and feed those children, than to see them out there in the street begging for bread! But when you have a lady that will just stay on welfare, and figure that welfare is enough for them, I don't buy it! I don't go along with that."[32]

The reference to children deserves note. Much has been made of the erosion of the nuclear family in inner cities. It is important to recognize that extended families, typically headed by older women, some including fictive kin, and many of which depend at least in part on financial contributions from males—fathers, sons, brothers, husbands—are a critical source of material sustenance in the struggle for survival. Emotional sustenance as well. "Kin matter enough to sacrifice for," observes Katherine Newman. Indeed, gang members frequently cite family obligations as justification for their drug dealing. As one young street dealer in Chicago put it, "It's about doing something for me and my family, taking care of them." Or to repeat the angry comments of a cocaine dealer quoted earlier: "I have to feed my family. . . . Do I work? I work. See, don't . . . bring me that bullshit. I been working since I was fifteen years old. I had to work to take care of my mother and father and my sisters. See, so can't, can't nobody bring me that bullshit about I ain't looking for no job."[33]

The goal is rarely just survival. The inner-city poor share with the well-to-do a belief in the American Dream, in the possibility of upward mobility. The majority of poor blacks, Jennifer Hochschild has found, "still believe that everyone in America can be successful, that achievement lies within one's own hands." Or, in the words of William Julius Wilson: "What is so striking is that despite the overwhelming joblessness and poverty, black residents in inner-city ghetto neighborhoods actually verbally endorse, rather than undermine, the basic American values concerning individual initiative." A young man in Chicago—a former drug dealer "born and reared in urban squalor," and someone who had never held a mainstream job—assured the sociologist Alford A. Young that America is the land of opportunity: "You just try to be what you want to be, that's it." Success meant "not accepting 'no' that's all." He also asserted that race prejudice was not a significant barrier to upward mobility. "To me it's up to the person, you know. I don't think it's a racial thing. Everything is possible."[34]

In the inner city, just as in middle-class suburbs, success is measured by material possessions. Children learn early on to ridicule signs of poverty:

Your house so poor I rung your doorbell, the whole house fell down.

I went to your house to go to the bathroom, the roaches said, "Hey, wait your turn."

I asked you how to find your house, and you said, "Next street on the left, second cardboard box on the right."[35]

The dream for drug dealers no less than fast food workers includes suburban homes, nice clothes, luxury cars. Indeed, the allure of material possessions explains why many young men in the inner cities become involved in illicit activity in the first place. They are convinced it offers greater opportunity for social mobility than work in the mainstream economy. As one street hustler put it:

What kin' of job coul' I fin' that' woul' provide me with, able to take care of fam'ly, pay my bills an' a home, ya know, two-car garage? You know? What kin' of job coul' I fin' with the education I got? They given' them away? Ya know what I'm sayin,' it ain't like I was goin' to college to try to be a doctor or lawyer, you know what I'm sayin,' or somethin' like tha' . . . I mean, it's har' for a brotha to sit up there an' say, "Well, I'mma leave this alone an' fin' me a minimum wage job."[36]

Or a Chicago drug dealer:

I want to have me a car man, you know, have my shit on, live in a nice place where all them people working downtown live, you know, you ain't got no trash on the streets, everyone's driving the Lexuses and the Benzes. You think they come back to this shit [he says pointing to the housing projects in which he resides]. Fuck no, nigger! They ain't worried about getting no heat, no food on their plate. I'm tired of hustling man, want the good life. You ever been to the suburbs man? It's boring as hell, but it's nice 'cause they all working, they ain't worried about niggers shooting at night. It's like I always tell you, you got to have a paycheck. You ain't made it man until you get that fat check.[37]

As Sudhir Venkatesh and Steven Levitt found in their investigation of an inner-city gang in Chicago, "Members spoke of their gang affiliation and their drive to earn income in ways that resonated with representations of work in the mainstream corporate firm. Many approached involvement as an institutionalized path of socioeconomic mobility for down-and-out youth, not simply as a refuge from the available low-paying work in the mainstream but as an avenue in which to craft one's identity and realize dominant values based in consumption, monetary accumulation, and individuality."[38]

Hustlers often overextend themselves—purchasing expensive brand-name clothing, flashy jewelry, "wheels that look the deal"—in an attempt to make neighbors think they have already achieved financial well-being. But, then, such is the power of the American Dream, which validates personal worth on the basis of material possessions. The question for ghetto residents is not whether the Dream is worth pursuing but how it is best to be achieved. A scene from the Blaxploitation classic *Superfly* slyly makes the point. The drug-dealing antihero, Priest, has decided to make one last million-dollar score so he can settle into a life of comfortable respectability. His partner, Eddie, is incredulous: "You're gonna give all this up? Eight-track stereo, color TV in every room, and can snort a half a piece of dope everyday? That's the American Dream, nigga!"[39]

★

In 1982 Ronald Reagan announced his "War on Drugs." Since then more than 31 million Americans have been arrested for drug-related offenses—possession in the great majority of cases, and possession of marijuana much more frequently than possession of hard drugs like heroin and crack. Few of the men and women incarcerated are "kingpins or major traffickers." It is the arrest and conviction of "low-level non-violent offenders" that largely explains why the prison and jail population of the United States now stands at more than 2.3 million. Include individuals on parole and probation and the total rises to over 7.3 million. A decade into the twenty-first century, more than 3 percent of all adult Americans are under control of the correctional system.[40]

The War on Drugs has hardly been colorblind. In 2003, to take a not untypical year, blacks represented 54 percent of all Americans imprisoned for drug offenses. The average black offender spends a third longer in prison than the average white offender. And among children and teenagers charged with drug crimes, blacks are forty-eight times more likely to be incarcerated than whites. The United States has adopted what Loïc Wacquant has sardonically referred to as a "de facto policy of 'carceral affirmative action.'" The rate of incarceration for black Americans, he contends, "has soared to levels unknown in any other society and is higher now than the total incarceration rate in the Soviet Union at the zenith of the Gulag and in South Africa at the height of the anti-apartheid struggle."[41]

It might seem reasonable to conclude that, because Ronald Reagan declared his War on Drugs at the very time that trafficking in crack was growing rapidly in the inner cities, substance abuse must principally be a black problem. That is simply not the case. According to a report in 2000 by the National Institute on Drug Abuse, white students use powder cocaine at seven times the rate of black students, use crack cocaine at eight times the rate of black students, and use heroin at seven times the rate of black students. A study by Human Rights Watch in 2008 found that although blacks represented approximately 22 percent of cocaine users in Georgia, they accounted for 79 percent of those arrested for possession of the drug. And the National Household Survey on Drug Abuse in 2000 determined that white teenagers are significantly more likely to deal in drugs than black teenagers.[42]

That the War on Drugs has produced a disproportionate number of black casualties is, in part, a result of the way in which legislation enacted in its name has been framed. Most notorious is the Anti–Drug Abuse Act of 1986. Often referred to as the "100-to-1" law, it called for the sale of a single gram of crack to be treated the same as the sale of one hundred grams of powder cocaine. In other words, elaborates the legal scholar Michael Tonry, the "sale of five grams of crack, a typical low-level street transaction, was punished as severely as sale of a half-kilogram of powder, an amount typical of high-level distributors." Since blacks have been more heavily involved in the trafficking of crack, and whites more heavily involved in the trafficking of powder cocaine, the law effectively mandated differential punishment along racial lines.[43]

The other major explanation for the high proportion of blacks in prison is racial profiling by police. Two landmark studies of highway patrol stops and searches, one along the New Jersey Turnpike, the other along a stretch of Interstate 95 near Baltimore, serve as useful illustrations. Blacks represented fewer than 15 percent of all drivers along the turnpike, yet they made up 42 percent of those pulled over and 73 percent of those arrested. In Maryland, only 17 percent of the drivers were black yet they accounted for 70 percent of those stopped and searched. In a recent study, psychologists showed police officers pictures of black and white males and asked, "Who looks criminal?" The officers identified the black men as more criminal-looking than the white men. In this, they were simply reflecting the views of the broader American society. A survey in 1995 asked individuals to "close your eyes for a second, envision a drug user, and describe that person." Ninety-five percent of respondents pictured the drug user as black.[44]

Not all blacks, it must be stressed, are equally at risk for arrest and prosecution. As legal scholar Michelle Alexander explains, it is "in the poverty-stricken, racially segregated ghettos, where the War on Poverty has been abandoned and factories have disappeared, that the drug war has been waged with the greatest ferocity. SWAT teams are deployed here; buy-and-bust operations are concentrated here; drug raids of apartment buildings occur here; stop-and-frisk operations occur on the streets here. Black and brown youth are the primary targets. It is not uncommon for a young black teenager living in a ghetto community to be stopped, interrogated, and frisked numerous times in the course of a month, or even a single week, often by paramilitary units."[45]

In 2010, police officers in New York pulled over and frisked more than 600,000 people. Eight-four percent of those targeted were either black or Hispanic. In half the cases, the officers justified their actions on grounds that the person had engaged in "furtive movements." Here is testimony from one of the black men stopped for questioning, a twenty-three-year-old:

Last May, I was outside my apartment building on my way to the store when two police officers jumped out of an unmarked car and told me to stop and put my hands up against the wall. I complied. Without my permission, they removed my cellphone from my hand, and one of the officers reached into my pockets, and removed my wallet and keys. He looked through my wallet, then handcuffed me. The officers wanted to know if I had just come out of a particular building. No, I told them, I lived next door. One of the officers asked which of the keys they had removed from my pocket opened my apartment door. Then he entered my building and tried to get into my apartment with my key. My 18-year-old sister was inside with two of our younger siblings; later she told me she had no idea why the police were trying to get into our apartment and was terrified. She tried to call me, but because they had confiscated my phone, I couldn't answer. Meanwhile, a white officer put me in the back of the police car. I was still handcuffed. The officer asked if I had any marijuana, and I said no. He removed and searched my shoes and patted down my socks. I asked why they were searching me, and he told me someone in my building complained that a person they believed fit my description had been ringing their bell. After the other officer returned from inside my apartment building, they opened the door to the police car, told me to get out, removed the handcuffs and simply drove off. I was deeply shaken.[46]

There is a simple reason why authorities target residents of the inner cities. As one former prosecutor put it, "It's a lot easier to go out to the 'hood, so to speak, and pick somebody than to put your resources in an undercover [operation in a] community where there are potentially politically powerful people." Which explains why the lifetime risk of imprisonment for college-educated blacks actually declined over the last decades of the twentieth century. By contrast, in 2002, fully 70 percent of men between the ages of eighteen and forty-five living in the impoverished North Lawndale neighborhood of Chicago had spent time in prison, the great majority for drug offenses. Bruce Western concludes: "Mass imprisonment has institutionalized the marginality of poor blacks, setting them apart from white society and crystallizing social inequality within the African American community."[47]

It is very true that police are more likely to pull over a middle-class black male behind the wheel of a luxury car than a middle-class white male. But if the driver is well-dressed, well-spoken, and a business executive or professional, he is extremely unlikely to face arrest. The NAACP president Benjamin Jealous tells the story of a retired federal judge who was stopped by a police officer because he had rap music blaring from his car. When the judge produced his credentials, the officer grew deferential and offered to escort him home. A taped slur by Mark Fuhrman, whose record of racist statements was so damaging to the prosecution at the O. J. Simpson trial, further illustrates the point, although in a backhanded and perverse way: "Nigger drivin' a Porsche that doesn't look like he's got a $300 suit on, you always stop him." Johnnie Cochran won an acquittal for Simpson in part by exposing race prejudice within the Los Angeles Police Department. But as Richard Thompson Ford has pointed out, he had to be selective in his treatment of the evidence. "Police *had* regularly hassled and manhandled poor blacks from South Central, but for the most part they handled rich blacks from Brentwood [where Simpson lived] the same way they treated rich whites: with kid gloves."[48]

Even among the black poor, justice is not colorblind. Police are inclined to assume that very dark-skinned blacks are more criminally inclined than light-skinned blacks. In addition, as the familiar inner-city saying goes, "The lighter the skin, the lighter the sentence." Research into the court system in Georgia between 1995 and 2002 found that while light-skinned blacks received sentences "statistically indistinguishable" from those of whites, blacks with a medium skin tone or dark skin received substantially harsher sentences. And an investigation of criminal proceedings in Florida found that blacks with very dark skin and "Afrocentric" facial characteristics fared worse than defendants who were light in complexion and had what are commonly thought of as "white" features.[49]

★

The penalty paid by inner-city residents convicted of drug offenses extends well beyond the term of their imprisonment. Most states require a parolee to "maintain gainful employment," yet the great majority also allow companies to discriminate against job applicants who have a criminal record. In addition, employers in a growing number of professions are barred by state licensing agencies from hiring ex-offenders. As a result, upon completing their sentences, prisoners routinely discover that, if they can find employment at all—rare enough in the inner cities—the jobs pay poorly and offer little opportunity for advancement.[50]

Many parolees are also burdened with heavy expenses. In 2007, the Justice Center of the Council of State Governments produced a study of debt obligations carried by newly released prisoners. A *New York Times* editorial summarized the findings:

> Often, the lion's share of the debt is composed of child support obligations that continue to mount while the imprisoned parent is earning no money. The problem does not stop there. The corrections system buries inmates in fines, fees and surcharges that can amount to $10,000 or more. According to the Justice Center study, for example, a person convicted of drunken driving in New York can be charged a restitution fee of $1,000, a probation fee of $1,800 and 11 other fees and charges that range from $20 to nearly $2,200. In some jurisdictions, inmates are also billed for the DNA testing that proves their guilt or innocence, for drug testing and even for the drug treatment they are supposed to receive as a condition of parole. These fees are often used to run the courts, the sheriffs' offices or other parts of the corrections system. A former inmate living at or even below the poverty level can be dunned by four or five departments at once—and can be required to surrender 100 percent of his or her earnings.[51]

Meanwhile, the Personal Responsibility and Work Opportunity Reconciliation Act, passed during the first Clinton administration, significantly limits the access that ex-prisoners have to public assistance. Under the law, the federal government gives block grants to the individual states, which then take responsibility for designing and administering welfare programs. But the states are prohibited from extending benefits to anyone who has been convicted of a drug-related felony. "Accordingly," writes Michelle Alexander, "pregnant women, women raising young children, people in drug treatment or recovery, and people suffering from HIV/AIDS are ineligible for food assistance for the rest of their lives."[52]

Additional federal legislation, enacted during Clinton's second term, makes ex-prisoners ineligible for public housing for at least five years. And Department of Housing and Urban Development guidelines require that all public-housing leases include a clause providing for the eviction of a tenant if any member of his or her household, or any guest, engages in drug-related or other criminal activity on or off the premises. Indeed, authorities have the right to bar anyone from public housing whom they *suspect* of using banned substances. Given the financial difficulties under which ex-prisoners who return to the inner cities operate, it can hardly be considered surprising that many resort to off-the-books ventures to get their hands on some cash. Or that, as a result, a majority sooner or later find themselves back behind bars.[53]

Most prisoners who have completed their sentences also find themselves stripped of their political rights. Thirty-five states disenfranchise convicted offenders who are on parole, and of those thirty-five, thirty also disenfranchise individuals on probation. In four states, ex-offenders are permanently barred from voting. As Marc Mauer, executive director of the Sentencing Project, has pointedly noted, "In no other democracy are convicted offenders who have completed their sentences disenfranchised for life." Currently 13 percent of black men, 1.4 million in total, are ineligible to vote because they have a criminal record. The Sentencing Project estimates that, given present rates of incarceration, three in ten black men in the next generation can expect to be disenfranchised at some point in their lives.[54]

The case of Clinton Drake, who served in the U.S. Army during the Vietnam War, is instructive. In 1988 he was arrested for possession of marijuana while employed as a cook at the Air Force base in Montgomery, Alabama. Five years later, caught with just ten dollars' worth of the drug, he was arrested again. Facing between ten and twenty years in prison as a repeat offender, he took the advice of the public defender assigned to his case and, in return for a guilty plea, received a sentence of "only" five years. On the eve of the 2000 presidential election Drake lamented:

> I put my life on the line for this country. To me, not voting is not right; it lead [sic] to a lot of frustration, a lot of anger. My son's in Iraq. In the army just like I was. My oldest son, he fought in the first Persian Gulf conflict. He was in the Marines. This is my baby son over there right now. But I'm not able to vote. They say I owe $900 in fines. To me, that's a poll tax. You got to pay to vote. . . . I know a lot of friends got the same cases like I got. Not able to vote. A lot of guys doing the same thing like I was doing. Just marijuana. They treat marijuana in Alabama like you committed treason or something. I was on the 1965 voting rights march from Selma. I was fifteen years old. At eighteen, I was in Vietnam fighting for my country. And now? Unemployed and they won't allow me to vote.[55]

Beyond the disproportionate costs that incarceration imposes on those like Drake who have been convicted of minor drug offenses, it also contributes to the destabilization of inner-city family life. Although the number of black women sent to prison increased rapidly under the War on Drugs, "the main effect of the prison boom on gender relations is due precisely to the proximate fact that men go to prison, and women are left in free society to raise families and contend with ex-prisoners returning home after release." Complained a seventeen-year-old Philadelphia mother with a new baby: "I'm so fed up with him [the baby's father] going in and out of the jail I couldn't take it no more. Five years is a long time to be waiting. . . . I waited for a year and a half the first time, when we first started going together before I had my son. . . . He got out, he was doing fine. I got pregnant, and then he was just in and out of jail the whole pregnancy." The fathers of more than one million black children were in prison or jail in 2000. As Bruce Western has observed: "Just as incarceration has become a normal life event for disadvantaged young black men, parental incarceration has become commonplace for their children."[56]

★

In *The New Jim Crow,* Michelle Alexander invites Americans

to think of the criminal justice system—the entire collection of institutions and practices that comprise it—not as an independent system but rather as a gateway into a much larger system of racial stigmatization and permanent marginalization. This larger system, referred to here as mass incarceration, is a system that locks people not only behind actual bars in actual prisons, but also behind virtual bars and virtual walls—walls that are invisible to the naked eye but function nearly as effectively as Jim Crow laws once did at locking people of color into a permanent second-class citizenship. The term mass incarceration refers not only to the criminal justice system but also to the larger web of laws, rules, policies, and customs that control those labeled criminals both in and out of prison. Once released, former prisoners enter a hidden underworld of legalized discrimination and permanent social exclusion. They are members of America's new undercaste.[57]

Under cover of the War on Drugs, the United States has resurrected state-sponsored discrimination against Americans of African descent. But the "new Jim Crow" is markedly different in its reach from the "old Jim Crow." The segregation laws of the pre-Civil-Rights-Era South, as C. Vann Woodward once noted, "rigidified practice, eliminated exceptions, and applied to all on the basis of race alone. [They] took no account of status, class, or behavior, but applied to all alike." The "new Jim Crow" does not apply to the upper echelons of black

America. It is true, of course, that black professionals and business executives at times find themselves victims of racial profiling, and not just along stretches of highway. But the eminent black scholar who is arrested in his own home by an officer responding to a report of suspected burglary is more likely to get invited to the White House for a beer than find himself incarcerated. The lawmakers and police, the prosecutors, judges, and juries who are the principal executors of the new Jim Crow have chosen to concentrate their attention on the inner-city poor, especially those with dark skin and purportedly Afrocentric features. In the process they have become key agents in the rewriting of the American racial script.[58]

9 • The "Privileged Class"

"We were looking forward to meeting our friends for dinner," writes the actor and social commentator Joseph Phillips. "We chose a nice, intimate Italian place, just right for doing a lot of catching up. During the evening's conversation, our friend's wife broached the topic of equal opportunity. According to our friends who are black and quite wealthy, there is no such thing. For black folks, the deck is stacked. If you have never experienced it, there is nothing quite as bizarre as millionaires sitting around, sipping Merlot, and talking about the lack of equal opportunity and how the system doesn't work. Needless to say, that is when the fun stopped and the throbbing in my temples began."[1]

The integration of the upper echelon of the black middle class into the power structure of America has surely been the most striking long-term result of the Civil Rights Movement. Beyond the election of Barack Obama and the appointment of blacks to high-ranking government positions, there are now black partners at the most prestigious Wall Street law firms, black surgeons at the leading American hospitals, and black professors with endowed chairs at Ivy League universities. Black executives have headed the Ford Foundation, the National Baseball League, the College Board, Fannie Mae, and major corporations such as Time Warner, American Express, Merrill Lynch, Merck, Xerox, and Beatrice Foods. Yet as Joseph Phillips's provocative comments suggest, many highly successful black men and women who built their careers in the wake of the Civil Rights Movement are convinced that their lives have been severely circumscribed by racial discrimination. "Succeeding more and enjoying it less" is the way Jennifer Hochschild puts it.[2]

★

A diverse range of studies conducted during the 1990s revealed that black business executives and professionals at integrated firms believed discrimination was an ever-present feature of their lives. A survey of fifty members of the Executive Leadership Council, a Washington, D.C.–based organization of black executives, mostly vice presidents or higher at Fortune 500 companies, found that most regarded "covert, elusive, and heavily masked" racism as the "major restraining force" on their career advancement. Monique Taylor, who conducted interviews among the "black gentry" of Harlem, reported "a shared feeling that race is, if not an exclusionary barrier, always a factor in their job experiences. Race matters, they say, in terms of how their performances are evaluated and in interactions with co-workers." In a survey of more than two hundred successful middle-class blacks, the sociologist Joe R. Feagin and psychologist Melvin Sikes found that respondents were "alternately baffled, frustrated, shocked, and outraged that the strong evidence of their hard work and personal achievements does not protect them from white discrimination."[3]

Suspicions of discriminatory treatment were not limited to individuals who had faced disappointment in their careers. Francine Soliunas was legal counsel for Illinois Bell when Ellis Cose interviewed her for *The Rage of a Privileged Class.* "I've had three promotions in the twelve years I've been here," she told him. "That's two more than the average lawyer." Yet as far as she was concerned, corporate America had violated its "contract" with blacks to reward hard work and excellence on the job. "People quietly make you aware at meetings that they doubt you know what you're talking about. Executives totally outside your area of expertise endeavor to prove that they are more expert than you." The message from those in authority was "unmistakable": "You think you have power? You don't really have power, because I can take away that power anytime I want."[4]

Respondents to the surveys raised a variety of complaints, prominent among them that they had been denied earned promotions and faced a "glass ceiling," that their business analysis and policy recommendations were not taken seriously, and that they had been automatically slotted into "black jobs" of limited influence where they were "used simply as communication links and representatives of blacks." While obviously not every charge of racism should be taken at face value, and conditions varied from industry to industry and, often, from company to company, discrimination undeniably remained a hard fact of life in corporate America at the beginning of the twenty-first century. The

$192 million that Coca-Cola agreed to pay in 2000 to settle a class-action law-suit for racial discrimination provides striking confirmation.[5]

Nor were complaints of black professionals and business executives limited to their experiences at work. Many sounded even angrier when describing their treatment in stores and on city streets. A senior partner in a Washington law firm told Cose that the rage he and other blacks felt was "not just [about] the money." It was about going into a shop "where there's a white redneck who treats me like I make two cents and am uneducated." Women charged that if they dropped into an expensive clothing or jewelry store, they were more likely to be trailed by a security guard than offered assistance by salespeople. Men charged that strangers cowered when they entered elevators, cabdrivers refused to stop for them. To many blacks of the "privileged class," here was proof that a quarter century beyond the Civil Rights Era, race still mattered.[6]

But exactly *how* did it matter? Go back to Benjamin Jealous's anecdote about the retired judge and the police officer. Once a black professional or business executive established his or her credentials, typically he or she received at least superficially respectful treatment and perhaps even an apology. Indeed, successful middle-class blacks knew that they could minimize their chances of being viewed as dangerous or unworthy by dressing conservatively, and by speaking and acting in a nonthreatening manner. As Jill Nelson wrote in 1993: "The more successful of us refashion ourselves in the image of white men. We go to Ivy League colleges and socialize primarily with white folks. We wear sober, preppy clothes, earth tones, seldom bright colors. . . . Mostly we down-play ourselves, try to out-white the white folks."[7]

The phrase "try to out-white the white folks" is tinged with bitterness, but in its own way it speaks to the fundamental way in which the life chances of up-wardly mobile blacks advanced in the last decades of the twentieth century. The very nature of racial subordination in earlier times dictated that, no mat-ter how much wealth a black man or woman might accumulate, no matter how faithfully they adopted the clothes, speech, and manners of elite whites— no matter, in other words, how far they went to "out-white the white folks"— they would never be allowed entry into the upper ranks of the American Estab-lishment. And that simply is no longer the case.

★

There is a subtext to complaints by blacks who built successful careers as professionals and business executives in the late twentieth century. We see it in a personal confession by William Julius Wilson:

I am an internationally known Harvard professor, yet a number of unforgettable experiences remind me that, as a black male in America looking considerably younger than my age, I am also feared. For example, several times over the years I have stepped into the elevator of my condominium dressed in casual clothes and could immediately tell from the body language of the other residents in the elevator that I made them feel uncomfortable. Were they thinking, "What is this black man doing in this expensive condominium? Are we in any danger?" I once sarcastically said to a nervous elderly couple who hesitated to exit the elevator because we were all getting off on the same floor, "Not to worry, I am a Harvard professor and I have lived in this building for nine years." When I am dressed casually, I am always a little relieved to step into an empty elevator, but I am not apprehensive if I am wearing a tie. I get angry each time I have an experience like the encounter in the elevator. It would be easy to say that the residents' reaction to me is simply another manifestation of racism. However, when I lived in a middle-class Chicago neighborhood that bordered a ghetto neighborhood, I, too, would tense up when I walked my dog at night and saw a black man or a group of black male teenagers approaching me on the street.[8]

The fear Wilson experienced when he encountered ghetto residents provides a clue to the rage that many successful blacks of his generation feel when they face discrimination in the course of their daily lives. Barack Obama wrote candidly on this subject in *Dreams from My Father:* "We're never so outraged as when a cabbie drives past us or the woman in the elevator clutches her purse, not so much because we're bothered by the fact that such indignities are what less fortunate coloreds have to put up with every single day of their lives—although that's what we tell ourselves—but because we're wearing a Brooks Brothers suit and speak impeccable English and yet have somehow been mistaken for an ordinary nigger."[9] "An ordinary nigger." Many privileged blacks, when giving vent to their anger, drop the adjective. The economist Glenn Loury has drawn out the implication in transparent terms:

The strategies of social identity manipulation used by racially marked people to inhibit being stereotyped—their methods of "partial passing"—are endless: affectations of speech; dressing up to shop at a downtown store; writing more equations on the blackboard than needed, to show a skeptical audience that one does indeed have complete command of the discipline's technical apparatus; "whistling Vivaldi" while walking along a city's mean streets so as not to be mistaken for a thug—most generally, adopting styles of self-presentation that aim to communicate "I'm not one of THEM; I'm one of YOU!"[10]

Meaning, of course: it is my class that should determine my public identity, not the color of my skin. In a society that has historically insisted on race as the central determinant of social categories, the statement "I'm not one of THEM; I'm one of YOU!" is merely a first, but arguably a very long, step toward the claim that ghetto residents and suburban professionals, though they share African descent, nonetheless belong to different communities.[11]

★

It is understandable that a black vice president at a bank might suspect discrimination was involved if a promotion he or she expected went to a white colleague with less experience. It is also understandable that black lawyers, doctors, and professors feel offended when they do not receive courteous treatment from police and salespeople, the kind of respect that white lawyers and doctors expect as a matter of course. What is not so easy to understand is why, according to surveys undertaken two and three decades after the Civil Rights Era, successful middle-class blacks were much more likely than ghetto residents to view their disappointments through the lens of racism. In 1992 researchers at UCLA's Center for the Study of Urban Poverty undertook an investigation into "ethnic alienation from American society." The questionnaire they distributed asked respondents to assess the accuracy of the following statements:

American society owes people of my ethnic group a better chance in life than we currently have.

American society has provided people of my ethnic group a fair opportunity to get ahead in life.

I am grateful for the special opportunities people of my ethnic group have found in America.

American society just hasn't dealt fairly with people from my background.[12]

As it happens, the riots in South Central Los Angeles erupted while the project was still under way, so the research team was able to document how the violence affected respondents' answers. Their findings included an "unexpected twist": not only did affluent blacks exhibit a higher degree of alienation than poor blacks before the rioting broke out, afterward they testified to a much greater rise in discontent.[13]

These results, while they may have caught the researchers by surprise, only anticipated what other scholars would later document more fully. Jennifer Hochschild observed in 1995: "Well-off African Americans see *more* racial discrimination than do poor blacks, see less decline in discrimination, expect less improvement in the future, and claim to have experienced more in their own lives." And more than a decade later—into the twenty-first century now—the sociologist Karyn Lacy concluded: "Wealthier blacks report more discrimination than poor blacks, are less optimistic about racial progress, and are less inclined to believe that whites positively type blacks."[14]

Why should a bank executive with a home in the suburbs, children in private schools or perhaps an Ivy League college, a Lexus for himself and a Mercedes Benz for his wife, feel more bitterness about racial discrimination than, say, a twenty-year-old unmarried mother, a part-time employee at McDonald's, who also works off the books—perhaps even selling her body—so she can help feed not only her own son and daughter, but her brother and mother as well? Orlando Patterson thinks the anger of the bank executive and others in similarly favored circumstances is an expression of what might be termed the "outrage of liberation." As Patterson explains it: "A formerly oppressed group's sense of outrage at what has been done to them increases the more equal they become with their former oppressors." The writer Debra Dickerson is more cynical: "The better off some blacks become, the harder we look for reasons to remain discontented. Survivor's guilt and bourgeois self-involvement, I think."[15]

The two interpretations, as different as they are, highlight the need to go beyond the actual discrimination experienced by corporate executives and professionals if we want to fully understand why affluent blacks often sound more bitter than the poor. We must look as well at how the opening up of mainstream opportunities has posed new challenges about the meaning of racial identity for upwardly mobile black men and women. Was it possible, a young manager in training asked the psychologist Ron Brown, to hold on to her "black identity" and be "a success in the white corporate world?" Her question captures a widespread concern among black professionals and executives. In the words of Joseph Phillips: "Balancing individualism while staying grounded in 'black culture' in ever-increasing integrated environments is an issue many black families face as they gain economic affluence and political and cultural clout." It is why many middle-class blacks who work among whites prefer to live in black-majority suburbs. As a systems administrator for the federal government who lives outside Washington explained: "I choose to have [my son and daughter] grow up around blacks so they can experience culture, their *own* culture."[16]

"Their *own* culture." But what, exactly, *is* "black culture"? Shared religious traditions? Shared music? Shared foods? Shared language? Two distinguished black professors of philosophy have expressed deep doubts that the ties binding Americans of African descent are principally, if at all, cultural. Kwame Anthony Appiah: "African-American culture, if this means shared beliefs, values, practices, does not exist." Tommie Shelby: "One can acknowledge the importance of learning black history and appreciating the beauty of black cultures without treating cultural blackness, however delimited, as defining who one is as a person or allowing it to set the boundaries of one's lifestyle or self-understanding." And again: "Although some are reluctant to admit this, many blacks do not feel particularly at home in even the most revered black cultural spaces. For example, the traditions and modes of expression that are characteristic of many black churches are widely thought to be paradigmatically black. There is no reason, however, to assume that those committed to other faiths or to no religion at all will find peace and security in black churches simply because these institutions embody black cultural traditions."[17]

In addition, it is often overlooked that what may seem central to the cultural definition of one generation can be of recent origin, and perhaps short-lived. Glenn Loury recalls walking in the woods near his New England home with his three-year-old son on a winter afternoon:

We happened upon a small pond, which, having frozen solid, made an ideal skating rink. Dozens of men, ranging in age from late teens to early thirties, were distributed across the ice in clusters of ten or so, playing, or preparing to play hockey. They glided over the pond's surface effortlessly, skillfully passing and defending, stopping and turning on a dime, moving with such power, speed, and grace that we were spellbound as we watched them. Little Glenn would occasionally squeal with delight as he marveled at one astounding feat after another, straining against my grip, which alone prevented him from running out onto the ice to join in the fun. All of these men were white—every last one of them. Few took notice of us at the pond's edge, and those who did were not particularly generous with

their smiles, or so, at least, it seemed to me. I sensed that we were inter-
lopers, that if we had come with sticks and skates we would not necessarily have been welcome. But this may be wrong; I do not really know what
they thought of our presence; no words were exchanged. I do know that
my son very much enjoyed watching the game, and I thought to myself
at the time that he would, someday too soon, come asking for a pair of
skates, and for his dad to teach him how to use them. I found myself
consciously dreading that day. The thought of my son's playing hockey on
that frozen pond did not sit well with me. I much preferred to think of
him on a basketball court. Hockey, we all know, is a white man's game.[18]

Basketball was invented by a Canadian physical education teacher of Scottish
descent at a branch of the YMCA in Springfield, Massachusetts, in the early
1890s. Although the game would become popular in urban centers during the
first decades of the twentieth century, no blacks were allowed into the National
Basketball Association during its first six years of operation, from 1944 through
1949. Looking back on the history of the sport during the age of Michael Jordan, *Ebony* magazine declared, "As wild as it may seem today, Black basketball
players were once oddities in a White man's game."[19]

"A white man's game." Glenn Loury's comments would seem to bear out a
widely quoted aphorism: "Identity is memory." But at the outset of the twenty-
first century, how alike were the memories of wealthy suburban business executives and the inner-city poor? Even during the era of Jim Crow in the South
and enforced residential segregation in the North, the life experiences of the
well-to-do diverged dramatically from those of Wilson's "truly disadvantaged."
Still, as the political scientist Cathy J. Cohen has observed, the historic record
of slavery and discrimination produced "common narratives of exclusion, self-
reliance, and struggle" among black Americans of differing material circumstances, and that in turn, especially in the century following the Civil War,
produced a sense among many influential members of the middle class that
they and the poor had a "linked fate." But in an age when the United States
has formally repudiated racial privilege and the upper echelon of black society
has been admitted to the corridors of power, the sense of having a shared
destiny has inevitably eroded. Contrast the sentiments expressed by Jill Nelson with a rant, years earlier, by her father, a prosperous dentist who was dark-
skinned and had been born into a poor family in Washington, D.C. First, her
father, addressing Jill, her sister, and two brothers in their comfortable West
End Avenue home in Manhattan:

Nelson Rockefeller wouldn't let his dog shit in here! What we have, compared to what Rockefeller and the people who rule the world have, is nothing. Nothing! Not even good enough for his dog. You four have to remember that and do better than I have. Not just for yourselves but for our people, black people.

And Jill, on accepting the offer of a job at the *Washington Post:*

I finally took to heart the words of evangelist Reverend Ike: "The only thing I have to say about poor people is don't be one of them."[20]

As Ellis Cose discovered when he conducted interviews for *The Rage of a Privileged Class,* "the resentment many black professionals feel at being expected to accept responsibility for the underclass is palpable." What one university administrator told him accurately captures a widespread attitude: "In every society there are underdogs and there is an underclass. And I am not going to take on the black underclass as a special burden of mine as a black man, although I am concerned. And I will demonstrate my concern. But don't hang that one on me." Such feelings, it should be noted, are especially strong among those with light skin.[21]

So back to the puzzle of the surveys: why do the privileged individuals of Nelson's generation—including Nelson herself, at least when she was working at the *Post*—express more anger over the role of race prejudice in their lives than do those blacks who patently have suffered most from discrimination? Here we might return to Cathy Cohen's observation about the "narratives of exclusion, self-reliance, and struggle" that have historically underwritten the sense of identity of the wealthy as well as the poor. Booker T. Washington made the point in his autobiography when asserting pride in his race: "I have learned that success is to be measured not so much by the position that one has reached in life as by the obstacles which he has overcome while trying to succeed." It was a sentiment repeated by the tennis star Arthur Ashe, whose boyhood was spent in the Jim Crow South: "Proud to be an American, I am also proud to be an African American. I delight in the accomplishments of fellow citizens of my color. When one considers the odds against which we have labored, we have achieved much."[22]

In that sense, the accomplishments of the upper echelons of the black population would seem to be the basis for race pride. Here, after all, are individuals who have apparently fulfilled the American Dream, a goal widely shared by the great majority of blacks. But more often than not, "the very fact of success, especially when it stems substantially from white support," opens the Wall Street lawyer or banker to the charge that he or she is "a sellout," "an oreo," an "Uncle Tom" (or "Aunt Thomasina"), a "pseudo." Malcolm Jamal Warner, who played Theo Huxtable on *The Cosby Show*, told a reporter for *TV Guide* how surprised he was by letters from viewers claiming the show depicted a "false reality": a two-career professional black couple living a comfortable middle-class life with their children. "The unspoken message," he said, "is not just that black people don't live like the Huxtables, but that black people can't live that way. Or shouldn't." Randall Kennedy: "If racial loyalty is deemed essential and morally virtuous, then a black person's adoption of positions that are deemed racially disloyal will be seen by racial loyalists as a supremely threatening sin, one warranting the harsh punishments that have historically been visited upon alleged traitors." In Sterling Anthony's novel *Cookie Cutter*, a serial killer stalks influential conservative blacks, leaving each corpse clutching an Oreo cookie.[23]

Still, the past includes numerous examples of less fortunate blacks, especially those with dark skin, accusing successful businessmen of being untrustworthy, "inauthentic." What makes the current period unusual, and perhaps unique, is the degree of soul-searching that many members of the privileged class are doing about the meaning of race. When the young manager asked Ron Brown whether it was possible to have a career in business and hold on to her "black identity," she was doing more than seeking guidance about how the "white corporate world" operates. She was asking as well, if rhetorically, "Where does race fit into my definition of myself?" In a society that finally, after almost two centuries, has formally repudiated white privilege, instituted affirmative action, and opened the doors of executive suites to educated blacks, a narrative of "exclusion, self-reliance, and struggle" must inevitably lose some of its salience for those who have apparently realized the American Dream. It is possible, of course, to complain, as many successful blacks of the post–World War II generation do, and often with justification, that they are not paid what they deserve, passed over for deserved promotions, given assignments of little importance, face a "glass ceiling." But these are grievances that have been raised by Catholics and Jews, by diverse immigrant groups, by women, and now increasingly openly by gay men and lesbians. They do not speak to the fundamentally distinct character of the "up from slavery" narrative. And in their own way they serve to highlight the much deeper deprivation of the "truly disadvantaged."

But then the deprivation of the "truly disadvantaged" in its own way serves to highlight the distinctive good fortune of the black privileged class. Shelby Steele has commented, "Since it was our victimization more than any other variable that identified and unified us, it followed logically that the purest black was the poor black." This statement is misleading in the sense that "self-reliance and struggle" have always existed alongside "exclusion"—victimization —in the narrative of black identity. But it does underscore a fundamental problem faced by the well-to-do. If the central characteristic of the black experience has been overcoming obstacles—rising "up from slavery"—then, practically if perversely speaking, the poor of the inner cities are in the best position to live an "authentic" black life, since they must "struggle" each day and show "self reliance" just to survive. Think of the women living "off the books" in Maquis Park. Successful blacks can assert their own claim to racial authenticity, as they do from time to time, by accusing the poor of lacking character and by trumpeting their own achievements. It is a way of saying, "We represent the 'up' in the 'up from slavery.' We have overcome." But the claim can ring hollow—the wealthy can seem like "sellouts"—to those whose struggles are ongoing. And it is not hard to imagine that in some instances—and the stress should be on the adjective *some*—the extent of the "rage" expressed by the "privileged class" has less to do with the reality of discrimination in their lives than an unconscious need to fulfill the historic black narrative.[24]

"The black American story," the novelist Charles Johnson has written,

> had a clearly defined conflict. And our ancestors fought *daily* for generations, with courage and dignity, to change this narrative. That was the *point* of their lives, their sacrifices, each and every day they were on this earth. We cannot praise enough the miracle they achieved, the lifelong efforts of our leaders and the anonymous men and women who kept the faith, demonstrated, went to jail, registered black people to vote in the Deep South, changed unjust laws, and died in order that Americans of all backgrounds might be free. I have always seen their fight for us as noble.

But it is time, he continues, to acknowledge that the battle ended in victory:

> It simply is no longer the case that the essence of black American life is racial victimization and disfranchisement, a curse and a condemnation, a destiny based on color in which the meaning of one's life is thinghood, created even before one is born. This is not something we can assume.

The specific conflict of this narrative reached its dramatic climax in 1963 in Birmingham, Alabama, and at the breathtaking March on Washington; its resolution arrived in 1965, the year before I graduated from high school, with the Voting Rights Act. Everything since then has been a coda for almost half a century. We call this long-extended and still ongoing anticlimax the post-civil-rights period.

Problems persist, "among them poor schools and far too many black men in prison and too few in college. But these are problems based more on the inequities of class." "Despite being an antique," however,

> the old black American narrative of pervasive victimization persists, denying the overwhelming evidence of change since the time of my parents and grandparents, refusing to die as doggedly as the Ptolemaic vision before Copernicus or the notion of phlogiston in the 19th century, or the deductive reasoning of the medieval schoolmen. It has become ahistorical. For a time it served us well and powerfully, yes, reminding each generation of black Americans of the historic obligations and duties and dangers they inherited and faced, but the problem with any story or idea or interpretation is that it can soon fail to fit the facts and becomes an ideology, even kitsch.[25]

★

It is understandable that black men and women who came of age during the protests of the 1960s and then rose to prominent positions in the post–Civil Rights Era should have the narrative of "exclusion, self-reliance, and struggle" in mind as they attempt to interpret the circumstances of their lives. And it is understandable as well that, given the power of that narrative, they worry, as they build successful careers in the no-longer-exclusively-white Establishment, about whether they are losing their "black identity." The tacit conflict between their ambitions and fears plays itself out most clearly in the way many of them raise their children.

They are determined to give their daughters and sons the best possible opportunity to enjoy the full benefits of the American Dream. This means providing them comfortable lives in safe—usually suburban—neighborhoods, with all the material benefits that upper-middle-class white children take for granted. It means, as well, ensuring that they attend the kind of elite schools where they will gain the knowledge—and the exposure to white children from privileged backgrounds—likely to maximize their opportunities for success later in life. As Ulric Haynes, dean of the Hofstra University School of Business, confided to Ellis Cose: "When my children became of school age . . . I wanted them to be in an educational environment that offered quality education as well as cultural diversity. I couldn't find it in any public school in any of the communities in which I lived. . . . The paradox is that in order to find the socioeconomic and the ethnic diversity and the quality education for my children, I had to send them to private schools." As for higher education, it is now increasingly common for exceptional students to go to the Ivy League or Stanford rather than prestigious historic black colleges such as Howard, the Atlanta universities, and Fisk.[26]

Still, as much as parents want their sons and daughters to feel comfortable among whites, they expect them to face discrimination. Comments Ellis Cose, "Though everyone knows that times are changing, most also know (or think they do) that the world their children will inherit will remain a racially troubled place." At the same time, they worry that immersion in a world of whites will cause their children to lose their "black identity." Said an accountant who lives in a majority-white Washington suburb, speaking of her three children: "I just don't want them to ever, *ever* think they are something they are not. . . . Sometimes you get caught up into—if you think you 'made it,' then suddenly you forget where you came from." Added a neighbor, "I don't mind white friends, but do you know who *you* are? If they thought they had to change something about themselves to be with [a] group of white friends, then it would bother me. . . . Forgetting that you're black . . . I wouldn't like that." Karyn Lacy summarizes the dilemma confronting many parents: "On the one hand, [they] seek for themselves and their children the option of attending a white college or university, working in a predominantly white occupational category, or living in a majority-white neighborhood. On the other hand, they express concern that complete immersion in the white world will subject the children to racial discrimination, alienate them from the larger black community, and generate nagging doubts about their racial identity and black authenticity."[27]

Parents adopt various strategies to try and ensure that their children grow up "authentically" black. Immersing them in "black history," for example. Not surprisingly, well-to-do blacks account for much of the dramatic increase in tourism to Africa. And many parents see to it that at home or in special programs after school or on weekends, children learn about heroic figures in the black American past: Harriet Tubman, Nat Turner, Sojourner Truth, Frederick Douglass, Martin Luther King, Jr. One weekend after she had moved to Washington, D.C., Jill Nelson suggested to her daughter Misu that they take a tour of Virginia slave plantations. The resulting exchange between the two of them, as set down by Nelson herself, could be taken as evidence of how perceptions are changing across generations (although, granted, it may have more to do with a familiar and timeless element of parent-child dynamics):

> "Sorry, Mom. Me and my friends are going to the mall."
>
> "The mall? You can go to the mall anytime. Let's go check out the plantations."
>
> "I don't think so . . ."
>
> "Don't you want to see the slave shanties, the shackles, the land our ancestors slaved on, died for?"
>
> "Yeah sure. I guess so. But not this weekend. I want to hang out with my friends."
>
> "Look. We can drive around Virginia, then stay in a hotel, order chocolate shakes and cheeseburgers from room service, even watch one of the pay movies." I resort to bribery.
>
> "That'd be nice. Mom. But how about another weekend? This weekend, the mall's where it's at."
>
> "The mall? The mall? How disgusting. Are you becoming a D.C. airhead, only interested in lurking around some tacky shopping center, ogling boys and giggling?" I am nearly screaming. I know I'm losing it, turning into every teenager's version of the parent from hell, but I can't control myself. "What about history, culture, the sacrifices of our ancestors? I mean, where would we be if Harriet Tubman hung out at the mall instead of freeing her people?"
>
> That's when Misu turns, looks me dead in the eye, and in a voice so dry it could wither a cactus says, "Mom, get a life."[28]

Above all, parents arrange for their children to spend time in social settings that are exclusively black. They believe, observes Karyn Lacy, "that blacks who do not have ongoing interactions with other black people are not authentically black. It is only through active participation in black spaces that black children learn what being black is all about." For some, this means taking their children to weekly religious services at inner-city churches. For others, it means sending them to "black camps" in "the 'hood," where, writes Debra Dickerson derisively, they have the opportunity to "mingle with 'thug' children." Most parents, however, are fearful that their children will pick up "ghetto habits" if they are exposed to the inner-city poor. And so they enroll them in social institutions open only to middle-class black families—indeed, in many cases, open only to families from their own privileged stratum of the middle class. Jack and Jill of America, for example, whose website summarizes its purpose: "Power and Potential: Parents Empowering Youth through Leadership Development, Cultural Heritage and Community Service." The organization, now seventy-five years old, has just thirty thousand members nationwide.[29]

Moving back and forth between predominantly white and exclusively black middle-class worlds can be disorienting. "I remember how schizophrenic our existence was," writes Lawrence Otis Graham of his childhood. "Friday night parties with the white neighborhood kids; Saturday expeditions to black plays and museums in Harlem with the black Jack and Jill kids; tennis outings at segregated Westchester country clubs with a white classmate's family; a first date with a black girl from the local NAACP teen chapter; weekend sleepaways with the kids from the white Boy Scout troop; summertime sleepovers with cousins and black friends from church. It was all a cultural seesaw."[30]

Not all children adapt well to a "cultural seesaw." And inevitably many have come to question the assumptions on which their parents raised them. Young black Harvard MBAs, Ellis Cose has found, see "a far different, rosier universe" than did the professionals and business executives he interviewed in the 1990s: "They see a world with prejudice but ultimately no limits—a place where race has costs and benefits but what ultimately happens is up to them." As a thirty-year-old woman, an executive at a major hotel chain, told him: "I'm tired of this blasted term [glass ceiling]. . . . It just conjures up images of being shackled and held back. How can we excel if we perceive ourselves as trapped? I'm beginning to wonder if we are the caged birds who don't realize the cage door is open."[31]

Eugene Robinson attributes the emerging "generational divide" to the rapid and profound change produced by the Civil Rights Movement:

> The baby boomers were the first generation of African Americans to know desegregated schools and neighborhoods. Subsequent generations of Mainstream African Americans have known nothing else. To the boomers, race was important, inescapable, urgent. To their children, race means much less. There is no cultural gap between black children who grew up in suburban, middle-class settings and their white classmates from down

the street. From kindergarten through high school, they are taught about tolerance and diversity; they don't just learn about Christmas, they decorate their classrooms for Hanukkah and Kwanzaa, too. Born mostly in the 1980s, this so-called millennial generation is as far removed from the tumult of the civil rights struggle as my generation is from the Great Depression. They can read about that time in history books, but there is no way they could have a feeling for what it was like, no way they could really connect.[32]

Privileged members of the "millennial generation" will of necessity write a new narrative of self-identity, one that presumably will depart in significant ways from the narrative that sustained their ancestors. Glenn Loury offers a personal opinion on this prospective development, with a backward glance at his distress that his son might choose to play hockey ("a white man's game") instead of basketball:

We had carefully considered the implications for our children of our decision to buy a house in a predominantly white suburb. We joined and became active in a church with many black families like our own, in part so that our boys would be provided with suitable racial peers. We are committed to ensuring that their proper education about black history and culture, including their family history, is not left to chance. We are ever vigilant concerning the effect on their developing psyches of racial messages that come across on television, in their books, at their nursery school, and so on. On all of this Linda [his wife] and I are in full accord. But she thought my concerns about hockey were taking things a bit too far. . . . The fact is that, given the class background of our children and the community in which we have chosen to make our lives, it is inevitable that their racial sensibilities will be quite different from ours. Moreover, it is impossible to predict just what self-definition they will settle upon. This can be disquieting to contemplate for those of our generation concerned about retaining a "genuinely black" identity in the face of the social mobility we have experienced within our lifetimes. But it is not, I think, to be feared.[33]

★

What *is* feared by many parents, mothers in particular, is that their children—their sons especially—will marry outside the race.

"Bring me home a Black girl." It's one of those commandments Ugo has heard from me most of his life, right up there with "Don't do drugs," "Finish school" and "Use a condom."

The words belong to Audrey Edwards, in an article for *Essence* magazine in the fall of 2002. Ugo is her stepson.

Over the years he has rolled his eyes, sighed in exasperation, muttered that I was racist or been mortified whenever I'd blurt out things like "Dark, light, shades in between—it doesn't matter to me as long as she's Black." But Ugo has also grown up to be very clear about what that edict really means. Don't even think about marrying a White girl.[34]

From the founding of the nation through to the 1970s, there was little occasion for black parents, no matter how wealthy, to fear (or hope) that their children would bring home a white friend, let alone a white husband or wife. Legal and de facto segregation ensured that young blacks and whites very rarely attended school together or shared social spaces, and never truly as equals. Many states, too, included provisions in their constitutions or passed laws barring marriage across racial lines. But then, in 1967, the U.S. Supreme Court, in *Loving v. Virginia,* ruled that "anti-miscegenation" legislation was unconstitutional. And while it can hardly be said that attitudes changed overnight, by the end of the first decade of the twenty-first century, a considerable majority of whites were telling pollsters that they approved of interracial marriage. Indeed, today there is more opposition among whites to a son or daughter marrying an atheist than to that son or daughter marrying someone of another race.[35]

At every period in the nation's history black Americans have been more supportive of intermarriage than whites. Given the laws prohibiting slaves from marrying and given the clearly discriminatory intent of anti-miscegenation legislation, it was only logical that black men and women would see restrictions on their choice of marriage partners as a fundamental denial of their "inalienable rights" as citizens. But the proportion of blacks claiming to "be fine with" a relative marrying someone from another race dropped from over 80 percent in 2001 to 72 percent in 2009. The reason for the growth in opposition to intermarriage was a new social reality created by the success of the Civil Rights Movement: interracial dating was now commonplace and increasing numbers of black men, especially from the privileged class, were marrying white women.[36]

Some historical perspective is in order here: from the end of slavery through the Civil Rights Era, marriages involving a black man and white woman, or a black woman and white man, were extremely rare. Studies of major cities around 1900 found that such unions accounted for less than 1 percent of all black marriages. Since the *Loving v. Virginia* decision, however, the number of black-white marriages has increased steadily, decade by decade, from 65,000 in 1970 to 167,000 in 1980; 213,000 in 1990; and 363,000 in 2000. Compared to other groups, the intermarriage rate remains low. But the trend seems clear.[37]

There are certain themes that parents stress when counseling their children to avoid forming romantic attachments with whites. One is that their partners will inevitably come to look down on them, hold them in contempt. Commented one mother, a senior marketing executive: "I don't care what anybody says, there's not a White person in America who doesn't feel superior to a former slave. Why would I want my son to marry someone who will probably always subconsciously feel she's better than him just because she's White."[38]

A second, and related, theme is that for a black man or woman to marry a white person is to "betray their race." To psychology professor Halford Fairchild, "for black men to date and marry white women in the face of our lingering debt to each other is irresponsible. . . . We are under siege. We are at war. To sleep with the enemy is treason. Racial treason." Here, though, gender must enter the conversation. The outrage expressed by Fairchild notwithstanding, it is black women like Audrey Edwards, not black males, who react most bitterly to the sight of interracial couples. And it is mainly women who press home to children the importance of marrying within the race. The historian Renee Romano accounts for the "gender divide" that emerged in the aftermath of the Civil Rights Era in this way: "In their attacks on interracial marriage, many black women expressed the idea that the key to racial progress was unity. Equality and racial advancement would best be achieved by blacks who built strong black families and worked together in their communities. Individual goals might have to be sacrificed for the good of the race. Many black men, in contrast, argued that racial liberation was contingent upon personal freedom. Only when black people could act like individuals would the race truly be free." To which we can add this observation by Alvin Poussaint, "The black woman in some ways sees herself as guardian of the black experience, keeper of the culture and the black family role." And this remark by Alice Walker: "To me, the black woman is our essential mother—the blacker she is the more she is us."[39]

Walker's comment serves as a reminder of how much physical appearance is wrapped up in perceptions of black identity. Many women testify to a felt need to have children, and grandchildren, who are "visibly African American." Ellen Holly, herself light-skinned, recalled her reaction when her white boyfriend proposed marriage just as he was about to board a plane for Paris:

> It wasn't going to work. I knew it even as I watched his plane disappear in the clouds. For one thing, my romantic imagination and political passion were too bound up with the idea of black men to commit to a white one. Then there was the matter of children. Even though I had not yet had them, I had always seen my children. They were so real to me I felt I could touch them. When I held them in my arms and looked into their little faces, I could even feel the warm little burst of moist air on my cheek as they expelled their breath. But these children were a silky chocolate brown, with great large dark eyes. I wanted them very, very badly, and with John I felt that I would lose them. Combined, we would be too pale. . . . I was just as afraid of losing those children if I were to marry a light-skinned black man.[40]

Now consider her reflections on the black actor J. A. Preston, another romantic interest: "In my mind's eye I will always see him as a Masai prince in the characteristic saffron robes and the intricate collar of beads, watching the sun go down on a Kenya horizon, all alone." For many black women, as in the past, dark-skinned men are "more authentic." A college student put it this way: "The way I hear [black women] talk about it is that they like the darker guys, that that's what makes them sexy or attractive. The darker guys seem more tied down to where they came from. They might wear African attire, not that they are necessarily from Africa."[41]

Ironically, the rapid and dramatic advancement of middle-class black women in recent decades has complicated their chances of finding a black husband, whether dark-skinned or light-skinned. As of 2006, there were more than 1.4 million black women in college, but fewer than 900,000 black men. And since the dropout rate is higher for men, each year black women earn twice as many bachelor's degrees as black men. The "gender gap" extends to the highest levels of the educational pyramid. In 2008 black women received 751 medical degrees, black men 396; black women received 1,893 law degrees, black men 1,109. Today approximately six of every ten black professionals and business executives are women, up from barely more than two in ten fifty years ago. Additionally, among black college graduates, women's earnings have been rising much more rapidly than men's.[42]

"With 70 percent of all college degrees awarded to African Americans going to women," laments sociologist Patricia Hill Collins, "how do middle-class Black women marry within the 'race'?" The answer is, in many cases they take husbands who are less well-educated than themselves. More than a quarter of black women who have graduated from university are married to black men who never attended college, and 4 percent are married to black men who did not finish high school. Comments Michael Eric Dyson: "While black women may prefer mates who are educationally compatible, they have often chosen mates whose lower achievement makes their marriages vulnerable to divorce and spousal abuse."[43]

It is perhaps not surprising, then, that many successful black women say they would rather stay single than settle for a black man "who doesn't meet their standards or expectations." In time, perhaps, we might expect that a growing number will show an openness to romantic involvement with accomplished white men—professionals or businessmen they meet during their university years or come to know through work. But for now, many suspect—fear—that if a white man shows interest in them, it is because he has bought into the age-old stereotype of black women as "super-sensual." And many more say that the sexual abuse previous generations of black women suffered at the hands of white men—in particular, slave women at the hands of their owners—makes falling in love with a white man out of the question. A college senior expressed it this way: "Well, there have been historical relationships between blacks and whites that really turned me off about white men. This history is just too present to me. Just the idea of being in a relationship with a white man is just so uncomfortable to me." And so while the number of intermarried couples has increased dramatically in recent decades, the proportion of black men marrying white women has far eclipsed the proportion of black women marrying white men. As it is, a significant minority of successful middle-class women choose to remain single. Which, along with the high divorce rate for black couples, explains why 70 percent of black professional women were unmarried a decade into the twenty-first century.[44]

Of course, a single woman may still choose to have children. But it turns out that highly educated black women are much more likely to remain childless than highly educated white women. Ralph Richard Banks, who conducted extensive interviews with professional black women, writes that he "was struck time and again by the cultural conservatism they exhibited." Even "the most financially secure" were reluctant to have children while they remained unmarried. At the same time, the number of babies from interracial unions has grown dramatically in recent decades. Before the days of *Loving v. Virginia,* the small percentage of men and women who married across the color line tended to do so later in life. Not infrequently, either the bride or groom, perhaps both, had been through a divorce. "In recent years, though," Randall Kennedy has observed, "interracial couples have been marrying at younger ages than their pioneering predecessors, and have shown a greater inclination to raise children and pursue all the other 'normal' activities that married life offers." From the early 1970s to the early 1990s, the number of babies with one black parent and one white parent grew fivefold. And in the great majority of cases it was the mother of the newborn who was white.[45]

★

In 1930, when the U.S. Census Bureau instructed enumerators to enter every person "of mixed white and Negro blood . . . no matter how small the percentage of Negro blood" as a "Negro," Washington effectively gave its imprimatur to the notorious "one-drop rule." Two later modifications in the collection of census data, in 1970 and 2000, reveal how much popular perceptions of racial definitions have changed since the Civil Rights Era. In 1970, the Census Bureau decided to abandon the practice of sending enumerators door to door. Instead, each household received forms by mail that residents were required to complete and return. This had the practical effect of allowing individuals to determine for themselves which box to check in the column designating "race." Granted, there were only five boxes on the form and respondents were asked to pick just one. But the new approach to gathering data effectively acknowledged that there might be a difference in how race was perceived by observer and observed, and, by implication, privileged the judgment of the observed.[46]

In 2000, following new guidelines issued by the Office of Management and Budget, the Census Bureau gave individuals the option of checking more than one box. It became possible then for a man or woman to self-identify as both black and white. This change reflected the new politics of race that emerged following the Civil Rights Era. During the 1980s and 1990s a diverse array of associations were established, mostly by members of the middle class, to allow individuals who had married across racial lines to meet, share information, and discuss ways to promote their interests. Early on, two organizations with nationwide representation began to lobby government for recognition of what they argued was the intrinsic and distinct racial identity of Americans with mixed ancestry. Project RACE (Reclassify All Children Equally) largely directed its energies at state legislatures; the Association of MultiEthnic Americans concentrated on the federal government. A central goal of both organizations was getting the designation "multiracial" added as an option on official forms.[47]

Activists based their claim on the same appeal to individual liberty that had animated demonstrators during the Civil Rights Era. It is expressed rather poetically in the "Bill of Rights for Racially Mixed People" written by the clinical psychologist Maria P. P. Root:

I have the right . . .
    not to justify my existence in this world
    not to keep the races separate within me
    not to be responsible for people's discomfort with my physical ambiguity
    not to justify my ethnic legitimacy

I have the right . . .
    to identify myself differently than strangers expect me to identify
    to identify myself differently than how my parents identify me
    to identify myself differently than my brothers and sisters
    to identify myself differently in different situations

I have the right . . .
    to create a vocabulary to communicate about being multiracial
    to change my identity over my lifetime—and more than once
    to have loyalties and identify with more than one group of people
    to freely choose whom I befriend and love.[48]

Under the circumstances, it might seem ironic that among the leading opponents of the call to add "multiracial" as a census category were well-known black civil rights leaders and organizations, including Jesse Jackson, Kweisi Mfume, the Congressional Black Caucus, the NAACP, and the Urban League. But as the sociologists Kerry Ann Rockquemore and David L. Brunsma explain: "These opponents argued that the underlying purpose of legislative directives that mandate the collection of data on racial groups was to enable the enforcement of civil rights legislation and to document the existence of racial inequalities. Adding a multiracial category, they argued, would increase the difficulty of collecting accurate data on the effects of discrimination and, therefore, deviate from the legal directive given to the Census Bureau. Mfume reminded those in the movement that 'the fight for freedom still needs freedom fighters.'"[49]

The decision to allow individuals to check more than one box on the race section of the 2000 census form did not address the concerns of black leaders. Nor did it give multiracial activists exactly what they had requested—specifically, it denied that people of mixed ancestry represented a single racial category. All the same, it did effectively signal government abandonment of the one-drop rule. In the end, a total of 784,764 Americans identified themselves as both "black" and "white" in the census. By 2010 that figure had shot up 134 percent, to 1,834,212. Add in the 230,848 who filled in the three separate boxes for "black," "white," and "American Indian or Alaska Native" and you have a total of over 2 million Americans who presumably would have been classified as "Negro" and, later, "black" in every census between 1930 and 1990. Of course, with almost 39 million individuals checking just the single box "black" in 2010, a case can be made that the one-drop rule has shown great staying power. But here a couple of caveats should be noted. First, given that typically the census forms would have been filled out by an adult or adults in any given household, we cannot assume that children would have necessarily agreed with the racial identity ascribed to them by their parents or other household head. It is note-worthy that a survey carried out several years before the 2000 census found that 40 percent of adolescents with one black parent and one white parent claimed a different racial identity at school than they did at home.[50]

Second, and perhaps related, the statistics do not provide a window onto the experiences of young adults of privileged circumstances who have a high de-gree of social interaction with white Americans. Kerry Ann Rockquemore and David Brunsma surveyed 230 students from colleges and universities across the United States, each with one biological parent who was black, one who was white. Their findings are suggestive. Only 13 percent of the students self-identified as "exclusively black." Three percent self-identified as "exclusively white." Slightly fewer than 15 percent rejected race as a defining element of their identity. Seven percent admitted that they adopted different identities at different times, depending on the circumstances—for example, they declared themselves to be "black" or "white" on forms according to which description they thought would best serve their interests. Most respondents, however, al-most 60 percent, described themselves as "biracial."[51]

Rockquemore and Brunsma found that "a common set of experiences" linked the "biracial" majority.

Many of the individuals were middle to upper-middle-class, educated in private schools, raised in predominantly white neighborhoods, and with

predominantly white friends and relatives composing their social networks. In many of these cases, they were the only one (or one of few)
nonwhites within their schools and communities. Many were popular
and active in sports and school activities and/or held leadership positions
in their educational institutions. It is within this particular type of social
context, combined with a homogeneous set of social networks, that these
individuals were able to develop a racial identity as "biracial," an understanding that was not previously/historically available—or at the very least
was not validated by others.[52]

As early as the 1990s some prominent individuals of mixed European and
African descent felt emboldened to celebrate their diverse origins. Barack
Obama, most obviously, and Tiger Woods, and the 1995 Miss USA Beauty
Pageant winner Chelsi Smith, who told an interviewer, "If people are going to
know me, it's important for them to know that I'm black and white and that
it hasn't been a disadvantage." But many young adults with one white parent
and one black parent have run headlong into the crumbling but still upright
wall of the one-drop rule. A woman in the Rockquemore and Brunsma study
who had Irish ancestry and identified herself as "biracial" acknowledged that
because of her dark skin, "I experience the world as a black woman." She felt
"resigned," the two sociologists noted, "to the fact that there would always be
a chasm between her self-identification (as biracial) and society's identification
of her (as black)."[53]

For some young adults, it was their treatment by blacks that proved most
difficult to bear. In his autobiography, Obama makes mention of a woman
named Joyce with "green eyes and honey skin" who lived in his dorm at Occidental College in Los Angeles:

One day I asked her if she was going to the Black Students' Association
meeting. She looked at me funny, then started shaking her head like a
baby who doesn't want what it sees on the spoon. "I'm not black," Joyce
said. "I'm multiracial." Then she started telling me about her father, who
happened to be Italian and was the sweetest man in the world; and her
mother, who happened to be part African and part French and part Native
American and part something else. "Why should I have to choose between
them?" she asked me. Her voice cracked, and I thought she was going to
cry. "It's not white people who are making me choose. Maybe it used to be
that way, but now they're willing to treat me like a person. No—it's black

people who always have to make everything racial. They're the ones making me choose. They're the ones who are telling me that I can't be who I am."[54]

★

The movement to allow Joyce and others of mixed African and European ancestry to declare themselves "biracial" has been championed by couples in which one partner (usually the husband) is black and the other is white, and by their children. But it is arguably only a matter of time before light-skinned individuals of privilege who have little knowledge of, and perhaps interest in, the "white" branches of their family trees nonetheless insist on a racial status that distinguishes them from the dark-skinned poor. In doing so, they would be merely returning to the position of black American elites—their own ancestors, in many instances—before the one-drop rule was adopted. Recall the words of a Boston man who met with the writer John Daniels at the beginning of the twentieth century: "Tell about us who are neither Negroes or whites, but an ambiguous something-between;—a people not yet known or named." Now consider the unambiguous self-presentation of Xavier Upton. Born in 1949, his parents were both highly educated and light-skinned professionals, his father a doctor, his mother a schoolteacher. When he went to college in the late 1960s, at the height of the Black Power movement, he was, in his own words, a "militant mulatto." When white students would ask him what blacks thought about some issue or other, he would reply, "I don't know. Why don't you ask one." Thirty years later, now a writer and a teacher, he began to self-identify as "multiracial."[55]

Reimagining America

In 2007 more than 1,500 black Americans were asked the following question as part of a survey carried out for the Pew Research Center:

> Which of these statements comes closer to your view—even if neither is exactly right: Blacks today can no longer be thought of as a single race because the black community is so diverse or Blacks can still be thought of as a single race because they have so much in common.[1]

Fully 37 percent of respondents answered that they believe blacks do not represent "a single race." This figure, so surprising to commentators—Eugene Robinson reported the finding "made my jaw drop"—obviously attests to the uncertainty that many black Americans today feel about the defining characteristics of "black identity." But the very question itself is revealing, because by its use of the adverbs "no longer" and "still," it illustrates the widespread misconception that people of African descent in the United States have always felt they belonged to a "single" race.[2]

★

Return to where we began, with the arrival of the first African slaves in Virginia during the early seventeenth century. To the colonists, they were "Negroes." When in time slave women gave birth to children fathered by English settlers, and English and Irish indentured servants gave birth to children fathered by slaves, the colonists referred to the offspring as "mulattoes." They did not assume that "mulattoes" and "Negroes" belonged to the same racial community. To have mixed ancestry was to be different from, and of greater human worth than, a person of pure African ancestry. But the tobacco-based economy depended on the labor of both "Negro" and "mulatto" slaves, and the continuing authority of the emerging planter elite depended on securing and retaining the goodwill of the growing number of English and Irish servants who had served out the terms of their indentures. Both needs were addressed by legislating what were considered two distinct "racial" entities—"mulattoes" and "Negroes"—into a single debased social caste.

The other colonies took diverse paths to the same end, and although slavery was abolished in the northern states shortly after the Revolution, the belief that people of mixed European and African ancestry were distinct from, and supe-rior to, people of pure African ancestry remained widespread throughout the new nation. The idea that all people with African ancestry represented a single racial community began to emerge in the last decade before the Civil War. But it was not until the early twentieth century that it became national dogma. To put it all in perspective: three centuries passed between the day the first Afri-cans were sold to English colonists in Jamestown and the U.S. Census Bureau gave formal sanction to the one-drop rule. It would be just another three gen-erations before the bureau effectively reversed itself, allowing that an individual might well belong to more than one race.[3]

★

During the first half of the nineteenth century, the prevailing belief that people of mixed ancestry were superior to individuals of pure African lineage allowed for the rise of a small elite among the free Negro population in the South. Most of the men belonging to this "colored aristocracy" were artisans or were involved in service trades. They depended heavily on the patronage of influential whites, including, not infrequently, planters who were blood rela-tives. In the North, too, some men of mixed ancestry were able to build a com-fortable existence by serving a white clientele. In both sections of the country, the families of such men created exclusive organizations—"exclusive" not only in the sense that you needed to have a certain standard of living to join, but also in that you needed to have light skin. The idea took hold among mem-bers of the elite that they represented a separate people, though "a people not yet known or named." Parents impressed upon their children the necessity of choosing marriage partners with a suitably elevated pedigree.[4]

Now move ahead a century, to a time when the one-drop rule has cemented itself on the nation. The privileged class has grown in size, the number of ex-clusive social organizations has proliferated. Some dark-skinned businessmen and professionals in the urban centers of the North have acquired substantial wealth serving the ghetto-bounded population. But as in the past, the upper echelon of the middle class is made up largely of men and women who carry conspicuous physical evidence of European ancestry. And marriage choices still reveal, among black men in particular, a preference for partners with light skin and straight hair. Something has changed, however, something funda-mental. Instead of seeking recognition as a racially distinct people, the elite now define themselves as natural leaders of all people of African ancestry. In that capacity they take it upon themselves to "uplift" those members of "our race" who remain mired in poverty and illiteracy, to teach them the habits and values necessary to succeed in America. At the same time, they serve as bro-kers with the white establishment, seeking to win the concessions they be-lieve are necessary to allow all members of their newly imagined community to flourish.[5]

Now move ahead once again, to our own time. Since the Civil Rights Era, unprecedented opportunities have opened up for black Americans of education and means, especially those with light skin. They can buy homes in wealthy suburban neighborhoods and find jobs as lawyers on Wall Street, as executives working for multinational firms, as officials at the highest level of government. Their children attend the best private schools and are targeted by administra-tors of affirmative action programs at Ivy League universities. And some of these same children are choosing to exercise a right historically available to European immigrants, Native Americans, and even alien citizens, but until now denied to everyone of discernible African ancestry: the right to define themselves as "not black." We can assume that their own children and grand-children—the great majority of them, anyway—will attend integrated schools and colleges and, if they are able to replicate the career success of their parents and grandparents, enjoy a life of privilege. Many will fall in love with and marry descendants of Irish, Italian, or Jewish immigrants, Hispanic Americans, and, yes, even descendants of the Pilgrims. They will benefit from privileges once only available to "whites." But like so many who have enjoyed those privileges, they will maintain that race is not an important part of their self-identity. They will think of themselves primarily, and simply, as "Americans."

★

The social ascent of the upper echelon of the black middle class has led some observers to suggest that race is beginning to lose its salience in the United

States—that the nation is, if not yet, at least on the way to becoming "post-racial." But the tragic conditions of life in the inner cities render that hope il-lusory. It is not just that ghetto residents continue to suffer the residual effects of past racism: a grossly underfunded public school system and enduring ste-reotypes that perpetuate discriminatory hiring practices. The state has legis-lated and selectively enforced a War on Drugs that renders the possibility of escape from poverty little more than an illusion and strips many young blacks, men especially, of rights that supposedly belong to every American. This is "the new Jim Crow" described by Michelle Alexander. It targets the black poor, especially those with dark skin and so-called Afrocentric features. In doing so, it is redefining the public understanding of "blackness" in the United States, enclosing it in the not-yet-gentrified inner cities. And so the myth persists that to be "authentically" black is to be poor. But not only that. To be "authentically" black is also to be lacking in the very values that define what it takes to succeed in America.[6]

Most people with African ancestry are neither "truly disadvantaged" nor "privileged." Many would define themselves as middle class, but their situa-tion is precarious. Few have significant financial resources. A considerable majority are vulnerable in times of severe economic downturn. A study by the Pew Research Center in 2007 found that 45 percent of blacks born into the middle class in the 1960s eventually fell into poverty or near poverty, three times the rate for whites. "Poverty is much more real" to middle-class blacks than to middle-class whites, observes Juan Williams. "They're more likely to have family or friends who've been through an experience like eviction, where their clothes and furniture are put out on the street in an embarrassing dis-play. In truth, the primary fear is of falling into some economic mishap that would take away our dignity, of reducing us merely to another poor black face. Just another 'nigger.'" A fortunate few will build prosperous careers, find their way to comfortable suburban living. But most will live on the edge of poverty, both in a geographic and economic sense. Their public identity will continue to be defined by their "black" neighbors in the inner cities, not by "biracial" or "multiracial" residents of the suburbs.[7]

★

The rising incidence of intermarriage and what Glenn Loury calls the "out-migration" of professionals and business executives through "acts of selective self-presentation" will, some have argued, deprive the "black community" of valuable resources and needed leaders. It is true that during the ascendancy of the one-drop rule, successful black men and women, most of them light-skinned, took prominent roles in campaigns against racism. The successes of the Civil Rights Movement owed a great deal to their activism. With rare exceptions, however, privileged individuals have been, as Monique Taylor characterizes them, "class actors," much more comfortable pressing for an end to discrimination than for empowerment of the downtrodden and redistribution of material resources. As Reverend Carl W. Kenney II, minister at a middle-class Baptist church in Durham, North Carolina, asked rhetorically, with a tinge of despair: "We are accustomed to marching and picketing when the issue is about racial difference. People will protest when their brothers and sisters are being denied equal opportunity, but what happens when the enemy is poverty?"[8]

If the United States is to end discrimination against all citizens of African ancestry and not just the privileged few, more will be needed than laws and judicial rulings mandating integration and outlawing blatantly racist practices. Efforts will have to be directed at eliminating the class inequality in racial guise created by slavery and perpetuated in other forms once slavery was abolished. As a first step, it will be necessary to acknowledge a truth expressed by Randall Kennedy: "The difficulties that disproportionately afflict black Americans are not 'black problems' whose solutions are the special responsibility of black people. They are *our* problems, and their solution or amelioration is the responsibility of us all, irrespective of race."[9]

Beyond that, it would be well to turn once again to the "dream" of Martin Luther King, Jr. Not, however, the dream as he described it at the March on Washington. Listen, instead, to his words a year and a half earlier, at the annual convention of the AFL-CIO, in Miami Beach. He looked forward "confidently," he said,

> to the day when we shall bring into full realization the dream of our American democracy—a dream yet unfulfilled. A dream of equality of opportunity, of privilege and property widely distributed; a dream of a land where men will not take necessities from the many to give luxuries to the few; a dream of a land where men do not argue that the color of a man's skin determines the content of his character; a dream of a nation where all our gifts and resources are held not for ourselves alone but as instruments of service for the rest of humanity; the dream of a country where every man will respect the dignity and worth of all human personality—that is the dream.[10]

Familiar themes from the March on Washington speech are here: faith in the promise of American democracy, anticipation of a day when skin color will not be read for the "content" of "character." But there are also themes that King left unmentioned when he spoke on the steps of the Lincoln Memorial: material well-being carries social responsibility, the obligation to be of service to others. And "privilege and property" must be "widely distributed." "Men will not take necessities from the many to give luxuries to the few."[11]

To some Americans today this version of King's dream will no doubt sound radical. But, in truth, it is as old and venerable as the nation itself. The author of the Declaration of Independence himself believed that the survival of the new republic depended on the wide distribution of property. Thomas Jefferson advocated a highly progressive tax system to prevent the growth of inequality. As he wrote to James Madison from France in the fall of 1785: "The small landholders are the most precious part of a state." Unlike King, Jefferson did not advocate eliminating class exploitation as a necessary step to destroying race prejudice. In his vision of the American future, there would be no black landowners. Slaves and free Negroes, belonging as they did to what he understood to be an inherently inferior race, would be shipped across the Atlantic, "back" to the land of their ancestors. But the fact that Jefferson's vision was clouded by white supremacist assumptions should not prevent us from recognizing that he and Martin Luther King, Jr. shared a fundamental conviction: all citizens need to have a propertied stake in the society. The gravest internal threat to the full realization of liberty in America is the concentration of power and privilege in the hands of a few.[12]

At a time when inequality in the United States has reached heights unseen since the Gilded Age, there can be little cause to believe that the nation is at the dawn of a post-racial era. The boundaries of black America may be changing, but the conditions of life for those residing within those boundaries have become yet more confining. Still, it is worth keeping in mind that during past decades of extreme inequality—the Gilded Age itself, for example—popular movements have arisen to protect the interests of the middle class and attempt to secure a life of dignity for the poor. It is true that in those earlier times, reformers typically gave little attention to the distinctive set of problems faced by "truly disadvantaged" black Americans. But we might hope for better from champions of progressive change born after the Civil Rights Era. And in any case, as history has repeatedly demonstrated, our race—the human race—is remarkably resourceful and creative. Individuals have the capacity to reimagine themselves. So too, then, do nations.[13]

Notes

A PERSONAL INTRODUCTION

1. Wayne and Shuster debuted on the *Ed Sullivan Show* in May of 1958. Over the following decade they appeared on the show sixty-seven times, far more than any other performers.

2. As a result, throughout *Imagining Black America,* I have deliberately refrained from using the term "African American." I do write of "Americans of African ancestry" (also "Americans of African descent"), but with a purely geographical intent, meaning simply individuals who have at least one ancestor who crossed the Atlantic from Africa sometime after the beginning of the seventeenth century.

3. Michael Wayne, *The Reshaping of Plantation Society: The Natchez District, 1860–1880* (Louisiana State University Press, 1983).

4. Michael P. Johnson and James L. Roark, *Black Masters: A Free Family of Color in the Old South* (Norton, 1984). See also the related work Michael P. Johnson and James L. Roark, eds., *No Chariot Let Down: Charleston's Free People of Color on the Eve of the Civil War* (University of North Carolina Press, 2001).

5. Johnson and Roark elaborate on the need for clarity in racial terminology in *Black Masters,* xv–xvi. See also Randall Kennedy, *Sellout: The Politics of Racial Betrayal* (Vintage, 2008), 8, fn.

6. "Black" was frequently used in earlier times as an *adjective* to describe all people of African ancestry and I have borrowed that practice here ("black Americans," "black women," "the black population," and so forth). I have, of course, left passages I quote from other authors unedited.

A WORD ABOUT RACE

1. Richard Redon et al., "Global Variation in Copy Number in the Human Genome," *Nature* 444 (Nov. 23, 2006): 444–54. Humans also share over 98 percent of our DNA

with chimpanzees (not to mention over 25 percent with dandelions); see the Chimpanzee Sequencing and Analysis Consortium, "Initial Sequence of the Chimpanzee Genome and Comparison with the Human Genome," *Nature* 437 (Sept. 1, 2005): 69–87; Jonathan Marks, *What It Means to Be 98% Chimpanzee: Apes, People, and Their Genes* (University of California Press, 2002), introduction. It is worth noting that genetic diversity in human populations is low relative to diversity in many other species. See L. B. Jorde et al., "The Distribution of Human Genetic Diversity: A Comparison of Mitochondrial, Autosomal, and Y-Chromosome Data," *American Journal of Human Genetics* 66, no. 3 (2000): 979; Richard C. Lewontin, "The Apportionment of Human Diversity," in T. Dobzhansky, M. K. Hecht, and W. C. Steers, eds., *Evolutionary Biology* 6 (Appleton-Century-Crofts, 1972): 381–98; and R. C. Lewontin, Steven Rose, and Leon J. Kamin, *Not in Our Genes* (Pantheon, 1984), 126. Not that there had been universal support for the view that race was a real biological division of humanity. Charles Darwin voiced misgivings in *The Descent of Man*. The distinguished anthropologist Franz Boas also challenged the conventional view about race in the 1930s as did, later and more directly, his student Ashley Montagu, especially in *Man's Most Dangerous Myth: The Fallacy of Race* (Columbia University Press, 1942).

2. Among the studies confirming Lewontin's findings in principle if not exact detail are Guido Barbujani et al., "An Apportionment of Human DNA Diversity," *Proceedings of the National Academy of Sciences* 94 (Apr. 1997): 4516–19; L. B. Jorde et al., "Distribution of Human Genetic Diversity"; Noah A. Rosenberg et al., "Genetic Structure of Human Populations," *Science* 298, no. 5602 (Dec. 20, 2002): 2381–85; and D. Serre and S. Pääbo, "Evidence for Gradients of Human Genetic Diversity within and among Continents," *Genome Research* 14, no. 9 (Sept. 2004): 1679–85. Jeffrey C. Long and Rick A. Kittles contend that only in sub-Saharan Africa do local populations commonly contain fully 85 percent of all human genetic variation. See Long and Kittles, "Human Genetic Diversity and the Nonexistence of Biological Races," *Human Biology* 75, no. 4 (Aug. 2003): 466–67.

3. See L. Luca Cavalli-Sforza, Paolo Menozzi, and Alberto Piazza, *The History and Geography of Human Genes* (Princeton University Press, 1994). Elements of their findings were anticipated by Frank B. Livingstone in "On the Nonexistence of Human Races," *Current Anthropology* 3 (1962): 279–81 and by C. Loring Brace in "A Nonracial Approach towards the Understanding of Human Diversity," in Ashley Montagu, ed., *The Concept of Race* (Free Press, 1964), 313–20. See also American Association of Physical Anthropologists, "Statement on Biological Aspects of Race," *American Journal of Physical Anthropology* 101 (1996): 570: "Partly as a result of gene flow, the hereditary characteristics of human populations are in a state of perpetual flux."

4. American Anthropological Association, "Statement on Race," *American Anthropologist* 100, no. 3 (Sept. 1998): 712. A survey of members of the American Anthropological Association taken in 1999 found that 69 percent of physical anthropologists and

80 percent of cultural anthropologists disagreed with the statement "There are biological races in the species Homo sapiens." See Leonard Lieberman, Rodney C. Kirk, Alice
Littlefield, "Exchange across Difference: The Status of the Race Concept—Perishing
Paradigm: Race—1931–99," *American Anthropologist* 105, no. 1 (Mar. 2003): 111–12. See
also the results of a survey of anthropologists and biologists conducted by the sociologist Ann Morning in 2001 and 2002: "On Distinction," http://raceandgenomics.ssrc
.org/Morning, accessed Feb. 15, 2013. For the argument that evidence may arise in the
future justifying the use of race as a biological category, but acknowledging that any
racial definitions will inevitably depart from "common lay conceptualizations," see
Long and Kittles, "Human Genetic Diversity," 469. There remain a small number of
scholars who contend that race is a true division of humanity, a product of natural selection. See, most notably, Vincent Sarich and Frank Miele, *Race: The Reality of Human
Differences* (Westview, 2005), and J. Phillipe Rushton, *Race, Evolution, and Behavior: A
Life History Perspective* (Transaction, 1994). But the main argument in favor of preserv-
ing race as a category of biological analysis comes from those who, in the words of the
biological anthropologist Alan Goodman, are "de facto" as opposed to "true" believers.
"They understand races as statistical approximations rather than natural types, asserting race as a de facto stand-in for the messy patterns of human biological variation."
See Alan Goodman, "Two Questions about Race," http:raceandgenomics.ssrc.org/
Goodman, accessed July 4, 2013. Such scholars argue that while genetic differences
between races may be small, those differences take on significance in a select number
of fields, most notably medicine. Two articles representative of this viewpoint are Ar-
mand Marie Leroi, "A Family Tree in Every Gene," *New York Times*, Mar. 14, 2005, A23,
and Sally Satel, "I Am a Racially Profiling Doctor," *New York Times Magazine* (May 5,
2002), 56. Counterarguments can be found in Serre and Pääbo, "Evidence for Gradients of Human Genetic Diversity"; Richard S. Cooper, Jay S. Kaufman, and Ryk Ward,
"Race and Genomics," *New England Journal of Medicine* 348, no. 12 (Mar. 20, 2003):
1166–70; Robert S. Schwartz, "Racial Profiling in Medical Research," *New England
Journal of Medicine* 344, no. 18 (May 3, 2001): 1392; and Stephen P. Fortmann, "Race,
Ethnicity, Biology, and Medical Research: A Modest Proposal," *Current Cardiovascular
Risk Reports* 2, no. 3 (May 2008): 167–68. Fortmann comments: "Confusion between
the social and biologic origins of race permeates medical science. . . . Many examples
of mechanistic studies comparing 20 or 30 individuals from different racial or ethnic
backgrounds infer a genetic basis for the observed differences despite the obvious limitations of sampling error and unmeasured confounding by social and cultural factors.
Indeed, the very definition of race and ethnicity is never clear and is usually based on
self-designation by the study participants. Such self-designation may well reflect important social differences and cultural identity but may be unrelated to genetic ancestry, especially in the diverse US population where an increasing proportion has parents
from different racial and ethnic groups."

5. Joseph L. Graves, *The Race Myth: Why We Pretend Race Exists in America* (Plume, 2005), 17; J. H. Relethford, "Human Skin Color Diversity Is Highest in the Sub-Saharan African Populations," *Human Biology* 72, no. 5 (Oct. 2000): 773–80; Stephen Molnar, *Human Variation: Races, Types, and Ethnic Groups*, 5th ed. (Prentice Hall, 2002), 250–52; Long and Kittles, "Human Genetic Diversity," 467; Jorde et al., "Distribution of Human Genetic Diversity," 981–85.

1. BIRTH OF A RACE

1. On "black" as a myth, see Joseph L. Graves, *The Race Myth: Why We Pretend Race Exists in America* (Plume, 2005); Alain Corcos, *The Myth of Human Races* (Michigan State University Press, 1997); Ashley Montagu, especially in *Man's Most Dangerous Myth: The Fallacy of Race* (Columbia University Press, 1942). For "black" as fiction, consider that the French journalist Jean Finot wrote as early as 1906: "Races are irreducible categories existing only as fictions in our brains," quoted in Corcos, *Myth of Human Races*, 20. See also Timothy Caulfield, "Media Hype Threatens Research," *Toronto Star*, May 23, 2006, A23. On "black" as an invention, see David Brion Davis, "Constructing Race: A Reflection," *William and Mary Quarterly*, 3rd ser., 54, no. 1 (1997): 7; Audrey Smedley, "'Race' and the Construction of Human Identity," *American Anthropologist* 100, no. 3 (Sept. 1998): 690; and Paul Gilroy, *Between Camps: Race, Identity and Nationalism at the End of the Colour Line* (Allen Lane, 2000), 31. For the term as an illusion, see *Race—The Power of an Illusion* (California Newsreel, VHS, 2003). On "black" as a delusion, consider Kerry Ann Rockquemore and David L. Brunsma, *Beyond Black: Biracial Identity in America*, 2d ed. (Rowman & Littlefield, 2008), 109. On "black" as chimera, see Colin Kidd, *The Forging of Races: Race and Scripture in the Protestant Atlantic, 1600–2000* (Cambridge University Press, 2006), 10; and as a four-letter word, see C. Loring Brace, *"Race" Is a Four-Letter Word: The Genesis of the Concept* (Oxford University Press, 2005). Kirsten Fischer gives a representative prefatory statement in *Suspect Relations: Sex, Race, and Resistance in Colonial North Carolina* (Cornell University Press, 2002), 7: "Informed by the extensive scholarship on race as a social construct, 'races' appear here as socially defined categories." K. Anthony Appiah has complained (although granted he is referring to "educated Americans" in general rather than scholars in particular): "Talk of the 'social construction of race' has become standard in the last few years, but this is a slogan, not the expression of a coherent understanding"—see Appiah, *The State and the Shaping of Identity*, The Tanner Lectures on Human Values, delivered at Clare Hall, Cambridge, Apr. 30 and May 1, 2001, 287, http://www.tannerlectures.utah.edu/lectures/documents/Appiah_02.pdf, accessed Dec. 2, 2011. For the Eric Foner quotation, see Foner, *Give Me Liberty! An American History* (Norton, 2005), 52. In a later edition (2d Seagull ed., Norton, 2009), Foner wrote: "The first Africans, twenty in all, arrived in Virginia in 1619" (98). But see William Thorndale, "The Virginia Census of 1619," *Maga-*

zine of Virginia Genealogy 33 (1995): 155–70 for evidence that Africans were in Virginia prior to the arrival of the Dutch ship mentioned by Foner. Africans were also on Portuguese ships that crossed the North Atlantic in the sixteenth century, including a pilot who, in 1525, sailed up what today is known as the Hudson River. See Graham Russell Hodges, *Root and Branch: African Americans in New York and East Jersey, 1613–1863* (University of North Carolina Press, 1999), 6–7.

2. Warren M. Billings, ed., *The Old Dominion in the Seventeenth Century: A Documentary History of Virginia, 1606–1689* (University of North Carolina Press, 1975), 155. *The Generall Historie of Virginia, New England and the Summer Isles.* was published in 1624, but here Smith was referring to events in 1619. Engel Sluiter, "New Light on the '20. and Odd Negroes' Arriving in Virginia, August 1619," *William and Mary Quarterly*, 3rd ser., 54 (1997): 395–96. See also Lisa Rein, "Mystery of Va.'s First Slaves Is Unlocked 400 Years Later," *Washington Post*, Sept. 3, 2006, A1.

3. Sluiter, "New Light," 395–98. See also J. Douglas Deal, *Race and Class in Colonial Virginia: Indians, Englishmen, and Africans on the Eastern Shore during the Seventeenth Century* (Garland, 1993), 164.

4. John Thornton, "The African Experience of the '20. and Odd Negroes' Arriving in Virginia in 1619," *William and Mary Quarterly*, 3rd ser., 55 (1998): 426, 432–33. On the difficulty of determining the self-identity of Africans caught in the slave trade, see Lorena S. Walsh, "The Chesapeake Slave Trade: Regional Patterns, African Origins, and Some Implications," *William and Mary Quarterly*, 3d ser., 58 (2001): 142; Gwendolyn Midlo Hall, *Slavery and African Ethnicities in the Americas: Restoring the Links* (University of North Carolina Press, 2005), 48.

5. Nor, for that matter, would they have thought of themselves as "African." See David Eltis, *The Rise of African Slavery in the Americas* (Cambridge University Press, 2000), 224, 226. My use of the term "African" has a purely geographic connotation: "Africans" are people from the continent of Africa, independent of how they identified themselves. For a piercing satirical piece on contemporary writing about Africa, see Binyavanga Wainaina, "How to Write about Africa," http://www.granta.com/Archive/92/How-to-Write-about-Africa/Page-1.

6. Thornton, "The African Experience," 431, 426; Michael A. Gomez, *Exchanging Our Country Marks: The Transformation of African Identities in the Colonial and Antebellum South* (University of North Carolina, 1998), 155, 157, 165–66; Eltis, *Rise of African Slavery*, 227–29. See also Philip D. Morgan, *Slave Counterpoint: Black Culture in the Eighteenth-Century Chesapeake & Lowcountry* (University of North Carolina Press, 1998), 448–49, 459. Few subjects in the history of the American slave trade have caused as much heated debate as the effect of the Middle Passage on the culture of the enslaved. See, for example, Stanley Elkins, *Slavery: A Problem In American Institutional and Intellectual Life* (University of Chicago Press, 1959); Sidney W. Mintz and Richard Price, *The Birth of an African-American Culture: An Anthropological Perspective* (Beacon, 1992); John

Thornton, *Africa and Africans in the Making of the Atlantic World, 1400–1680* (Cambridge University Press, 1992); Gomez, *Exchanging Our Country Marks;* Hall, *Slavery and African Ethnicities;* Douglas B. Chambers, "Ethnicity in the Diaspora: The Slave Trade and the Creation of African 'Nations' in the Americas," *Slavery and Abolition* 22, no. 3 (Dec. 2001): 25–39. For a recent work on the Middle Passage, see Emma Christopher, *Slave Ship Sailors and Their Captive Cargoes* (Cambridge University Press, 2006). Ira Berlin has argued that many of the earliest individuals brought from Africa to the Chesapeake were "Atlantic creoles," men and women who had spent years in contact with Europeans along the coast of Africa or in the Caribbean and were familiar with Portuguese, Spanish, or English culture, maybe all three. That now appears quite unlikely, however. See Ira Berlin, *Many Thousands Gone: The First Two Centuries of Slavery in North America* (Harvard University Press, 1998), introduction, chap. 1; James H. Sweet, "Spanish and Portuguese Influences on Racial Slavery in British North America, 1492–1619," paper presented at "Collective Degradation: Slavery and the Construction of Race," the Fifth Annual Gilder-Lehrman Center International Conference, Yale University, Nov. 7–8, 2003, 25–29, http://www.yale.edu/glc/events/race/Sweet.pdf, accessed Dec. 2, 2011. Berlin claims that some of the "20. and odd Negroes" were creoles, apparently on the basis of speculation by Wesley Frank Craven more than thirty-five years ago. Since he (Berlin) indicates in a footnote that he has consulted Sluiter's compelling and much more recent article, it is difficult to see why he supports Craven's supposition. See Wesley Frank Craven, *White, Red, and Black: The Seventeenth-Century Virginian* (University of Virginia Press, 1971), 77–81.

7. "Race," Ira Berlin observes, "is continually defined." It very much matters "who does the defining and why" (Berlin, *Many Thousands Gone,* 1). See also Barbara J. Fields, "Ideology and Race in American History," in J. Morgan Kousser and James M. McPherson, eds., *Region, Race, and Reconstruction: Essays in Honor of C. Vann Woodward* (Oxford University Press, 1982), 150; Benedict Anderson, *Imagined Communities: Reflections on the Origin and Spread of Nationalism* (Verso, 1983). Colin Kidd observes, "All racial taxonomies—whether popular or scientific—are the product not of nature but of the imagination combined with inherited cultural stereotyping as well—to be fair—as the empirical observation of genuine (though superficial, trivial and inconsequential) biological differences" (Kidd, *Forging of Races,* 9).

8. Winthrop D. Jordan, *White over Black: American Attitudes toward the Negro, 1550–1812* (Penguin, 1969), 583–85. As Sheila Skemp, Jordan's former colleague at the University of Mississippi, wrote after his death, "Elegantly written, breathtaking in its scope, [*White over Black*] became—and remains—the starting place for anyone who wanted to examine the meaning and origins of race in America" (http://www.historians .org/Perspectives/issues/2007/0705/0705mem1.cfm, accessed Dec. 2, 2011).

9. Jordan, *White over Black,* 4, 7.

10. Since Jordan wrote his celebrated study we have learned, among other things,

that negative associations with the color black can be found "not only in antiquity and in Western culture in general but also among various Asian, Native American, and even sub-Saharan African peoples" (quoted in David Brion Davis, *Inhuman Bondage: The Rise and Fall of Slavery in the New World* [Oxford University Press, 2006], 57). See also Lloyd A. Thompson, *Romans and Blacks* (Routledge, 1989), 110. We have learned as well that while the literature of western Europe in the late sixteenth century does indeed include a wealth of derogatory references to sub-Saharan Africans, it also offers us the myth of Prester John as well as "saintly and heroic" African figures—see George M. Fredrickson, *Racism: A Short History* (Princeton University Press, 2002), 26–28. Recent works that explore color consciousness in Elizabethan England include Kim F. Hall, *Things of Darkness: Economies of Race and Gender in Early Modern England* (Cornell University Press, 1995) and Sujata Iyengar, *Shades of Difference: Mythologies of Skin Color in Early Modern England* (University of Pennsylvania Press, 2005).

11. Sweet, "Spanish and Portuguese Influences on Racial Slavery," 8–9. David M. Goldenberg traces the linkage of black skin and slavery back to the Islamic conquest of Africa in the seventh century in *The Curse of Ham: Race and Slavery in Early Judaism, Christianity, and Islam* (Princeton University Press, 2003), 170. See also William Waller Hening, *Statutes at Large; Being a Collection of All the Laws of Virginia from the First Session of the Legislature in the Year 1619* (R. and W. and G. Bartow, 1823), http://www .vagenweb.org/hening/, 1 (1639): 226, accessed Mar. 23, 2013; Deal, *Race and Class in Colonial Virginia*, 341; "An Act Concerning Negroes and Other Slaues," Archives of Maryland Online 1 (1664): 533, http://www.aomol.net/html/index.html, accessed Mar. 23, 2013; and Hening, *Statutes at Large*, 3 (1692): 102.

12. T. H. Breen and Stephen Innes, *"Myne Owne Ground": Race and Freedom on Virginia's Eastern Shore, 1640–1676* (Oxford University Press, 1980), 72–77; Billings, *The Old Dominion in the Seventeenth Century*, 164–65; and Philip Morgan, *Slave Counterpoint*, 156. Morgan also comments, "At least through the 1680s, Virginians came close to" seeing free people of African ancestry as "members or potential members of their community" (*Slave Counterpoint*, 12). See also Martha Hodes, *White Women, Black Men: Illicit Sex in the Nineteenth-Century South* (Yale University Press, 1997), 28–29; A. Leon Higginbotham, Jr., *In the Matter of Color: Race and the American Legal Process: The Colonial Period* (Oxford University Press, 1978), 42; and A. Leon Higginbotham, Jr. and Barbara K. Kopytoff, "Racial Purity and Interracial Sex in the Law of Colonial and Antebellum Virginia," *Georgetown Law Journal* 77 (1989): 1990–91. In 1666, almost 11 percent of people of African ancestry were landholders in Northampton County, Virginia, compared to fewer than 18 percent of residents of European ancestry. "This disparity," argues Theodore Allen, "is no more than normal considering that 53.4 percent of the European-American landholders, but none of the African-Americans came as free persons." See Allen, *The Invention of the White Race*, vol. 2: *The Origin of Racial Oppression in Anglo-America* (Verso, 1997), 240–44, 184.

13. I would suggest that "Negroes" also was used as a synonym for slaves in the famous first reference to the term in the official record, from the *Minutes of the Judicial Proceedings of the Governor and Council:* "September 17th, 1630. Hugh Davis to be soundly whipped, before an assembly of Negroes and others for abusing himself to the dishonor of God and shame of Christians, by defiling his body in lying with a negro; which fault he is to acknowledge next Sabbath day" (Hening, *Statutes at Large* 1 [1630]: 146). Through the seventeenth century, most commentators argued that extended residence in temperate climates would result in the descendants of Africans becoming ever lighter in complexion; see Jordan, *White over Black,* 16; Fischer, *Suspect Relations,* 2. The early colonial experiences of African slaves in a northern colony are explored in Thelma Wills Foote, *Black and White Manhattan: The History of Racial Formation in Colonial New York City* (Oxford University Press, 2004); see also Hodges, *Root and Branch.* For a useful overview of the proslavery argument in the decades leading up to the Civil War, see Drew Gilpin Faust, *The Ideology of Slavery: Proslavery Thought in the Antebellum South, 1830–1860* (Louisiana State University Press, 1981).

14. Even Winthrop Jordan notes, "In the early years, the English settlers most frequently contrasted themselves with Negroes by the term *Christian*" (Jordan, *White over Black,* 93). See also Kathleen M. Brown, *Good Wives, Nasty Wenches, and Anxious Patriarchs: Gender, Race, and Power in Colonial Virginia* (University of North Carolina Press, 1996), 135. Africans had a vibrant religious life. See, for example, Thornton, *Africa and Africans,* 235–53; Suzanne Preston Blier, *African Vodun: Art, Psychology, and Power* (University of Chicago Press, 1995); John Iliffe, *Africans: The History of a Continent* (Cambridge University Press, 1995), 85–93.

15. Warren M. Billings, "The Cases of Fernando and Elizabeth Key: A Note on the Status of Blacks in Seventeenth-Century Virginia," *William and Mary Quarterly,* 3rd ser, 30 (1973): 469–70; Anthony S. Parent, Jr., *Foul Means: The Formation of a Slave Society in Virginia, 1660–1740* (University of North Carolina Press, 2003), 112–13; and Higginbotham, *In the Matter of Color,* 21. See also H. L. McIlwaine, ed., *Minutes of the Council and General Court of Colonial Virginia, 1622–1632, 1670–1676, with Notes and Excerpts from Original Council and General Court Records into 1683, Now Lost* (Virginia State Library, 1926), 477. Hening, *Statutes at Large,* 2 (1667), 260; "An Act for the Encourageing the Importacon of Negros and Slaues into This Province," Archives of Maryland Online 2 (1671), 272; "An Act Relating to Servants and Slaves," Archives of Maryland Online 26 (1704), esp. 259–60; and "An Act Relating to Servants and Slaves," Archives of Maryland Online 30 (1715), esp. 289–90.

16. Brown, *Good Wives,* 223, 220; Lorena S. Walsh, *From Calabar to Carter's Grove: The History of a Virginia Slave Community* (University of Virginia Press, 1997), 112, 152.

17. Jordan, *White over Black,* 97–98; Kidd, *Forging of Races,* 57.

18. Of particular interest to historians has been a 1643 law in Virginia ordering that "all negro women at the age of sixteen years" be included among the "tithable" persons

(Hening, *Statutes at Large* 1 [1643]: 242; Deal, *Race and Class in Colonial Virginia*, 181). Alden Vaughan is the most outspoken proponent of the view that racism existed from the earliest days of settlement in Virginia. See especially Alden T. Vaughan, *Roots of American Racism: Essays on the Colonial Experience* (Oxford University Press, 1995), chap. 7, and Alden T. Vaughan and Virginia Mason Vaughan, "Before *Othello:* Elizabethan Representations of Sub-Saharan Africans," *William and Mary Quarterly*, 3rd ser., 54, no. 1 (1997): 19–44. See also Hening, *Statutes at Large* 1 (1660), 532; Fischer, *Suspect Relations*, 42–54. In Massachusetts Bay, the Puritans hanged four Quakers. See Sarah Crabtree, "'A Beautiful and Practical Lesson of Jurisprudence: The Transatlantic Quaker Ministry in the Age of Revolution,' *Radical History Review* 99 (Fall 2007): 52–53. For additional Virginia laws concerning the Quakers, see Hening, *Statutes at Large* 2 (1662): 48, 180–83. The Maryland legislature took steps against the Quakers two years earlier than Virginia, in 1658; see Archives of Maryland Online 3 (1658): 352.

19. Even T. H. Breen and Stephen Innes, who claim that skin color was a factor of secondary importance in seventeenth-century Virginia, contend that "the sudden shift in the ratio of blacks to whites" in the early eighteenth century "either generated racist ideas or brought to the surface latent racist assumptions" (Breen and Innes, "*Myne Owne Ground*," 107–108). According to Walsh, *From Calabar to Carter's Grove:* "As late as 1690 Africans or their descendants were no more than seven percent of the total population in Virginia and Maryland, which then numbered about 75,000" (25). See also Parent, *Foul Means*, 74; Archives of Maryland Online 23 (1698): 499; Hugh Jones, *The Present State of Virginia, from Whence Is Inferred a Short View of Maryland and North Carolina*, ed. Richard L. Morton (University of North Carolina Press, 1956), 75–76; and Morgan, *Slave Counterpoint*, 61.

20. On the experiences of free people of African descent in different British colonies, see Allen, *Invention of the White Race*, vol. 2, 240–44.

21. Walsh, *From Calabar to Carter's Grove*, 114. Russell Menard notes that there were "frequent references in the immigrant lists to servants sixteen years old and under as poor, friendless, or orphaned" (Russell R. Menard, *Migrants, Servants and Slaves: Unfree Labor in Colonial British America* [Ashgate, 2001], 128, also chap. 9).

22. Edmund S. Morgan, *American Slavery, American Freedom: The Ordeal of Colonial Virginia* (Norton, 1975), 236, 320–25; Deal, *Race and Class in Colonial Virginia*, 116; and Menard, *Migrants, Servants and Slaves*, chap. 9, 128. See also Gloria Main, *Tobacco Colony: Life in Early Maryland, 1650–1720* (Princeton University Press, 1982), 100. In response to complaints from residents of the counties of York, Gloucester, and Middlesex about the "great numbers of felons and other desperate villaines sent hither from the several prisons in England," the General Court of Virginia prohibited further importation of "any jaile birds or such others, who for notorious offences have deserved to dye in England" (Hening, *Statutes at Large* 2 [1671]: 509–10). See also Darrell B. Rutman and Anita H. Rutman, *A Place in Time: Middlesex County, Virginia, 1650–1750* (Norton, 1984), 130.

23. On the abuse of servants, see, for example, Deal, *Race and Class in Colonial Virginia*, 111, 115, 167; Morgan, *American Slavery, American Freedom*, 126–28; Brown, *Good Wives*, 152; Rutman and Rutman, *A Place in Time*, 136; Breen and Innes, *"Myne Owne Ground,"* 64; Main, *Tobacco Colony*, 114–15; Hening, *Statutes at Large* 2 (1662): 117; and Billings, *Old Dominion in the Seventeenth Century*, 138. A problem for the historian is explaining how planters could justify to themselves treating Christian men and women as if they had no meaningful rights—in other words, as if they were heathens. The answer may lie in contested notions about what constituted "true" Christianity. In 1652, the Kent County (Maryland) Court recorded the following testimony in a case involving the death of a servant: "In one of the depositions, it is stated, that a servant had run away, and upon being taken back, Mistress Ward did whip her with a peach tree rod & after she had done, she took water and salt, and salted her, and when she was adoing the same the maid cried out, and desired her Mistress to use her like a Christian, and she replied and said: 'Oh! ye you.' 'Do you liken yourself like a Christian?'" Archives of Maryland Online 54 (1652): 9.

24. Hening, *Statutes at Large* 2 (1670): 280. That same year Lord Baltimore issued a proclamation taking the vote away from every free male in Maryland who held less than fifty acres or an estate worth less than forty pounds. See Menard, *Migrants, Servants and Slaves*, chap. 2, 60.

25. In the summer of 1640, six servants and a slave named Emanuel stole guns, weapons, and a boat and made an abortive attempt to escape to the Dutch colony of New Amsterdam. See McIlwaine, *Minutes of the Council*, 467; Morgan, *Slave Counterpoint*, 9; Morgan, *American Slavery, American Freedom*, 327. See also Berlin, *Many Thousands Gone*, 26, 44; Deal, *Race and Class in Colonial Virginia*, 179, 293–94; Merton L. Dillon, *Slavery Attacked: Southern Slaves and Their Allies, 1619–1865* (Louisiana State University Press, 1990), 8; Allen, *Invention of the White Race*, vol. 2, 151, 154–58; Walsh, *From Calabar to Carter's Grove*, 34; Breen and Innes, *"Myne Owne Ground,"* 28–29, 106; Parent, *Foul Means*, 56; Billings, *Old Dominion in the Seventeenth Century*, 140. A remarkable case came before the courts in Maryland when two English servants belonging to John Hawkins, one of his former servants, and two of his slaves, "John the Negro" and "Tony the Negro," went on trial in 1671 for "voluntarily & wickedly feloniously and Traitorously" bludgeoning him to death with an axe. One of the servants confessed to the murder, but the other servant as well as the freedman and "John the Negro" pleaded not guilty. The final accused, "Tony the Negro," the clerk recorded, "could Speake no English" and his case was taken up separately. As if to confound our expectations, the jury convicted all the accused except for "Tony the Negro." See Archives of Maryland Online 65 (1671): 2–8.

26. The quotation is from Allen, *Invention of the White Race*, vol. 2, 214. See also Morgan, *Slave Counterpoint*, 9, 308; Morgan, *American Slavery, American Freedom*, 269; and Walsh, *From Calabar to Carter's Grove*, 34.

27. Menard, *Migrants, Servants and Slaves*, chap. 3, 362–63; Main, *Tobacco Colony*, 105; Allan Kulikoff, *Tobacco and Slaves: The Development of Southern Cultures in the Chesapeake, 1680–1800* (University of North Carolina Press, 1986), 40; Rutman and Rutman, *A Place in Time*, 165; Morgan, *American Slavery, American Freedom*, 308.

28. Hening, *Statutes at Large* 3 (1692): 102–03; 3 (1705): 448–51, 460–61; and 6 (1748): 112. Masters were instructed to give "to every male servant, ten bushels of indian corn, thirty shillings in money, or the value thereof, in goods, and one well fixed musket or fuzee, of the value of twenty shillings, at least: and to every woman servant, fifteen bushels of indian corn, and forty shillings in money, or the value thereof, in goods" (Hening, *Statutes at Large* 3 [1705]: 451).

29. In 1705, "Negroes," "mulattoes," and American Indians were barred by law from serving as witnesses in any case. See Hening, *Statutes at Large* 3 (1705): 298. A 1732 law amended that prohibition to allow their testimony in capital cases involving slaves. (It also noted that "negros, mullatos, and Indians" who professed themselves Christians had been allowed to testify in spite of the earlier statute.) See Hening, *Statutes at Large* 4 (1732): 326–27. Twelve years later a new law allowed them to testify in all cases involving slaves (Hening, *Statutes at Large* 5 [1744]: 245). Yet another law, in 1748, stipulated that if any "negroe, mulattoe, or Indian" shall give false testimony he shall "have one ear nailed to the pillory, and there to stand for the space of one hour, and then the said ear to be cut off, and thereafter the other ear nailed in like manner, and cut off at the expiration of one other hour" (Hening, *Statutes at Large* 6 [1748]: 106–107; 3 [1705]: 449–50). Exception to the restriction on bearing arms was made for "every free negro, mulatto, or Indian, being a house-keeper, or listed in the militia" as well as those "living at any frontier plantation," provided they obtained a permit. See Hening, *Statutes at Large* 4 (1723): 131, 133–34; 3 (1705): 250–51.

30. In 1752 the Maryland Assembly did prohibit slaveowners from freeing slaves on their deathbeds or in their wills—see Archives of Maryland Online 50 (1752): 76–78. This seems to have been done, however, largely to prevent elderly slaves from becoming a burden on society. On the relatively advantageous conditions (compared to Virginia) faced by free people of African descent in Maryland, see David Skillen Bogen, "The Maryland Context of *Dred Scott:* The Decline in the Legal Status of Maryland Free Blacks, 1776–1810," *Journal of American Legal History* 34 (1990): 383–85; Brown, *Good Wives*, 214–216. As evidence of the ambivalence lawmakers felt, Brown points out that in 1705 the House of Burgesses passed a bill offering free people of African ancestry some protection from enslavement.

31. Hening, *Statutes at Large* 2 (1662): 170. Prior to 1662 at least some magistrates in Virginia had ruled that legal status was dictated by paternity, meaning that the child of a free father was free. See Billings, "The Cases of Fernando and Elizabeth Key," 472; Archives of Maryland Online 1 (1664): 533–34. The legislators in Maryland came to adopt the Virginia position regarding the status of a newborn in 1681; see Archives of

Maryland Online 7 (1681): 203–205; Hening, *Statutes at Large* 3 (1691): 86–87. In 1681, the Maryland Assembly complained that "diuerse ffreeborne Englishe or Whitewoman sometimes by the Instigacon Procuremt or Conievance of theire Masters Mistres or dames, & always to the Satisfaccon of theire Lascivious & Lustfull desires, & to the disgrace not only of the English butt allso of many other Christian Nations, doe Inter-marry with Negroes & Slaues by which meanes diuerse Inconveniencys Controuersys & suites may arise Touching the Issue or Children" (Archives of Maryland Online 7 [1681]: 204). The first law mentioning mulattoes—which defined who was tithable—was passed by the House of Burgesses in 1672; see Hening, *Statutes at Large* 2 (1672): 296. There are earlier references to mulattoes in court records: consider Joel Williamson, *New People: Miscegenation and Mulattoes in the United States* (Free Press, 1980), 8; Mc-Ilwaine, *Minutes of the Council,* 504; Hening, *Statutes at Large* 3 (1705): 252; Thomas D. Morris, *Southern Slavery and the Law, 1619–1860* (University of North Carolina Press, 1998), 22–23. Peter Wallenstein notes that the 1705 Virginia statute "probably sufficed at the time to exclude virtually all Virginians with any traceable African ancestry." See Peter Wallenstein, *Tell the Court I Love My Wife: Race, Marriage, and Law—An American History* (Palgrave Macmillan, 2002), 18. Joshua D. Rothman explores the planters' un-certainty about racial categorization at length, and demonstrates how it continued into the antebellum period, in *Notorious in the Neighborhood: Sex and Families across the Color Line in Virginia, 1787–1861* (University of North Carolina Press, 2003), chap. 6.

32. Archives of Maryland Online 30 (1715): 289; 33 (1717): 112; Williamson, *New People,* 11.

33. Gordon S. Wood, "Without Him, No Bill of Rights," *New York Review of Books* 53, no. 19 (Nov. 30, 2006): 54.

34. As William M. Wiecek observes, "Statutory law at any time is in a process of de-velopment, with legislatures usually acting in response to particular problems per-ceived as urgent." See William M. Wiecek, "The Statutory Law of Slavery and Race in the Thirteen Mainland Colonies of British North America," *William and Mary Quar-terly* 3rd ser., 34 (1977): 259. Which is not to say that planter influence over the rest of society was limited to legislation. Along with court rulings, however, laws are the main evidence available from the early colonial period. As a number of scholars have shown, the planters of the Revolutionary era and the nineteenth century found a variety of ways to influence the perceptions held by other members of society. See, for example, Rhys Isaac, *The Transformation of Virginia, 1740–1790* (University of North Carolina Press, 1999); Eugene Genovese, *The World the Slaveholders Made* (Wesleyan University Press, 1988); Eugene Genovese, *Roll, Jordan, Roll: The World the Slaves Made* (Vintage, 1976); and Michael Wayne, *Death of an Overseer: Reopening a Murder Investigation from the Plantation South* (Oxford University Press, 2001). The planters in the Chesapeake, at least prior to the 1680s, had "modest genealogies." But their wealth and the political offices they controlled gave them unparalleled authority in the society. See Breen and

Innes, *"Myne Owne Ground,"* 46–47; Kulikoff, *Tobacco and Slaves,* 270. Planters had particular reason to be skeptical of the "Herrenvolk democracy" that came into being in the nineteenth century. Pierre van den Berghe has defined "Herrenvolk democracies" as regimes "that are democratic for the master race but tyrannical for the subordinate groups." See his *Race and Racism: A Comparative Perspective* (John Wiley & Sons, 1967), 18.

35. It is one of the more notable ironies of American history that "Negroes" appear in the official record long before "whites." Indeed, the designation "white" receives first mention in the statutes of Maryland only in 1681 and in Virginia only in 1691. See Jordan, *White over Black,* 96, fn. 125. Nancy Shoemaker speculates that the transition from "Christian" to "white" first took place in Barbados. See her *A Strange Likeness: Becoming Red and White in Eighteenth Century North America* (Oxford University Press, 2004), 129.

36. Among the influential works on the survival of African traditions and practices are Morgan, *Slave Counterpoint;* Berlin, *Many Thousands Gone;* Gomez, *Exchanging Our Country Marks;* Hall, *Slavery and African Ethnicities;* Thornton, *Africa and Africans;* Eltis, *Rise of African Slavery;* Walsh, *From Calabar to Carter's Grove;* John Michael Vlach, *By the Work of Their Hands: Studies in Afro-American Folklife* (University of Michigan Press, 1991); Robert Farris Thompson, *Flash of the Spirit: African and Afro-American Art and Philosophy* (Random House, 1983); Mechal Sobel, *The World They Made Together: Black and White Values in Eighteenth-Century Virginia* (Princeton University Press, 1989); Sterling Stuckey, *Slave Culture: Nationalist Theory and the Foundations of Black America* (Oxford University Press, 1987); and Jason R. Young, *Rituals of Resistance: African Atlantic Religion in Kongo and the Lowcountry South in the Era of Slavery* (Louisiana State University Press, 2007). For the methodology used by Berlin, see Ira Berlin, "Time, Space, and the Evolution of Afro-American Society on British Mainland North America," *American Historical Review* 85 (1980): 44–78.

37. Kulikoff, *Tobacco and Slaves,* 319. Prior to the 1680s, more than 80 percent of the slaves in Maryland worked in groups that included English or European indentured servants. Main, *Tobacco Colony,* 106, 124. See also Rutman and Rutman, *A Place in Time,* 166; Walsh, *From Calabar to Carter's Grove,* 34.

38. Kulikoff, *Tobacco and Slaves,* 65. The growth of the slave population by natural increase, Philip Morgan notes, was "an unprecedented development" in the history of slave societies in the Western Hemisphere: see Morgan, *Slave Counterpoint,* 81. Allan Kulikoff observes that "Before 1740 few quarters housed more than thirty slaves, but by the 1770s and 1780s the wealthiest gentlemen ran home plantations with more than one hundred slaves and quarters with thirty to fifty"—see Kulikoff, *Tobacco and Slaves,* 337, as well as Berlin, *Many Thousands Gone,* 127, 129. Philip Morgan maintains that there was a creole majority in Virginia as early as 1720 (Morgan, *Slave Counterpoint,* 61). For the struggles of newly arrived Africans, see Brenda E. Stevenson, *Life in Black*

and White: Family and Community in the Slave South (Oxford University Press, 1996), 169. For the reminiscences of Charles Ball see *Slavery in the United States: A Narrative of the Life and Adventures of Charles Ball, a Black Man, Who Lived Forty Years in Maryland, South Carolina and Georgia, as a Slave under Various Masters, and was One Year in the Navy with Commodore Barney, during the Late War* (John S. Taylor, 1837), 21, http:// docsouth.unc.edu/neh/ballslavery/ball.html, accessed Dec. 2, 2011. There is also some evidence of friction between individuals from different African societies. See Morgan, *Slave Counterpoint,* 457–58, 614.

39. Lorena Walsh comments that by the middle of the eighteenth century, "as creole children—who ranged from the first to the third or fourth generation born in Virginia—began to replace their African-born elders, any conflicts resulting from the merging of the two groups of creoles and recently arrived Africans faded." Walsh, *From Calabar to Carter's Grove,* 116.

40. Kulikoff, *Tobacco and Slaves,* 432; Brown, *Good Wives,* 214.

41. Deal, *Race and Class in Colonial Virginia,* 211, 286–89; Morgan, *Slave Counterpoint,* 485; Hening, *Statutes at Large* 3 (1691): 87–88; Parent, *Foul Means,* 158; Brown, *Good Wives,* 221.

42. Breen and Innes, *"Myne Owne Ground,"* 97–100. Notes Douglas Deal, "The sparse information we have about the religious beliefs of the freedmen permits no more than the cautious supposition that they adopted, albeit in their own fashion, the Anglicanism of the English majority" (Deal, *Race and Class in Colonial Virginia,* 212). See also Brown, *Good Wives,* 214, 225–26. The quotation by the attorney about Benjamin Banneker can be found in Bogen, "The Maryland Context of *Dred Scott,*" 385. Morgan, *Slave Counterpoint,* 485–86 provides the quotation by James Madison.

43. Williamson, *New People,* 13. See also Morgan, *Slave Counterpoint,* 488.

44. Williamson, *New People,* 7; Deal, *Race and Class in Colonial Virginia,* 184; Morgan, *American Slavery, American Freedom,* 336.

45. Jordan, *White over Black,* 170.

46. Morgan, *Slave Counterpoint,* 521–22; Kulikoff, *Tobacco and Slaves,* 340–44, 350; Walsh, *From Calabar to Carter's Grove,* 114; James Sidbury, *Ploughshares into Swords: Race, Rebellion, and Identity in Gabriel's Virginia, 1730–1810* (Cambridge University Press, 1997), 20–21.

2. ON IMMIGRATION, CITIZENSHIP, AND BEING "NOT-BLACK"

1. Act of Mar. 26, 1790, ch. 3, 1 Stat. 103; Eric Foner, "Response to Arnesen," *International Labor and Working-Class History* 60 (Fall 2001): 57. Ian F. Haney López comments, "In 1935, Hitler's Germany limited citizenship to members of the Aryan race, making Germany the only country other than the United States with a racial restriction on naturalization." See Haney López, *White by Law: The Legal Construction of Race* (New

York University Press, 1996), 44. A movement in Congress during 1870 to make naturalization available to all free persons regardless of race was defeated in the Senate by a vote of 26 to 12; see Desmond King, "Making Americans: Immigration Meets Race," in Gary Gerstle and John Mollenkopf, eds., *E Pluribus Unum? Contemporary and Historical Perspectives on Immigrant Political Incorporation* (Russell Sage Foundation, 2001), 161.

2. Benjamin Franklin, "Observations Concerning the Increase of Mankind, Peopling of Countries, &c." (1751), http://www.historycarper.com/resources/twobf2/increase .htm, accessed Dec. 3, 2011. It is worth pointing out that Franklin did add, "But perhaps I am partial to the Complexion of my Country, for such Kind of Partiality is natural to Mankind." See Haney López, *White By Law*, 67. Nell Irvin Painter explores the history of the meaning of "whiteness" from ancient times in *The History of White People* (Norton, 2010).

3. Two especially important pioneering works are Alexander Saxton, *The Rise and Fall of the White Republic: Class Politics and Mass Culture in Nineteenth-Century America* (Verso, 1990), and David R. Roediger, *The Wages of Whiteness: Race and the Making of the American Working Class* (Verso, 1991). See also Noel Ignatiev, *How the Irish Became White* (Routledge, 1995); Karen Brodkin, *How Jews Became White Folks and What That Says about Race in America* (Rutgers University Press, 1998); Thomas S. Guglielmo, *White on Arrival: Italians, Race, Color, and Power in Chicago, 1890–1945* (Oxford University Press, 2003); James R. Barrett and David Roediger, "Inbetween Peoples: Race, Nationality and the 'New Immigrant' Working Class," *Journal of American Ethnic History* 16 (Spring 1997): 3–44. For Foner's quotation, see his "Response to Arneson," 57–58. Ariela Gross has concluded, based on a study of American trial records during the nineteenth and twentieth centuries, that "European Americans were always white before the law." See Gross, *What Blood Won't Tell: A History of Race on Trial in America* (Harvard University Press, 2008), 7.

4. Matthew Frye Jacobson, *Whiteness of a Different Color: European Immigrants and the Alchemy of Race* (Harvard University Press, 1998), esp. chap. 2. The quotations are the words of Francis A. Walker, president of M.I.T. and superintendent of the Census, from an 1896 article in the *Atlantic Monthly*, quoted in Richard Alba and Victor Nee, *Remaking the American Mainstream: Assimilation and Contemporary Immigration* (Harvard University Press, 2003), 68. For "not not-white," see Haney López, *White by Law*, 28–29.

5. The Irish immigrant experience is well captured in Kerby A. Miller, *Emigrants and Exiles: Ireland and the Irish Exodus to North America* (Oxford University Press, 1988).

6. Maria Monk, *The Awful Disclosures of Maria Monk* (Standard Publications, 2006). On the Philadelphia riots see Michael Feldberg, *The Philadelphia Riots of 1844: A Study of Ethnic Conflict* (Greenwood, 1975) and http://www.philaplace.org/story/316, accessed Apr. 23, 2013.

7. The Irish were also ridiculed as drunks. A joke from a Southern newspaper captures the stereotype: "An Irishman coming from the Fourth of July considerably bewildered, and seeing the houses and everything else going around in a queer manner, concluded that the easiest way to get home was to 'stand still till his own home passed him and then make a dive for it.'" Michael Wayne, *Death of an Overseer: Reopening a Murder Investigation from the Plantation South* (Oxford University Press, 2001), 19. For the quotation, see Eric Foner, *Give Me Liberty! An American History* (Norton, 2005), 482.

8. Roediger, *Wages of Whiteness*, 140–44. On the Irish and the Democrats see also Ignatiev, *How the Irish Became White;* Jean Baker, *Affairs of Party: The Political Culture of Northern Democrats in the Mid-Nineteenth Century* (Fordham University Press, 1998). See also Desmond King, *Making Americans: Immigration, Race, and the Origins of the Diverse Democracy* (Harvard University Press, 2000), 64–65. The full text of the Dillingham Commission Report can be found at http://archive.org/stream/dictionaryofrace oounitrich/dictionaryofraceoounitrich_djvu.txt, accessed Feb. 27, 2013.

9. The text of the treaty can be viewed at http://www.mexica.net/guadhida.php, accessed Dec. 3. 2011. See, too, Tomás Almaguer, *Racial Fault Lines: The Historical Origins of White Supremacy in California* (University of California Press, 1994), 54 (quotation from the California Constitutional Convention on p. 56); Mae M. Ngai, *Impossible Subjects: Illegal Aliens and the Making of Modern America* (Princeton University Press, 2004), 51. Seventy-six years after the treaty was signed, the Johnson-Reed Act of 1924, which placed restrictions on immigration according to national origin, also effectively classified Mexicans as whites.

10. Almaguer, *Racial Fault Lines*, 54–55, 57. Working-class Mexicans were often simply classified as Indians for legal purposes. Neil Foley has found that in early twentieth-century Texas, "most whites viewed practically all Mexicans as unambiguously nonwhite." See Foley, *The White Scourge: Mexicans, Blacks, and Poor Whites in Texas Cotton Culture* (University of California Press, 1997), 41.

11. Patricia Nelson Limerick, *The Legacy of Conquest: The Unbroken Past of the American West* (Norton, 1987), 235–43.

12. Foner, *Give Me Liberty!*, 681; Limerick, *Legacy of Conquest*, 243–45.

13. David G. Gutiérrez, *Walls and Mirrors: Mexican Americans, Mexican Immigrants, and the Politics of Ethnicity* (University of California Press, 1995), 76.

14. The quotation is from Ngai, *Impossible Subjects*, 74; see also Gutiérrez, *Walls and Mirrors*, 76–77. LULAC is still in operation. Its website is http://lulac.org.

15. James L. Slayden, "Some Observations on Mexican Immigration," *Annals of the American Academy of Political and Social Science* 93 (Jan. 1921): 125; Gutiérrez, *Walls and Mirrors*, 131.

16. The quotation from the immigrant is from Gutiérrez, *Walls and Mirrors*, 89. Sometimes they were treated worse than aliens. Some restaurants in the Southwest exhibited signs that read "No Dogs or Mexicans Allowed"—see Gutiérrez, *Walls and*

Mirrors, 131. For the quotation by the veteran, see George J. Sánchez, *Becoming Mexican American: Ethnicity, Culture and Identity in Chicano Los Angeles, 1900–1945* (Oxford University Press, 1993), 211.

17. Ngai, *Impossible Subjects*. See also Foley, *White Scourge*, 63; and Gutiérrez, *Walls and Mirrors*, 129. Two years after the trial, a California Court of Appeal overturned the verdicts. Eerie echoes of the public response to the Sleep Lagoon case reverberated after the murder of a black teenager in Los Angeles in 2007. See Roberto Lovato, "The Smog of Race War in LA," *The Nation*, Apr. 7, 2007, 20–24.

18. Ngai, *Impossible Subjects*, 8. Their association with Mexicans in the minds of white Americans led some Latinos to conclude, perhaps inevitably, that "the only way to stop this indiscriminate lumping of American citizens with newly arrived Mexican immigrants was to take a stand against continuing large-scale immigration from Mexico" (Gutiérrez, *Walls and Mirrors*, 75).

19. Erika Lee, *At America's Gates: Chinese Immigration during the Exclusion Era, 1882–1943* (University of North Carolina Press, 2003), 25; Haiming Liu, "The Social Origins of Early Chinese Immigrants: A Revisionist Perspective," in Susie Lan Cassel, ed., *The Chinese in America: A History from Gold Mountain to the New Millennium* (AltaMira Press, 2002), 21, 25. For the commentary by Mae M. Ngai, see her "History as Law and Life: *Tape v. Hurley* and the Origins of the Chinese American Middle Class," in Sucheng Chan and Madeline Y. Hsu, eds., *Chinese Americans and the Politics of Race and Culture* (Temple University Press, 2008), 67.

20. Sucheng Chan, *Asian Americans: An Interpretive History* (Twayne, 1991), 45; Lee, *At America's Gates*, 25, 29; Ngai, "History as Law and Life," 67–68; *Congressional Globe* 40, 6 (1870): 5156.

21. Chan, *Asian Americans*, 54. The full text of the Page Act of 1875 can be seen at http://www-rohan.sdsu.edu/dept/polsciwb/brianl/docs/1875Immigration%20Act .pdf, accessed Feb. 15, 2013. The law was designed to keep out convicted felons, prostitutes, and individuals who had entered into contracts "for lewd and immoral purposes." Not incidentally, it also included a provision stating "that if any citizen of the United States, or other person amenable to the laws of the United States shall take, or cause to be taken or transported, to or from the United States any subject of China, Japan, or any Oriental country, without their free and voluntary consent, for the purpose of holding them to a term of service, such citizen or other person shall be liable to be indicted therefore, and, on conviction of such offense, shall be punished by a fine not exceeding two thousand dollars and be imprisoned not exceeding one year" (Lee, *At America's Gates*, 35).

22. In 1920 Japan also agreed to deny passports to "picture brides," women selected for Japanese (and Korean) laborers in the United States by matchmakers who worked from photographs and family recommendations (Chan, *Asian Americans*, 55). The Johnson-Reed Act was passed seven years after Congress had enacted a law prohibiting

immigration from what was termed the "Asiatic Barred Zone," a vast region covering almost all of East and South Asia, including India, Arabia, Afghanistan, and parts of Russia. Filipinos were not barred until 1934. Congress finally repealed the Chinese exclusion laws in 1943, largely to counter Japanese wartime propaganda that the United States was anti-Asiatic. Exclusion of all other nationalities, including the Japanese, came to an end with passage of the McCarran-Walter Act in 1952.

23. For the census data, see http://www2.census.gov/prod2/decennial/documents/ 33973538v2p1ch6.pdf and http://www2.census.gov/prod2/decennial/documents/ 33973538v2p1ch2.pdf, both accessed Sept. 30, 2013. The Japanese had a more favorable balance between the sexes, which accounts for the more rapid growth in their numbers. A bare majority of the individuals of Chinese ancestry lived in California, as well as almost three-quarters of the individuals of Japanese ancestry.

24. The full text of the ruling can be found at http://supreme.justia.com/us/260/178/ case.html, accessed Dec. 3, 2011. For commentary, see Ngai, *Impossible Subjects,* 42–44; Haney López, *White by Law,* 131. A small number of Asian immigrants were able to secure naturalization before local courts in the 1870s, effectively establishing a claim to whiteness. But that avenue to citizenship was closed off by a circuit court decision, *In re Ah Yup,* in 1878—see Chan, *Asian Americans,* 47.

25. Xiao-Huang Yin, "Writing a Place in American Life: The Sensibilities of American-born Chinese as Reflected in Life Stories from the Exclusion Era," in Sucheng Chan, ed., *Chinese American Transnationalism: The Flow of People, Resources, and Ideas between China and America during the Exclusion Era* (Temple University Press, 2006), 212–14; Chan, *Asian Americans,* 117. The JACL is still in operation; see http://www.jacl.org.

26. King, "Making Americans," 159. See also Gary Gerstle, *American Crucible: Race and Nation in the Twentieth Century* (Princeton University Press, 2001), 112; Scott Kurashige, *The Shifting Grounds of Race: Black and Japanese Americans in the Making of Multiethnic Los Angeles* (Princeton University Press, 2008), 56, 24; Ngai, *Impossible Subjects,* 170; Andrea Louie, "Searching for Roots in Contemporary China and Chinese America," in Chan and Hsu, *Chinese Americans and the Politics of Race and Culture,* 203. Comments Erika Lee, "Born in the United States, [Chinese Americans] were nevertheless lumped together with other Chinese as 'Orientals' or foreigners" (Lee, *At America's Gates,* 239–40).

27. Ngai, *Impossible Subjects,* 175. The text of the report can be seen at http://www .du.edu/behindbarbedwire/decision_to_evacuate.html, accessed Dec. 3, 2011.

28. Roosevelt's executive order can be found at http://historymatters.gmu.edu/d/ 5154, accessed Dec. 3, 2011. For commentary, see Chan, *Asian Americans,* 126. Chan also notes that "Though Hawaii was in much greater danger of being attacked and martial law was declared immediately following the bombing of Pearl Harbor, no mass evacuation of the 150,000 Japanese took place there, because to have removed them, when they comprised 37 percent of the islands' total population and an even larger

proportion of its skilled labor force, would have disrupted the islands' economy too much and would, moreover, have tied up too many ships" (126). The treatment of individuals whose ancestry linked them to the European wartime allies of Japan stands in stark contrast. While Roosevelt empowered the army to detain individuals of Italian or German ancestry, military officials used that authority hesitantly. In the end, only about 3,200 resident aliens of Italian background were arrested and just 300 interned. About 11,000 German residents (among them some naturalized citizens) were arrested and just 5,000 interned—see http://historymatters.gmu.edu/d/5154, accessed Dec. 3, 2011.

29. Chan, *Asian Americans*, 139.

30. For the full text of these constitutional provisions, see http://www.usconstitution .net/const.html#Article1 and http://www.usconstitution.net/const.html#Am14, both accessed Dec. 3, 2011. Congress granted all Native Americans full rights of citizenship only in 1924, with passage of the Indian Citizenship Act; see http://digital.library.ok state.edu/kappler/vol4/html_files/v4p1165.html, accessed Dec. 3, 2011. Questions subsequently arose regarding the citizenship of Indians born after the law went into effect. These questions were finally resolved under the Nationality Act of 1940, which granted citizenship to all those born in the United States "to a member of an Indian, Eskimo, Aleutian, or other aboriginal tribe." The Supreme Court ruling in 1884 came in the case *Elk v. Wilkins*, available online at http://supreme.justia.com/cases/federal/ us/112/94/case.html, accessed Feb. 15, 2013. See also Robert F. Berkhofer, Jr., *The White Man's Indian: Images of the American Indian from Columbus to the Present* (Vintage, 1978), 176–77; and Alan Trachtenberg, *Shades of Hiawatha: Staging Indians, Making Americans, 1880–1930* (Hill and Wang, 2004), 124, 213.

31. Henry Knox to George Washington, July 7, 1789, http://www.pbs.org/george washington/collection/pres_1789jul7.html, and for the comments to the American Indians of Ohio, http://www.shelbycountyhistory.org/schs/indians/coljohnhardin.htm, both accessed Dec. 3, 2011. See also Reginald Horsman, *Race and Manifest Destiny: The Origins of American Racial Anglo-Saxonism* (Harvard University Press, 1981), 107.

32. William G. McLoughlin, *Cherokee Renascence in the New Republic* (Princeton University Press, 1992), 37. Jefferson's views on women and the civilizing of Indians are explored in Brian Steele, "Thomas Jefferson's Gender Frontier," *Journal of American History* 95, no. 1 (June 2008): 17–42.

33. Bernard W. Sheehan, *Seeds of Extinction: Jeffersonian Philanthropy and the American Indian* (Norton, 1973), 174.

34. Berkhofer, *White Man's Indian*, 149–51. The Civilization Fund Act can be found in the *U.S. Statutes at Large*, 3:516–17, available online at http://www.digitalhistory.uh .edu/native_voices/voices_display.cfm?id=45, accessed Dec. 3, 2011. The government used most of the money to subsidize missionary societies dedicated to establishing schools and providing Indians with instruction in agricultural and domestic arts. As Bernard Sheehan wryly observes, "authorities in the state governments, especially

Georgia, Alabama, and Mississippi, failed to appreciate the attractions of Jeffersonian philanthropy" (Sheehan, *Seeds of Extinction,* 243). The Northwest Ordinance of 1787 included the following article: "Religion, morality, and knowledge, being necessary to good government and the happiness of mankind, schools and the means of education shall forever be encouraged. The utmost good faith shall always be observed towards the Indians; their lands and property shall never be taken from them without their consent; and, in their property, rights, and liberty, they shall never be invaded or disturbed, unless in just and lawful wars authorized by Congress; but laws founded in justice and humanity, shall from time to time be made for preventing wrongs being done to them, and for preserving peace and friendship with them" (http://www.early america.com/earlyamerica/milestones/ordinance/text.html, accessed Dec. 3, 2011). For the Sheehan quotation, see his *Seeds of Extinction,* 268. On the difficulty in restraining the settlers see Horsman, *Race and Manifest Destiny,* 114, 193–95.

35. Berkhofer, *White Man's Indian,* 157–58; Philip J. Deloria, *Playing Indian* (Yale University Press, 1998), 103–104. Thomas Jefferson, in 1803, had been the first public figure to propose that Indians be given territory across the Mississippi in return for title to their lands in the East.

36. Horsman, *Race and Manifest Destiny,* 196; Deloria, *Playing Indian,* 103–104. Lancaster schools were grammar schools organized along lines established by the English Quaker reformer Joseph Lancaster. The other four tribes were the Chickasaw, Choctaw, Creek, and Seminole. Fay Yarborough deals with racial attitudes among the Cherokee before the Civil War in *Race and the Cherokee Nation: Sovereignty in the Nineteenth Century* (University of Pennsylvania Press, 2008), chaps. 1–3.

37. The Indian Removal Act is detailed at http://memory.loc.gov/cgi-bin/ampage?coll Id=llsl&fileName=004/llsl004.db&recNum=458, and Jackson's activities are described at http://www.tngenweb.org/cessions/jackson.html, both accessed Dec. 3, 2011. For a good, concise history, see Theda Perdue and Michael Green, *The Cherokee Nation and the Trail of Tears* (Penguin, 2008). The other "civilized tribes" were also forced to relocate across the Mississippi.

38. The population of both Montana and Idaho doubled, the population of both Nebraska and Washington tripled, the population of both Arizona and Colorado quadrupled. By 1880 white settlers outnumbered Indians in Dakota Territory by more than six to one. See Frederick E. Hoxie, *A Final Promise: The Campaign to Assimilate the Indians, 1880–1920* (Cambridge University Press, 1989), 43. In 1871 Washington ceased to recognize Indian tribes as independent nations and began to treat them rather as "wards of the state." In practical terms, this meant that rights and responsibilities on both sides were now determined not by treaties but by congressional legislation and by agents working for the Bureau of Indian Affairs (see Berkhofer, *White Man's Indian,* 171). The federal government continued to have commissioners negotiate with tribal leaders, but the documents they produced were called "agreements," not treaties.

39. Dee Brown, *Bury My Heart at Wounded Knee: An Indian History of the American West* (Henry Holt, 1970), 189.

40. The Morgan quotation is from Horsman, *Race and Manifest Destiny*, 206–207. Michael Rogin has argued that destruction of the Indians "symbolized the American experience. The conquest of the Indians made the country uniquely American." See Rogin, *Fathers and Children: Andrew Jackson and the Subjugation of the American Indian* (Knopf, 1975), 7.

41. Berkhofer, *White Man's Indian*, 168–69. The first Indian reservations established by the federal government were in California, in 1853.

42. Hoxie, *Final Promise*, 42. For the quotation by Morgan, see http://www.alaskool .org/native_ed/historicdocs/use_of_english/prucha.htm, accessed Dec. 3, 2011. See also Berkhofer, *White Man's Indian*, 172.

43. For Morgan's comments, see the online version of Francis Paul Prucha, ed., *Documents of United States Indian Policy* (Lincoln: University of Nebraska Press, 1990), at http://www.alaskool.org/native_ed/historicdocs/use_of_english/prucha.htm, accessed Dec. 3, 2011.

44. Hoxie, *Final Promise*, 53–54.

45. For the full quotation by Pratt, see the online resource "History Matters," at http://historymatters.gmu.edu/d/4929, accessed Dec. 3, 2011.

46. Ibid.

47. By 1900, fully 10 percent of Native American children had been placed in 307 schools based on the Carlisle model. See King, "Making Americans," 155–56. For analysis of Pratt's comments, see Berkhofer, *White Man's Indian*, 171–72. Writes Alan Trachtenberg, "Horatio Alger was proffered as the model for survival. Native children in off-reservation boarding schools would be taught 'character'; like Ragged Dick they would climb or fall by their own efforts. They would learn this new way of thinking, this need to look out for themselves, by the hard knocks of the street and the market" (Trachtenberg, *Shades of Hiawatha*, 39). See also Hoxie, *Final Promise*, 95, 209.

48. Berkhofer, *White Man's Indian*, 174.

49. For the text of the Dawes Act, see http://public.csusm.edu/nadp/a1887.htm, accessed Dec. 3, 2011. For the quotation by Deloria, see his *Playing Indian*, 104.

50. On the Dawes Act's goal of promoting nuclear families and breaking down traditional clan and tribal loyalties, see King, "Making Americans," 154. Frederick Hoxie also notes: "Despite the power it exerted over Indian-white relations for nearly half a century, the Dawes Act was little more than a statement of intent. It contained no timetables and few instructions as to how it would be implemented. At its core, the law was an assertion that the gap between the two races would be overcome and that Indians would be incorporated into American society." It is worth noting that the Dawes Act resulted in far less land loss for Native Americans than seven major cessions arranged between 1880 and 1895 (Hoxie, *Final Promise*, 77, 44—and for the phrase "a campaign

to integrate native resources into the American economy," p. 187). For more on how the lands changed ownership, see Berkhofer, *White Man's Indian*, 175.

51. To view the Reorganization Act in its entirety, see http://www.cskt.org/gov/docs/ reorganizationact.pdf, accessed Dec. 3, 2011. After passage of the act, Indians recovered over two million acres. For the quotation, see Hoxie, *A Final Promise*, 142.

52. Deloria, *Playing Indian*, 103–104, 64.

53. Berkhofer, *White Man's Indian*, 88; Geo. Catlin, *Illustrations of the Manners, Customs, and Condition of the North American Indians: With Letters and Notes Written during Eight Years of Travel and Adventure among the Wildest and Most Remarkable Tribes Now Existing* (Henry G. Bohn, 1850), 260.

54. Trachtenberg, *Shades of Hiawatha*, xxiii, 264; Deloria, *Playing Indian*, 90.

55. For the letters of Franklin Lane, see http://www.fullbooks.com/The-Letters-of -Franklin-K-Lane5.html, accessed Dec. 3, 2011.

56. Orlando Patterson, *Freedom*, vol. 1: *Freedom in the Making of Western Culture* (Basic Books, 1991), xiii. Notes Morgan with irony, "The Virginia assembly voted in 1780 to reward its soldiers in the fight for freedom with a bounty of 300 acres of land *and* a slave." See Edmund S. Morgan, *American Slavery, American Freedom: The Ordeal of Colonial Virginia* (Norton, 1975), 376, 385. Slavery served to underwrite freedom in another way as well. As Sir Augustus John, an English diplomat posted to the United States during the Jefferson administration, observed, Virginians "can profess an unbounded love of liberty and of democracy in consequence of the mass of the people, who in other countries might become mobs, being there nearly altogether composed of their own Negro slaves" (quoted in John Ashworth, *Slavery, Capitalism, and Politics in the Antebellum Republic*, vol. 1: *Commerce and Compromise, 1820–1850* [Cambridge University Press, 1996], 32).

57. Writes Edmund Morgan, "Racism made it possible for white Virginians to develop a devotion to the equality that English republicans had declared to be the soul of liberty" (Morgan, *American Slavery, American Freedom*, 386). In a stand-up routine he performed in the 1960s, the comedian Dick Gregory complained that Thomas Jefferson "forgot to write 'for whites only'" on the Declaration of Independence. See the cut entitled "Black Rioters" on disc 2 of the CD set produced by Collectables: *Dick Gregory: The Light Side: The Dark Side*. In a short story by Charles Johnson set during the Revolution, "A Soldier for the Crown," one slave takes hope from the preamble to the Declaration of Independence, with its promise of natural rights to "all men." To which his friend replies, "Alex, those are just *words*. White folks' words for other white folks" (Charles Johnson, *Soulcatcher and Other Stories* [Harvest Original, 1998], 37). The distinguished mathematician (and sometime science fiction writer) Chandler Davis once quipped to me that Francis Scott Key should have written "Oh say, does that star-spangled banner yet wave / O'er the land of the free, not to mention the slave?"

58. Among the works exploring how racial ideology was used to win broad support

for slavery among nonslaveholding white Southerners are J. Mills Thornton III, *Politics and Power in a Slave Society: Alabama, 1800–1860* (Louisiana State University Press, 1978); Lacy K. Ford, *Origins of Southern Radicalism: The South Carolina Upcountry, 1800–1860* (Oxford University Press, 1991); J. William Harris, *Plain Folk and Gentry in a Slave Society: White Liberty and Black Slavery in Augusta's Hinterlands* (Louisiana State University Press, 1998). For the quotations, see the speech at http://www.pbs.org/wgbh/aia/part4/4h3439t.html, accessed Dec. 3, 2011.

59. For a survey of the discriminatory legislation against Northern blacks, see Leon F. Litwack, *North of Slavery: The Negro in the Free States, 1790–1860* (University of Chicago Press, 1965). David Roediger comments, "The existence of slavery (and increasingly of open Northern campaigns to degrade free Blacks) gave working Americans both a wretched touchstone against which to measure their fears of unfreedom and a friendly reminder that they were by comparison not so badly off" (Roediger, *Wages of Whiteness*, 13, 49). Leonard L. Richards looks at anti-abolition activity in the North in *"Gentlemen of Property and Standing": Anti-Abolition Mobs in Jacksonian America* (Oxford University Press, 1971).

60. Ralph Ellison, *Shadow and Act* (Random House, 1964), 116. The comment comes from an article that Ellison originally published in the *New Leader* in Dec. 1963.

61. James R. Grossman, *Land of Hope: Chicago, Black Southerners, and the Great Migration* (University of Chicago Press, 1989), 3–4; Ngai, *Impossible Subjects*, 251. To cite just one example, between 1910 and 1920 the black population of Detroit grew over 600 percent.

62. For Washington's speech, see http://web.cn.edu/kstooksbury/atlanta_exposition_address.htm, accessed July 15, 2013. In the view of Wilson Jeremiah Moses, "This was Washington's tour de force, his suggestion that Protestant English speaking blacks were culturally superior to non-American whites" (Moses, *The Golden Age of Black Nationalism, 1850–1925* [Oxford University Press, 1988], 98). See also Matthew Pratt Guterl, *The Color of Race in America, 1900–1940* (Harvard University Press, 2001), 108; Grossman, *Land of Hope*, 171; 325, fn. 24. The phrase in the *Defender* was also used by Archibald J. Carey, influential minister of the African Methodist Episcopal Church.

63. W. E. B. Du Bois wrote with disgust in "The Souls of White Folks" that "America trains her immigrants to this despising of 'niggers' from the day of their landing" (http://www.gutenberg.org/files/15210/15210-h/15210-h.htm#Chapter_II, accessed Dec. 3, 2011). Note James Barrett and David Roediger, "Most [immigrants in the late nineteenth and early twentieth centuries] did not arrive with conventional United States attitudes regarding 'racial' difference, let alone its significance and implications in the context of industrial America. Yet most, it seems, [in the words of an elderly Italian American] 'got caught up in . . . this racial thing'" (Barrett and Roediger, "Inbetween Peoples," 3). For the quotations in this paragraph, see Randall Kennedy, *Nigger: The Strange Career of a Troublesome Word* (Vintage, 2003), 14; Arnold R. Hirsch, *Making the*

Second Ghetto: Race and Housing in Chicago, 1940–1960 (University of Cambridge Press, 1983), 80; and Roediger, *Wages of Whiteness*, 136.

64. On the role of immigrant communities in the creation and perpetuation of black ghettoes, see, for example, Gilbert Osofsky, *Harlem: The Making of a Ghetto* (Harper, 1963); Thomas L. Philpott, *The Slum and the Ghetto: Neighborhood Deterioration and Middle Class Reform, Chicago, 1880–1930* (Oxford University Press, 1978); Kenneth L. Kusmer, *A Ghetto Takes Shape: Black Cleveland, 1870–1930* (University of Illinois Press, 1976); Hirsch, *Making the Second Ghetto;* John T. McGreevy, *Parish Boundaries: The Catholic Encounter with Race in the Twentieth-Century Urban North* (University of Chicago Press, 1996); Thomas J. Sugrue, *The Origins of the Urban Crisis: Race and Inequality in Postwar Detroit* (Princeton University Press, 1996). For the Langston Hughes quotation, see his *The Big Sea* (Hill and Wang, 1940), 33. On Chicago's week of rioting, see William J. Tuttle, *Race Riot: Chicago in the Red Summer of 1919* (University of Illinois Press, 1970); also Chicago Commission on Race Relations, *The Negro in Chicago: A Study of Race Relations and a Race Riot* (University of Chicago Press, 1922).

65. Quoted in Hirsch, *Making the Second Ghetto*, 78–81.

66. Quoted in Sugrue, *Origins of the Urban Crisis*, 79, 212. See also Russell A. Kazal, *Becoming Old Stock: The Paradox of German-American Identity* (Princeton University Press, 2004), 269.

67. Foley, *The White Scourge*, 11, 41, 209. Mexican American and white farmers joined together in many locals of the Socialist Renters' Union and Land League.

68. The quotation is from Alba and Nee, *Remaking the American Mainstream*. See also James W. Loewen, *The Mississippi Chinese: Between Black and White* (Harvard University Press, 1971), chaps. 3 and 4.

69. See Kurashige, *The Shifting Grounds of Race*, 20, 41. The article in the *Times* appeared in Feb. 1907.

70. Ibid., 62; Gunnar Myrdal, *An American Dilemma: The Negro Problem and Modern Democracy*, vol. 1 (Harper Torchbooks, 1962), 54.

71. On the early colonial practice of treating Africans and Indians as a single social entity, see, for example, Peter Wallenstein, *Tell the Court I Love My Wife: Race, Marriage, and Law—An American History* (Palgrave Macmillan, 2002), 14–15. For the quotation by Gerstle, see his *American Crucible*, 22.

72. Lothrop Stoddard, *The Rising Tide of Color against White World-Supremacy* (Charles Scribner's Sons, 1921), 126–27; Trachtenberg, *Shades of Hiawatha*, xxiv. On p. 26 Trachtenberg also writes: "In the South, the claim of bloodline descent from Pocahontas or other Indian princess was a matter of pride and status, while any sign of African descent could be fatal."

73. On the Oklahoma experience, see Murray R. Wickett, *Contested Territory: Whites, Native Americans and African Americans in Oklahoma, 1865–1907* (Louisiana State University Press, 2000), 196. "In the South," notes Matthew Jacobson, "anyone not legally

black was regarded as white for the purposes of segregation law" (Jacobson, *Whiteness of a Different Color*, 187). A white Baptist minister from Clarksdale told James Loewen, who had come to Mississippi in the 1960s to do research for his Harvard doctoral dissertation on the experiences of Chinese immigrants and their descendants, "You're either a white man or nigger, here. Now, that's the whole story" (quoted in James W. Loewen, *Mississippi Chinese*, frontispiece). The union president is quoted in Tuttle, *Race Riot*, 142. For the quotation by Senator Inouye, see Richard J. Stillman II, *Integration of the Negro in the U.S. Armed Forces* (Praeger, 1968), 31. It particularly galled black soldiers that German prisoners of war were allowed to eat in restaurants legally off limits to Negroes.

74. Bernard Bailyn deals with the philosophical underpinnings of Revolutionary thought in *The Ideological Origins of the American Revolution* (Harvard University Press, 1967). Ivan Hannaford traces the development of racial thinking in *Race: The History of an Idea in the West* (Johns Hopkins University Press, 1996). See also George M. Fredrickson, *Racism: A Short History* (Princeton University Press, 2002), chap. 1. Nikhil Pal Singh's quotation is from his *Black Is a Country: Race and the Unfinished Struggle for Democracy* (Harvard University Press, 2004), 22.

3. THE NEGRO, "INCARNATION OF AMERICA"

1. The quotation by Clay can be found in James T. Campbell, *Middle Passages: African American Journeys to Africa, 1787–2005* (Penguin, 2006), 44. The American Colonization Society evolved into an institution designed to ensure the security of slavery in the South by siphoning off Negroes who were free. For an overview of the ACS, see Eric Burin, *Slavery and the Peculiar Solution: A History of the American Colonization Society* (University Press of Florida, 2005).

2. For the response of Negroes in Philadelphia, see Scott J. Hammond, Kevin R. Hardwick, and Howard L. Lubert, eds., *Classics of American Political and Constitutional Thought: Origins through the Civil War* (Hackett, 2007), 951–53.

3. J. Forten and Russel Perrott, "An Address to the Humane and Benevolent Inhabitants of the City and County of Philadelphia" (http://www.blackpast.org/?q=1817-j -forten-russel-perrott-address-humane-and-benevolent-inhabitants-city-and-county -philadelphia, accessed Dec. 4, 2011). In a fictional recreation of the meeting, the author Charles Johnson has all the black leaders arguing forcefully for leaving America for Africa only to be repudiated by those in attendance. See Johnson, *Soulcatcher and Other Stories* (Harvest Original, 1998), 67–73. See also Mia Bay, *The White Image in the Black Mind: African-American Ideas about White People, 1830–1925* (Oxford University Press, 2000), 22–23. At a meeting in Richmond, representatives of the free black population declared that, while they were willing to consider emigration, "we prefer being colonized in the most remote corner of the land of our nativity, to being exiled in a foreign country." They asked for land on the Missouri River. See James Brewer Stewart, *Holy*

Warriors: The Abolitionists and American Slavery (Hill and Wang, 1976), 30; also http://www.pbs.org/wgbh/aia/part3/3h484t.html, accessed Dec. 4, 2011.

4. Campbell, *Middle Passages*, 20, 28–29.

5. J. Douglas Deal, *Race and Class in Colonial Virginia: Indians, Englishmen, and Africans on the Eastern Shore during the Seventeenth Century* (Garland, 1993), 378. The Watkins quotation can be found in Mary Frances Berry and John W. Blassingame, *Long Memory: The Black Experience in America* (Oxford University Press, 1982), 299.

6. Even some slaves resisted opportunities to go to Liberia, usually because of a desire to remain with family and friends. See Burin, *Slavery and the Peculiar Institution,* chap. 3. For the complete text of David Walker's appeal, see Walker, *Walker's Appeal, in Four Articles; Together with a Preamble, to the Coloured Citizens of the World, but in Particular, and Very Expressly, to Those of the United States of America, Written in Boston, State of Massachusetts, September 28, 1829* (David Walker, 1830), 73, available online at http://docsouth.unc.edu/nc/walker/walker.html, accessed Dec. 4, 2011. For a biography of Walker, see Peter P. Hinks, *To Awaken My Afflicted Brethren: David Walker and the Problem of Antebellum Slave Resistance* (Pennsylvania State University Press, 1997). The quotation from Leonard I. Sweet is from his *Black Images of America, 1784–1870* (Norton, 1976), 40. The sermon by Peter Williams comes from Albert J. Raboteau, *Canaan Land: A Religious History of African Americans* (Oxford University Press, 2001), 27.

7. Campbell, *Middle Passages*, 63–64. See also Sterling Stuckey, *Slave Culture: Nationalist Theory and the Foundations of Black America* (Oxford University Press, 1987), chap. 4. Fear among free Negroes that they would be compelled to emigrate was strengthened when Andrew Jackson oversaw the forced removal of the Cherokees. See Bay, *The White Image in the Black Mind,* 23.

8. On Negroes and the American Colonization Society, see Burin, *Slavery and the Peculiar Institution,* 30. For the observation by James H. Meriwether, see his *Proudly We Can Be Africans: Black Americans and Africa, 1935–1961* (University of North Carolina Press, 2002), 13. The letter from Frederick Douglass to Harriet Beecher Stowe can be found in Frederick Douglass, *The Life and Times of Frederick Douglass, Written by Himself* (Park, 1882), 355, and at http://www.teachingamericanhistory.org/library/index.asp?document=771 (accessed Mar. 1, 2013).

9. Robert S. Levine, ed., *Martin R. Delany: A Documentary Reader* (University of North Carolina Press, 2003), 482–83.

10. At the National Emigration Convention of Colored Men, held in Cleveland in 1854, Delany argued for emigration to Central and South America or the Caribbean. See ibid., 2, 245–79. Tommie Shelby explores what he sees as Delany's "pragmatic" black nationalism in *We Who Are Dark: The Philosophical Foundations of Black Solidarity* (Harvard University Press, 2005), chap. 1. For the quotation by James Campbell, see his *Middle Passages,* 90. See also Wilson Jeremiah Moses, *Afrotopia: The Roots of African American Popular History* (Cambridge University Press, 1998), 123–24.

11. Campbell, *Middle Passages*, 104, 109–110, 123. Turner took four trips to Africa but never settled there himself; see Robin D. G. Kelley, *Freedom Dreams: The Black Radical Imagination* (Beacon, 2002), 21. James Meriwether notes, "Although Crummell later in life shifted away from strongly advocating emigration, he nevertheless continued to support the need for black Americans to help redeem Africans from heathenism and barbarism" (Meriwether, *Proudly We Can Be Africans*, 13). See also Wilson Jeremiah Moses, *Alexander Crummell: A Study of Civilization and Discontent* (Oxford University Press, 1989). Garnet lobbied to have himself appointed minister to Liberia as he was dying. His wish was granted. He landed in Monrovia on Dec. 28, 1881, and died on Feb. 12, 1882. According to Crummell, Garnet said, "Please the Lord I can only safely cross the ocean, land on the coast of Africa, look around upon its green fields, tread the soil of my ancestors, live if but a few weeks; then I shall be glad to lie down and be buried beneath its sod" (see http://www.africawithin.com/bios/henry_garnet.htm, accessed Dec. 4, 2011). The quoted passage about Crummell is from Waldo E. Martin, Jr., *The Mind of Frederick Douglass* (University of North Carolina Press, 1984), 211–12. For an older study of emigration see Edwin S. Redkey, *Black Exodus: Black Nationalist and Back-to-Africa Movements, 1890–1910* (Yale University Press, 1969).

12. On the lack of support among Negroes for colonization, see Martin, *The Mind of Frederick Douglass*, 210; Meriwether, *Proudly We Can Be Africans*, 23; and Eric Foner, *The Fiery Trial: Abraham Lincoln and American Slavery* (Norton, 2010), 19. Steven Hahn does identify a surge in interest in colonization during Reconstruction, however. See his *A Nation under Our Feet: Black Political Struggles in the Rural South from Slavery to the Great Migration* (Harvard University Press, 2003), chap. 7. The remarks by Douglass can be found at http://www.teachingamericanhistory.org/library/index.asp?document =1034, accessed Mar. 1, 2013. See also William S. McFeely, *Frederick Douglass* (Norton, 1991), 377–80.

13. Like Turner and Delany, Douglass sought the cultural antecedents of black Americans in ancient Egypt, not sub-Saharan Africa. See Martin, *The Mind of Frederick Douglass*, 203, 208; Moses, *Afrotopia*, 80, 85; Kelley, *Freedom Dreams*, 21–23; and Campbell, *Middle Passages*, 110–11. Unlike most advocates of emigration, Edward Wilmot Blyden advocated adopting elements of traditional African culture.

14. Booker T. Washington, *Up from Slavery* (Doubleday, Page, 1901); Robert J. Norrell, *Up from History: The Life of Booker T. Washington* (Harvard University Press, 2009), 86. For the comment by Louis R. Harlan, see his *Booker T. Washington: The Making of a Black Leader, 1856–1901* (Oxford University Press, 1972), 253. At least one commentator referred to Washington as the Benjamin Franklin of his race. See Wilson Jeremiah Moses, *Creative Conflict in African American Thought* (Cambridge University Press, 2004), 155.

15. Louis R. Harlan, *Booker T. Washington: The Wizard of Tuskegee, 1901–1915* (Oxford University Press, 1983), 244–51; Moses, *Creative Conflict*, 164, 148; Robert Park,

quoted in Norrell, *Up from History*, 373–74. Park and Washington published their findings in *The Man Farthest Down* (Doubleday, Page, 1912). Park worked at Tuskegee with Washington for almost a decade in the early twentieth century. Later he moved to the University of Chicago where he produced influential works on race relations and urban sociology.

16. Quoted in Cary D. Wintz, ed., *African American Political Thought, 1890–1930: Washington, Du Bois, Garvey, and Randolph* (M. E. Sharpe, 1996), 171. Washington responded to Garvey, Louis Harlan notes, with "vague encouragement" (Harlan, *Wizard*, 280). See also Moses, *Creative Conflict*, 163.

17. See, for example, the "Exchange on Black Nationalism" between Theodore Draper and Eric Foner in the *New York Review of Books* 15, no. 10 (Dec. 3, 1970). The quotation from Garvey is from Marcus Garvey, *The Philosophy and Opinions of Marcus Garvey; or, Africa for the Africans,* compiled by Amy Jacques Garvey (Frank Cass, 1967), pt. 1, 10.

18. Harlan, *Wizard*, 266–77, quotation on p. 275. See also Moses, *Creative Conflict*, 163; and Louis R. Harlan, Raymond W. Smock, and Geraldine McTigue, *The Booker T. Washington Papers*, vol. 11 (University of Illinois Press, 1981), 72–73. Andrew Zimmerman, in his *Alabama in Africa: Booker T. Washington, the German Empire, and the Globalization of the New South* (Princeton University Press, 2012) tells the story of an expedition from Washington's Tuskegee Institute to the German colony of Togo in 1901.

19. Garvey, *Philosophy and Opinions of Marcus Garvey*, pt. 2, 136–37; E. David Cronon, *Black Moses: The Story of Marcus Garvey and the Universal Negro Improvement Association* (University of Wisconsin Press, 1960), 183–85. The Sherrill quotation is from Judith Stein, *The World of Marcus Garvey: Race and Class in Modern Society* (Louisiana State University Press, 1986), 109; the Garvey quotation can be seen on p. 37. "We do not want all the Negroes in Africa," Garvey said in 1924. "Some are no good here and naturally will be no good there." On Marcus Garvey's influence in the American South, see Mary H. Rolinson, *Grassroots Garveyism: The Universal Negro Improvement Association in the Rural South, 1920–1927* (University of North Carolina Press, 2007).

20. The quoted passage from the Declaration is from Garvey, *Philosophy and Opinions of Marcus Garvey*, pt. 2, 136–37. The quotation from the Peace Conference can be seen in Wintz, *African American Political Thought*, 188.

21. Garvey, *Philosophy and Opinions of Marcus Garvey*, pt. 2, 72, 67–68; Shelby, *We Who Are Dark*, 75. Garvey did favor limitations on the amount of capital that individuals and corporations could possess.

22. For Du Bois's criticism of Washington, see especially W. E. B. Du Bois, *The Souls of Black Folk* (Norton, 1999), chap. 3. The "vicious attack" is from *The Crisis*, May 1924, and quoted in Wintz, *African American Political Thought*, 129. Garvey was equally scathing in his personal attacks on Du Bois. He wrote in *The Negro World*, Jan. 1, 1921: "As we study the personality of Du Bois, we find that he only appreciates one type of men, and that is the cultured, refined type which lingers around universities and attends

pink tea affairs. The men of dynamic force of the Negro race, the men with ability to sway and move the masses, Dr. Du Bois cannot appraise their face value, and that is why the author of 'The Souls of Black Folk,' while the idol of the drawing room aristocrats, could not thus far become the popular leader of the masses of his own race." And on Feb. 13, 1923: "It is no wonder that Du Bois seeks the company of white people, because he hates Black as being ugly. . . . Yet this professor, who sees ugliness in being Black, essays to be a leader of the Negro people and has been trying for over fourteen years to deceive them in connection with the National Association for the Advancement of Colored People. Now what does he mean by advancing Colored people if he hates Black so much? In what direction must we expect his advancement? We can conclude in no other way that it is in the direction of losing our Black identity and becoming, as nearly as possible, the lowest Whites by assimilation and miscegenation" (http://afgen.com/garvey_dubois.html, accessed Dec. 4, 2011). Judith Stein's observation is from *The World of Marcus Garvey*, 216. The kind words Du Bois had for Washington can be found in *Souls of Black Folk*, 45; and for Garvey in *The Crisis*, Feb. 1928 (quoting an article from Jan. 1921), see David Levering Lewis, ed., *W. E. B. Du Bois: A Reader* (Henry Holt, 1995), 343.

23. Du Bois wrote: "Since the death of the leaders of the past there have come mighty changes in the nation. The gospel of money has risen triumphant in church and state and university. The great question which Americans ask today is, 'What is he worth?' or 'What is it worth?' The ideals of human rights are obscured, and the nation has begun to swagger about the world in its useless battleships looking for helpless peoples whom it can force to buy its goods at high prices. The wave of materialism is temporary; it will pass and leave us all ashamed and surprised; but while it is here it strangely maddens and blinds us" (in *World Today*, Apr. 26, 1904). And writing in *The Crisis*, July 1921: "The American Federation of Labor, as representing the trade unions in America, has been grossly unfair and discriminatory toward Negroes and still is. American Socialism has discriminated against black folk and before the war was prepared to go further with this discrimination." A month earlier Du Bois wrote, "The NAACP has been accused of not being a 'revolutionary' body. This is quite true. We do not believe in revolution. We expect revolutionary changes in many parts of this life and this world, but we expect these changes to come mainly through reason, human sympathy, and the education of children, and not by murder." The passages cited here and in the text can be found in Lewis, *W. E. B. Du Bois*, 329, 555, 533.

24. From *The Crisis*, June 1921, reprinted in Lewis, *W. E. B. Du Bois*, 555. Black culture too, he suggested, would be the salvation of America. That is how best to understand his famous identification of the "double-consciousness," the "two-ness" experienced by Negroes: "an American; a Negro; two souls, two thoughts, two unreconciled strivings; two warring ideals in one dark body, whose dogged strength alone keeps it from being torn asunder." Do not be misled by the phrase "warring ideals." His point

was not (at least not when he first coined the phrase "double-consciousness") that American and black identities stood somehow in opposition. Quite the contrary, he contended that black culture would be the ultimate fulfillment of American destiny: "There are today no truer exponents of the pure human spirit of the Declaration of Independence than the American Negroes; there is no true American music but the wild sweet melodies of the Negro slave; the American fairy tales and folklore are Indian and African; and, all in all, we black men seem the sole oasis of simple faith and reverence in a dusty desert of dollars and smartness. Will America be poorer if she replace [sic] her brutal, dyspeptic blundering with lighthearted but determined Negro humility? or her coarse and cruel wit with loving jovial good-humor? or her vulgar music with the soul of the Sorrow Songs? Merely a concrete test of the underlying principles of the great republic is the Negro Problem, and the spiritual striving of the freedmen's sons is the travail of souls whose burden is almost beyond the measure of their strength, but who bear it in the name of an historic race, in the name of this the land of their fathers' fathers, and in the name of human opportunity." His ideas on black double-consciousness appeared first in an essay entitled "Strivings of the Negro People," published in the *Atlantic Monthly*, 1897. See Wintz, *African American Political Thought*, 86–87.

25. Shelby, *We Who Are Dark*, 67.

26. Matthew Guterl sees the publication of Du Bois's novel *Dark Princess* in 1928 as marking a symbolic break for him with his earlier faith in "pluralism, civilization, and white folks." See Matthew Pratt Guterl, *The Color of Race in America, 1900–1940* (Harvard University Press, 2001), 145. For the story of Du Bois's life after World War I, see David Levering Lewis, *W. E. B. Du Bois, 1919–1963: The Fight for Equality and the American Century* (Henry Holt, 2001). Harvard Sitkoff's comments are from his *A New Deal for Blacks: The Emergence of Civil Rights as a National Issue: The Depression Decade*, 30th anniversary ed. (Oxford University Press, 2009), 26–27. For the quotation by Hill, see *New York Times*, Apr. 5, 1931.

27. Robin D. G. Kelley, *Freedom Dreams*, 45. Harrison joined the Socialist Party in 1911 but was expelled in 1914. His career and contribution to black thought are explored in Jeffrey B. Perry, *Hubert Harrison: The Voice of Harlem Radicalism, 1883–1918* (Columbia University Press, 2008). See also Kevin K. Gaines, *Uplifting the Race: Black Leadership, Politics, and Culture in the Twentieth Century* (University of North Carolina Press, 1996), chap. 9. Randolph's career is examined in Paula F. Pfeffer, *A. Philip Randolph, Pioneer of the Civil Rights Movement* (Louisiana State University Press, 1996) and Jervis Anderson, *A. Philip Randolph: A Biographical Portrait* (University of California Press, 1986).

28. The quotations in the text are from Sitkoff, *A New Deal for Blacks*, 106–107. Eugene Debs asserted, "We have nothing special to offer the Negro"—see Nikhil Pal Singh, *Black Is a Country: Race and the Unfinished Struggle for Democracy* (Harvard University Press, 2004), 27. It was only in 1933 that the Socialist Party explicitly began to

address the problems of racial discrimination. As for the African Blood Brotherhood, its militancy, Judith Stein notes, "was vocal but floated above popular issues in a vain search for a constituency" (Stein, *World of Marcus Garvey*, 141). James Ford, black vice-presidential candidate for the Communist Party in 1932, observed that prior to that year, the party was "completely isolated from the basic masses of the Negro people" (quoted in Sitkoff, *A New Deal for Blacks*, 109). See also Rick Halpern, *Down on the Killing Floor: Black and White Workers in Chicago's Packinghouses, 1904–54* (University of Illinois Press, 1997), 108.

29. The authoritative account of the trial and its aftermath is Dan T. Carter, *Scottsboro: A Tragedy of the American South*, rev. ed. (Louisiana State University Press, 2007). See also "A Trial Account" by Douglas Linder at http://www.law.umkc.edu/faculty/projects/Ftrials/scottsboro/scottsb.htm, accessed Mar. 1, 2013; James A. Miller, *Remembering Scottsboro: The Legacy of an Infamous Trial* (Princeton University Press, 2009); and James Goodman, *Stories of Scottsboro* (Vintage, 1995).

30. Mark Naison, *Communists in Harlem during the Depression* (University of Illinois Press, 1983), chap. 3. The quotation about the communists in Chicago is from St. Clair Drake and Horace G. Cayton, *Black Metropolis: A Study of Negro Life in a Northern City* (University of Chicago Press, 1993), 86–87. See also Earl Lewis, *In Their Own Interests: Race, Class, and Power in Twentieth-Century Norfolk, Virginia* (University of California Press, 1991), 129–30; Halpern, *Down on the Killing Floor*, 108–109. The black press, not having the financial resources to send reporters to Scottsboro, relied heavily on communists for their information; see Sitkoff, *A New Deal for Blacks*, 111. The quotation by Hudson is from Nell Irvin Painter, *The Narrative of Hosea Hudson: His Life as a Negro Communist in the South* (Harvard University Press, 1979), 100. The quotation by Robert Black is from Robert Rodgers Korstad, *Civil Rights Unionism: Tobacco Workers and the Struggle for Democracy in the Mid-Twentieth-Century South* (University of North Carolina Press, 2003), 125–26.

31. The *Chicago Defender* excerpt can be seen in Halpern, *Down on the Killing Floor*, 109. The *Oklahoma Black Dispatch* quote comes from Sitkoff, *A New Deal for Blacks*, 117. The description of the event in Harlem where Ellington played is in Earl Ofari Hutchinson, *Blacks and Reds: Race and Class in Conflict, 1919–1990* (Michigan State University Press, 1995), 70. See also Robin D. G. Kelley, *Hammer and Hoe: Alabama Communists during the Great Depression* (University of North Carolina Press, 1990), 119–22; Sitkoff, *A New Deal for Blacks*, 113–14. The best-known instance of Communists and liberals working together came when the ILD and the NAACP cooperated on the second appeal to the Supreme Court involving the Scottsboro Boys.

32. The quotation is from Naison, *Communists in Harlem*, 279–83. Notes Mark Naison, "Very few Harlemites participated in the general social and cultural life of the Communist movement—its May Day marches, fraternal organizations, summer camps—except when those institutions emphasized racial themes, and the emancipatory vision

of socialism seems to have touched black intellectuals far more than it did black workers." Richard Wright describes his growing disillusionment with the Communist Party in his *American Hunger* (Harper & Row, 1977). Indeed, many black intellectuals who joined the party in the 1930s came to have doubts about its understanding of the distinctive aspects of the black experience and black culture. On the exaggerated membership numbers and high turnover, see Hutchinson, *Blacks and Reds*, 71; Painter, *Hosea Hudson*, 18–20. On black votes for Roosevelt, see Nancy J. Weiss, *Farewell to the Party of Lincoln: Black Politics in the Age of FDR* (Princeton University Press, 1983), 205–207, 286–88, 233–34. The percentage vote for Roosevelt in 1932 was Harlem, 51 percent; Pittsburgh, 41 percent; Philadelphia, 28 percent; Detroit, 31 percent. In Knoxville, Roosevelt's vote rose from 30 percent in 1932 to 56 percent in 1936. Communists hesitated to attack Roosevelt during the 1936 campaign because of his popularity with the black community. Robin Kelley points out that when Roosevelt was in office, support for the Communist Party in Alabama declined (Kelley, *Hammer and Hoe*, 132).

33. Sitkoff, *A New Deal for Blacks*, 59–62. See also Weiss, *Farewell to the Party of Lincoln*, chap. 7.

34. Weiss, *Farewell to the Party of Lincoln*, 299, also chap. 10.

35. Sitkoff, *New Deal for Blacks*, 57, 249, 53, 54.

36. Ibid., 36–43. Writes Earl Ofari Hutchinson, "Franklin Delano Roosevelt would be well into his second term as president before blacks saw any appreciable change in their plight" (Hutchinson, *Blacks and Reds*, 59).

37. Sitkoff, *New Deal for Blacks*, 53, 246–47. In the South, discrimination against Negroes remained widespread under the WPA. See, for example, Kelley, *Hammer and Hoe*, 152–58.

38. Walter White, *A Man Called White: The Autobiography of Walter White* (Viking, 1948), 169–70. See also Weiss, *Farewell to the Party of Lincoln*, chap. 5, 240–49. Under pressure from his wife, Roosevelt did once give a radio address at which he condemned lynch law as "murder." This was in late 1933 at a conference of the Federated Council of Churches and followed the lynching of two white men in San Jose, California.

39. Weiss, *Farewell to the Party of Lincoln*, 217–20. Two star players in the National Football League during the 1950s and 1960s were Roosevelt Brown, an offensive lineman for the New York Giants, and Roosevelt Grier, a defensive lineman for the Los Angeles Rams.

40. Quoted in Weiss, *Farewell to the Party of Lincoln*, 298.

41. Robin D. G. Kelley, *Race Rebels: Culture, Politics, and the Black Working Class* (Free Press, 1994), chap. 5; Hutchinson, *Blacks and Reds*, 97–98. The *Daily Worker*, improbably enough, designated Ford the "Frederick Douglass of 1936."

42. Theodore Kornweibel, Jr., "Apathy and Dissent: Black America's Negative Responses to World War I," *South Atlantic Quarterly* 80, no. 3 (Summer 1981): 332; Anderson, *A. Philip Randolph*, 106. Randolph and Chandler Owen, co-publishers of the

socialist journal *The Messenger,* were convicted of violating the Espionage Act for publishing an article entitled "Pro-Germanism among Negroes." They were sentenced to two and a half years in jail, but the judge released them, apparently assuming that, being Negroes themselves, they were not smart enough to write the article or understand it. After Randolph organized the march on Washington, Roosevelt, to avoid what he saw as the potentially disruptive consequences of a protest by black Americans in the nation's capital, issued Executive Order 8802 banning discrimination in the federal government and in private companies that held defense contracts, and creating the Fair Employment Practices Committee to monitor hiring and treatment of laborers. The standard account of the March on Washington Movement is Herbert Garfinkel, *When Negroes March: The March on Washington Movement in the Organizational Politics for FEPC* (Free Press, 1959).

43. On the history of black military service, see Jack D. Foner, *Blacks and the Military in American History: A New Perspective* (Praeger, 1974); Bernard C. Nalty, *Strength for the Fight: A History of Black Americans in the Military* (Free Press, 1989); Gerald Astor, *The Right to Fight: A History of African Americans in the Military* (Da Capo, 2001); Gail Lumet Buckley, *American Patriots: The Story of Blacks in the Military from the Revolution to Desert Storm* (Random House, 2002). Black soldiers took part in a total of perhaps 450 battles during the Civil War, of which almost forty were major engagements. Among the works that deal with their experiences are Benjamin Quarles, *The Negro in the Civil War* (Da Capo, 1989); Noah Andre Trudeau, *Like Men of War* (Castle, 2002); Dudley Cornish, *The Sable Arm: Black Troops in the Union Army, 1861–1865* (University of Kansas Press, 1987); and Joseph T. Glatthaar, *Forged in Battle: The Civil War Alliance of Black Soldiers and White Officers* (Free Press, 1990). The Philadelphia address appeared in *Frederick Douglass' Monthly,* Mar. 2, 1863, and is quoted in Frederic May Holland, *Frederick Douglass: The Colored Orator* (Funk & Wagnalls, 1895), 300–301, available online at http://docsouth.unc.edu/neh/holland/holland.html, accessed Dec. 4, 2011.

44. Ida B. Wells worked actively to help mobilize a unit in Illinois: "All of us were anxious that they should have the opportunity of helping to furnish a part of the national guard of the state. I went to Springfield with my children and stayed with the regiment until finally it was mustered into the service, and I saw them entrain for Cuba" (*Crusade for Justice: Autobiography of Ida B. Wells* [University of Chicago Press, 1970], 254). See also Glenda Elizabeth Gilmore, *Gender and Jim Crow: Women and the Politics of White Supremacy in North Carolina, 1896–1920* (University of North Carolina Press, 1996), 63, 78–82. In addition to the four black regular army regiments that had been posted across the Mississippi and had considerable combat experience through their service in the Indian Wars, as many as ten thousand black men volunteered. For the quoted editorial, see Berry and Blassingame, *Long Memory,* 305–307. See also Gary Gerstle, *American Crucible: Race and Nation in the Twentieth Century* (Princeton University Press, 2001), 33; Anthony Powell, "An Overview: Black Participation in the Spanish-American

War," available online at http://www.spanamwar.com/AfroAmericans.htm, accessed Dec. 4, 2011. The 24th Infantry played a major role in the charge up San Juan Hill. Many black families displayed prints of the military operation on the walls of their homes. The quotations by Washington are in Foner, *Blacks and the Military*, 73; Berry and Blassingame, *Long Memory*, 305; and Norrell, *Up from History*, 138, respectively.

45. Quoted in Ethel Waters with Charles Samuels, *His Eye Is on the Sparrow* (Da Capo Press, 1992), 122. James Weldon Johnson told the following anecdote: "One coloured [*sic*] man came into a Harlem barber-shop where a spirited discussion of the war was going on. When asked if he wasn't going to join the Army and fight the Germans, he replied amidst roars of laughter: 'The Germans ain't done nothin' to me, and if they have, I forgive 'em.'" Horace Cayton recalled many years later, "I wasn't against the war, nor was I very bitter about the many injustices dealt out to Negro soldiers. It seems to me I felt much as all Negroes felt: this was their war, and since they weren't willing to accept us as civilians, then let them fight it. It was something that didn't concern Negroes. It was a white-folks' war." See Theodore Kornweibel, Jr., "Apathy and Dissent: Black America's Negative Responses to World War I," *South Atlantic Quarterly* 80, no. 3 (Summer 1981): 324–25. It is worth noting that Cayton recorded his reflections many years after the war.

46. Works arguing that Negroes supported the war effort include Arthur E. Barbeau and Florette Henri, *The Unknown Soldiers: African-American Troops in World War I* (Da Capo, 1996), chap. 1; Foner, *Blacks and the Military*, 109–12; John Hope Franklin, Jr. and Alfred A. Moss, Jr., *From Slavery to Freedom: A History of African Americans*, 7th ed. (McGraw-Hill, 1994), chap. 16; Richard M. Dalfiume, *Desegregation of the U.S. Armed Forces: Fighting on Two Fronts* (University of Missouri Press, 1969), 8–10. For a contrary view, see Kornweibel, "Apathy and Dissent." Some Negroes went north to Canada and enlisted in the Canadian Army. The quotation from the Kansas editor was printed in *The Crisis* (June 1918): 68. The material from Ida Wells is from *Crusade for Justice*, 368. For more on black support for the war effort, see Joe William Trotter, Jr., *The African American Experience* (Houghton Mifflin, 2001), 375; and William J. Tuttle, *Race Riot: Chicago in the Red Summer of 1919* (University of Illinois Press, 1970), 219. According to Mary B. Talbert, president of the National Association of Colored Women, black women alone bought more than $5 million worth of bonds in the third (of five) Liberty Loan drives. Black insurance companies were major purchasers of bonds. North Carolina Mutual Life, for instance, acquired $300,000 worth in less than two years.

47. The story of the East St. Louis riot is told in Harper Barnes, *Never Been a Time: The 1917 Race Riot That Sparked the Civil Rights Movement* (Walker & Co., 2008). For the Ida B. Wells quotation, see *Crusade for Justice*, 383–84; see also Wintz, *African American Political Thought*, 116. Du Bois's editorial ran in July 1918. The controversy surrounding the editorial, which included the charge that Du Bois had written it in return for a captain's commission in the army, is described in David Levering Lewis, *W. E. B. Du*

Bois: Biography of a Race, 1868–1919 (Henry Holt, 1993), 555–60. See also Chad L. Williams, *Torchbearers of Democracy: African American Soldiers and the Era of the First World War* (University of North Carolina Press, 2010), 74–77.

48. *The Crisis* 14, no. 2 (June 1917): 58.

49. Wilson Jeremiah Moses, *The Golden Age of Black Nationalism* (Oxford University Press, 1988), 246–47; Dalfiume, *Desegregation of the U.S. Armed Forces*, 8–9; Foner, *Blacks and the Military*, 109. The Central Committee of Negro College Men report is available in full at www.archives.gov.on.ca/en/explore/online/dan_hill/papers/big_001_military.aspx, accessed July 16, 2013.

50. On the violence, see Grif Stockley, *Blood in their Eyes: The Elaine Massacres of 1919* (University of Arkansas Press, 2004). James Weldon Johnson's quotation is from *Along This Way: The Autobiography of James Weldon Johnson* (Da Capo, 2000), 341.

51. Dalfiume, *Desegregation of the U.S. Armed Forces*, 108. The Schuyler and *Crisis* quotations can be found in Azza Salama Layton, *International Politics and Civil Rights Policies in the United States, 1941–1960* (Cambridge University Press, 2000), 39. Another black columnist claimed that the war was a blessing because now the whites could "mow one another down" (see Phillip McGuire, *Taps for a Jim Crow Army: Letters from Black Soldiers in World War II* [ABC-Clio, 1983], xxvii). The quotation about hoping the Japanese will "dish out" comes from Gerstle, *American Crucible*, 190. After Pearl Harbor, one black sharecropper told his landlord, the Japanese "done declared war on you white folks" (quoted in Trotter, *African American Experience*, 491).

52. The *California Eagle* quotation is from Scott Kurashige, *The Shifting Grounds of Race: Black and Japanese Americans in the Making of Multiethnic Los Angeles* (Princeton University Press, 2008), 102–103; *The Crisis* excerpt appears in Patrick S. Washburn, *The African American Newspaper: Voice of Freedom* (Northwestern University Press, 2006), 147.

53. Quoted in Gerstle, *American Crucible*, 211–12. According to Benjamin Quarles, black men volunteered for induction "in record numbers" (see his foreword in McGuire, *Taps for a Jim Crow Army*, xxix). In Los Angeles, army officials felt it necessary to issue a statement to the black press, "IT IS ABSOLUTELY UNTRUE THAT WE ARE RECRUITING NEGROES INTO THE REGULAR ARMY" (see Kurashige, *Shifting Grounds of Race*, 134).

54. Gerstle, *American Crucible*, 213; Trotter, *African American Experience*, 493, 514. Neil A. Wynn's comment is from his book *The Afro-American and the Second World War*, rev. ed. (Holmes & Meier, 1993), 103.

55. Trotter, *African American Experience*, 514. Although the U.S. Treasury did not track purchases according to race or ethnicity, according to Gerstle, *American Crucible*, 198 (and 194): "Impressionistic evidence suggests that groups with the greatest stake in the war's outcome—Jews, Poles, and African Americans, for example—purchased the most bonds." Many Negroes signed up for plans at the companies where they worked to allow regular amounts to be deducted from their wages for the purchase of

bonds (see Franklin and Moss, *From Slavery to Freedom,* 450). Perhaps no black leader spoke with more patriotic fervor than Mary McLeod Bethune, who stated: "No blood more red, nor more loyal penetrates the veins of mankind; America can depend on us. I know that at a time like this, every Negro man, woman and child will stand straight up without reservations to his responsibility to his country" (quoted in Berry and Blassingame, *Long Memory,* 320).

56. *The Crisis* is quoted in Washburn, *African American Newspaper,* 147. On discrimination in the military, see McGuire, *Taps for a Jim Crow Army;* Foner, *Blacks and the Military,* chap. 7; and Dalfiume, *Desegregation of the U.S. Armed Forces,* chaps. 3 and 4. The most notable wartime racial violence was in Detroit. See, for example, Thomas J. Sugrue, *The Origins of the Urban Crisis: Race and Inequality in Postwar Detroit* (Princeton University Press, 1996), chap. 2. The editorial in *Opportunity* is cited in Garfinkel, *When Negroes March,* 27. Some Negroes chose to resist induction. Yet, as Lester Granger of the Urban League commented, "The quest of the Negro for full partnership in the war is an expression of his desire to assume full citizenship responsibilities" (quoted in Wynn, *The Afro-American and the Second World War,* 25–26, 101). See also Drake and Cayton, *Black Metropolis,* 748.

57. Pat Washburn, "The Pittsburgh Courier's Double-V Campaign in 1942," paper presented at the Annual Meeting of the Association for Education in Journalism" (Lansing, Mich., Aug. 1981), 3, available online at http://www.eric.ed.gov/PDFS/ED205956.pdf, accessed Dec. 4, 2011.

58. Ibid. In June the paper hired the cafeteria worker who had inspired the Double V initiative, James G. Thompson, to run the Double V campaign (Washburn, *The African American Newspaper,* 152). The editorial from the *New York Age* can be found in Berry and Blassingame, *Long Memory,* 321. A conservative faction within the black population argued that Negroes should not agitate for integration during the war, but its members were decidedly unrepresentative of popular opinion (see McGuire, *Taps for a Jim Crow Army,* xl–xli). Wynn, *The Afro-American and the Second World War,* 100–101, and Dalfiume, *Desegregation of the U.S. Armed Forces,* 126, note the widespread support for the war in the black population.

59. Gerstle, *American Crucible,* 211.

60. Gunnar Myrdal, *An American Dilemma: The Negro Problem and Modern Democracy,* vol. 1 (Harper & Row, 1962), 4; Sweet, *Black Images of America,* 147; Waldo E. Martin, Jr., *No Coward Soldiers: Black Cultural Politics in Postwar America* (Harvard University Press, 2005), 36.

61. On the "special appreciation of the freedom dear to republicans," see Edmund S. Morgan, *American Slavery, American Freedom: The Ordeal of Colonial Virginia* (Norton, 1975), 376. The quotation from the escaped slave can be found in Benjamin Drew, *A North-Side View of Slavery: The Refugee; or, The Narratives of Fugitive Slaves in Canada. Related by Themselves, with an Account of the History and Condition of the Colored Popula-*

tion of Upper Canada (John P. Jewett and Company, 1856), 43. Writes Wilson Jeremiah Moses, "Reductionist critics have derided black American adherence to the Protestant ethic as a thoughtless aping of Anglo-American bourgeois values, designed to curry favor with the dominant race. Nothing is so simple. Nationalists and militant separatists have been among the most vocal advocates of the Calvinistic approach to racial uplift. The emphasis that black perfectionists placed on personal character had very little to do with the idea of making one's self acceptable to whites" (Moses, *Afrotopia*, 146).

62. Paul Bohannan and Philip Curtin have pointed out that "the median date for the arrival of America's African ancestors—the date by which half had arrived and half were still to come—is remarkably early, about 1780. The similar median date for the arrival of our European ancestors was remarkably late—about the 1890s" (Bohannan and Curtin, *Africa and Africans*, 4th ed. [Prospect Heights, Illinois: Waveland Press, 1995]), 13. Gary Younge has observed, "Bar a handful of pilgrims and the Native American Indians, African-Americans are the ethnic group with the longest, geographical attachment to the US. Unlike other racial minorities in the west, they are not relatively recent immigrants. So, in times of national crisis, they rally around their flag in a way that those of Arab descent in France, say, or of Caribbean descent in Britain could not imagine" (Younge, "Different Class," *The Guardian*, Nov. 23, 2002). The quotation regarding the public housing disagreement is from John T. McGreevy, *Parish Boundaries: The Catholic Encounter with Race in the Twentieth-Century Urban North* (University of Chicago Press, 1996), 77; James Baldwin's words are from his *The Fire Next Time* (Vintage International, 1991), 98.

63. Quoted in Wintz, *African American Political Thought*, 49. It is noteworthy that Washington confines his vision of Americans to "the white and black man." Clearly he shared the perception of Asians and Hispanic Americans as "alien citizens" and Native Americans as a vanishing people.

64. W. E. B. Du Bois, *The Gift of Black Folk: The Negroes in the Making of America* (Square One, 2009), 57.

65. Quoted in Sondra Kathryn Wilson, ed., *In Search of Democracy: The NAACP Writings of James Weldon Johnson, Walter White, and Roy Wilkins (1920–1977)* (Oxford University Press, 1999), 116.

66. Quoted in Wilson, *In Search of Democracy*, 399.

67. Quoted in Wintz, *African American Political Thought*, 310.

4 · COLOR AND CLASS

1. Consistency was lacking about who was a "mulatto." Instructions to census enumerators in 1850 and 1860 did not define the term. In 1870 and 1880, mulattoes were to include "quadroons, octoroons, and all persons having any perceptible trace of African

blood." In 1890 enumerators were instructed: "Be particularly careful to distinguish between blacks, mulattoes, quadroons, and octoroons. The word 'black' should be used to describe those persons who have three-fourths or more black blood; 'mulatto,' those persons who have from three-eighths to five-eighths black blood; 'quadroon,' those persons who have one-fourth black blood; and 'octoroon,' those persons who have one-eighth or any trace of black blood." In 1910 the U.S. Census Bureau distinguished "full blooded Negroes" from "mulattoes," who were defined as "all other persons having some proportion or perceptible trace of negro blood." The census for 1900 made no provision for listing "mulattoes." That year enumerators were told simply to mark a "'B" for black "(negro or negro descent)." Instructions to enumerators for every census between 1790 and 2010 can be found at http://www.census.gov/history/www/through _the_decades/census_instructions/1930_instructions.html, accessed Sept. 30, 2013. Jennifer L. Hochschild and Brenna M. Powell examine changing racial categories in the federal census in "Racial Reorganization and the United States Census 1850–1930: Mulattoes, Half-Breeds, Mixed Parentage, Hindoos, and the Mexican Race," available online at http://scholar.harvard.edu/jlhochschild/publications/racial-reorganization -and-united-states-census-1850–1930-mulattoes-half-br, accessed Apr. 24, 2013. Individual states followed a similar path. From 1785 until 1910, a "mulatto" in Virginia was defined as a person with at least "one-fourth part or more of negro blood." In 1910, the state legislature defined a "colored person" as anyone with at least one-sixteenth black blood. In 1924 it categorized a "white person" as someone with "no trace whatsoever" of black blood. Six years later a "colored" person was determined to be someone "in whom there is ascertainable any negro blood." See Trina Jones, "Shades of Brown: The Law of Skin Color," *Duke Law Journal* 49, no. 6 (Apr. 2000): 1512–13. The remark from the man in South Carolina can be found in Martha Hodes, *White Women, Black Men: Illicit Sex in the Nineteenth Century South* (Yale University Press, 1997), 199. According to Joel Williamson, the one-drop rule was effectively in place by 1915 (Williamson, *New People: Miscegenation and Mulattoes in the United States* [Free Press, 1980], 108). See also James F. Davis, *Who Is Black? One Nation's Definition* (Pennsylvania State University Press, 1991), chap. 4. In "The Devil and the One-Drop Rule: Racial Categories, African Americans, and the U.S. Census," *Michigan Law Review* 95, no. 5 (Mar. 1997): 1161–1265, Christine B. Hickman argues that the one-drop rule has served to unify Americans of African descent.

2. Charles H. Parrish, "Color Names and Color Notions," *Journal of Negro Education* 15, no. 1 (Winter 1946): 13–20. See also Kathy Russell, Midge Wilson, and Ronald Hall, *The Color Complex: The Politics of Skin Color among African Americans* (Anchor, 1993), 66. Katheryn B. Davis, Maurice Daniels, and Letha A. (Lee) See, "The Psychological Effects of Skin Color on African Americans' Self-Esteem," *Journal of Human Behavior in the Social Environment* 1, nos. 2, 3 (June 1998): 63–90 includes a table partly adapted from Parrish's findings. The historian Lawrence Levine has found reference to the fol-

lowing shades in black secular songs during the first decades of the twentieth century: "deep black, ashy black, pale black, dead black, chocolate-brown, coffee, sealskin-brown, deep brown, dark brown, reddish brown, deep yella brown, chocolate, high-brown, low-brown, velvet brown, bronze, gingerbread, fair light brown, tan, olive, copper, pink, banana, cream, brightskin, high yaller, lemon." See Levine, *Black Culture and Black Consciousness: Afro-American Folk Thought from Slavery to Freedom* (Oxford University Press, 1977), 285–86.

3. Walter Johnson, *Soul by Soul: Life inside the Antebellum Slave Market* (Harvard University Press, 1999), 139.

4. Ibid., 150–51. As Johnson also notes, extremely light-skinned men were regarded with suspicion. Reports by planters to the police about runaway slaves provide further evidence of a deep sensitivity to subtle distinctions in skin color. See Joshua D. Rothman, *Notorious in the Neighborhood: Sex and Families across the Color Line in Virginia, 1787–1861* (University of North Carolina Press, 2003), 204. Not all, or even most, members of the elite were willing to risk the domestic upheaval likely to follow public acknowledgment that they had fathered slave children. Mary Chesnut famously wrote in her diary, "Like the patriarchs of old our men live all in one house with their wives and their concubines, and the mulattoes one sees in every family exactly resemble the white children—every lady tells you who is the father of all the mulatto children in everybody's household, but those in her own she seems to think drop from the clouds, or pretends so to think" (C. Vann Woodward, ed., *Mary Chesnut's Civil War* [Yale University Press, 1993], 29). Some planters did acknowledge their slave offspring, however. "In the Last Will I made I left to you, over & above my other children Sally Johnson the mother of Louisa & all the children of both," wrote a wealthy slaveholder to his son shortly before the Civil War. "Sally says Henderson is my child. It is probable, but I do not believe it. Yet act on her's [*sic*] rather than my opinion. Louisa's first child *may* be mine. I think not. Her second I believe is mine. Take care of her other children who are both of *your* blood and not of mine & of Henderson. The services of the rest will I think compensate for indulgence to these. I cannot free these people & send them North. It would be cruelty to them. Nor would I like that any but my own blood should own as [slaves] my own blood or Louisa. I leave them to your charge, believing that you will best appreciate & most independently carry out my wishes in regard to them. Do not let Louisa or any of my children or probable children be the Slaves of Strangers. Slavery *in the family* will be their happiest earthly condition" (Williamson, *New People*, 55–56).

5. See Eugene Genovese, *Roll, Jordan, Roll: The World the Slaves Made* (Pantheon, 1974) 328–365 and 388–98 for discussion of the circumstances of house servants and artisans, respectively. On the fact that on some plantations skilled trades and house servant positions were kept within certain slave families, see Johnson, *Soul by Soul*, 150, and Douglas R. Egerton, *Gabriel's Rebellion: The Virginia Slave Conspiracies of 1800 and 1802* (University of North Carolina Press, 1993), 21.

6. Certainly there were domestic servants who did not enjoy notable privileges. Eugene Genovese notes, "Those who might have formed an elite status group on the plantations constituted only a small minority of the total number of house slaves. Five percent of the total of adult slaves or 20 percent of the total number of house slaves would seem the highest reasonable estimate, although the figure would have to be much higher for the South Carolina and Georgia low country, the Natchez district, and a few pockets here and there" (Genovese, *Roll, Jordan, Roll*, 328–29). The William Wells Brown excerpts are from his *Clotel; or, The President's Daughter* (Dover, 2004), 57, 59. Asked by a WPA interviewer in the 1930s about life on the plantation where she had lived as a slave more than seventy years earlier, Rosa Starke replied, "Dere was just two classes to de white folks—buckra slave owners and poor white folks dat didn't own no slaves. Dere was more classes 'mongst de slaves. De fust class was de house servants. Dese was de butler, de maids, de nurses, chambermaids, and de cooks. De nex' class was de carriage drivers and de gardeners, de carpenters, de barber and de stable men. Then come the nex' class, de wheelwright, wagoners, blacksmiths and slave foremen. De nex' class I 'members is de cow men and de niggers dat have care of de dogs. All dese have good houses and never have to work hard or git a beatin'. Then come the cradlers of the wheat, de threshers, and de millers of de corn and de wheat, and de feeders of de cotton gin. De lowest class was de common field niggers." From James Mellon, ed., *Bullwhip Days: The Slaves Remember; an Oral History* (Grove Press, 2002), 136.

7. Regarding holidays on the plantations, see Roger Abrahams's examination of the corn-shucking festival in his *Singing the Master: The Emergence of African American Culture in the Plantation South* (Pantheon, 1992). See also Genovese, *Roll, Jordan, Roll*, 332–41. Michael Wayne, *Death of an Overseer: Reopening a Murder Investigation from the Plantation South* (Oxford University Press, 2001) recounts the story of a murder on an estate near Natchez, Mississippi, carried out in 1857 by a carriage driver, carpenter, and field hand apparently acting with the approval, and on behalf, of the entire slave force.

8. Ira Berlin, *Slaves without Masters: The Free Negro in the Antebellum South* (Oxford University Press, 1974), 138–43; Michael P. Johnson and James L. Roark, *Black Masters: A Free Family of Color in the Old South* (Norton, 1984), 31–33. An influential work from an earlier period is John Hope Franklin, *The Free Negro in North Carolina, 1790–1860* (University of North Carolina Press, 1943).

9. The free Negroes of the Upper South were concentrated in the tidewater between Delaware and North Carolina. Free black women in the towns had a particularly difficult existence, the victims of "wretched poverty and persistent discrimination"—see Suzanne Lebsock, *The Free Women of Petersburg: Status and Culture in a Southern Town, 1784–1860* (Norton, 1984), 90. See also Berlin, *Slaves without Masters*, chaps. 7 and 10; and Johnson and Roark, *Black Masters*, 33.

10. See Loren Schweninger, *Black Property Owners in the South, 1790–1915* (Univer-

sity of Illinois Press, 1997); Johnson and Roark, *Black Masters*, 61–62; 192–94; Berlin, *Slaves without Masters*, 263–64; and Brenda E. Stevenson, *Life in Black and White: Family and Community in the Slave South* (Oxford University Press, 1996), 270–72. A legislative commission appointed to investigate the alleged Denmark Vesey–led insurrection in 1822 concluded that the mulatto elite were "a barrier between our own color and that of the black—and, in cases of insurrection, are more likely to enlist themselves under the banners of the whites. . . . Most of them are industrious, sober, hardworking mechanics, who have large families and considerable property; and so far as we are acquainted with their temper, and dispositions of their feelings, abhor the idea of association with the blacks in any enterprise that may have for its object the revolution of their condition. It must be recollected also, that the greater part of them own slaves, and are, therefore so far interested in this species of property as to keep them on the watch, and induce them to disclose any plans that may be injurious to our peace—experience justifies this conclusion" (Jones, "Shades of Brown," 1508–1509).

11. Cyprian Clamorgan, *The Colored Aristocracy of St. Louis*, ed. Julie Winch (University of Missouri Press, 1999), 45–47, 49. Commenting on the complexion of the "colored aristocracy," Clamorgan wrote: "Many of them are separated from the white race by a line of division so faint that it can be traced only by the keen eye of prejudice—a line so dim indeed that, in many instances that might be named, the stream of African blood has been so diluted that the most critical observer can not detect it."

12. The census of 1830 listed 3,775 Negro slaveholders. Leonard P. Curry, *The Free Black in Urban America, 1800–1850: The Shadow of the Dream* (University of Chicago Press, 1981), appendix C includes statistics on black slaveowners in New Orleans, Charleston, Baltimore, Washington, and Louisville. See also Larry Koger, *Black Slaveowners: Free Black Slave Masters in South Carolina, 1790–1860* (University of South Carolina Press, 1995). Louisiana was the state with the single largest number of slaveholders, a product of its distinctive background as a Spanish and French colony. For a valuable study of one community of Louisiana mulatto planters, see Gary B. Mills, *The Forgotten People: Cane River's Creoles of Color* (Louisiana State University Press, 1977). On Ellison, see Johnson and Roark, *Black Masters*, 132–35. On Durnford, see David O. Whitten, *Andrew Durnford: A Black Sugar Planter in the Antebellum South* (Transaction, 1995), 64.

13. For the comments by Ira Berlin, see *Slaves without Masters*, 279. On William Johnson, see Edwin Adams Davis and William Ransom Hogan, *The Barber of Natchez* (Louisiana State University Press, 1973), and Davis and Hogan, *William Johnson's Natchez: The Ante-Bellum Diary of a Free Negro* (Louisiana State University Press, 1993). Olmsted concluded his observation: "There was no indication of their belonging to a subject race, except that they invariably gave the way to the white people they met." See Frederick Law Olmsted, *The Cotton Kingdom: A Traveller's Observations on Cotton and Slavery in the American Slave States* (Da Capo, 1996), 46–47.

14. Berlin, *Slaves without Masters*, 297–99, 312–13 (with the comment from the Baltimore minister appearing on p. 279); Stevenson, *Life in Black and White*, 316–17. For the quotation about the Friendly Moralist Society, see Johnson and Roark, *Black Masters*, 214. The Brown Fellowship Society, also of Charleston, was similarly exclusive.

15. Johnson and Roark, *Black Masters*, 212–13, 207. Barred from the Brown Fellowship Society and the Friendly Moralist Society, well-to-do free blacks in Charleston formed their own social club: The Humane Brotherhood. Membership was restricted to no more than thirty-five "respectable Free Dark Men." For the history of William Johnson, see Davis and Hogan, *William Johnson's Natchez*; for the quotation by Johnson, see Douglas Walter Bristol, *Knights of the Razor: Black Barbers in Slavery and Freedom* (The John Hopkins University Press, 2009), 85. The words of Durnford's son are documented in Whitten, *Andrew Durnford*, 111 (emphasis added).

16. The entire speech by Eggart can be viewed online at http://mulattodebate.forum chitchat.com/post/Michael-T.-Eggart-on-Mixed-People-5528890, accessed July 16, 2013. See also Johnson and Roark, *Black Masters*, 215–17, 26; Bernard E. Powers, Jr., *Black Charlestonians: A Social History, 1822–1885* (University of Arkansas Press, 1994), 58. The concept of privileged mulattoes as a middle caste was most fully developed in Louisiana and had a great deal to do with policies developed under the Spanish and French before the United States came into possession of the territory. See Virginia Dominguez, *White by Definition: Social Classification in Creole Louisiana* (Rutgers University Press, 1993).

17. The great majority of Negro men in the North did not get the vote until ratification of the Fifteenth Amendment in 1870. The history of Reconstruction is best told by Eric Foner in *Reconstruction: America's Unfinished Revolution, 1863–1877* (Harper Perennial Modern Classics, 2002). The consequences of enfranchising the freedmen have been a subject of intense debate among historians since Reconstruction came to an end more than 130 years ago. During the first decades of the twentieth century, the "Dunning school" argued that the freedmen were completely unprepared to have a political voice and became the pawns of Northern carpetbaggers and unscrupulous Southern whites—scalawags—who lined their own pockets while bankrupting the state governments. W. E. B. Du Bois challenged this interpretation in 1935 in his epic *Black Reconstruction in America, 1860–1880*, highlighting what he claimed were the many advances that had been made under the Reconstruction governments. Reconstruction, Du Bois famously claimed, was a "splendid failure." Because white supremacist assumptions were widespread in the historical profession prior to World War II, *Black Reconstruction* was largely ignored at the time of its publication. During the 1960s, however, Du Bois's scholarship was effectively resurrected, and it deeply influences the dominant studies of Reconstruction today. The crippling debt problems experienced during the period—and they were very real—were not a product of corruption underwritten by black voters, but largely of the desperate and ultimately hopeless attempt by

the Republican leadership in the South to attract *white* voters by subsidizing costly development schemes. See, for example, Mark W. Summers, *Railroads, Reconstruction, and the Gospel of Prosperity: Aid under the Radical Republicans, 1865–1877* (Princeton University Press, 1984). A small number of slaves—mostly urban artisans, mostly mulattoes—had acquired literacy before the war and were also favorably situated to gain office. The best analysis of the political role played during Reconstruction by former slaves from the plantations and farms is Steven Hahn, *A Nation under Our Feet: Black Political Struggles in the Rural South from Slavery to the Great Migration* (Harvard University Press, 2003), pt. 2.

18. Thomas Holt, *Black over White: Negro Political Leadership in South Carolina during Reconstruction* (University of Illinois Press, 1977). Sixty percent of the population of South Carolina was black. Another valuable study is Joel Williamson, *After Slavery: The Negro in South Carolina during Reconstruction, 1861–1877* (University of North Carolina Press, 1965). For developments in the state directly to the south see Edmund L. Drago, *Black Politicians and Reconstruction in Georgia: A Splendid Failure* (University of Georgia Press, 1992). Eric Foner, *Freedom's Lawmakers: A Directory of Black Officeholders during Reconstruction* (Louisiana State University Press, 1996) is a directory of America's first generation of black public officials. It is worth noting that not all members of the antebellum free mulatto elite chose to support the Republican Party. See, for example, Johnson and Roark, *Black Masters,* 326–27. On the success of mulattoes winning Congressional seats, see Jennifer L. Hochschild and Vesla Weaver, "The Skin Color Paradox and the American Racial Order," *Social Forces* 86, no. 2 (Dec. 2007): 650.

19. Holt, *Black over White*, 59, 126, 143–44, 148–50, 160–62, 188–91. There is substantial evidence of tension between mulattoes and individuals of unmixed African ancestry during Reconstruction. In the campaign for the constitutional convention in 1868—this was the first occasion on which Negroes were able to vote—a mulatto candidate declared, "I never ought to have been a slave, for my father was a gentleman." He added, "If ever there is a nigger government—an unmixed nigger government—established in South Carolina, I shall move" (59).

20. Michael Perman, *Struggle for Mastery: Disfranchisement in the South, 1888–1908* (University of North Carolina Press, 2000); Murray Wickett, *Contested Territory: Whites, Native Americans, and African Americans in Oklahoma, 1865–1907* (Louisiana State University Press, 2000), chap. 7. R. Volney Riser tracks court cases in which Negroes fought disenfranchisement laws in the days before the emergence of the NAACP—see Riser, *Defying Disfranchisement: Black Voting Rights Activism in the Jim Crow South, 1890–1908* (Louisiana State University Press, 2010). Not incidentally, disenfranchisement also resulted in a significant proportion of poor whites losing the vote. The voice of black rural laborers had become increasingly insistent during Reconstruction. See Hahn, *A Nation under Our Feet*, chap. 5; C. Vann Woodward, *The Strange Career of Jim Crow* (Oxford University Press, 2001); Howard N. Rabinowitz, *Race Relations in the Urban South,*

1865–1890 (University of Georgia Press, 1996); and Wickett, *Contested Territory*, chap. 7. For the quotation by the Virginia spokesman, see Willard B. Gatewood, *Aristocrats of Color: The Black Elite, 1880–1920* (University of Arkansas Press, 2000), 192.

21. Karen Ferguson, *Black Politics in New Deal Atlanta* (University of North Carolina Press, 2002), 4. See also Adolph Reed, Jr., *Stirrings in the Jug: Black Politics in the Post-Segregation Era* (University of Minnesota Press, 1999), 20. Nor did this "group of literate spokespeople" include only men. As Glenda Gilmore has demonstrated, after disenfranchisement women among the elite formed a network of groups to promote the cause of black rights. "In a nonpolitical guise, black women became the black community's diplomats to the white community." From Glenda Elizabeth Gilmore, *Gender and Jim Crow: Women and the Politics of White Supremacy in North Carolina, 1896–1920* (University of North Carolina Press, 1996), 147–48. It is likely unnecessary to add that many working-class Negroes declined to recognize the elite as their legitimate spokesmen. See, for example, Earl Lewis, *In Their Own Interests: Race, Class, and Power in Twentieth-Century Norfolk, Virginia* (University of California Press, 1991).

22. The population statistics are from the U.S. Census Bureau; see http://www2 .census.gov/prod2/decennial/documents/1860a-15.pdf, accessed Dec. 5, 2011. On the circumstances of well-to-do Northern Negroes, see Leon F. Litwack, *North of Slavery: The Negro in the Free States, 1790–1860* (University of Chicago Press, 1961), 182, 186 (the source of the Grimké quotation); also Gatewood, *Aristocrats of Color*, 157. For an examination of how black character was understood by whites in both the South and the North, see George M. Fredrickson, *The Black Image in the White Mind: The Debate on Afro-American Character and Destiny, 1817–1914* (Harper and Row, 1971). Certain individuals of African descent acquired significant wealth. A listing of "some wealthy citizens of Philadelphia" in 1846 mentioned at least four, including the sailmaker James Forten and a lumber merchant, Stephen Smith, whose property was evaluated at $100,000 (Curry, *The Free Black in Urban America*, 42–43).

23. On the continuing sense of superiority among the old elite, see David M. Katzman, *Before the Ghetto: Black Detroit in the Nineteenth Century* (University of Illinois Press, 1973), 158–62; Kenneth L. Kusmer, *A Ghetto Takes Shape: Black Cleveland, 1870–1930* (University of Illinois Press, 1976), 98–99. Complained Nannie Burroughs, a dark-skinned educator, "Many Negroes have colorphobia as badly as the white folks have Negrophobia" (quoted in Gatewood, *Aristocrats of Color*, 158). Gatewood, Kusmer, and Katzman also provide evidence on the efforts of the elite to wall themselves off from other Negroes. See also Peter Gottlieb, *Making Their Own Way: Southern Blacks' Migration to Pittsburgh, 1916–30* (University of Illinois Press, 1987), 197–98; James Grossman, *Land of Hope: Chicago, Black Southerners, and the Great Migration* (University of Chicago Press, 1989), 128–30. Among the clubs that restricted membership along color as well as class lines were Cleveland's Caterers Club and Social Circle (renamed the Euchre Club in 1904); Chicago's Old Settler's Club, Appomattox Club, Prudence

Crandall Club, and Manasseh Society (which was restricted to men of African descent with white wives); and Detroit's Summer Club, Dumas Literary Society, and Oak and Ivy Club. For the words of Ray Stannard Baker, see his *Following the Color Line: An Account of Negro Citizenship in the American Democracy* (Doubleday, Page, 1908), 218. The comments of the man interviewed by John Daniels can be found in Daniels, *In Freedom's Birthplace: A Study of Boston Negroes* (Arno, 1969), 183. Like the mulatto elite of the South, the aristocrats of Cleveland referred to their social set as "our people."

24. Daniels, *In Freedom's Birthplace*, 182. See also Gatewood, *Aristocrats of Color*, 332.

25. There are many studies detailing the emergence of the ghetto. Classic works include Gilbert Osofsky, *Harlem: The Making of a Ghetto*, 2d ed. (Harper Torchbooks, 1971); Allan H. Spear, *Black Chicago: The Making of a Negro Ghetto, 1890–1920* (University of Chicago Press, 1967); and Kusmer, *A Ghetto Takes Shape*. The comments of Hall can be found in Grossman, *Land of Hope*, 131.

26. Grossman, *Land of Hope*, 129. See also Kusmer, *A Ghetto Takes Shape*, 76, 81, 103.

27. Important works dealing with the Great Migration include Grossman, *Land of Hope;* Gottlieb, *Making Their Own Way;* James N. Gregory, *The Southern Diaspora: How the Great Migrations of Black and White Southerners Transformed America* (University of North Carolina Press, 2007); Davarian L. Baldwin, *Chicago's New Negroes: Modernity, the Great Migration, and Black Urban Life* (University of North Carolina Press, 2007); and Isabel Wilkerson, *The Warmth of Other Suns: The Epic Story of America's Great Migration* (Random House, 2010). In Harlem, West Indian immigrants represented another group of newcomers with unfamiliar ways. See Osofsky, *Harlem*, 131–35; Joe William Trotter, Jr., "Blacks in the Urban North: The 'Underclass Question' in Historical Perspective," in Michael B. Katz, ed., *The Underclass Debate: Views from History* (Princeton University Press, 1993), 67; and Joe William Trotter, Jr., *River Jordan: African American Urban Life in the Ohio Valley* (University Press of Kentucky, 1998), 90. Anti-Southern sentiment among Negroes in the North traced back to well before the Civil War. When an English traveler arrived in Philadelphia in 1846, two porters greeted him and offered to carry his baggage. While one claimed he was "in de cheap line," the other retorted: "Cheap! neber mind him, Sa; he's only a nigga from Baltimore, just come to Philadelphy." He then continued: "I'se born here, Sa, and know de town like a book. Dat ere nigga not seen good society yet knows nuffin habn't got do polish on. Git out, nigga, and clean you self," at which he turned upon his heel, and laughed heartily "yhaw, yhaw, yhaw." Alex. Mackay, *The Western World; or, Travels in the United States in 1846–47*, 3d ed., vol. 1 (3 vols.; Richard Bentley, 1850), 133, available online at http://www .archive.org/stream/westernworldortro1mackrich/westernworldortro1mackrich_djvu. txt, accessed Dec. 5, 2011. The remark about migrants creeping along "like a disease" can be found in Grossman, *Land of Hope*, 139. Nor was sectional prejudice confined to the North. When Ethel Waters toured the South for the first time, she was "shocked to find out that [Southern] Negroes were prejudiced against those of their own people like

me who lived in the North." On the railways: "Those Southern Negroes, knowing I was from the North, would do everything to pressure me out of my seat, spitting and poking, elbowing and knocking my hat off." Ethel Waters with Charles Samuels, *His Eye Is on the Sparrow* (Da Capo, 1992), 92–94.

28. Wallace Thurman, *The Blacker the Berry* (Dover, 2008), 23.

29. Ralph Ellison, *Invisible Man* (Vintage International, 1990), 327–29. The narrator replies, with contempt: "That's enough out of you, you piece of yellow gone-to-waste."

30. Kusmer, *A Ghetto Takes Shape*, 253, 106–107. The *Chicago Defender*, which actively promoted the migration, nonetheless complained, "It is evident that some of the people coming to this city have seriously erred in their conduct in public places, much to the humiliation of all respectable classes of our citizens, and by so doing, on account of their ignorance of laws and customs necessary for the maintenance of health, sobriety and morality among our people in general, have given our enemies ground for complaint." The *Defender* quotation can be seen in Spear, *Black Chicago*, 168; the Urban League pamphlet information is from Grossman, *Land of Hope*, 150.

31. Kusmer, *A Ghetto Takes Shape*, 214–15; Osofsky, *Harlem*, 20; Williamson, *New People*, 129–30; E. Franklin Frazier, *The Negro Family in the United States* (University of Notre Dame Press, 2001), chap. 22. The Powell quotation is from Jervis Anderson, *This Was Harlem: A Cultural Portrait, 1900–1950* (Farrar, Straus and Giroux, 1982), 340. "Color tax" parties were a familiar feature of fraternities at prestigious black colleges such as Howard and Fisk—the darker your date, the higher the tax you had to pay.

32. St. Clair Drake and Horace R. Cayton, *Black Metropolis: A Study of Negro Life in a Northern City* (Harcourt, Brace, 1945), 500–501, 496. Billie Holiday reported in her autobiography that she encountered just such color prejudice when her mother began dating a man from "a very high-class family." His sisters "were very light-skinned and thought it was terrible he was taking up with Mom and me, because we were a shade or two darker" (Billie Holiday with William Dufty, *Lady Sings the Blues* [Penguin, 1992], 15). As it was, Holiday herself was sufficiently light-skinned that she was once asked by management at a club in Detroit to darken her skin before performing.

33. Gatewood, *Aristocrats of Color*, 192–95; Ferguson, *Black Politics in New Deal Atlanta*, 35. Noted Mary Church Terrell of the National Association of Colored Women, "It is unfortunate, but it is true, that the dominant race in this country insists upon gauging the Negro's worth by his most illiterate and vicious representatives rather than by the more intelligent and worthy classes. Colored women of education and culture know that they cannot escape altogether the consequences of the acts of their most depraved sisters. They see that even if they were wicked enough to turn a deaf ear to the call of duty, both policy and self-preservation demand that they go down among the lowly, the illiterate and even the vicious, to whom they are bound by the ties of race and sex, and put forth every possible effort to reclaim them" (http://womenshistory.about .com/library/etext/bl_mary_church_terrell_1902_essay.htm, accessed Dec. 5, 2011). Evelyn Higginbotham explores the role of the "talented tenth" of women in *Righteous*

Discontent: The Women's Movement in the Black Baptist Church, 1880–1920 (Harvard University Press, 1994).

34. Reverend H. H. Proctor, "The Need of Friendly Visitation," in W. E. B. Du Bois, ed., *Social and Physical Condition of Negroes in Cities*, Atlanta University Publications, no. 2 (Atlanta University Press, 1897), 44–45.

35. Crummell is quoted in Gatewood, *Aristocrats of Color*, 224–25. For the comments of Kevin K. Gaines, see his *Uplifting the Race: Black Leadership, Politics, and Culture in the Twentieth Century* (University of North Carolina Press, 1996), 2–3. See also Grossman, *Land of Hope*, 146; Gilmore, *Gender and Jim Crow*, 75; and Kusmer, *A Ghetto Takes Shape*, 106. The insights of Thomas J. Sugrue are from his *Sweet Land of Liberty: The Forgotten Struggle for Civil Rights in the North* (Random House, 2008), 9.

36. Thurman's observations are noted in *The Blacker the Berry*, 86. W. E. B. Du Bois found similar evidence of resentment in Philadelphia a decade later. See W. E. B. Du Bois, *The Philadelphia Negro: A Social Study* (University of Pennsylvania Press, 1996), 316–19. See also Katzman, *Before the Ghetto*, 162. The narrator in *Invisible Man* gives expression to the resulting disillusionment felt by so many members of the elite. Here he is commenting on his days as a university student in the South: "How all of us at the college hated the black-belt people, the 'peasants,' during those days! We were trying to lift them up and they . . . did everything it seemed to pull us down" (Ellison, *Invisible Man*, 47). Ethel Waters's recollections can be found in *His Eye Is on the Sparrow*, 4, 78, 93. Waters herself "always liked the ordinary working fellows." "Dictys and the others among my own people who despise Negroes who are poor and ignorant and condemned to live like animals arouse my fury as no white people ever can. We Negroes have lived through so much together—centuries of slavery, terror, segregation, and unending concentrated abuse—that I'll never understand how some of us who have one way or another been able to lift ourselves a little above the mass of colored people can be so insanely brutal as to try to knock the hell out of our own blood brothers and sisters." The term "dicty" or "dickty" gained currency during the 1920s. Its origin is unknown. Dick Gregory's comments are from his *Nigger* (Washington Square Press, 1964), 61.

37. For Chase, see Gatewood, *Aristocrats of Color*, 166–73. Bruce's life is examined in Ralph Crowder, *John Edward Bruce: Politician, Journalist, and Self-Trained Historian of the African Diaspora* (New York University Press, 2004). The elite were not infrequently the subject of ridicule in popular culture. "Colored aristocracy" was the name of a cakewalk dance performed in black minstrel shows in the late nineteenth century.

38. Waters, *His Eye Is on the Sparrow*, 196; James Baldwin's short story is in *Going to Meet the Man* (Vintage, 1993), 151.

39. The senator's quotation is from Holt, *Black over White*, 60. A Northern visitor to Charleston around the same period of time reported hearing a black field hand say of a light-colored urban Negro: "Dat whitewashed nigger am just like a mule. He ain't got no country and no ancestor." Williamson, *After Slavery*, 315. For Lena Horne's reflec-

tions, see Lena Horne and Richard Schickel, *Lena* (Doubleday, 1965), 31. For a recent, and highly critical, life of Horne see James Gavin, *Stormy Weather: The Life of Lena Horne* (Atria, 2009). Her daughter, Gail Lumet Buckley, looks back over six generations in *The Hornes: An American Family* (Applause, 2002). The remark by John Edward Bruce can be found in Crowder, *John Edward Bruce,* 15. Bruce also described the "aristocrats of color" as "neither fish, nor fowl, nor good red herring." They were, he said, just "hybrids." Gatewood, *Aristocrats of Color,* 164–65. Elaine Brown learned when she was in junior high school in the 1950s that although her mother was "low class," her biological father was Dr. Horace Scott, son of Emmett Scott, Booker T. Washington's successor at the Tuskegee Institute. He and his family, she has written, "were the kind of people who thought light-skinned blacks were 'trash,' as the obvious product of illicit relations with Caucasians" (Elaine Brown, *A Taste of Power: A Black Woman's Story* [Anchor, 1992], 50). The quotation from Drake and Cayton can be found in their *Black Metropolis,* 500. The remark by the "dark skinned boy" to Charles S. Johnson can be found at Charles S. Johnson, *Growing Up in the Black Belt: Negro Youth in the Rural South* (Washington: American Council on Education, 1941), 262.

40. Marcus Garvey, *The Philosophy and Opinions of Marcus Garvey; or, Africa for the Africans,* compiled by Amy Jacques Garvey (Frank Cass, 1967), 56, 29–30. Garvey's criticism was aimed particularly at W. E. B. Du Bois and the NAACP.

41. Linton's observations are documented in Williamson, *New People,* 118. In 1940, thirty-one states had laws prohibiting marriage across the color line but only six states barred interracial sex; see Renee C. Romano, *Race Mixing: Black-White Marriage in Postwar America* (Harvard University Press, 2003), 5. On the history of legislation prohibiting miscegenation, see Peggy Pascoe, *What Comes Naturally: Miscegenation Law and the Making of Race in America* (Oxford University Press, 2009); Peter Wallenstein, *Tell The Court I Love My Wife: Race, Marriage, and Law—An American History* (Palgrave Macmillan, 2002); and Werner Sollers, *Interracialism: Black-White Intermarriage in American History, Literature, and Law* (Oxford University Press, 2000), pt. 1. Ariela J. Gross, *What Blood Won't Tell: A History of Race on Trial in America* (Harvard University Press, 2008) examines, among other things, court cases concerning the one-drop rule. The European ancestry of twentieth-century mulattoes could be traced back, in the vast majority of cases, to sexual relations between indentured servants and slaves during the colonial period and to sexual exploitation of slaves by their owners (and by the friends and relatives of their owners) in the antebellum South.

42. For the review of *Shuffle Along,* see Matthew Pratt Guterl, *The Color of Race in America, 1900–1940* (Harvard University Press, 2001), 132; see also James Haskins et al., *Black Stars of the Harlem Renaissance* (John Wiley & Sons, 2002), 31. *Shuffle Along* had songs by the celebrated team of Noble Sissle and Eubie Blake and included performances by Josephine Baker and Paul Robeson. For Johnson's commentary, see "The Vanishing Mulatto," *Opportunity* 3, no. 34 (Oct. 1925): 291.

43. Etta James and David Ritz, *Rage to Survive: The Etta James Story* (Da Capo, 1998), 22.

44. Drake and Cayton, *Black Metropolis*, 496–97. Drake and Cayton also note that "When 'fair' (i.e., light-skinned) Negroes seem inordinately proud of their skin-color, or when darker Negroes have a predilection for associating with very light ones or encouraging their children to do so, Bronzeville calls them 'color-struck.'" See also Zora Neale Hurston, *Their Eyes Were Watching God* (HarperPerennial, 1990), 149. The term persists to the present day. See Margaret L. Hunter, *Race, Gender, and the Politics of Skin Tone* (Routledge, 2005), 109.

45. George S. Schuyler, *Black No More* (Modern Library, 1999), 4–5. "Ofay" was, and to some extent still is, a derogatory term applied to whites. The *Oxford English Dictionary* doubts the popular view that the word derives from the pig Latin for "foe." Some commentators believe it has African origins, but no corresponding term in an African language has yet been identified.

46. Quoted in Russell et al., *Color Complex*, 112. "Jim, proud of his treasure—a white wife,—tried hard to fulfil [*sic*] his promises and furnished [Mag] with a more comfortable dwelling, diet, and apparel," wrote Harriet Wilson in *Our Nig*. Published in 1859, *Our Nig* is regarded as the first novel written by an American woman of African descent. See Wilson, *Our Nig: Sketches from the Life of a Free Black* (Dover, 2005), 14. In *Black No More*, Max Disher's obsession with a white woman dictates the course of his life.

47. Gatewood, *Aristocrats of Color*, 184–85; see also Drake and Cayton, *Black Metropolis*, 138; Romano, *Race Mixing*, 85–89. The two quotations about Douglass can be found in Randall Kennedy, *Interracial Intimacies: Sex, Marriage, Identity, and Adoption* (Pantheon, 2003), 73. Douglass himself remarked sadly to Ida B. Wells: "I want to tell you that you are the only colored woman save Mrs. Grimké who has come into my home as a guest and has treated Helen as a hostess has a right to be treated by her guest. Each of the others, to my sorrow, acted as if she expected my wife to be haughty or distant, and they all began by being so themselves." Quoted in Ida B. Wells, *Crusade for Justice: Autobiography of Ida B. Wells* (University of Chicago Press, 1970), 72. Although Walter White, president of the NAACP between 1931 and 1955, is estimated to have had no more than one sixty-fourth African ancestry, he too faced condemnation when he took a white wife; see Thomas Dyja, *Walter White: The Dilemma of Black Identity in America* (Ivan R. Dee, 2008), 181–82. In the years between the two world wars, some prominent Communists, among them James Ford and Harry Haywood, married white women. They suffered criticism from black women, some of whom requested that the party ban interracial marriage. See Mark Naison, *Communists in Harlem during the Depression* (University of Illinois Press, 1983), 280.

48. The quotation from Redding is from Faith Berry, ed., *A Scholar's Conscience: Selected Writings of J. Saunders Redding* (University Press of Kentucky, 1992), 32; the work

song is reprinted in Zora Neale Hurston, *Mules and Men* (HarperPerennial, 1990), 269. One young Bronzeville man confessed to Drake and Cayton, "I never go out with dark women because they just don't interest me. I prefer a light person for a sweetheart or a wife . . . I don't look for coal mines; I look for gold mines" (Drake and Cayton, *Black Metropolis*, 498). Kathy Russell, Midge Wilson, and Ronald Hall, in *Color Complex*, observe: "The desire for lighter skin is nearly universal. Throughout Central and South America, Asia, and even Africa, society is prejudiced against those with dark skin, especially young dark women" (41). See also John Solomon Otto and Augustus M. Burns, "The Use of Race and Hillbilly Recordings as Sources for Historical Research: The Problem of Color Hierarchy among Afro-Americans in the Early Twentieth Century," *Journal of American Folklore* 85, no. 338 (Oct.–Dec. 1972): 347–49.

49. Gwendolyn Brooks, "The Ballad of Chocolate Mabbie," in *A Street in Bronzeville* (Harper & Brothers, 1945), 12. Reprinted By Consent of Brooks Permissions.

50. Brown—light brown, in particular—was the preferred choice in skin color; see Williamson, *New People*, chap. 3. Various songs heard in the South between the world wars capture the prevailing view. From the 1920s: "Some say give me a high yaller, / I say give me a teasin' brown / For it takes a teasin' brown to satisfy my soul. / I don't want no coal-black woman for my regular, / Give me brown, Lawd, Lawd, give me brown." And a decade later: "I don't want no jet black woman for my regular, / O give me brown, and oh my Lord, give me brown. / For black is evil, evil, yella so low down, / When you git in trouble, and oh my Lord, yella can't be found " (both in Levine, *Black Culture and Black Consciousness*, 286). For the studies on skin color and preferences in partners, see Drake and Cayton, *Black Metropolis*, 503–506; Johnson, *Growing Up in the Black Belt*, 262; Davis, *Who Is Black?*, 60. For general information on the products advertised, see Kusmer, *A Ghetto Takes Shape*, 107; for the advertisements quoted, see Russell et al., *The Color Complex*, 49–50.

51. Thurman, *The Blacker the Berry*, 79.

52. For one such survey, see Charles S. Johnson, *Growing Up in the Black Belt*, 260–61, table 18. Thurman, *The Blacker the Berry*, 1–2.

53. Levine, *Black Culture and Black Consciousness*, 287; Otto and Burns, "The Use of Race and Hillbilly Recordings," 354.

54. James, *Rage to Survive*, 64, 184.

55. For the history of "Strange Fruit," written by Abel Meeropol, as well as its role in Holiday's life, see David Margolick, *Strange Fruit: Billie Holiday, Café Society, and an Early Cry for Civil Rights* (HarperCollins, 2001). Complained a black woman from Brooklyn in a letter to the NAACP in 1949, "Soon as Negroes men [sic] get in a position to support a family they must find a white wife or some one next to same complexion while the poor black devils of womanhood suffer on bread lines with there [sic] brats" (Romano, *Race Mixing*, 86–88, 242). Thurman's *The Blacker the Berry* quotations are from pp. 128–29. It presumably goes without saying that there were some women who

simply discounted skin color in taking the measure of a potential partner. Sarah and Elizabeth Delany, born in the late nineteenth century, had a light-complexioned mother and a dark father, both educators at a college in Raleigh, North Carolina. The two daughters recounted in their memoir: "Some colored women who were as light as Mama would not have gotten involved with a dark-skinned man, but Mama didn't care. She said he was the cream of the crop, a man of the highest quality. Oh, Mama was a smart woman. It takes a smart woman to fall in love with a good man." Sarah L. Delany and A. Elizabeth Delany with Amy Hill Hearth, *Having Our Say: The Delany Sisters' First 100 Years* (Dell, 1994), 59–60. It is worth noting that middle-class Negroes seeking to adopt children often requested boys or girls who were light-skinned with "good" hair. See Kennedy, *Interracial Intimacies*, 3–4, 524–25, fn. 8; Davis, *Who Is Black?*, 60.

56. Wilma King, *The Essence of Liberty: Free Black Women during the Slave Era* (University of Missouri Press, 2006), 46. The quotation from *Anglo-African Magazine* is in Litwack, *North of Slavery*, 183. Elaine Brown's comments are in her *A Taste of Power*, 31, 427. In those days Brown dreamed of being white. Observes the journalist Patrice Gaines, "In the North Carolina projects where my mother grew up, if your hair was kinky you were dirty or deranged, too crazy to care about your appearance" (Patrice Gaines, *Laughing in the Dark: From Colored Girl to Woman of Color—A Journey from Prison to Power* [Anchor, 1994], 94). See also Maxine Leeds Craig, *Ain't I a Beauty Queen? Black Women, Beauty, and the Politics of Race* (Oxford University Press, 2002), 25–26.

57. The descriptions of the advertisements can be found in Russell et al., *The Color Complex*, 44, 46. Ayana D. Bird and Lori Tharps examine how Africans and their American descendents viewed and arranged their hair in *Hair Story: Untangling the Roots of Black Hair in America* (St. Martin's Press, 2001). See also Kusmer, *A Ghetto Takes Shape*, 107. On the inclusion of the ad in Garvey's *The Negro World,* see Robert A. Hill, ed., *The Marcus Garvey and Universal Negro Association Papers*, vol. 5: *Sept. 1922–Aug. 1924* (University of California Press, 1986), 228, fn. 7.

58. The story of Madam Walker is told in A'Lelia Bundles, *On Her Own Ground: The Life and Times of Madam C.J. Walker* (Scribner, 2001); see also http://www.madam cjwalker.com/bios/madam-c-j-walker, accessed July 5, 2013. For Walker's contribution to the development of the beauty industry in the United States, see Kathy Lee Peiss, *Hope in a Jar: The Making of America's Beauty Culture* (Metropolitan, 1998).

59. Charles W. Chesnutt, *The House behind the Cedars* (University of Georgia Press, 2000), 198. In *Their Eyes Were Watching God*, the snobbish Mrs. Turner says to Janie Starks, "You oughta meet mah brother. He's real smart. Got dead straight hair" (Hurston, *Their Eyes Were Watching God*, 140–42).

60. James, *Rage to Survive*, 27.

61. Malcolm X with Alex Haley, *The Autobiography of Malcolm X* (Ballantine, 1992), 64; Levine, *Black Culture and Black Consciousness*, 291–92. Notes Maxine Leeds Craig, "The painful straightening of Malcolm's hair was a rite of passage that marked his

transformation from hick to hipster, from rural adolescence to a distinctively black style of manhood" (Craig, *Ain't I a Beauty Queen?*, 111).

62. Bundles, *On Her Own Ground*, 268–69.

63. Ellison, *Invisible Man*, 101.

64. Gatewood, *Aristocracy of Color*, 195.

65. Plessy later rode the railroad as a white man. On the historical context and legal underpinnings of Plessy's arguments, see Rebecca J. Scott, "Public Rights, Social Equality, and the Conceptual Roots of the *Plessy* Challenge," *Michigan Law Review* 106 (Mar. 2008): 777–804. The freelance writer Keith Weldon Medley provides a compelling description of the court case in *We as Freemen: "Plessy v. Ferguson"* (Pelican, 2003).

5. THE CIVIL RIGHTS MOVEMENT

1. Eric J. Sundquist examines the origins of the speech, its context, and consequences in *King's Dream: The Legacy of Martin Luther King's "I Have a Dream" Speech* (Yale University Press, 2009). See also Drew Hansen, *The Dream: Martin Luther King, Jr., and the Speech That Inspired a Nation* (Harper Perennial, 2005); Taylor Branch, *Parting the Waters: America in the King Years, 1954–63* (Simon & Schuster, 1988), chap. 22; James H. Cone, *Martin and Malcolm and America: A Dream or a Nightmare* (Orbis, 1991), chap. 3; and Jim Cullen, *The American Dream: A Short History of an Idea That Shaped a Nation* (Oxford University Press, 2003), chap. 4.

2. For the full text of the speech, see http://mlk-kpp01.stanford.edu/kingweb/publications/papers/vol1/440500-The_Negro_and_the_Constitution.htm, accessed Dec. 7, 2011.

3. The letter can be viewed in its entirety at http://mlk-kpp01.stanford.edu/index.php/resources/article/annotated_letter_from_birmingham, accessed Dec. 7, 2011. For a penetrating analysis see Jonathan Rieder, *Gospel of Freedom: Martin Luther King, Jr.'s Letter from Birmingham Jail and the Struggle That Changed a Nation* (Bloomsbury, 2013).

4. For his complete speech at the March on Washington, see http://mlk-kpp01.stanford.edu/index.php/encyclopedia/documentsentry/doc_august_28_1963_i_have_a_dream, accessed Dec. 7, 2011.

5. Thomas Jefferson, *Notes on the State of Virginia* (University of North Carolina Press, 1954), 137–38; Fawn M. Brodie, *Thomas Jefferson: An Intimate History* (Norton, 1998), 38, 118. Lincoln said in 1858—this was during his debate with Stephen Douglas at Charleston, Illinois: "While I was at the hotel to-day, an elderly gentleman called upon me to know whether I was really in favor of producing perfect equality between the negroes and white people. While I had not proposed to myself on this occasion to say much on that subject, yet as the question was asked me, I thought I would occupy perhaps five minutes in saying something in regard to it. I will say then that I am not, nor ever have been, in favor of bringing about in any way the social and political equal-

ity of the white and black races, that I am not, nor ever have been, in favor of making voters or jurors of negroes, nor of qualifying them to hold office, nor to intermarry with white people; and I will say in addition to this that there is a physical difference between the white and black races which I believe will forever forbid the two races living together on terms of social and political equality. And inasmuch as they cannot so live, while they do remain together there must be the position of superior and inferior, and I as much as any other man am in favor of having the superior position assigned to the white race" (part of Lincoln's "Fourth Joint Debate at Charleston," which can be viewed at http://www.bartleby.com/251/41.html, accessed Mar. 26, 2013). Eric Foner notes that before the Civil War, Lincoln seemed to have assumed that most slaves, once freed, would voluntary leave the United States, something which he believed would be in the interests of both races. But while he "never became a full-fledged racial egalitarian," Lincoln did become more vocal over time about the need to ensure that people of African descent received all the protections accorded to citizens in the Constitution. And by the latter stages of the war he had increasingly come to think that emigration would be an option only for those Negroes—a distinct minority, he now imagined—who could never reconcile themselves to staying in the United States. See Eric Foner, *The Fiery Trial: Abraham Lincoln and American Slavery* (Norton, 2010), 127–28, 257.

6. Frederick Douglass, "The Present and Future of the Colored Race in America," address delivered June 1863 and available online at http://teachingamericanhistory.org/library/index.asp?document=777, accessed Dec. 7, 2011. For Douglass's comments at the Chicago World's Fair, see William S. McFeely, *Frederick Douglass* (Norton, 1991), 371.

7. Notes Jason Sokol, "Many whites seemed to believe that rights were mutually exclusive, and finite. Whites would lose freedom for every right that blacks gained" (Sokol, *There Goes My Everything: White Southerners in the Age of Civil Rights* [Vintage, 2007], 217). See also Numan V. Bartley, *The Rise of Massive Resistance: Race and Politics in the South during the 1950s* (Louisiana State University Press, 1999); Clive Webb, ed., *Massive Resistance: Southern Opposition to the Second Reconstruction* (Oxford University Press, 2005). The procession at the Evers funeral is shown in *Eyes on the Prize: America's Civil Rights Movement,* PBS video, series 1, episode 5: "Mississippi: Is This America? (1962–1964)."

8. Civil rights leaders came to understand well the role of television in advancing their cause. Protests were consciously designed to provoke the kind of angry response from Southern whites that would be carried on national news broadcasts. The Southern Christian Leadership Conference named its series of marches and boycotts in Birmingham, "Operation C," the "C" standing for "Confrontation." Nikhil Singh has written: "With the onset of the Cold War, U.S. State Department officials routinely argued that white supremacy was the 'Achilles heel' of U.S. foreign relations. From the highest levels of government and social policy, it appeared that the stability of the expanded American realm of action in the world was linked to the resolution of the crisis of racial discord and division at home"—see Nikhil Pal Singh, *Black Is a Country: Race and the*

Unfinished Struggle for Democracy (Harvard University Press, 2004), 7. Mary L. Dudziak, *Cold War Civil Rights: Race and the Image of American Democracy* (Princeton University Press, 2000) is a rich treatment of how the Civil Rights Movement was related to the Cold War. See also Penny von Eschen, *Satchmo Blows up the World: Jazz Ambassadors Play the Cold War* (Harvard University Press, 2006). Kevin K. Gaines, *African Americans in Ghana: Black Expatriates and the Civil Rights Era* (University of North Carolina Press, 2006) explores the nature of transnational views of black identity in Ghana. Kwame Nkrumah and many other African leaders had attended university in the United States and had close contacts with black American scholars and newspaper executives. Notes James Campbell, *Ebony* magazine was "an important source of information about black America for Africans. A pilgrimage to Johnson Publishing's gleaming Chicago headquarters [where *Ebony* was produced] . . . became de rigueur for touring African heads of state." James T. Campbell, *Middle Passages: African American Journeys to Africa, 1787–2005* (Penguin, 2006), 313.

9. Sokol, *There Goes My Everything*, 83, 90. Carter's views are documented in Ann Waldon, *Hodding Carter: The Reconstruction of a Racist* (Algonquin Books of Chapel Hill, 1993), 249. Carter was called to answer questions before a Mississippi committee on un-American activities in 1959. King's association with Jack O'Dell and Stanley Levison was frequently used to bring his loyalty into question. See, for example, David Garrow, *Bearing the Cross: Martin Luther King, Jr. and the Southern Christian Leadership Conference* (Perennial Classics, 2004).

10. Roy Wilkins, "Undergirding the Democratic Ideal," *The Crisis* (Dec. 1951): 647–650.

11. Dudziak, *Cold War Civil Rights*, 124–25. The Roberts quotation is from *Eyes on the Prize*, series 1, episode 2: "Fighting Back (1957–1962)." On the integration of Central High, see Elizabeth Jacoway, *Turn Away Thy Son: Little Rock, the Crisis That Shocked the Nation* (Free Press, 2007). Ralph Ellison wrote of the Central High drama, "The skins of those thin-legged little girls who faced the mob in Little Rock marked them as Negro, but the spirit which directed their feet is the old universal urge toward freedom. For better or worse, whatever there is of value in Negro life is an American heritage, and as such it must be preserved." Quoted in Debra J. Dickerson, *The End of Blackness: Returning the Souls of Black Folk to Their Rightful Owners* (Pantheon, 2004), 257.

12. Lyndon Johnson, remarks at the Howard University Commencement (June 4, 1965), available online at http://millercenter.org/scripps/archive/speeches/detail/3387, accessed Dec. 7, 2011. The promised conference took place in Washington on June 1 and 2, 1966.

13. Branch, *Parting the Waters*, 887 (see also Sundquist, *King's Dream*, 2); Singh, *Black Is a Country*, 4.

14. The "many surveys" include Pew Research Center, "Optimism about Black Progress Declines: Blacks See Growing Values Gap between Poor and Middle Class," Nov. 13,

2007, 3, 51, http://pewsocialtrends.org/files/2010/10/Race-2007.pdf, accessed Dec. 7, 2011; John R. Logan, Brian J. Stults, and Reynolds Farley, "Segregation of Minorities in the Metropolis: Two Decades of Change," *Demography* 41, no. 1 (Feb. 2004): 2; Thomas J. Sugrue, *Sweet Land of Liberty: The Forgotten Struggle for Civil Rights in the North* (Random House, 2008), 247–48, 536; Richard Thompson Ford, *The Race Card: How Bluffing about Bias Makes Race Relations Worse* (Picador, 2009), 26–27; Jennifer L. Hochschild, *Facing Up to the American Dream: Race, Class, and the Soul of the Nation* (Princeton University Press, 1995), 56–60; Michael K. Brown et al., *Whitewashing Race: The Myth of a Colorblind Society* (University of California Press, 2003), 36; Renee C. Romano, *Race Mixing: Black-White Marriage in Postwar America* (Harvard University Press, 2003), 191–92, 2, 45, 207; Pew Research Center, "Marrying Out: One-in-Seven Marriages is Interracial or Interethnic," June 15, 2010, http://pewsocialtrends.org/files/2010/10/755 -marrying-out.pdf, accessed Dec. 7, 2011; Orlando Patterson, *The Ordeal of Integration: Progress and Resentment in America's "Racial" Crisis* (Civitas/Counterpoint, 1997), 194; Susan Welch et al., *Race and Place: Race Relations in an American City* (Cambridge University Press, 2001), 115–16. Ford also notes: "Today racism is socially, as well as legally, unacceptable: for most businesses the biggest cost of a claim of racism isn't the legal liability—it's the bad publicity" (Ford, *The Race Card*, 348). Adds the economist Glenn Loury, "Things have changed a great deal since the 1950s. Racial discrimination in the public sphere is a relatively straightforward, universally recognized moral problem. Almost everyone now agrees that such discrimination should be proscribed in the interest of creating a 'level playing field.'" Loury, *The Anatomy of Racial Inequality* (Harvard University Press, 2002), 94.

15. Ellen Holly, *One Life: The Autobiography of an African American Actress* (Kodansha International, 1996), 104.

16. Ibid. It is worth noting that not all black Americans looked with approval on the Civil Rights Movement. The iconoclastic, and by the 1960s proudly conservative, columnist George Schuyler notoriously protested the awarding of the Nobel Peace Prize to Martin Luther King, Jr. And Lawrence Otis Graham has written that his great-grandmother, a privileged member of the "blue-veined crowd," complained, "I don't see anything civil about a bunch of nappy-headed Negroes screaming and marching around the streets." Graham, *Our Kind of People: Inside America's Black Upper Class* (Harper-Perennial, 2000), 2–3.

6. BLACK POWER

1. The commonly used term "race riot" is an unfortunate one in that its meaning has changed dramatically over the course of American history. What are routinely referred to as "race riots" in the first half of the nineteenth century were actually outbreaks of mob violence by whites against Negroes. The "race riots" of the urban North

following World War I often included battles between gangs of whites and gangs of Negroes, sometimes spanning several neighborhoods. The "race riots" of the 1960s, by contrast, were acts of looting and violence by inner-city blacks directed largely against white-owned property owners and frequently sparked by conflict with white police. The worst riot took place in the summer of 1967 in Detroit. Over nearly six days of fighting, forty-three people died and a thousand were wounded. Property damage was $250 million, with 1,300 buildings destroyed by fires. Five thousand blacks were left homeless.

2. Peniel E. Joseph, *Waiting 'Til the Midnight Hour: A Narrative History of Black Power in America* (Henry Holt, 2006), chap. 7; Clayborne Carson, *In Struggle: SNCC and the Black Awakening of the 1960s* (Harvard University Press, 1995), chap. 13. Before Carmichael spoke, his close associate Willie Ricks told the crowd to expect a call for "black power." SNCC workers who had come to Mississippi predisposed to distrust King found him to be approachable and friendly. Commented Cleveland Sellers: "He turned out to be easygoing with a delightful sense of humor. His mind was open and we were surprised to find that he was much less conservative than we initially believed." Sellers with Robert Terrell, *The River of No Return: The Autobiography of a Black Militant and the Life and Death of SNCC* (Scholarly Book Services, 2002), 164. Carmichael himself later described King as "a warm, funny, likeable, unpretentious human being who shared many of our values" (Joseph, *Waiting 'Til the Midnight Hour*, 137). The "black power" slogan had been used before, by Richard Wright and by Congressman Adam Clayton Powell, Jr.

3. The full text of Carmichael's speech is available online at http://voxygen.net/classes/contemporary-public-address/stokely-carmichael-black-power-speech, accessed Dec. 7, 2011.

4. Joseph, *Waiting 'Til the Midnight Hour*, 142.

5. Robin D. G. Kelley, *Freedom Dreams: The Black Radical Imagination* (Beacon, 2002), 60–109 looks at the influence of Marxist and Communist writings—and of revolutionary movements in Asia, Latin America, and Africa—on the thought of American activists. Kelley gives particular attention to the Revolutionary Action Movement (RAM), "what might loosely be called the first black Maoist-influenced organization in history." For a biography of the man whose life inspired RAM and who was elected its president in exile, see Timothy B. Tyson, *Radio Free Dixie: Robert F. Williams and the Roots of Black Power* (University of North Carolina Press, 2001). Huey Newton was convicted of voluntary manslaughter and sentenced to two to fifteen years in prison. Two years later, however, the California Appellate Court overturned the verdict and ordered a new trial. After two subsequent mistrials, California dropped the case. Hoover's claim about the threat posed by the Panthers was hyperbolic—see Nikhil Pal Singh, "The Black Panthers and the 'Undeveloped Country' of the Left," in Charles E. Jones, ed., *The Black Panther [Reconsidered]* (Black Classic Press, 1998), 82.

6. William L. Van Deburg, *New Day in Babylon: The Black Power Movement and Ameri-*

can Culture, 1965–1975 (University of Chicago Press, 1992), 162; Floyd W. Hayes, III, and Francis A. Kiene, III, "'All Power to the People': The Political Thought of Huey P. Newton and the Black Panther Party," in Jones, *The Black Panther [Reconsidered]*, 171. The "Resolutions" and "Ten-Point Program" can be found in Huey Newton, *To Die for the People*, ed. Toni Morrison (City Lights, 2009), 42, 3–6, respectively. Eldridge Cleaver, the party's minister of information, claimed that the Panthers offered a "Yankee-Doodle-Dandy version of socialism." Robin Kelley has observed, "Although [the Black Panther Party] was the most visible black organization promoting Mao's thought, by some accounts its members were probably the least serious about reading Marxist, Leninist, or Maoist writings and developing a revolutionary ideology" (Kelley, *Freedom Dreams*, 93). The comedian Dick Gregory, linking the urban upheavals of the 1960s to the legacy of the Founding Fathers, did a routine in front of white college students in which he advised them to sit their parents in front of the television, turn on news coverage of the riots, and then read aloud from the Declaration of Independence. Dick Gregory, "Black Rioters," *The Light Side: The Dark Side* (Collectibles CD, 1997).

7. Gary Gerstle has estimated that the membership of the Panthers, SNCC, Core, the Nation of Islam, and "other black nationalist organizations" probably never exceeded 50,000: see Gerstle, *American Crucible: Race and Nation in the Twentieth Century* (Princeton University Press, 2001), 300. Given that the Panthers' critique of American capitalism was influenced by Marxist thought, whether they should be classified as "black nationalists" is open to debate. Stokely Carmichael attempted to merge SNCC with the Panthers in the late 1960s but eventually abandoned the experiment, unhappy that the Panther leadership was willing to work with radical organizations that included whites (see Joseph, *Waiting 'Til the Midnight Hour*, 243–47). On the concept of "cool pose" see Richard Majors and Janet Mancini Billson, *Cool Pose: The Dilemmas of Black Manhood in America* (Touchstone, 1992). As Thomas Sugrue has observed, "The television news was the ideal stage for the performance of black power—and it gave viewers the impression that the Panthers were more numerous and influential than they actually were" (Sugrue, *Sweet Land of Liberty: The Forgotten Struggle for Civil Rights in the North* [Random House, 2008], 345–46). The FBI files on the Panthers can be found at Federal Bureau of Investigation, *Black Panther Party—The FBI Files*, vols. 1–7 (FBI Files, 2009). The quotation from Huey P. Newton is from his autobiography *Revolutionary Suicide* (Wildwood House, 1974), 329. Many commentators have argued that, in one critical sense, the Panthers and other Black Power organizations were insufficiently radical: they failed to challenge the patriarchal assumptions underlying mainstream American gender relations. When asked the proper place for a woman in SNCC, Stokely Carmichael infamously answered "prone" (Carson, *In Struggle*, 148). Elaine Brown, who for a time during the 1970s headed the Panthers, later charged, "A woman in the Black Power movement was considered, at best, irrelevant. A woman asserting herself was a pariah. A woman attempting the role of leadership was, to my

proud black Brothers, making an alliance with the 'counter-revolutionary, man-hating, lesbian, feminist white bitches.' It was a violation of some Black Power principle that was left undefined. If a black woman assumed a role of leadership, she was said to be eroding black manhood, to be hindering the progress of the black race. She was an enemy of black people" (Brown, *A Taste of Power: A Black Woman's Story* [Doubleday, 1992], 357). Black females took particular offense at Eldridge Cleaver's collection of essays *Soul on Ice* (Dell, 1991), in which, among other things, he revealed how he had prepared himself for raping white women by raping black women. The most famous black feminist critique of the day was by Michele Wallace, *Black Macho and the Myth of the Superwoman* (Verso, 1990). Waldo E. Martin, Jr., author of *No Coward Soldiers: Black Cultural Politics in Postwar America* (Harvard University Press, 2005), has noted that "even amid the militant racial separatism and antiwhite rhetoric" of the Black Power era, there remained "a hopeful commitment among blacks to the American project" (33). In *Freedom Dreams*, Robin Kelley has commented on the failure of groups like RAM "to build a strong base in black urban communities" (107–108). And Barack Obama recalls in his memoir how, as a student at Occidental College in Los Angeles during the 1980s, he "stumbled upon one of the well-kept secrets about black people: that most of us weren't interested in revolt"—see Barack Obama, *Dreams from My Father: A Story of Race and Inheritance* (Three Rivers, 2004), 98.

8. "Invisibly divided by race" is from Sugrue, *Sweet Land of Liberty,* 131; see also Harvard Sitkoff, *The Struggle for Black Equality, 1954–1992,* rev. ed. (Hill and Wang, 1993), 192. The Kerner Commission's findings are in *Report of the National Advisory Commission on Civil Disorders* (Mar. 1, 1968), 73, 76, available online at http://www.eisenhower foundation.org/docs/kerner.pdf, accessed July 5, 2013.

9. Conley's comment can be found in Josh Sides, "Straight into Compton: American Dreams, Urban Nightmares, and the Metamorphosis of a Black Suburb," *American Quarterly* 56, no. 3 (Sept. 2004): 591. For the observations and reaction of Martin Luther King, Jr., see *The Autobiography of Martin Luther King, Jr.,* ed. Clayborne Carson (Warner, 1998), 291.

10. *Report of the National Advisory Commission on Civil Disorders,* 76; Lawrence Otis Graham, *Our Kind of People: Inside America's Black Upper Class* (HarperPerennial, 2000), 32. Jack and Jill is a club for children of the upper echelon of the black middle class (see Chapter 9).

11. George Wallace, who ran as an independent and won 13 percent of the vote, was even more direct than Nixon in mining white resentment of gains made by blacks during the Kennedy and Johnson years.

12. Sugrue, *Sweet Land of Liberty,* 265, 501; Manning Marable, *Race, Reform, and Rebellion: The Second Reconstruction and Beyond in Black America, 1946–2006,* 3d ed. (University Press of Mississippi, 2007), 122; Steven F. Lawson, *Running for Freedom: Civil Rights and Black Politics in America since 1941,* 2d ed. (McGraw-Hill, 1997), 163–80;

Adolph Reed, Jr., *Stirrings in the Jug: Black Politics in the Post-Segregation Era* (University of Minnesota Press, 1999), 79. Andrew Hacker, *Two Nations: Black and White, Separate, Hostile, Unequal* (Scribner, 2003), 237, includes a list of cities that had elected black mayors as of 2002 and the percentage of their populations that were black. The number of elected black officials at all levels of government rose from just 33 in 1941 to 193 in 1965, 764 in 1970, 1,909 in 1980, and over 8,000 in 1993. See Jennifer L. Hochschild, *Facing Up to the American Dream: Race, Class, and the Soul of the Nation* (Princeton University Press, 1995), 40.

13. J. Phillip Thompson, III, *Double Trouble: Black Mayors, Black Communities, and the Call for a Deep Democracy* (Oxford University Press, 2006), 4; also Reed, *Stirrings in the Jug*, 97. An example of a mayor implementing affirmative action: under Maynard Jackson, the percentage of contracts in Atlanta awarded to black firms increased from 2 to 13 percent. And Jackson refused to allow expansion of Atlanta International Airport until black firms were assured 25 percent of the work (Lawson, *Running for Freedom*, 165–66). Thomas J. Sugrue examines the restructuring of the northern economy and its impact on black residents of cities in *The Origins of the Urban Crisis: Race and Inequality in Postwar Detroit* (Princeton University Press, 1996). On cuts to urban funding during the Reagan years, see William Julius Wilson, *More Than Just Race: Being Black and Poor in the Inner City* (Norton, 2009), 34–35; Marable, *Race, Reform, and Rebellion*, 206–208; and William Julius Wilson, *When Work Disappears* (Knopf, 1996), 49. Steps had already been taken in this direction by Richard Nixon, whose administration began to distribute federal funding through block grants, which did not mandate that local officials direct financial resources to the inner-city poor. See Michael K. Brown et al., *Whitewashing Race: The Myth of a Colorblind Society* (University of California Press, 2003), 97–98.

14. Sugrue, *Sweet Land of Liberty*, 503–504.

15. Jennifer L. Hochschild and Vesla Weaver, "The Skin Color Paradox and the American Racial Order," *Social Forces* 86, no. 2 (Dec. 2007): 650–51.

16. Sugrue, *Sweet Land of Liberty*, 504–505. "The logic of pro-growth politics," Adolph Reed has argued, "denies broad progressive redistribution as a policy." Reed lists Goode, along with Coleman Young (Detroit), Andrew Young (Atlanta), Marion Barry (Washington), Kenneth Gibson and Sharpe James (Newark), "Dutch" Morial and Sidney Barthelemy (New Orleans), and Richard Arrington (Birmingham) as mayors who "governed on programs centered on making local government the handmaiden to private development interests." See Reed, *Stirrings in the Jug*, 88–89, 100–101. In 1988, after Andrew Young's second term in office, 47 percent of census tracts in Atlanta were deemed to be "high poverty"; the figure in 1970, three years before Maynard Jackson was elected as the city's first black mayor, had been 28 percent. Between 1973, when Atlanta, Detroit, and Washington elected their first black mayors, and 2003, the black youth unemployment rate rose from 70 to 78 percent. Thompson, *Double Trouble*, 59–60, 11–12, 49.

17. Comments J. Phillip Thompson, "Black voters who had been initially excited by the election of blacks as mayors now became increasingly disenchanted. Conditions in their neighborhoods and lives changed little. This created, in turn, incentives for black officials to demobilize the black poor, or to allow demobilization to occur. Those most disheartened by their conditions failed to or ceased to participate. Alienation of the black urban poor from politics set in motion a cycle of political withdrawal. Black political participation declined, particularly in poor neighborhoods" (*Double Trouble*, 4–5, 58–60, 41–44). Barack Obama was deeply impressed by the support he saw for Harold Washington when he went to work in the inner city of Chicago after college. Ordinary blacks looked at Washington with "a familiarity and affection normally reserved for a relative. His picture was everywhere . . . displayed prominently, like some protective totem" (Obama, *Dreams from My Father*, 135). The minister's lament can be found in Sudhir Alladi Venkatesh, *Off the Books: The Underground Economy of the Urban Poor* (Harvard University Press, 2006), 235. When Washington ran for reelection in 1987, the voter turnout was 14 percent lower in poor wards than it had been four years earlier. Still, the support he received from inner-city voters played an important part in securing his return to office. He died just eight months after the election, leaving open the question of whether over time he might have been able to effect more radical change.

18. Brown wrote the song with Alfred Ellis in 1968. It was released under the King Records label. The comments of the Detroit riot participant can be found in *Report of the National Advisory Commission on Civil Disorders*, 76. The sociologist Robert Merton argued at the time, "When a nation, race, ethnic group, or any other powerful collectivity has long extolled its own admirable qualities and, expressly or by implication, deprecated the qualities of others it invites and provides the potential for counterethnocentrism. And when a once largely powerless collectivity acquires a socially validated sense of growing power, its members experience an intensified need for self-affirmation. Under such circumstances, collective self-glorification, found in some measure among all groups, becomes a predictable and intensified counterresponse to long-standing belittlement from without. So it is that, in the United States, the centuries-long institutionalized premise that 'white (and for some, presumably only white) is true and good and beautiful' induces, under conditions of revolutionary change, the counterpremise that 'black (and for some, presumably only black) is true and good and beautiful.'" See Merton, "Insiders and Outsiders: A Chapter in the Sociology of Knowledge," *American Journal of Sociology* 8, no. 1 (July 1972): 18–19.

19. Henry Louis Gates, "The Two Nations: The Best of Times, the Worst of Times," *Brookings Review* 16, no. 2 (Spring 1998): 6.

20. Payton is quoted in Maxine Leeds Craig, *Ain't I a Beauty Queen? Black Women, Beauty, and the Politics of Race* (Oxford University Press, 2002), 139.

21. Craig, *Ain't I a Beauty Queen?*, 97. See also Kathy Russell, Midge Wilson, and

Ronald Hall, *The Color Complex: The Politics of Skin Color among African Americans* (Anchor, 1993), 47.

22. Jill Nelson's comments are from her book *Volunteer Slavery: My Authentic Negro Experience* (Penguin, 1993), 18–19. Patrice Gaines, who like Nelson became a writer at the *Washington Post*, reflected in her autobiography: "In 1969, I thought my Afro separated me from the Negroes and the coloreds and pulled my head higher, so that I walked straighter, a pure and visible version of the African princess I thought I was until the age of five" (Gaines, *Laughing in the Dark: From Colored Girl to Woman of Color—A Journey from Prison to Power* [Anchor, 1994], 94). Remembers the writer Debra Dickerson: "Rain was my fiercest enemy. Fat, tangled, nappy roots swelled and bulged and made me hate myself. This battle black women fight with our hair is a large part of the reason why so few black women over the age of thirty can swim—chemical relaxers had yet to be invented and we simply would not subject ourselves to the public humiliation of nappy hair." See Dickerson, *An American Story* (Pantheon, 2000), 35.

23. Marita Golden's reminiscences are from her book *Don't Play in the Sun: One Woman's Journey Through the Color Complex* (Anchor, 2004), 4, 12, 35–36. It was not only girls who were warned to stay out of the sun. Lawrence Otis Graham recalls his great-grandmother calling to him and his brother "in a kindly, overprotective tone": "You boys stay out of that terrible sun. God knows you're dark enough already" (Graham, *Our Kind of People*, 2). On the emergence of "Black is Beautiful," see Craig, *Ain't I a Beauty Queen?*, chap. 2.

24. Russell et al., *The Color Complex*, 98–99.

25. Golden, *Don't Play in the Sun*, 35–36. See also Craig, *Ain't I a Beauty Queen?*, 41–42. Mark E. Hill, "Skin Color and the Perception of Attractiveness among African Americans: Does Gender Make a Difference?" *Social Psychology Quarterly* 65, no. 1 (Mar. 2002): 87. A study of the 1978 edition of *Who's Who among Black Americans* found that the men profiled had lighter skin than the general black population and that their wives were frequently lighter still. The *Village Voice* quotation comes from Randall Kennedy, *Interracial Intimacies: Sex, Marriage, Identity, and Adoption* (Pantheon, 2003), 115. Michele Wallace wrote in 1978: "Some black women would laugh low in their throats when they saw a black man with a white woman and make cracks about his high-water pants or his flat head or his walk, anything that might suggest that he was inadequate: 'Only the rejects crawl for white pussy.'" Others feigned incredulity: "I mean really. How could he want a white woman when black women fuck better, cook better, dance better, party better"—Wallace, *Black Macho and the Myth of the Superwoman*, 10. And this from Marita Golden: "The Black Panthers made regular forays onto campus to recruit members from among the Black student population. In their black leather jackets and black berets, with their huge Afros and militant attitudes, the Panthers were irresistible to the Black girls on campus. But we soon realized that most of the Panther brothers preferred White girls, or as we bitterly and crudely joked, 'white meat'" (Golden, *Don't Play in the Sun*, 34).

26. Golden, *Don't Play in the Sun*, 13–14. See also Ralph Richards Banks, *Is Marriage for White People? How the African American Marriage Decline Affects Everyone* (Dutton, 2011), 139.

27. On the continuing disadvantages of individuals with dark skin, see Michael Hughes and Bradley R. Hertel, "The Significance of Color Remains: A Study of Life Chances, Mate Selection and Ethnic Consciousness among Black Americans," *Social Forces* 68, no. 4 (June 1990): 1105–20. Based on data collected from the National Survey of black Americans conducted in 1980 as well as interviews with two thousand individuals, Hughes and Hertel concluded that "dark-skinned blacks suffer much the same disadvantages relative to light-skinned blacks that blacks, in general, suffer relative to whites." Other relevant works include Margaret L. Hunter, *Race, Gender, and the Politics of Skin Tone* (Routledge, 2005), which is the source of the Hunter quotation cited (p. 53); Maxine S. Thompson and Verna M. Keith, "The Blacker the Berry: Gender, Skin Tone, Self-Esteem and Self-Efficacy," *Gender and Society* 15, no. 3 (June, 2001): 336–37; Russell et al., *The Color Complex;* and Hill, "Skin Color and the Perception of Attractiveness." Margaret Hunter points out that what are deemed to be "African" facial features— full lips; broad, flat noses—are also correlated with economic disadvantage. Jokes about what were thought of as typically African facial features were commonplace in the post–Black Power era. See Carl Husemoller Nightingale, *On the Edge: A History of Poor Black Children and Their American Dreams* (Basic Books, 1993), 117. In recent decades, there have been representations in American popular culture of the conflict between dark-skinned blacks with nappy hair and light-skinned blacks with straight hair. A powerful example is the song-and-dance sequence between the Jigaboos and Wannabees in Spike Lee's *School Daze* (Sony Pictures, 1988).

28. Craig, *Ain't I a Beauty Queen?*, 104–106; Golden, *Don't Play in the Sun*, 35.

29. Craig, *Ain't I a Beauty Queen?*, 156. See also Russell et al., *The Color Complex*, 47, 91; Chris Rock, "Good Hair" (Lionsgate Home Entertainment, 2009, DVD); Maxine Leeds, "Young African-American Women and the Language of Beauty," in Karen A. Callaghan, *Ideals of Feminine Beauty: Philosophical, Social, and Cultural Dimensions* (Greenwood, 1994), 156.

30. As James T. Campbell wrote in *Middle Passages: African American Journeys to Africa, 1787–2005* (Penguin, 2006), 318: "Ghanaian independence was front-page news in every leading black newspaper and magazine in the United States. *Ebony* produced a lavish pictorial. The *Pittsburgh Courier* published a thirty-two-page supplement, 'Salute to Ghana.'" In a front-page editorial, the *Courier* underscored the special meaning that Ghana's independence had for African Americans: "Ghana's contributions, as a free nation, to peace, to art, to industry, to government, will be regarded by American Negroes as symbols of their own worth and potential. When we, American Negroes, shake hands with Ghana today, we say not only 'Welcome!' but also, 'Your opportunity to prove yourself is our opportunity to prove ourselves.'" See also Saidiya Hartman,

Lose Your Mother: A Journey along the Atlantic Slave Route (Farrar, Straus and Giroux, 2007), 34–37. On the *Roots* phenomenon, see Alex Haley, *Roots: The Saga of an American Family* (Doubleday, 1976). Haley won both the Pulitzer Prize and the National Book Award for his fictionalized work, which spurred unprecedented interest among blacks in genealogy. A serialized version of *Roots*, which aired on ABC in January of 1977, drew a larger audience than any previous television program and won nine Emmy awards. William L. van de Burg explores the diverse expressions of "soul" in *New Day in Babylon*. Photographs of ghetto murals are found in Camilo José Vergara, *The New American Ghetto* (Rutgers University Press, 1995), 135–37. The term "African American," commonly used by writers today, emerged during the 1980s.

31. An annotated directory of current academic programs on the African diaspora can be found at http://www-sul.stanford.edu/depts/ssrg/africa/african-diaspora/african-diaspora-studies.html, accessed Mar. 3, 2013.

32. The term "Afrocentricity" is also used. By his own count, Asante has directed more than 140 doctoral dissertations. The websites of the two scholars are http://www.asante.net/biography and http://www.maulanakarenga.org, both accessed Mar. 3, 2013. Asante has written a biography of Karenga: *Maulana Karenga: An Intellectual Portrait* (Polity Press, 2009). While Asante brought the term "Afrocentrism" to public consciousness in the United States during the 1980s, it seems to have originated as early as 1962 in the *Encyclopedia Africana* project under W. E. B. Du Bois, then living in Ghana. The term originally had a geographic rather than racial focus. See Wilson Jeremiah Moses, *Afrotopia: The Roots of African American Popular History* (Cambridge University Press, 1998), 226.

33. Molefi Kete Asante, *Afrocentricity: The Theory of Social Change* (African American Images, 2003), 4–5.

34. Ibid., 30.

35. Ibid., 86–87. A "non-Afrocentric" black man or woman, Asante writes, "unable to call upon the power of ancestors, because one does not know them; without an ideology or heritage, because one does not respect one's own prophets . . . is like an ant trying to move a large piece of garbage only to find that it will not move" (3).

36. The official Kwanzaa website is http://www.officialkwanzaawebsite.org/index.shtml, accessed Mar. 3, 2013. For Gerald Early's comment, see his "Dreaming of a Black Christmas," *Harper's* 294, no. 1760 (Jan. 1997): 58. It "is a romanticism of agrarian life," Early adds wryly, "that only urban people who have never farmed for a living could hold with a straight face."

37. For more on Kwanzaa, see the official Kwanzaa website. The procedures for celebrating Kwanzaa are outlined there, at www.officialkwanzaawebsite.org/celeb-procedures.shtml, accessed Dec. 7, 2011.

38. The quotation is from Asante, *Afrocentricity*, 2. Critiques of Afrocentrism include Tunde Adeleke, *The Case against Afrocentrism* (University Press of Mississippi, 2009),

and Clarence E. Walker, *We Can't Go Home Again: An Argument about Afrocentrism* (Oxford University Press, 2001). Comments bell hooks: "Many African-centered critiques trash Eurocentrism for its unitary representations of culture, the universalizing of white experience, its erasure of African ways of knowing, while constructing within these same narratives a unitary utopian representation of Africa as paradise, a motherland where all was perfect before white imperialism brought evil and corruption. Utopian Afrocentric evocations of an ancient high culture of black kings and queens erase the experiences of servants and slaves in the interest of presenting contemporary black folks with superheroic models of black subjectivity." See bell hooks, *Killing Rage: Ending Racism* (Henry Holt, 1995), 243–44.

39. Karenga's words are from "Annual Founder's Kwanzaa Message," *Los Angeles Sentinel*, Dec. 24, 2009, A7, available online at http://www.officialkwanzaawebsite.org/documents/PrinciplesandPracticesofKwanzaa.pdf, accessed Mar. 3, 2013. For William Oliver's comment, see his "Black Males and Social Problems: Prevention through Afrocentric Socialization," *Journal of Black Studies* 20, no. 1 (Sept. 1989): 29. Jennifer Hochschild discusses ways in which Afrocentrism appears (and appears not) to be compatible with traditional American values in her *Facing Up to the American Dream*, 137–38.

40. Early, "Dreaming of a Black Christmas," 60.

41. For the comment by Joseph C. Phillips, see Phillips, *He Talk Like a White Boy: Reflections on Faith, Family, Politics, and Authenticity* (Running Press, 2006), 204. See also Shelby Steele, *The Content of Our Character: A New Vision of Race in America* (Harper Perennial, 1990). Oprah Winfrey, comments the feminist author Patricia Hill Collins, "reinforces an individualistic ideology of social change that counsels her audiences to rely solely on themselves. Change yourself and your personal problems will disappear, advises Winfrey. If we each took personal responsibility for changing ourselves, social problems in the United States would vanish" (Collins, *Black Sexual Politics: African Americans, Gender, and the New Racism* [Routledge, 2004], 143). For the comment by bell hooks, see *Killing Rage*, 165; for the quotation by Hochschild, see *Facing Up to the American Dream*, 140.

42. On perceptions of Africa during the Black Power era, see Campbell, *Middle Passages*, chap. 9. Among the most prominent figures emigrating to Africa were W. E. B. Du Bois, who settled in Ghana in 1961 at the invitation of President Kwame Nkrumah, and Stokely Carmichael, who went to Guinea in 1969 and changed his name to Kwame Ture in honor of Nkrumah and the Guinean prime minister Ahmed Sékou Touré. Cheryl Bentsen interviewed Gates for "Head Negro in Charge," *Boston Magazine* (Apr. 1998): 70. For the reflections by Keith Richburg, see Richburg, *Out of America: A Black Man Confronts Africa* (Basic Books, 1997), 233. Richburg relates that during his three years in Africa he "never met an African who celebrated Kwanza [*sic*] or could even tell me what it was" (236). See also Phillips, *He Talk Like a White boy*, 223–24.

43. The "Chicago actor" is quoted in Russell et al., *The Color Complex*, 71. As Paul Sniderman and Thomas Piazza note, based on interviews with 756 blacks in Chicago in 1997: "It is curiously hard for some to acknowledge that the operative word in 'African American' is 'American.'" See Paul M. Sniderman and Thomas Piazza, *Black Pride and Black Prejudice* (Princeton University Press, 2002), 112. And Orlando Patterson: American blacks "are among the most American of Americans, and the emphasis on their Africanness is both physically inappropriate and culturally misleading." See Patterson, *The Ordeal of Integration: Progress and Resentment in America's "Racial" Crisis* (Civitas/Counterpoint, 1997), xi. Whoopi Goldberg's comments are from her *Book* (William Morrow, 1997), 105. Morgan Freeman on *60 Minutes* in 2005 said: "I don't want a black history month. Black history is American history" (see http://www.today.com/id/10482634/site/todayshow/ns/today-entertainment/t/freeman-calls-black-history-month-ridiculous/#.URe5ume4r1M, accessed Feb. 10, 2013). And John McWhorter writes: "We are centuries beyond Africa; Nigerians and Botswanans are foreign to us—we are at heart a distinctly American people." See McWhorter, *Authentically Black: Essays for the Black Silent Majority* (Gotham, 2004), 33.

44. On the importance of Africa to many black Americans, see Joe R. Feagin and Melvin P. Sikes, *Living with Racism: The Black Middle-Class Experience* (Beacon Press, 1994), 356–58; Graham, *Our Kind of People*, 26; Campbell, *Middle Passages*, 371. For the quote by John L. Jackson, see his *Harlemworld: Doing Race and Class in Contemporary Black America* (University of Chicago Press, 2001), 43.

7. BLACK AMERICANS

1. The U.S. Census Bureau estimated the "black or African American" population of the United States at 39,641,000 in 2009. The bureau also estimated that there were an additional 2,163,000 individuals who would self-identify both as "black or African American" and a member of another race—"white," say, or "Asian." The decision to allow citizens to check off multiple boxes in the section of the 2000 census form set aside for race is discussed in Chapter 9. See also Bob Herbert, "Too Long Ignored," *New York Times*, Aug. 20, 2010; Michael K. Brown et al., *Whitewashing Race: The Myth of a Colorblind Society* (University of California Press, 2003), 79. The employment data are from "African American Unemployment," http://www.blackdemographics.com/employment.html, accessed Dec. 8, 2011. See also Pew Research Center, "Optimism about Black Progress Declines: Blacks See Growing Values Gap between Poor and Middle Class," Nov. 13, 2007, 4, http://pewsocialtrends.org/files/2010/10/Race-2007.pdf, accessed Dec. 8, 2011; Brown et al., *Whitewashing Race*, 68–69; and Michael Tonry, *Punishing Race: A Continuing American Dilemma* (Oxford University Press, 2011), 12.

2. The late Derek Bell is perhaps the best known of the scholars who have articulated the view that little of significance has changed. See, for example, *Faces at the Bottom of*

the Well: The Permanence of Racism (Basic Books, 1992). Writes the political scientist Cathy J. Cohen, "With the increasing formal incorporation of some African Americans into political, social, and economic institutions of this country and the resulting bifurcated, racialized experiences of, for instance, middle-class and poor African Americans, a unidimensional representation of this group may no longer be possible." See Cohen, *Boundaries of Blackness: AIDS and the Breakdown of Black Politics* (University of Chicago Press, 1999), 15.

3. The significance of ending legalized segregation was explored in C. Vann Woodward's celebrated *The Strange Career of Jim Crow,* published by Oxford University Press in 1955, just a year after the Supreme Court handed down its decision in *Brown v. Board of Education.* Martin Luther King, Jr. called *The Strange Career of Jim Crow* "the historical Bible of the Civil Rights Movement." On the demographic shifts, see Sabrina Tavernise and Robert Gebeloff, "Many U.S. Blacks Moving to South, Reversing Trend," *New York Times,* Mar. 24, 2011; and Dan Bilefsky, "For New Life, Blacks in City Head to South," *New York Times,* June 1, 2011. The term "ancestral homeland" was applied to the South by Isabel Wilkerson, author of *The Warmth of Other Suns: The Epic Story of America's Great Migration* (Random House, 2010). See also Eugene Robinson, *Disintegration: The Splintering of Black America* (Doubleday, 2010), 92; William H. Frey, "The New Great Migration: Black Americans Return to the South, 1965–2000" (Brookings Institution, 2004), 7; Tavernise and Gebeloff, "Many U.S. Blacks Moving South"; Art Golab, "Latest Census Shows Shrinking Chicago, Growing Collar Counties," *Chicago Sun-Times,* Mar. 17, 2011, http://www.suntimes.com/news/3838469-418/chicagos-population-drops-6.9-collar-counties-grow-census-shows, accessed Dec. 8, 2011; and Associated Press, "More Blacks Leave NYC, Chicago for the South," Feb. 15, 2011, http://www.crainsnewyork.com/article/20110215/FREE/110219914, accessed Dec. 8, 2011. For snapshots of some Southern cities where the middle class has grown rapidly, see http://www.blacksindallas.com; http://www.houstoninblack.com; http://www.blackdemographics.com/virginia Beach_norfolkblackdemographics.html; http://www.blackdemographics.com/charlotte blackdemographicscom.html; and http://www.blackdemographics.com/atlantablack demographics.html (all accessed Dec. 8, 2011).

4. Desmond King, *Making Americans: Immigration, Race, and the Origins of the Diverse Democracy* (Harvard University Press, 2000), 244. Like the Civil Rights Movement, the call for immigration reform benefited from the need for Washington to combat Soviet propaganda that America was a bridgehead for racism. See Richard Alba and Victor Nee, *Remaking the American Mainstream: Assimilation and Contemporary Immigration* (Harvard University Press, 2003), 172. Over the twenty-five years following passage of the Hart-Celler Act, new legislation made it still easier to gain immigrant status: The Immigration and Nationality Act of 1976; The Refugee Act of 1980; The 1986 Immigration Reform and Control Act, which made it possible for undocumented immigrants living in the United States to apply for legal status; the 1990 Immigration Act.

But restrictions on the total number of immigrants from the Western Hemisphere also led to more Mexicans crossing the border illegally.

5. Mae M. Ngai, *Impossible Subjects: Illegal Aliens and the Making of Modern America* (Princeton University Press, 2004), 265. Since 1980, Europeans have represented only about 10 percent of immigrants arriving each year. See Sam Roberts, "More Africans Enter U.S. Than in Days of Slavery," *New York Times*, Feb. 21, 2005.

6. Guyana, on the northeast coast of South America, is also an important source of immigrants. See Mary Mederios Kent, "Immigration and America's Black Population," *Population Bulletin* 62, no. 4 (Dec. 2007): 4–5, 7–8, http://www.prb.org/pdf07/62.4 immigration.pdf, accessed July 5, 2013; Roberts, "More Africans Enter U.S. Than in Days of Slavery." In 2002, when 60,000 Africans arrived in the United States, over 8,000 were from Nigeria, over 7,500 were from Ethiopia, more than 4,000 were from Somalia and Ghana (each), and over 3,000 were from Kenya. Colin Powell, whose parents came to New York in the 1920s, observed in his autobiography: "There is, undeniably, a degree of clannishness among West Indians, Jamaicans included. My family socialized and found friends almost entirely within the Jamaican community." See Colin Powell with Joseph E. Persico, *My American Journey* (Ballantine, 1995), 22. The author and civil rights activist Audre Lorde, whose father was from Barbados and mother from Grenada, described much the same pattern of behavior in her "mythobiography" *Zami: A New Spelling of My Name* (Crossing Press, 1982). Kent, "Immigration and America's Black Population," 3–4, 12; John R. Logan and Glenn Deane, "Black Diversity in Metropolitan America," 4–5, http://mumford1.dyndns.org/cen2000/BlackWhite/Black DiversityReport/Black_Diversity_final.pdf, accessed Mar. 3, 2013.

7. See Charles Johnson, "The End of the Black American Narrative," *American Scholar* (Summer 2008), available online at http://www.theamericanscholar.org/the -end-of-the-black-american-narrative, accessed Apr. 20, 2013. The comments by Mary Andom can be seen at http://community.seattletimes.nwsource.com/archive/?date =20030816&slug=nextculture17, accessed Apr. 20, 2013. On income and social differences between the groups, see Pamela R. Bennett and Amy Lutz, "How African American Is the Net Black Advantage? Differences in College Attendance among Immigrant Blacks, Native Blacks, and Whites," *Sociology of Education* 82, no. 1 (Jan. 2009): 73; and Logan and Deane, "Black Diversity in Metropolitan America," 6.

8. Mary C. Waters, *Black Identities: West Indian and Immigrant Dreams and American Realities* (Russell Sage Foundation, 1999), 65.

9. Powell, *My American Journey*, 22; Waters, *Black Identities*, 71 (the quotation from the "young woman" is on p. 73); John L. Jackson, *Harlemworld: Doing Race and Class in Contemporary Black America* (University of Chicago Press, 2001), 43.

10. Waters, *Black Identities*, 73–74; Robinson, *Disintegration*, 235, 9 (for the quoted "reply" by the immigrants, which is his paraphrase of testimony he's heard from immigrants, see p. 214); Logan and Deane, "Black Diversity in Metropolitan America," 5;

Kent, "Immigration and America's Black Population," 9–10. A more reliable estimate than the one provided by Robinson can be found in Douglas S. Massey et al., "Black Immigrants and Black Natives Attending Selective Colleges and Universities in the United States," *American Journal of Education* 13, no. 2 (Feb. 2007): 243–71. The authors found that children of immigrants from Africa and the West Indies represented 35 percent of black freshmen entering elite universities.

11. Thomas J. Sugrue, *Sweet Land of Liberty: The Forgotten Struggle for Civil Rights in the North* (Random House, 2008), 51, 388; Bart Landry, *The New Black Middle Class* (University of California Press, 1987), 121; Renee C. Romano, *Race Mixing: Black-White Marriage in Postwar America* (Harvard University Press, 2003), 213–14. "Public employment was crucial to the wage and salary gains made by African Americans relative to white workers in the 1960s because the wage gap between black and white workers is far narrower in the public sector. There is also evidence that, unlike white workers, black public employees were paid a higher salary than their counterparts in the private sector" (Brown et al., *Whitewashing Race*, 74).

12. Sugrue, *Sweet Land of Liberty*, 537. See also Andrew Hacker, *Two Nations: Black and White, Separate, Hostile, Unequal* (Scribner, 2003), 137.

13. David A. Thomas and Robin J. Ely, "Making Differences Matter: A New Paradigm for Managing Diversity," *Harvard Business Review* 5 (Sept.–Oct. 1996): 79–90.

14. Robinson, *Disintegration*, 7, 91, 93. Whites earning between $50,000 and $99,999 make up 37 percent of the white middle class; blacks in the same income category represent 31 percent of the black middle class. Karyn R. Lacy, *Blue-Chip Black: Race, Class, and Status in the New Black Middle Class* (University of California Press, 2007), 35. Every year *Black Enterprise* magazine lists the one hundred largest black-owned companies in seven different sectors of the economy. In 2008, the top one hundred industrial/service companies and one hundred leading auto dealers—the core of the "BE 100s"—collectively grossed more than $28 billion. See http://www.blackenterprise.com/2008/10/15/be-100s-the-2008-report, accessed Dec. 8, 2011.

15. From Lacy, *Blue-Chip Black*, 45, fig. 2, based on the U.S. Census and the American Housing Survey. Philadelphia is the only major city in which the proportion of the black population living in suburbs actually dropped between 1970 and 2000, from 23 percent to 22 percent.

16. Many literary works have testified to the dreams of escape, most notably Lorraine Hansberry's prize-winning *A Raisin in the Sun,* which debuted on Broadway in 1959. The text of the Fair Housing Act can be viewed at http://www.justice.gov/crt//about/hce/title8.php, accessed Dec. 8, 2011. On demographic changes during the period, see John R. Logan, Brian J. Stults, and Reynolds Farley, "Segregation of Minorities in the Metropolis: Two Decades of Change," *Demography* 41, no. 1 (Feb. 2004): 2. A survey conducted by the same organization in 1942 found that 84 percent of Americans believed there should be "separate sections in town and cities for Negroes to live in." See

Susan Welch et al., *Race and Place: Race Relations in an American City* (Cambridge University Press, 2001), 30–31. The journalist Jonathan Mahler has summarized developments in Detroit: "In the aftermath of Detroit's polarizing 1967 riots, the steady stream of white residents who were already leaving the city turned into a torrent. Yet many middle-class blacks opted to stay behind. Most of the suburbs remained off limits to African-Americans; what's more, the 1973 election of Detroit's first black mayor, Coleman Young—himself a former Ford line worker—seemed like cause for renewed optimism. But in the 1980s, as crime rates soared, the quality of schools and services plummeted and the number of crack houses multiplied, more and more middle-class blacks abandoned the city for the suburbs, or in some cases, left the Detroit area altogether." Jonathan Mahler, "G.M., Detroit and the Fall of the Black Middle Class," *New York Times Magazine*, June 24, 2009.

17. William Levitt had intended the community to be all white, arguing, "We can solve a housing problem or we can try to solve a racial problem, but we cannot combine the two" (quoted in Sugrue, *Sweet Land of Liberty*, 223). For the quotation by Sugrue, see his *Sweet Land of Liberty*, 201. In 1962, Catholic, Protestant, and Jewish leaders formed the Open Occupancy Conference in Detroit to promote residential integration, particularly in suburban communities. The conference stated that its primary goal was "to assist middle-class blacks to move into the larger community." Thomas J. Sugrue, *The Origins of the Urban Crisis: Race and Inequality in Postwar Detroit* (Princeton University Press, 1996), 193.

18. Richard D. Alba, John R. Logan, and Brian J. Stults, "How Segregated Are Middle-Class African Americans?" *Social Problems* 47, no. 4 (Nov. 2000): 543–558; Wilson, *When Work Disappears*, 47. For more on Michael Eric Dyson's "Afristocracy" label, see Dyson, *Is Bill Cosby Right? Or Has the Black Middle Class Lost Its Mind?* (Basic Civitas Books, 2005), xiv. Richard Thompson Ford, *The Race Card: How Bluffing about Bias Makes Race Relations Worse* (Picador, 2009), 287–88. Lacy, *Blue-Chip Black*, 5. Mitchellville is an unincorporated black-majority town in Prince George's County, Maryland, just outside Washington. The average cost for a home was over half a million dollars in 2007. Many of the residences boast more than 6,000 square feet of living space. The Country Club at Woodmore, designed by a team that included Arnold Palmer, is one of more than a dozen golf courses, public and private, in the county, making Prince George's "an epicenter of African American golf." See Woodmore's website at http://www.ccwoodmore.com, accessed Dec. 8, 2011. *Atlanta Magazine* 42, no. 12 (May 2003): 81–84. For more on the most affluent of blacks, see Robinson, *Disintegration*, 25, 78–79; Sugrue, *Sweet Land of Liberty*, 510–12; demographic information from http://www.blackdemographics.com/middle_class.html, accessed Dec. 8, 2011; and Bilefsky, "For New Life, Blacks in City Head South."

19. Landry, *The New Black Middle Class*, 86; Hacker, *Two Nations*, 117–18; Mahler, "GM, Detroit and the Fall of the Black Middle Class." Thirty-one percent of black middle-

class families match the Department of Housing and Urban Development's definition for "housing burdened," meaning they spend 30 percent or more of their after-tax income on housing expenses. For the Demos and Institute for Assets and Social Policy data, see Jennifer Wheary et al., "Economic (In)security: The Experience of the African-American and Latino Middle Classes," available at http://iasp.brandeis.edu/pdfs/Author/meschede-tatjana/By%20A%20Thread%20Report%202.pdf, accessed July 17, 2013. For Mary Pattillo's reflections, see her *Black Picket Fences: Privilege and Peril among the Black Middle Class* (University of Chicago Press, 1999), 6. See also Elijah Anderson, *Code of the Street: Decency, Violence, and the Moral Life of the Inner City* (Norton, 1999), introduction; Welch et al., *Race and Place*, 30–31; Alba et al., "How Segregated Are Middle-Class African Americans?"; and Lacy, *Blue-Chip Black*, 15, 2.

20. William Julius Wilson, *When Work Disappears* (Knopf, 1996), 195; Jennifer L. Hochschild, *Facing Up to the American Dream: Race, Class, and the Soul of the Nation* (Princeton University Press, 1995), 48–49; Phillip J. Bowman, Ray Muhammad, and Mosi Ifatunji, "Skin Tone, Class, and Racial Attitudes among African Americans," in Cedric Herring, Verna M. Keith, and Hayward Derrick Horton, eds., *Skin Deep: How Race and Complexion Matter in the "Color-Blind" Era* (University of Illinois Press, 2004), 134–35; Pew Research Center, "Optimism about Black Progress Declines," 13. In 1992 the wealthiest fifth of black families had 49 percent of the total black income while the wealthiest fifth of white families had 44 percent of the total white income. There was also greater inequality, including asset inequality, within the black population than between black Americans and white Americans. See Orlando Patterson, *The Ordeal of Integration: Progress and Resentment in America's "Racial" Crisis* (Civitas/Counterpoint, 1997), 24. Since the 1970s, more than half of all black families have lived in the poorest quarter of neighborhoods in consecutive generations; the figure for white families is just 7 percent. See Patrick Sharkey, "The Intergenerational Transmission of Context," *American Journal of Sociology* 113 (Jan. 2008): 933; Bowman et al., "Skin Tone, Class, and Racial Attitudes," 135; Wilson, *When Work Disappears*, 11–12; and Wilson, *More Than Just Race*, 59.

21. The term "hypersegregation" first appeared in a paper Massey and Denton published in 1989: Douglas S. Massey and Nancy A. Denton, "Hypersegregation in U.S. Metropolitan Areas: Black and Hispanic Segregation along Five Dimensions," *Demography* 26, no. 3 (Aug. 1989): 373–91. It achieved popular currency with publication of their study *American Apartheid and the Making of the Underclass* (Harvard University Press, 1993). Massey and Denton define hypersegregation in the following way: A group must be "very highly segregated" on at least four of the five following dimensions: 1. "Blacks may be distributed so that they are overrepresented in some areas and underrepresented in others, leading to different degrees of *unevenness*." 2. "[Blacks] may be distributed so that their racial *isolation* is ensured by virtue of rarely sharing a neighborhood with whites." 3. "Black neighborhoods may be tightly *clustered* to form

one large contiguous enclave or scattered about in a checkerboard fashion." 4. "[Blacks] may be *concentrated* within a very small area or settled sparsely throughout the urban environment." 5. "[Blacks] may be spatially *centralized* around the urban core or spread out along the periphery" (Massey and Denton, *American Apartheid and the Making of the Underclass*, 74). See also Rima Wilkes and John Iceland, "Hypersegregation in the Twenty-First Century, *Demography* 41, no. 1 (Feb. 2004): 23–26. Prior to 2000, only blacks could be found living in hypersegregated neighborhoods. The census for that year, however, showed that Los Angeles and New York were also hypersegregated for Latinos. See Alba et al., "How Segregated Are Middle-Class African Americans?"; Sugrue, *Origins of the Urban Crisis*, 199–203, 207; and Wilson, *When Work Disappears*, 14.

8. THE "TRULY DISADVANTAGED"

1. Some have taken to calling the well-to-do element "the truly advantaged." See, for example, Eric S. Brown, "The Black Professional Middle Class and the Black Community: Racialized Class Formation in Oakland and the East Bay," in Kenneth L. Kusmer and Joe William Trotter, eds., *African American Urban History since World War II* (University of Chicago Press, 2009), 282; John Sibley Butler, *Entrepreneurship and Self-Help among Black Americans: A Reconsideration of Race and Economics* (State University of New York, 2005), 325, 332.

2. Loïc Wacquant, "Inside the Zone: The Social Art of the Hustler in the Black American Ghetto," *Theory, Culture, & Society* 15, no. 2 (Feb. 1998): 2. A remarkable collection of photographs documenting the recent history of inner-city communities can be found in Camilo José Vergara, *The New American Ghetto* (Rutgers University, 1995).

3. On crack cocaine generally, see Sudhir Alladi Venkatesh, *Off the Books: The Underground Economy of the Urban Poor* (Harvard University Press, 2006), 243. For the street hustler's comments, see Wacquant, "Inside the Zone," 27. For the Philadelphia mother's lament, see Elijah Anderson, *Code of the Street: Decency, Violence, and the Moral Life of the Inner City* (Norton, 1999), 43.

4. William Julius Wilson, *When Work Disappears* (Knopf, 1996), 61. The "code of the street" can turn what may seem like petty provocations—for example, maintaining eye contact too long—into deadly confrontations. Notes Elijah Anderson, "there are always people around looking for a fight in order to increase their share of respect—or 'juice,' as it is sometimes called on the street" (Anderson, *Code of the Street*, 34, 73). Someone who has been disrespected and does not retaliate is widely known as a "sucker," "chump," or "punk." For more on young black males' experiences of violence and their responses to injury, see John H. Rich and Courtney M. Grey, "Pathways to Recurrent Trauma among Young Black Men: Traumatic Stress, Substance Abuse, and the 'Code of the Street,'" *American Journal of Public Health* 95, no. 5 (May, 2005): 818, 816; Bruce Western, *Punishment and Inequality in America* (Russell Sage Foundation, 2006), 169;

and Rondel Thompson and Sophia Parker, "The National Urban League Equality Index," in National Urban League, *The State of Black America, 2007: Portrait of the Black Male* (Beckham Publications, 2007), 25–26. For the insights of Jim Myers, see his "Notes on the Murder of Thirty of My Neighbors," *Atlantic Monthly* (Mar. 2000): 76.

5. The remark by Lafayette is quoted in Alex Kotlowitz, *There Are No Children Here: The Story of Two Boys Growing Up in the Other America* (Anchor, 1991), x; see also p. 32. Also see DeNeen L. Brown, "Getting Ready to Die Young; Children in Violent D.C. Neighborhoods Plan Their Own Funerals," *Washington Post*, Nov. 1, 1993; and Jim Myers, "Notes on the Murder of Thirty of My Neighbors," 82. One young man in Boston, who turned to marijuana for escape, recorded his emotional struggles in rap lyrics: "As the day darkens, / I'm feeling shook. / I guess that's why I stay high, / constantly fighting to keep the nightmares from turning to reality. / Nightmares of bloody days / and court dates circulating in my mind. / Nightmares seem to always turn into reality, / and reality seems to fade into nightmares" (Rich and Grey, "Pathways to Recurrent Trauma," 819). On average, during the summer of 1987, one person was beaten, shot, or stabbed every three days at the Henry Horner Homes. In just one week, the police confiscated 22 guns and 330 grams of cocaine. See Kotlowitz, *There Are No Children Here*, 32, x.

6. For the comments by Orlando Patterson, see *Rituals of Blood: Consequences of Slavery in Two American Centuries* (Civitas/Counterpoint, 1998), 139. As of 2000, about half of single black mothers had incomes below the poverty line. See Andrew Hacker, *Two Nations: Black and White, Separate, Hostile, Unequal* (Scribner, 2003), 94–95; Bob Herbert, "Too Long Ignored," *New York Times*, Aug. 20, 2010; Anderson, *Code of the Street*, 214; William Julius Wilson, *More Than Just Race: Being Black and Poor in the Inner City* (Norton, 2009), 128. At the beginning of the twenty-first century, close to two-thirds of black single mothers had never been married, nearly five times the proportion of the previous generation. In the early years of the twenty-first century, almost a third of all "persistently poor households" in the United States were headed by nonelderly black women. See Wilson, *More Than Just Race*, 101. Poor black women are much less likely than poor white women to have adequate prenatal care, which in part explains why infant mortality is almost twice as high among blacks as among whites. See Eugene Robinson, *Disintegration: The Splintering of Black America* (Doubleday, 2010), 129–30.

7. Wilson, *When Work Disappears*, 29–30; Thomas J. Sugrue, *Sweet Land of Liberty: The Forgotten Struggle for Civil Rights in the North* (Random House, 2008), 257; Thomas J. Sugrue, *The Origins of the Urban Crisis: Race and Inequality in Postwar Detroit* (Princeton University Press, 1996), 126–28; Anderson, *Code of the Street*, 314; Hacker, *Two Nations*, 118; and Wilson, *When Work Disappears*, 35. In 1986 North Lawndale also had 48 state lottery agents, 50 currency exchanges, and 99 licensed liquor stores and bars.

8. For the "left at home" quotation and the words of Marian Wright Edelman, see

"Losing Our Children in America's Cradle to Prison Pipeline," in National Urban League, *State of Black America, 2007,* 222–23. For additional information, see Wilson, *More Than Just Race,* 67. Twenty years ago Jonathan Kozol explored the inadequacies of public education in inner-city schools in *Savage Inequalities: Children in America's Schools* (Harper Perennial, 1992). See also Christopher Knaus, "Still Segregated, Still Unequal: Analyzing the Impact of No Child Left Behind on African American Students," in National Urban League, *State of Black America, 2007,* 106. Three-quarters of white students graduate from high school on time. See *Journal of Black Higher Education Weekly Bulletin,* Aug. 6, 2009, http://www.jbhe.com/latest/news/8–6-09/racialgap .html, accessed Dec. 8, 2011. In New York City in 2008, by contrast, just 38 percent of black high school students graduated on time (Herbert, "Too Long Ignored"). (Intriguingly, Hawaii, the birthplace of Barack Obama, is the only state where blacks are more likely than whites to graduate on time.) Black students are also three times more likely than white students, two times more likely than Hispanic and American Indian students, and five times more likely than students of Asian background to be suspended from school. See the Council of the Great City Schools, "A Call for Change: The Social and Educational Factors Contributing to the Outcomes of Black Males in Urban Schools," Oct. 2010, chap. 2, http://cgcs.schoolwires.net/cms/lib/DC00001581/Centricity/Domain/ 35/Publication%20Docs/callforchange.pdf, accessed Dec. 8, 2011.

9. Wilson, *More Than Just Race,* 77. One example of the decline in employment opportunities for high-school dropouts: the number of jobs requiring some college education increased by 38 percent in Philadelphia during the 1970s, while employment available to individuals without a high-school degree fell by 32 percent. See Carl Husemoller Nightingale, *On the Edge: A History of Poor Black Children and Their American Dreams* (Basic Books, 1993), 57; Renee Hanson, Mark McArdle, and Valerie Rawlston Wilson, "Invisible Men: The Urgent Problems of Low-Income African-American Males," in National Urban League, *State of Black America, 2007,* 210–12. For Bruce Western's work in this area, see Western, *Punishment and Inequality in America,* 91. "Employment rates of young black women now exceed those of young black men even though many of the women must also care for children" (Wilson, *More Than Just Race,* 76). See also Cedric Herring, "Skin Deep: Race and Complexion in the 'Color-Blind' Era," in Cedric Herring, Verna M. Keith, and Hayward Derrick Horton, eds., *Skin Deep: How Race and Complexion Matter in the "Color-Blind" Era* (University of Illinois Press, 2004), 6; and note Maxine S. Thompson and Verna M. Keith: "Employers view darker African American men as violent, uncooperative, dishonest, and unstable" (from "The Blacker the Berry: Gender, Skin Tone, Self-Esteem and Self-Efficacy," *Gender and Society* 15, no. 3 [June 2001]: 352). See also Wilson, *When Work Disappears,* 136.

10. Sugrue, *Origins of the Urban Crisis,* 144. Social workers who interviewed black teenagers in Detroit during the 1960s found that not a single one believed that skilled trades or office work would be available to them (Sugrue, *Sweet Land of Liberty,* 261;

Wilson, *When Work Disappears,* 58). In New Orleans, in the aftermath of Hurricane Katrina, with the local economy in ruins, a boy could earn $30 as a lookout during drug deals and up to $1,000 helping to transport drugs. See Mercedes R. Carnethon, "Black Male Life Expectancy in the United States: A Multi-Level Exploration of Causes," in National Urban League, *State of Black America, 2007,* 145; and Anderson, *Code of the Street,* 114. The drug trade, writes the journalist and author Nathan McCall, was "the black answer to urban capitalism." See Nathan McCall, *Makes Me Wanna Holler: A Young Black Man in America* (Vintage, 1995), 102.

11. For the Anderson quotation, see *Code of the Street,* 111. For the comment by Malcolm X, see Malcolm X as told to Alex Haley, *The Autobiography of Malcolm X* (Ballantine, 1965), 359. For the quotation by the gang leader, see Sudhir Alladi Venkatesh and Steven D. Levitt, "'Are We a Family or a Business?' History and Disjuncture in the Urban American Street Gang," *Theory and Society* 29, no. 4 (Aug. 2000): 451. Comments Katherine Newman: "Media attention given to the glamour of the drug trade suggests that it is an attractive magnet for kids who need money. But the young adults we met in Harlem are frightened of the drug lords and want to stay as far away from their business as possible. They know too many people who are dead, in jail, or permanently disabled from the ravages of drugs." See Newman, *No Shame in My Game: The Working Poor in the Inner City* (Vintage, 2000), 100–101.

12. Discussion of the concept of an "oppositional culture," especially as it manifests itself in the education system, can be found in John U. Ogbu, ed., *Minority Status, Oppositional Culture and Academic Engagement* (Routledge, 2008). For Anderson's insights, see his *Code of the Street.* Cosby's remarks at an NAACP awards ceremony in Washington commemorating the fiftieth anniversary of *Brown v. Board of Education*—he was one of the honorees—have drawn particular attention, and criticism. See Ta-Nehisi Coates, "This Is How We Lost to the White Man," *Atlantic Monthly* (May 2008), available online at http://www.theatlantic.com/magazine/archive/2008/05/-8216-this-is-how -we-lost-to-the-white-man-8217/6774, accessed Dec. 8, 2011; Michael Eric Dyson, *Is Bill Cosby Right? Or Has the Black Middle Class Lost Its Mind?* (Basic Civitas Books, 2005); and Cathy J. Cohen, *Democracy Remixed* (Oxford University Press, 2010), chap. 2.

13. Venkatesh, *Off the Books,* 92–93. "Maquis Park" is an invented name for a community of roughly ten square blocks on Chicago's South Side.

14. Ibid., 4–5. See also Jennifer L. Hochschild, *Facing Up to the American Dream: Race, Class, and the Soul of the Nation* (Princeton University Press, 1995), 161.

15. Newman, *No Shame in My Game,* xi. For the quotation by the Chicago mother, see Wacquant, "Inside the Zone," 10. A 28-year-old mother in one of the large housing projects in Chicago explained what her friends do when they turn desperate: "Shit, turn tricks, sell drugs, anything—and everything. Mind you, everyone is not a stick-up man, you know, but any and everything. Me myself I have sold marijuana, I'm not a drug pusher, but I'm just tryin' to make ends meet—I'm tryin' to keep bread on the

table—I have two babies." Wilson, *When Work Disappears*, 58. Another woman from the projects in Chicago netted as much as $700 running a monthly card game. See Kotlowitz, *There Are No Children Here*, 60.

16. Venkatesh, *Off the Books*, 25–26.

17. Newman, *No Shame in My Game*, 219.

18. Venkatesh, *Off the Books*, 218–19, 246, 162–63, 196. Barack Obama discovered the ad hoc nature of community governance when he worked as a neighborhood organizer in Chicago. See Barack Obama, *Dreams from My Father: A Story of Race and Inheritance* (Three Rivers, 2004), pt. 2. Jail can become a temporary refuge for hustlers needing shelter. Confessed one Chicago woman: "If you're poor, you *need* jail. You really do. That's where I disappear to. The food is good and it's better in the winter; the people are okay to you, except for the guards that try and get up in your kootchie. And you get some peace. I mean, you have to know when to go! You can't go right after [check day] when everyone's in there because they're drunk. No. You go middle of the week, slow time, get a few days, get rested, get warm. See, everyone around here does that. That's why we know the cops so well; we see them all the time. They're like our landlords."

19. Venkatesh, *Off the Books*, 187–89, 125, 58. Venkatesh notes: "Over the course of one bitterly cold winter stretch, I observed several hustlers bringing blankets to people sleeping in parks; some took homeless persons into their own illegal abode—however crowded it may have already been—and others canvassed the area persuading men and women to patronize the local shelters. None of them was paid for this work; none of them had a formal tie to an advocacy organization or transitional housing center. And they did not believe that the city's human service agencies would be following in their footsteps" (189).

20. Venkatesh and Levitt, "Are We a Family or a Business?" 428–29, 451–52. During the summer of 1987, police in Chicago estimated that the Conservative Vice Lords, a gang operating out of the Henry Horner Homes, grossed up to $100,000 each week. The gang had an arsenal that included pistols, Uzis, and grenades. Kotlowitz, *There Are No Children Here*, 41, 34, 37. For more, see Don Hazen, ed., *Inside the L.A. Riots: What Really Happened* (Institute for Alternative Journalism, 1992), 104–105; Monique M. Taylor, *Harlem between Heaven and Hell* (University of Minnesota Press, 2002), 123; Newman, *No Shame in My Game*, 110; Mary Pattillo, *Black on the Block: The Politics of Race and Class in the City* (University of Chicago Press, 2007), 272; Venkatesh, *Off the Books*, 286; and Kotlowitz, *There Are No Children Here*, 136, which includes the essay by the murdered gang leader. One gang leader told Elijah Anderson how upset he was when he found out that a woman who had bought crack from one of his dealers had children and had used all her welfare money for drugs. "He sought the woman out and gave her half her money back. His rationale was that business is business but that the kids shouldn't go hungry." See Anderson, *Code of the Street*, 121.

21. A young man in Harlem told the anthropologist John L. Jackson that when he

sees black people with suits on, "some days I just feel like I want to drop [punch] them" while at other times "it's like I feel a little proud." John L. Jackson, *Harlemworld: Doing Race and Class in Contemporary Black America* (University of Chicago Press, 2001), 118. See also Pattillo, *Black on the Block*, 104, which discusses the vicarious pleasure taken in the accomplishments of black professionals. On the conference, see Courtland Milloy, "Black Men's Dreams, Black Men's Reality," *Tampa Tribune*, May 27, 1991. Mansfield Frazier was a prisoner in a Kentucky penitentiary who immersed himself in writings on the "underclass" and wrote to numerous well-known black authors thinking they would be interested in an "enlightened exchange of ideas." He received not a single response. He subsequently complained in *Southern Exposure* that "middle class black writers . . . have been infected by 'arms-length liberalism.' They might champion the underclass, but they want nothing to do with them. They write passionately about the wrongs perpetrated by our racist society and how it marginalizes the have-nots, but they wouldn't care to live next door to the have-nots and, evidently, would not even correspond with them. My experience, unfortunately, isn't unique. There is a discernible pattern which I discovered talking to other convicts about their experiences with the outside world." See Frazier, "On Race, Rage, and the Underclass," *Southern Exposure* (Winter 1996): 57.

22. Complains a social worker who lives in New Rochelle but works in Harlem: "When I say my father was a lawyer and owned a restaurant and my mom was a nurse and teacher, and got her doctorate, and that I grew up in Connecticut and take the Metro North into work, people can start to act like 'oh, what could you ever tell me about anything.' Sometimes I lie or try to just be quiet. I just try to keep quiet, but sometimes it makes me upset that people think that they are the only ones who can say something because they are poor like that" (Jackson, *Harlemworld*, 83–84; for the quotation in the text by the "unemployed man," see p. 38). For a discussion about gentrification in Harlem between the author and journalist Herb Boyd and Roscoe Brown, director of the Center for Urban Education Policy at the CUNY Graduate Center, Jan. 31, 2007, see http://www.youtube.com/watch?v=ekJPbEoXjoM&feature=related, accessed Dec. 8, 2011. For the material from Taylor, see *Harlem between Heaven and Hell*, 87, 100. A writer told Taylor: "People like myself who have moved into the neighborhood want to see things happen. First of all, for selfish reasons. They are just like any other property owner, you know. They want to see the value of their property go up. We're buying these apartments, and, on an economic level, you want to see it go up rather than down. I mean, that's just basic stuff. People who had the good sense to invest want to see their stuff go up." See also Michael E. Crutcher, Jr., *Tremé: Race and Place in a New Orleans Neighborhood* (University of Georgia Press, 2010), chap. 7.

23. Pattillo, *Black on the Block*, 9–10. By 2006, a two-bedroom, two-bathroom condominium was bringing as much as $300,000.

24. Ibid., 207–208. Observes Pattillo: "The increased municipal revenue that comes

with the influx of middle-class residents could in theory equalize the structural land-scape by funding things like high-quality public preschools, wage increases for civil service workers, or investments in public transportation. But in practice such a redis-tribution of resources often takes a backseat to feeding the demands of the new gentry for public art, smoother streets, and support for more high-end housing, recreational, and commercial activity. Because both the public sector and the private market cater to the coveted middle-class citizen-consumer, the underlying structures of inequality are left intact. If gentrification is the point at which mixed-income communities tip up-ward, then whatever structural reforms had been enacted—better schools, more jobs, cleaner environment—now disproportionately benefit the incoming gentry rather than the outgoing poor residents" (107).

25. Oakland was identified as the single poorest of Chicago's seventy-seven commu-nities in terms of both median family income and the proportion of families who were poor. The University of Chicago police were invited in to help with policekeeping in North Kenwood-Oakland. Many of their efforts were directed to monitoring the public behaviour of the poor. See Pattillo, *Black on the Block*, 15, chaps. 4 and 5, 262–65, 88. Ruth Baxter-Brown, a young professional living in Harlem, recounted how her hus-band stopped people from eating chicken on the stoop of their brownstone. They "set our garbage can on fire and cursed us out a few times." Taylor, *Harlem between Heaven and Hell*, 121.

26. Taylor, *Harlem between Heaven and Hell*, 126; Chris Rock, "Bring the Pain" (Dream-works, 2002, DVD).

27. Pattillo, *Black on the Block*, 3. Not a few gentrifiers were also suffering from "in-tegration exhaustion": fatigue from living as black pioneers in white neighborhoods. See Sheryll Cashin, *The Failures of Integration: How Class and Race Are Undermining the American Dream* (PublicAffairs, 2004), 9. For the comment by the black college president, see Wilson, *When Work Disappears*, 130–31. See also Joleen Kirschenman, "African-American Employers' Attitudes toward African-American Workers," in Steven A. Tuch and Jack K. Martin, eds., *Racial Attitudes in the 1990s: Continuity and Change* (Praeger, 1997), 201–25; Newman, *No Shame in My Game*, 156–57.

28. Robin Kelley has written, "Contrary to the new 'culture of poverty' theorists who claim that the lifestyles of the so-called black 'underclass' constitute a significant de-viation from mainstream values, most gangsta rappers insist that the characters they rap about epitomize what America has been and continues to be." See Kelley, *Race Rebels: Culture, Politics, and the Black Working Class* (Free Press, 1994), 201. The Hochs-child quote is from her *Facing Up to the American Dream*, 160. For the survey's results, see Wilson, *When Work Disappears*, 179.

29. Newman, *No Shame in My Game*, 297, 209.

30. Venkatesh, *Off the Books*, 24–25.

31. Newman, *No Shame in My Game*, 97, 108–109 discusses how teenagers who work

at fast food restaurants deal with the taunts of peers. For the quotations in this paragraph, see Wilson, *When Work Disappears*, 75; and Venkatesh and Levitt, "Are We a Family or a Business?" 447.

32. Thomas B. Edsall and Mary D. Edsall, *Chain Reaction: The Impact of Race, Rights, and Taxes on American Politics* (Norton, 1992), 148. Reagan claimed the woman used 80 aliases, listed 30 different addresses, had a dozen Social Security cards, and was collecting veterans' benefits on four nonexistent deceased husbands. See Patricia Hill Collins, *Black Feminist Thought: Knowledge, Politics, and the Consciousness of Empowerment*, rev. 10th anniversary ed. (Routledge, 2000), 79. In a National Black Election Panel Study conducted in the 1980s, 74 percent of blacks contended that there was no need for government aid; blacks should help themselves. See Michael C. Dawson, *Behind the Mule: Race and Class in African-American Politics* (Princeton University Press, 1994), 190–91. On Kimberly Battle-Walters's conversations with the beauty-shop regulars, see Battle-Walters, *Sheila's Shop: Working-Class African American Women Talk about Life, Love, Race, and Hair* (Rowman & Littlefield, 2004), 41–45. Of 100 black single mothers receiving Aid to Families with Dependent Children, 61 admitted to feeling a sense of shame about having to resort to welfare to help support their families. (In 1997, Aid to Families with Dependent Children was replaced by the much more restrictive Temporary Assistance for Needy Families, which placed time limits on one's eligibility for welfare.)

33. Newman, *No Shame in My Game*, 189–198, 204; Anderson, *Code of the Street*, 38–39, 208–10; Wilson, *When Work Disappears*, 102, 58; Venkatesh and Levitt, "Are We a Family or a Business?" 447.

34. Hochschild, *Facing Up to the American Dream*, 159; Wilson, *When Work Disappears*, 179–80 (see also Wilson, *More Than Just Race*, 82–84); and Alford A. Young, Jr., *The Minds of Marginalized Black Men: Making Sense of Mobility, Opportunity, and Future Life Chances* (Princeton University Press, 2004), 180. Said another Chicago man, thirty-four years old: "Everybody get [sic] pretty much what they deserve because if everybody wants to do better they got to go out there and try. If they don't try, they won't make it." See also Ellis Cose, *The End of Anger: A New Generation's Take on Race and Rage* (HarperCollins, 2011), chap. 8.

35. Carl Husemoller Nightingale, *On the Edge: A History of Poor Black Children and Their American Dreams* (Basic Books, 1993), 160–61.

36. Wacquant, "Inside the Zone," 23; see also Anderson, *Code of the Street*, 151, 234.

37. Venkatesh and Levitt, "Are We a Family or a Business?" 447–48.

38. Ibid., 446–47, 428–29. Venkatesh and Levitt maintain that inner-city gangs underwent a fundamental change during the 1980s: "Their members were following their consumptive urges precisely at the time in which free market ideology and the romance of the 'bootstrap' mentality had produced a new phenomenal form of late capitalism, namely the individual yuppie who consumed with conspicuous and ferocious intent" (428–29).

39. *Superfly* (Warner Home Video, 2004, DVD). See also Wacquant, "Inside the Zone," 31, fn. 11; and Richard Majors and Janet Mancini Billson, *Cool Pose: The Dilemmas of Black Manhood in America* (Touchstone, 1992), 82–83. Writing about the lifestyle of the hustler during the era of Black Power, Julius Hudson argued: "The evolution of the hustler's society, and of the social type designated as the hustler, accounts for the unexpected (and to a certain extent shocking) wealthy life-styles found in the black ghetto. Although the hustling ethic appears to be diametrically opposed to the Protestant ethic, it is really an outgrowth of it." See Julius Hudson, "The Hustling Ethic," in Thomas Kochman, ed., *Rappin' and Stylin' Out: Communication in Urban Black America* (University of Illinois Press, 1972), 410–24. Hudson was more optimistic about the abilities of hustlers to achieve material well-being than later developments would justify.

40. Richard Nixon was the first president to use the term "war on drugs," in 1971. During the Nixon era, for the only time in the history of the "war," the majority of funding went toward treatment rather than law enforcement. See *Frontline*'s treatment of this issue at http://www.pbs.org/wgbh/pages/frontline/shows/drugs/cron, accessed Dec. 8, 2011. In 1980 there were just over 40,000 Americans in prison or jail for sale or possession of banned substances; today the number is half a million. See Alexander, *The New Jim Crow*, 59; Human Rights Watch, *Targeting Blacks: Drug Law Enforcement and Race in the United States* (Human Rights Watch, 2008), 1, 12, 10, available online at http://www.hrw.org/en/node/62236, accessed Dec. 8, 2011. Marijuana-related offenses accounted for 82 percent of the increase in drug arrests between 1990 and 2002 and "virtually all" of those arrested were charged with possession. See Ryan S. King and Marc Mauer, "The War on Marijuana: The Transformation of the War on Drugs in the 1990s," *Harm Reduction Journal*, Feb. 9, 2006, available online at http://www.harm reductionjournal.com/content/3/1/6, accessed Dec. 8, 2011. The 2.3 million prisoners represent an increase of 274 percent since Ronald Reagan's first term in office. See Pew Center on the States, "One in 31: The Long Reach of American Corrections," Mar. 2009, 4, available online at http://www.pewcenteronthestates.org/uploadedFiles/PSPP _1in31_report_FINAL_WEB_3-26-09.pdf, accessed Dec. 8, 2011. Between 1980 and 2000, Illinois constructed an average of one new prison each year. See Paul Street, *The Vicious Circle: Race, Prison, Jobs and Community in Chicago, Illinois, and the Nation* (The Urban League, 2002), 3.

41. Among blacks sent to prison in 2003, almost two in five were convicted of drug offenses; for whites the figure was one in four. See Human Rights Watch, *Targeting Blacks*, 3. As recently as 1978, about 80 percent of men and women arrested for drug offenses were white (Tonry, *Punishing Race*, 57–58). For the comments by Loïc Wacquant, see his "Deadly Symbiosis: Rethinking Race and Imprisonment in Twenty-first-Century America," *Boston Review* 27, no. 2 (Apr./May, 2002), available online at http://bostonreview.net/BR27.2/wacquant.html, accessed Dec. 8, 2011. The legal scholar Michelle Alexander writes: "The only country in the world that even comes close to the

American rate of incarceration is Russia, and no other country in the world incarcerates such an astonishing percentage of its racial or ethnic minorities" (Alexander, *The New Jim Crow*, 8).

42. The NIDA study and the National Household Survey on Drug Abuse are discussed in Alexander, *The New Jim Crow*, 97. The same National Institute on Drug Abuse study found that similar percentages of white and black high-school students use marijuana. The evidence collected by Human Rights Watch on cocaine use in Georgia can be found at Human Rights Watch, *Targeting Blacks*, 45. The same study noted that blacks accounted for 72 percent of all persons arrested for drug offenses in Illinois and that in Minnesota blacks are ten times more likely than whites to be arrested for drug-related offenses. A study for the National Urban League reported that white adults are nearly twice as likely to be binge drinkers as black adults. See Rondel Thompson and Sophia Parker, "The National Urban League Equality Index," in National Urban League, *The State of Black America, 2007*, 27.

43. The Fair Sentencing Act of 2010 reduced the ratio from 100-to-1 to 18-to-1. But, to quote Tonry again, under the new statute "a mandatory minimum five-year prison sentence awaits any low-level dealer convicted of selling 28 grams of crack. A powder cocaine dealer must sell a half kilogram to face such a destiny." Three-strikes laws, "dangerous offender" laws, and mandatory minimum sentences for violent and drug crimes also operate in a discriminatory fashion. See Michael Tonry, *Punishing Race: A Continuing American Dilemma* (Oxford University Press, 2011), 1, 4, 49–50. See also the report released by the American Civil Liberties Union on the twentieth anniversary of passage of the "100-to-1" law, at http://www.aclu.org/drug-law-reform/aclu-releases-crack-co caine-report-anti-drug-abuse-act-1986-deepened-racial-inequity, accessed Dec. 8, 2011.

44. The studies of highway patrol stops were carried out in the 1990s. In both states, as it turned out, whites were more often found in possession of illegal drugs than blacks (Alexander, *The New Jim Crow*, 130–31; see p. 103 for the survey of Americans "envisioning" drug offenders). See also Tonry, *Punishing Race*, 47. On police officers' attitudes, see Jennifer L. Eberhardt et al., "Seeing Black: Race, Crime, and Visual Processing," *Journal of Personality and Social Psychology* 87, no. 6 (Dec. 2004): 889–93. Respondents in the 1995 survey also identified the typical drug dealer as black.

45. Alexander, *The New Jim Crow*, 122. See also David K. Shipler, *The Rights of the People: How Our Search for Safety Invades Our Liberties* (Knopf, 2011), chap. 2. The creators of the celebrated television series *The Wire* have written: "What once began, perhaps, as a battle against dangerous substances long ago transformed itself into a venal war on our underclass. Since declaring war on drugs nearly 40 years ago, we've been demonizing our most desperate citizens, isolating and incarcerating them and otherwise denying them a role in the American collective. All to no purpose. The prison population doubles and doubles again; the drugs remain." See Ed Burns et al., "*The Wire's* War on the Drug War," *Time*, Mar. 05, 2008.

46. Nicholas K. Peart, "Why Is the N.Y.P.D. after Me?" *New York Times*, Dec. 17, 2011. See also Rich and Grey, "Pathways to Recurrent Trauma," 819.

47. The former prosecutor is quoted in Alexander, *The New Jim Crow*, 121–22. Note that in the late twentieth century middle-class blacks were still more likely to face imprisonment than whites. For Bruce Western's comment, see Western, *Punishment and Inequality in America*, 73, 194. See also Street, *The Vicious Circle*, 16.

48. Alexander, *The New Jim Crow*, 129. Comments the legal scholar John O. Calmore: "Even dark-skinned, nappy-headed African Americans like me can pass sociologically and culturally if we have the right history of socialization, the right credentials, a respectable job, an affluent income, and a proper street address or zip code." See Calmore, "Dismantling the Master's House: Essays in Memory of Trina Grillo: Random Notes of an Integration Warrior," *Minnesota Law Review* 81, no. 6 (June 1997): 1450. Cose, *The End of Anger*, 100. In response to Fuhrman's comment, the syndicated columnist Clarence Page wrote: "If ever I should have the occasion to drive a Porsche around Los Angeles, please remind me to wear a good suit." For more, see Clarence Page, "Chickens Coming Home to Roost with the Fuhrman Tapes and O. J.'s Case," *Chicago Tribune*, Sept. 3, 1995. On race and the meaning of the Simpson trial, see Toni Morrison and Claudia Brodsky Lacour, eds., *Birth of a Nation'hood: Gaze, Script, and Spectacle in the O. J. Simpson Case* (Pantheon, 1997). For the Richard Thompson Ford comment, see his *The Race Card: How Bluffing about Bias Makes Race Relations Worse* (Picador, 2009), 325.

49. Eberhardt et al., "Seeing Black," 888–89; Kathy Russell, Midge Wilson, and Ronald Hall, *The Color Complex: The Politics of Skin Color among African Americans* (Anchor, 1993), 38; and Jennifer L. Hochschild and Vesla Weaver, "The Skin Color Paradox and the American Racial Order," *Social Forces* 86, no. 2 (Dec. 2007): 649. The researchers into the Georgia court system controlled for type of offense and socioeconomic status. For the Florida study, see Irene V. Blair, Charles M. Judd, and Kristine M. Chapleau, "The Influence of Afrocentric Facial Features in Criminal Sentencing," *Psychological Science* 15, no. 10 (Oct. 2004): 674–679. The authors define "Afrocentric features" as "those physical features that are perceived as typical of African Americans (e.g., dark skin, wide nose, full lips)." They found that even among whites those characteristics resulted in more severe sentences. See also Tonry, *Punishing Race*, 7; Alexander, *The New Jim Crow*, 104.

50. Failure to secure and hold a job can result in a return to prison. See Alexander, *The New Jim Crow*, 145–46; Tonry, *Punishing Race*, 156. Of the 98 occupations requiring state licenses in Illinois in 2000, a full 57 limited or barred access to ex-offenders, in some cases even those convicted of just a misdemeanor. See Street, *The Vicious Circle*, 6; Western, *Punishment and Inequality in America*, 125.

51. *New York Times* (editorial), "Out of Prison and Deep in Debt," Oct. 6, 2007. See also Alexander, *The New Jim Crow*, 150–51. The Council of State Governments' Justice

Center report, entitled "Repaying Debts," can be found at justicecenter.csg.org/files/
RepayingDebts_Guide_final.pdf, accessed Dec. 8, 2011.

52. Public Law 104–193—Aug. 22, 1996 110 Stat. 2105, available online at http://
frwebgate.access.gpo.gov/cgi-bin/getdoc.cgi?dbname=104_cong_public_laws&docid
=f:publ193.104.pdf, accessed Dec. 8, 2011; Alexander, *The New Jim Crow*, 153.

53. Gwen Rubenstein and Debbie Mukamal, "Welfare and Housing—Denial of Benefits to Drug Offenders," in Marc Mauer and Meda Chesney-Lind, eds., *Invisible Punishment: The Collateral Consequences of Mass Imprisonment* (New Press, 2002), 44–45. Another law during Clinton's second term disqualified anyone convicted of a drug-related
offense from getting a student loan. See Jeremy Travis, *But They All Come Back: Facing the
Challenges of Prisoner Reentry* (Urban Institute Press, 2005), 69. See also Human Rights
Watch, *No Second Chance: People with Criminal Records Denied Access to Public Housing*
(Human Rights Watch, 2004), 7; and Alexander, *The New Jim Crow*, 141–45. Over 50
percent of all felons end up back in prison. See The Council of State Governments'
Justice Center, "Repaying Debts," 1. According to Michael Tonry, "accumulating evi-
dence suggests that sending people to prison makes them more likely to commit new
crimes than if they had been punished in some other way" (Tonry, *Punishing Race*, 21).

54. The Sentencing Project, *Felony Disfranchisement Laws in the United States*, Mar.
2011, available online at http://www.sentencingproject.org/doc/publications/fd_bs_fd
lawsinusMar11.pdf, accessed Dec. 8, 2011. See also the NAACP report "Defending
Democracy: Confronting Modern Barriers to Voting Rights in America," 25–28, http://
naacp.3cdn.net/67065c25be9ae43367_mlbrsy48b.pdf, accessed Dec. 20, 2011; Ryan S.
King, *Expanding the Vote: State Felony Disfranchisement Reform, 1997–2008* (Sentencing
Project, Sept. 2008), http://www.sentencingproject.org/doc/publications/fd_statedis
franchisement.pdf, accessed Dec. 8, 2011; Human Rights Watch and the Sentencing
Project, *Losing the Vote: The Impact of Felony Disfranchisement Laws in the United States,
1998*, http://www.hrw.org/reports98/vote, accessed Dec. 8, 2011; Jeff Manza and Christopher Uggan, *Locked Out: Felon Disfranchisement and American Democracy* (Oxford
University Press, 2008). For Marc Mauer's comments, see "Mass Imprisonment and
the Disappearing Voters," in Marc Mauer and Meda Chesney-Lind, eds., *Invisible Punishment*, 57. The percentage of black men denied the vote because they have a criminal
record is seven times the national average (The Sentencing Project, *Felony Disfranchisement Laws in the United States*, 3). It is worth noting that, because of felony convictions,
about 30 percent of black men are also banned for life from jury service (Alexander, *The
New Jim Crow*, 119).

55. "Five years for five joints," Michelle Alexander comments drily (Alexander, *The
New Jim Crow*, 154–55). In recent years prosecutors have increasingly used the threat
of higher charges with more severe penalties to secure guilty pleas. See Richard A.
Oppel, Jr., "Sentencing Shift Gives New Leverage to Prosecutors," *New York Times*,
Sept. 25, 2011.

56. For the quotation on the "main effect of the prison boom," see Western, *Punishment and Inequality in America*, 15. See also Donald Braman, "Families and Incarceration," in Marc Mauer and Meda Chesney-Lind, eds., *Invisible Punishment*, 50–58. For the comment by the young mother in Philadelphia, see Kathryn Edin and Maria Kefalas, *Promises I Can Keep: Why Poor Women Put Motherhood before Marriage* (University of California Press, 2005), 212, 86. As one woman from Chicago lamented: "It is difficult around here to find a good man. Most of them don't work. They just work the streets, you know. They just steal and deal and stud. That kind of thing is a drag. I mean, it's very risky and though it brings in a lot of money, they're going to lose it all and you know you're going down with them" (Wacquant, "Inside the Zone," 10). One black child out of eleven had a father in prison in 2000. The proportion was even higher for children under the age of ten. In roughly half of all cases, the fathers were living with the children at the time they were sentenced (Western, *Punishment and Inequality in America*, 138, which is also the source for the quotation in the text about parental incarceration). See also Marc Mauer and Meda Chesney-Lind, "Introduction," in Mauer and Chesney-Lind, eds., *Invisible Punishment*, 4. Survey data indicate that men who have spent time in prison are substantially more likely to commit domestic violence than men who have never been incarcerated (Western, *Punishment and Inequality in America*, 159–61).

57. Alexander, *The New Jim Crow*, 12–13. See also Wacquant, "The New 'Peculiar Institution.'"

58. C. Vann Woodward, *Thinking Back: The Perils of Writing History* (Louisiana State University Press, 1996), 96.

9. THE "PRIVILEGED CLASS"

1. Joseph C. Phillips, *He Talk Like a White Boy: Reflections on Faith, Family, Politics, and Authenticity* (Running Press, 2006), 159. Shelby Steele, like Phillips, a conservative, recounts a similar experience: "Not long ago, a friend of mine, black like myself, said to me that the term *black middle class* was actually a contradiction in terms. Race, he insisted, blurred class distinctions among blacks. If you were black, you were just black and that was that. When I argued, he let his eyes roll at my naïveté. Then he went on. For us, as black professionals, it was an exercise in self-flattery, a pathetic pretension, to give meaning to such a distraction. Worse, the very idea of class threatened the unity that was vital to the black community as a whole. After all, since when had white America taken note of anything but color when it came to blacks? He then reminded me of an old Malcolm X line that had been popular in the 60's. Question: What is a black man with a Ph.D.? Answer: A nigger." Steele, *The Content of Our Character: A New Vision of Race in America* (Harper Perennial, 1990), 93.

2. Manning Marable, *Race, Reform, and Rebellion: The Second Reconstruction and*

Beyond in Black America, 1946–2006, 3d ed. (University Press of Mississippi, 2007), 188; Eugene Robinson, *Disintegration: The Splintering of Black America* (Doubleday, 2010), 3, 8, 141; Andrew Hacker, *Two Nations: Black and White, Separate, Hostile, Unequal* (Scribner, 2003), 126–28; Sophia A. Nelson, *Black Woman Redefined: Dispelling Myths and Discovering Fulfillment in the Age of Michelle Obama* (BenBella, 2011), 20; Robert S. Boynton, "The New Intellectuals," *Atlantic Monthly* (Mar. 1995): 53–70. Ellis Cose did a survey recently of 193 black MBAs from Harvard Business School. Nearly 90 percent put their household income at over $100,000, 40 percent at over $300,000, and 30 percent at $400,000 or more. See Cose, *The End of Anger: A New Generation's Take on Race and Rage* (HarperCollins, 2011), 8, 12. For the quotation by Jennifer L. Hochschild, see her *Facing Up to the American Dream: Race, Class, and the Soul of the Nation* (Princeton University Press, 1995), 72. Such individuals, Hochschild added, "have grown disillusioned with and even embittered about the American dream."

3. The Executive Leadership Council survey results are in Ellis Cose, *The Rage of a Privileged Class* (HarperPerennial, 1995), 81–82. Monique M. Taylor's reflections on her interviews are in *Harlem between Heaven and Hell* (University of Minnesota Press, 2002), 62–63. Elijah Anderson carried out interviews at a major financial institution in Philadelphia. He concluded that "although some whites may pride themselves on seeing and treating blacks as individuals, blacks often remain unconvinced of their ability to do so." See Anderson, "The Social Situation of the Black Executive: Black and White Identities in the Corporate World," in Michèle Lamont, ed., *The Cultural Territories of Race: Black and White Boundaries* (University of Chicago Press, 1999), 19. For the results of the survey conducted by Joe R. Feagin and Melvin P. Sikes, see their *Living with Racism: The Black Middle-Class Experience* (Beacon, 1994), ix. Feagin and Sikes observe, "Our analysis suggests that racial hostility and discrimination make it impossible for any African American to achieve the full promise of the American dream." Compare Karyn R. Lacy, *Blue-Chip Black: Race, Class, and Status in the New Black Middle Class* (University of California Press, 2007), 72–77.

4. Cose, *The Rage of a Privileged Class,* 82–83.

5. For the survey results, see Cose, *The Rage of a Privileged Class,* 76–81; Anderson, "The Social Situation of the Black Executive," 18. On the Coca-Cola settlement, see Business and Human Rights Resource Center, "Case profile: Coca-Cola lawsuit (re racial discrimination in USA)," http://www.business-humanrights.org/Categories/Lawlawsuits/Lawsuitsregulatoryaction/LawsuitsSelectedcases/Coca-Colalawsuitre racialdiscriminationinUSA, accessed Dec. 9, 2011. And a report by the American Bar Association in 2006 found that black women were far more likely than white men to be the targets of demeaning comments or harassment. See Nelson, *Black Woman Redefined,* 63.

6. Cose, *The Rage of a Privileged Class,* 34. Even Oprah alleged that she has faced discrimination while shopping, at Hermès in Paris. Complaints about taxi drivers are

so common, claims Richard Thompson Ford, that they have become "a stock example of modern racial injustice"—see Ford, *The Race Card: How Bluffing about Bias Makes Race Relations Worse* (Picador, 2009), 59–76. Soon after announcing his candidacy for the presidency, Barack Obama appeared on *60 Minutes,* where he pointed out that cabs often failed to stop for him; see Randall Kennedy, *Sellout: The Politics of Racial Betrayal* (Vintage, 2008), 11–12. For an analysis of why the behavior of taxi drivers is not perhaps evidence of racism, see Glenn C. Loury, *The Anatomy of Racial Inequality* (Harvard University Press, 2002), 30–31. *Race Matters* is the title of a widely praised book by the philosophy professor and social critic Cornel West (Beacon Press, 1993).

7. Jill Nelson, *Volunteer Slavery: My Authentic Negro Experience* (Penguin, 1993), 86. See also Lacy, *Blue-Chip Black,* 75–76, 93–97. One middle-class student told Joe Feagin and Melvin Sikes that success meant becoming "Afro-Saxon." See Feagin and Sikes, *Living with Racism,* 93–94.

8. William Julius Wilson, *More Than Just Race: Being Black and Poor in the Inner City* (Norton, 2009), 1–2.

9. Barack Obama, *Dreams from My Father: A Story of Race and Inheritance* (Three Rivers Press, 2004), 100. bell hooks makes the same point in much more scathing terms: "Privileged black folks who are pimping black culture for their own opportunistic gain tend to focus on racism as though it were the great equalizing factor. For example, when a materially successful black person tells the story of how no cab will stop for him because of color he claims unity with the masses of black folk who are daily assaulted by white supremacy. Yet this assertion of shared victimhood obscures the fact that this racial assault is mediated by the reality of class privilege. However 'hurt' or even 'damaged' the individual may be by his failure to acquire a taxi immediately, that individual is likely to be more allied with the class interests of individuals who share similar status (including whites) than with the needs of those black folks whom racist economic aggression renders destitute, who do not even have the luxury to consider taking a taxi." See bell hooks, *Killing Rage: Ending Racism* (Henry Holt, 1995), 179–80.

10. Loury, *The Anatomy of Racial Inequality,* 50–51.

11. Individuals with particularly dark skin are especially attentive to matters of wardrobe, manners, and language, since their appearance makes winning acceptance that much harder. See Kathy Russell, Midge Wilson, and Ronald Hall, *The Color Complex: The Politics of Skin Color among African Americans* (Anchor, 1993), 131–32.

12. The UCLA questionnaire can be viewed in its entirety at http://ucdata.berkeley.edu/data_holdings/other/lacss/lac92qxn, accessed July 18, 2013.

13. Ibid. See also Cose, *The Rage of a Privileged Class,* 6–7.

14. Hochschild notes, as well, that black unskilled workers are less likely than black professionals and managers to complain about their work situations. Hochschild, *Facing Up to the American Dream,* 73, 161–62. See also Marable, *Race Reform and Rebellion,* 150–51. Now and then interviewers came across a person who seemed to be lacking a

sense of historical perspective. One young woman told Joe Feagin and Melvin Sikes: "I'm not saying that white people are all out to get us, because I don't think they think about us that much, where they sit down and actually plot, in some dark smoke-filled room, how they're going [to] stomp on black people. They don't have to because it's ingrained in the system. So things are like that. And white people call me paranoid and stuff, because I guess they look at things in regards to like the sixties when black people were like being beaten up every damn day, and crosses [were burned] in front of yards, and it was so blatant. But now it's changed. And just because it's not blatant any more doesn't mean it's not there. In fact, I think it's worse." See Feagin and Sikes, *Living with Racism*, 93. The comment by Karyn Lacy is in her *Blue-Chip Black*, 160. See also Pew Research Center, "Optimism about Black Progress Declines: Blacks See Growing Values Gap between Poor and Middle Class," Nov. 13, 2007, 32, http://pewsocialtrends.org/files/2010/10/Race-2007.pdf, accessed Dec. 8, 2011.

15. Orlando Patterson, *The Ordeal of Integration: Progress and Resentment in America's "Racial" Crisis* (Civitas/Counterpoint, 1997), 64; Debra J. Dickerson, *An American Story* (Pantheon, 2000), 257.

16. Cose, *The Rage of a Privileged Class*, 46. Phillips adds: "I have heard many white friends say that they have never seen me as black. This is meant as a compliment. . . . My response to these compliments is that while I am appreciative of their acceptance, I *am* black. So, here is yet another pose in the mental yoga that black people practice: Striving to realize our individual humanity while still holding tight to some portion of our racial identity. (I am quite certain my white friends and neighbours do not put themselves through those mental acrobatics. However, every black person I know is constantly involved in this type of intricate analysis.)" Phillips, *He Talk Like a White Boy*, 226, 211. The comments by the systems administrator are in Lacy, *Blue-Chip Black*, 167.

17. K. Anthony Appiah, *Race, Culture, Identity: Misunderstood Connections*, the Tanner Lecture on Human Values, delivered at the University of California at San Diego, Oct. 27 and 28, 1994, 125, available online at http://www.tannerlectures.utah.edu/lectures/documents/Appiah96.pdf, accessed Dec. 9, 2011; Tommie Shelby, *We Who Are Dark: The Philosophical Foundations of Black Solidarity* (Harvard University Press, 2005), 170, 179–80. Ninety years ago, George Schuyler, the iconoclastic newspaper columnist—this was long before the days when he cloaked himself in the cape of conservatism—wrote in *The Nation*: "True, from dark-skinned sources have come those slave songs based on Protestant hymns and Biblical texts known as the spirituals, work songs and secular songs of sorrow and tough luck known as the blues, that outgrowth of rag-time known as jazz (in the development of which whites have assisted), and the Charleston, an eccentric dance invented by the gamins around the public market-place in Charleston, S.C. No one can or does deny this. But these are contributions of a caste in a certain section of the country. They are foreign to Northern Negroes, West Indian Negroes, and African Negroes. They are no more expressive or character-

istic of the Negro race than the music and dancing of the Appalachian highlanders or the Dalmatian peasantry are expressive or characteristic of the Caucasian race." See George S. Schuyler, "The Negro-Art Hokum," *The Nation* 122 (June 16, 1926): 662–63. It is worth noting that the range of practices in black churches varies profoundly, as Barack Obama learned when he first arrived in Chicago: "Now [Reverend Philips] was explaining the history of churches in Chicago. There were thousands of them, and it seemed as if he knew them all: the tiny storefronts and the large stone edifices; the high-yella congregations that sat stiff as cadets as they sang from their stern hymnals, and the charismatics who shook as their bodies expelled God's unintelligible tongue" (Obama, *Dreams from My Father*, 273).

18. Glenn C. Loury, "Race and Identity in America: A Personal Perspective," excerpted from *One by One from the Inside Out: Essays and Reviews on Race and Responsibility in America*, available online at http://www.historyplace.com/pointsofview/loury.htm, accessed Dec. 9, 2011.

19. "Basketball," *Ebony* 47 (Aug. 1992): 62. On the origins of basketball, see Rob Rains, *James Naismith: The Man Who Invented Basketball* (Temple University Press, 2009). On the early years of blacks in the sport, see Bob Kuska, *Hot Potato: How Washington and New York Gave Birth to Black Basketball and Changed America's Game Forever* (University of Virginia Press, 2004). The YMCA in Springfield was one of only a handful of branches to allow black members during the 1890s. But there is no evidence that Naismith included blacks among the students he instructed. See Nina Mjagkij, *Light in the Darkness: African Americans in the YMCA, 1852–1946* (University Press of Kentucky, 1994), 40. On how the self-presentation of black basketball players has changed since the days of Michael Jordan, see Wesley Morris, "The Rise of the NBA Nerd: Basketball Style and Black Identity," http://www.grantland.com/story/_/id/7346656/the-rise-nba -nerd, accessed Dec. 13, 2011. The first man of African ancestry to play in the National Hockey League was Willie O'Ree, a Canadian. He made his debut, for the Boston Bruins, in Jan. 1958. Since then, more than seventy black players have appeared in the NHL, the great majority born and raised in Canada. As I am putting the finishing touches on this manuscript, in April 2013, one of the top-ranked prospects for the NHL draft this coming summer is a black American defenseman for the Portland Winterhawks of the Western Hockey League, Seth Jones. His father, Popeye Jones, had an eleven-year career in the NBA.

20. For Jill Nelson's reflections, see Nelson, *Volunteer Slavery*, 38, 30. For Cathy Cohen's comments, see *Boundaries of Blackness: AIDS and the Breakdown of Black Politics* (University of Chicago Press, 1999), 10. Writes bell hooks: "There is a shared history that frames the construction of our diverse black experiences" (hooks, *Killing Rage*, 247). Jill Nelson described her first date with a mortician from Harlem this way: "He took me to lunch at a fast food joint and bought me a chicken sandwich. I thought that was very grass roots. As always, I was looking for the authentic Negro experience,

which of course my own wasn't, since being bourgeois somehow negated being black. Since the late 1960s, when I'd risked baldness for an Afro, I'd been trying to understand how and where I fit into African-American culture. I wanted to party with the criminals and go home to a nice, safe apartment in a good neighborhood. I wanted to be able to talk just as comfortably with both a wino on the corner and a CEO, to sniff drugs until early in the morning and pump out a brilliant story the next afternoon. I wanted to be down with the get down, but not of it. I wanted to be a street sister by night, black princess by day. My first date with the Mortician—a poor man, in Harlem, dining on what my friend Judyie calls the 'black national foods,' salty, greasy, and fried—fit into the scenario. I was like a perverse anthropologist, looking for the real Negro outside myself instead of just looking in the mirror" (Nelson, *Volunteer Slavery*, 23).

21. Cose, *The Rage of a Privileged Class*, 105, 95. Bill Lawson has observed: "Many blacks feel a deep commitment to the general black community and want that community to flourish, and yet they believe that to stay in decaying and crime-ridden communities is over and beyond what is owed to the black community. It would be a supererogatory act, one is not obligated to do it, and in certain cases it would be foolhardy if one did." See Lawson, "Uplifting the Race: Middle-Class Blacks and the Truly Disadvantaged," in Bill E. Lawson, *The Underclass Question* (Temple University Press, 1992), 99. See also Russell et al., *Color Complex*, 72.

22. Booker T. Washington, *Up from Slavery* (Doubleday, Page, 1901), 39–40. It is revealing that the comedian and social activist Dick Gregory called the second of his two autobiographies *Up from Nigger* (Stein and Day, 1976). For the statements by Arthur Ashe, see Arthur Ashe and Arnold Rampersad, *Days of Grace: A Memoir* (Ballantine, 1993), 140. Ashe also commented, speaking of the pre–Civil Rights Era: "The cornerstone of identity in the African American world was the knowledge that we as a people had been historically wronged by the larger culture that dominated us" (155).

23. On the charge that well-to-do blacks are selling out, see Kennedy, *Sellout*, 5, 8; Anderson, "The Social Situation of the Black Executive," 26; Dickerson, *An American Story*, 130–31; and Joel Garreau, *Edge City: Life on the New Frontier* (Anchor, 1992), 167. The Warner quotation can be found in Ellen Holly, *One Life: The Autobiography of an African American Actress* (Kodansha International, 1996), 226. Randall Kennedy, "My Race Problem—And Ours," *Atlantic Monthly* (May 1997): 66; Sterling Anthony, *Cookie Cutter* (Ballantine, 1999).

24. Steele, *Content of Our Character*, 101. Observes the writer Joel Garreau: "Because for so long it was the same thing to be black and to be poor, some first generation middle-class black people are having trouble sorting out what it even means to be 'authentically' black in the absence of privation" (Garreau, *Edge City*, 167). Contrary to what Garreau suggests, there has always been an element of the black population that was well-off in a material sense. Still, societal constraints on middle-class blacks are now vastly reduced compared to before the Civil Rights Era. "Privation" can take different forms.

25. Charles Johnson, "The End of the Black American Narrative," *American Scholar. org* (Summer 2008), available online at http://theamericanscholar.org/the-end-of-the-black-american-narrative, accessed Dec. 9, 2011. Glenn Loury has written: "I no longer believe that the camaraderie engendered among blacks by our collective experience of racism constitutes an adequate basis for any person's self-definition. Even if I restrict attention to the question 'Who am I as a black American at the end of the twentieth century?,' these considerations of historical victimization and struggle against injustice do not take me very far toward finding an answer. I am made 'black' only in the most superficial way by virtue of being the object of a white racist's hate. The empathetic exchange of survivors' tales among 'brothers,' even the collective struggle against the clear wrong of racism, does not provide a tapestry sufficiently rich to give meaning and definition to the totality of my life. I am so much more than the one wronged, misunderstood, underestimated, derided, or ignored by whites. I am more than the one who has struggled against this oppression and indifference; more than a descendant of slaves now claiming freedom; more, that is, than either a 'colored person' (as seen by the racist) or a 'person of color' (as seen by the antiracist)" (Loury, "Race and Identity in America").

26. One resident of the exclusive Sherwood Park neighborhood outside Washington told Karyn Lacy: "Black parents look out and they say, 'Well, white people have it. Why shouldn't my kid have it?' If they're honest, that's what it will be reduced to. You look on television and you see all these happy, smiling white people with nice things and you say, 'Well, why should they have that and I shouldn't?' Or 'why should their kid have hundred-fifty dollar tennis shoes and mine shouldn't?'" Many of his neighbors feel pressure to buy cars for their children. Lacy, *Blue-Chip Black*, 145–47. For Haynes's comments to Cose, see Cose, *Rage of a Privileged Class*, 136–37. See also Sarah Susannah Willie, *Acting Black: College, Identity, and the Performance of Race* (Routledge, 2003), 25; Hacker, *Two Nations*, 177; and Robert S. Boynton, "The New Intellectuals," *Atlantic Monthly* (Mar. 1995): 64.

27. Cose, *Rage of a Privileged Class*, 137, 58–59; Lacy, *Blue-Chip Black*, 169–70, 152–54.

28. "An entire black heritage tourism industry emerged, complete with chartered flights, air-conditioned buses, and other amenities." See James T. Campbell, *Middle Passages: African American Journeys to Africa, 1787–2005* (Penguin, 2006), 372. For Jill Nelson's conversation with her daughter, see Nelson, *Volunteer Slavery*, 170. Not that all elite families think slavery should be part of their children's historical memory. Lawrence Otis Graham had assumed that most of the people in attendance at his brother's wedding were white, but it turned out they were part of the Washington light-skinned elite. "Emboldened" by this knowledge, he stepped to the microphone and coaxed his brother and new sister-in-law into performing "the hundred-year-old broom jumping ceremony in the center of the ballroom. The ceremony lasted no more than five minutes, but it turned into a total disaster. For all of us. What had normally been

considered one of the few lasting traditions from the pre-emancipation black southern culture was suddenly seen as a hostile and unwelcome gesture. 'Why would he bring a niggerish thing like that in here?' announced a woman as my new sister-in-law's dress was just clearing the elevated broom handle. 'These country-ass blacks always have to drag in this slave history crap,' added an older gentleman sitting just off the dance floor. 'Jesus Christ.'" See Lawrence Otis Graham, *Our Kind of People: Inside America's Black Upper Class* (HarperPerennial, 2000), 214–15.

29. Lacy, *Blue-Chip Black*, 156, 169–73, 177; Phillips, *He Talk Like a White Boy*, 227. Debra Dickerson adds: "Such parents [who send their children to "black camps" in the inner cities] worry that their children are 'missing out on reality and becoming generic.' One girl was sent to such a camp because she preferred classical music and didn't know the music and games that her elders had played as children. African American vernacular and cultural references often went over her head. Notice that all the anger and dislocation, the flaunted blackness, comes from the parents. Note the essentializations: 'reality' for blacks is poverty and danger, blacks don't listen to classical music, blacks sling slang, blacks are poor, blacks must seek out other blacks, however inorganically." See Debra J. Dickerson, *The End of Blackness: Returning the Souls of Black Folk to their Rightful Owners* (Pantheon, 2004), 211, 177. The website for Jack and Jill is http://jackandjillinc.org, accessed Apr. 10, 2013. Lawrence Otis Graham recalls a career day held for Jack and Jill members at a private school on Manhattan's Upper West Side. After the presentations, the teenagers and the speakers—who included, in addition to Graham (a lawyer), two physicians, a state assemblyman, a Fortune 500 executive, an architect, and an investment banker—moved to a Fifth Avenue apartment. "This was the first time," Graham recalled, "that I'd seen a Renoir, a Beardon, and a Picasso in someone's living room. It was the first time I'd been served by a butler who poured tea with white gloves." Graham, *Our Kind of People*, 20–22.

30. Graham, *Our Kind of People*, 252.

31. Cose, *The End of Anger*, 80–81. Her dreadlocks, the journalist and author Patrice Gaines recalls, embarrassed her daughter Andrea, "who as a preteen wanted nothing more than for herself and her family to blend in with everyone else." Patrice Gaines, *Laughing in the Dark: From Colored Girl to Woman of Color—A Journey from Prison to Power* (Anchor, 1994), 193. Robinson, *Disintegration*, 182. As Orlando Patterson writes: "Taking a long-term perspective, the important thing to note is that the children of the newly emerged Afro-American middle class will be second-and third-generation burghers with all the confidence, educational resources and, most of all, cultural capital to find a more secure niche in the nation's economy" (Patterson, *The Ordeal of Integration*, 25–26). Exclusive social spaces once off-limits to children from the very wealthiest of black families have largely become integrated. "In recent years certain elite white organizations have opened up a space for a black debutante who often has credentials that equal or outshine those of white participants. Such was the case when Harvard graduate

Candace Bond became the first black to be presented by St. Louis's exclusive, all-white Veiled Prophet debutante ball; when Yale graduate Elizabeth Alexander became queen of the mostly white Azalea Festival in Washington; and when Auldlyn Higgins became the first black in the Baltimore Junior League. Candace and Auldlyn were the daughters of prominent surgeons, and Elizabeth was the daughter of Clifford Alexander, who not only was a graduate of Harvard and Yale Law School but was also serving as secretary of the United States Army." Graham, *Our Kind of People*, 50.

32. Robinson, *Disintegration*, 77.

33. Loury, "Race and Identity in America." Eugene Robinson has observed in a similar vein: "My wife and I grew up in black neighborhoods; one result of integration is that our sons did not. Most of the friends they had while growing up were white. But times had changed, and what we once thought of as 'proprietary' black culture had spread beyond any narrow racial context. Blacks became not just acceptable but cool. Both of my sons have had white friends who spoke Ebonics much more fluently than they did. Likewise, young African Americans are acculturated and can easily converse in today's dialects of Valleyspeak. In black-majority Mainstream community [sic] like Prince George's or DeKalb, it is not impossible for white kids to be cool and popular. And it is likely that black students, even if they grow up in mostly black or all-black neighborhoods, will eventually find themselves on white-majority college campuses. The lifelong friend they meet in the dorms will be white, Asian, Latino—the law of averages says they're unlikely to be black. When these Mainstream kids go out with their friends to hear music, it will be in integrated venues—not an all-black nightclub like the Bohemian Caverns of old. My generation had many of these world-expanding college experiences, too. But we had lived through the civil rights movement, the assassination of Dr. King, the riots, the emergence of the Black Panthers. . . . We had the kind of race consciousness that comes from experience, not a history book. All of which is a long way of saying that race doesn't matter to our children's generation in the same way it does to ours. It matters less. Change is good. But even welcome, long-awaited changes aren't easy." Robinson, *Disintegration*, 103–104.

34. Edwards continues: "I myself became clear about this—or clear about a mother's role in imparting to male children what's expected when it comes to marriage—when I interviewed the son of a Black magazine publisher ten years ago. The publisher had three sons and a Black wife who had made it clear to her boys that they were not to bring home any White girls. 'We could have them as friends,' the eldest son recalled, 'but we were definitely not to marry them.'" Audrey Edwards, "Bring Me Home a Black Girl," *Essence* 33, no. 7 (Nov. 2002): 177. And then there was the woman who told her son: "If you love your mother, bring home a black girl." Ralph Richards Banks, *Is Marriage for White People? How the African American Marriage Decline Affects Everyone* (Dutton, 2011), 148.

35. Renee Romano notes: "The black-white divide is the most tenacious of all Ameri-

can color lines, and in many ways the regulation of black-white relationships and the taboo against them are unique. Relationships between blacks and whites were the first to be prohibited during the colonial era, and no matter what other groups were forbidden to marry by antimiscegenation laws, all of the laws that existed in one time or another forbade relationships between blacks and whites." Three major sociological studies of interracial couples who married during the 1940s and 1950s found only one couple out of 51 that met in high school or college. Romano, *Race Mixing: Black-White Marriage in Postwar America* (Harvard University Press, 2003), 321, fn. 5, 8. For a detailed treatment of the case *Loving v. Virginia*, 388 U.S. 1 (1967), see Phyl Newbeck, *Virginia Hasn't Always Been for Lovers: Interracial Marriage Bans and the Case of Richard and Mildred Loving* (Southern Illinois University Press, 2004). Despite the U.S. Supreme Court ruling, South Carolina removed the provision in its constitution barring racial intermarriage only in 1998; Alabama did so in 2000. See Peter Wallenstein, *Tell The Court I Love My Wife: Race, Marriage, and Law—An American History* (Palgrave Macmillan, 2002), 247. In a survey conducted by the Pew Research Center in 2009, 88 percent of whites ages 18–29 said they would "be fine with" a relative marrying a black man or woman. The figure for those aged 30–49 was 79 percent, those aged 50–64 was 55 percent, those aged 65 and over was 41 percent. See Pew Research Center, "Marrying Out: One-in-Seven Marriages Is Interracial or Interethnic," June 15, 2010, 27–29, http://pewsocialtrends.org/files/2010/10/755-marrying-out.pdf, accessed Dec. 9, 2011. In a Gallup Poll taken in 1958, only 4 percent of whites approved of marriage between whites and blacks. By 1997 the national figure had risen to 61 percent (Romano, *Race Mixing*, 2, 45). See also Susan Welch et al., *Race and Place: Race Relations in an American City* (Cambridge University Press, 2001), 115–16. Note, however, that a survey conducted by the *Washington Post*, the Kaiser Foundation, and Harvard University in 2001 found that nearly half of all whites—this was a higher percentage than in any other group—expressed the view that it is better for people to marry within their own race. See Kimberly McClain DaCosta, *Making Multiracials: State, Family, and Market in the Redrawing of the Color Line* (Stanford University Press, 2007), 91.

36. Pew Research Center, "Marrying Out," 27, 30. A 2001 poll published in the *Washington Post* found that nearly two-thirds of black men and half of black women had dated someone of another race. Romano, *Race Mixing*, 260. On the preponderance of the wealthy and well-educated among black men who marry white women, see Matthijs Kalmijn, "Trends in Black/White Intermarriage," *Social Forces* 72, no. 1 (Sept. 1993): 122; Michael Eric Dyson, "Sexual Fault Lines: Robbing the Love between Us," in National Urban League, *The State of Black America, 2007: Portrait of the Black Male* (Beckham Publications, 2007), 236–37; Banks, *Is Marriage for White People?*, 34; Nelson, *Black Woman Redefined*, 97. The other element of the black population with a strong tendency to marry whites is the foreign-born. See Romano, *Race Mixing*, 262.

37. Romano, *Race Mixing*, 215, 249–50; Kalmijn, "Trends in Black/White Intermar-

riage," 122–24. By 2008, 16 percent of all marriages involving a black person were inter-racial. The figures for Hispanic and Asian residents of the United States who married outside their ethnicity or race were 26 percent and 31 percent, respectively. Pew Re-search Center, "Marrying Out," 2. See also Randall Kennedy, *Interracial Intimacies: Sex, Marriage, Identity, and Adoption* (Pantheon, 2003), 127.

38. Edwards, "Bring Me Home a Black Girl," 179. See also DaCosta, *Making Multi-racials*, 95.

39. For the Fairchild comment, see Kennedy, *Interracial Intimacies*, 119. The Romano and Poussaint quotations are from Romano, *Race Mixing*, 242. See also Michael A. Fletcher, "Interracial Marriages Eroding Barriers," *Washington Post*, Dec. 28, 1998. In the eyes of Professor Russell Adams of the Department of Afro-American Studies at Howard University, the decision of Clarence Thomas to marry a white attorney, Vir-ginia Lamp, in 1987 represented "his rejection of the black community" (Kennedy, *Sellout*, 62–64). A survey of black women's perceptions conducted by a psychologist at the University of Michigan in the late 1990s found that the sight of black-white couples constituted the second most cited source of anxiety, ahead of financial worries (though behind lack of personal time). Meanwhile, a 1998 poll conducted by *Essence* found that almost two-thirds of black women were distressed by black men marrying or dating white women. Banks, *Is Marriage for White People?*, 34. The survey results bring to mind the "war council" scene in Spike Lee's "Jungle Fever" (Universal Studios, 2006, DVD). Still, it is possible today for a leading black spokesman to marry a white wife—Henry Louis Gates can serve as an example—without facing the opprobrium heaped on Frederick Douglass 130 years ago and without suffering a significant erosion in his authority to address black issues. And, perhaps needless to point out, there are many star athletes and entertainers who marry white women without suffering a loss to their celebrity status among blacks. For a compilation of "notable black/nonblack interracial couples, 1801–2001," see the list produced by Robert Fikes, Jr., of San Diego State University at http://www.afrocentricnews.com/html/interracial.html (accessed Dec. 9, 2011). Romano, *Race Mixing*, 242. The executive assistant to the CEO of a For-tune 500 company said that if she fell in love with, and married, a white man, "My black heart, I would need to turn it in." Banks, *Is Marriage for White People?*, 137; Alice Walker, *In Search of Our Mothers' Gardens* (Harcourt, 1983), 291.

40. Holly, *One Life*, 101–102.

41. Ibid., 157. See also Heather M. Dalmage, "'Mama, Are You Brown?': Multi Racial Families and the Color Line," in Cedric Herring, Verna M. Keith, and Hayward Der-rick Horton, eds., *Skin Deep: How Race and Complexion Matter in the "Color-Blind" Era* (University of Illinois Press, 2004), 83. The quotation by the "college student" is in Margaret L. Hunter, *Race, Gender, and the Politics of Skin Tone* (Routledge, 2005), 107–108. A woman Ralph Richard Banks interviewed also spoke of wanting "chocolate" babies (Banks, *Is Marriage for White People?*, 159). See also Mark E. Hill, "Skin Color and the

Perception of Attractiveness among African Americans: Does Gender Make a Difference?" *Social Psychology Quarterly* 65, no. 1 (Mar. 2002): 77–91.

42. Banks, *Is Marriage for White People?*, 38–39. Black women began to outnumber black men at institutions of higher learning in the early 1960s. The gender gap has grown since then. See Hacker, *Two Nations*, 204–205. This development is not unique to black Americans. As Orlando Patterson has pointed out: "In all other ethnic groups, women have been catching up with, and surpassing, men in the acquisition of bachelor's degrees since about the early eighties." But "Afro-American women had passed this milestone years earlier and simply widened the gap with the enhanced opportunities that came with the seventies." See Patterson, *Rituals of Blood: Consequences of Slavery in Two American Centuries* (Civitas/Counterpoint, 1998), 16–17. See also Richard Fry and D'Vera Cohn, "Women, Men and the New Economics of Marriage," Pew Research Center, *Social and Demographic Trends Report*, Jan. 19, 2010, 21, 23–24, available online at http://pewsocialtrends.org/files/2010/10/new-economics-of-marriage.pdf, accessed Dec. 9, 2011; Valerie Ralston Wilson, "On Equal Ground: Causes and Solutions for Lower College Completion Rates among Black Males," in National Urban League, *The State of Black America, 2007*, 124; and Wilson, *More Than Just Race*, 66–67. "With the exception of Asian Americans in the legal profession, where both genders are near parity, only among Afro-Americans do we find men substantially below parity in the fields of medicine, dentistry, law, and business" (Patterson, *Rituals of Blood*), 17–18. See also Natalie Nitsche and Hannah Brueckner, "Opting Out of the Family? Social Change in Racial Inequality in Family Formation Patterns and Marriage Outcomes among Highly Educated Women," paper presented at the annual meeting of the American Sociological Association, San Francisco, Aug. 8, 2009, 1, available online at http://www.yale.edu/ciqle/Nitsche_brueckner_Executive%20summary.pdf. See also Banks, *Is Marriage for White People?*, 42; Hacker, *Two Nations*, 136. Among whites, men outnumber women in the professions and in managerial positions (Patterson, *Rituals of Blood*, 37). By 2000 the average black woman with a bachelor's degree was earning $1,117 for every $1,000 earned by a white woman with a bachelor of arts degree; the average black man $784 for every $1,000 earned by a white man with a bachelor of arts. See Hacker, *Two Nations*, 112, 119. See also Michael Tonry, *Punishing Race: A Continuing American Dilemma* (Oxford University Press, 2011), 174.

43. Patricia Hill Collins, *Black Sexual Politics: African Americans, Gender, and the New Racism* (Routledge, 2004), 249–50, where she also writes: "By comparison, nearly seventy percent of white women with a college degree married men who also had a college degree, and only twelve percent of white women with a college degree married men who never went to college"; Dyson, "Sexual Fault Lines," 233.

44. In a survey of 540 professional women conducted by Sophia Nelson and Kellyanne Conway, 66 percent said they would remain single rather than marry a black man who falls short of their expectations. Forty-one percent of the women said that relation-

ships with black men were challenging because black women "earn more money/have more financial security" and "have achieved a higher level of success." See Nelson, *Black Woman Redefined*, 29, 89, 91. Derrick Bell, "The Sexual Diversion: The Black Man/Black Woman Debate in Context," in Don Belton, ed., *Speak My Name: Black Masculinity and the American Dream* (Beacon Press, 1995), 149. For the comment by the "college senior," see Tricia Rose, *Longing to Tell: Black Women Talk about Sexuality and Intimacy* (Picador, 2003), 308. A woman told Ralph Richard Banks: "I do see white men as the oppressor. Even within my own family black women have been the victim of sexual violence by white men. I think it's still very prevalent, this desire for white men to want to conquer or tame exotic women." Banks, *Is Marriage for White People?*, 152. Until the last decades of the twentieth century, the number of black men and women who were involved in interracial marriages was roughly equal (Romano, *Race Mixing*, 230). In 2005, about 9 percent of American blacks were married to someone of another race. But of that 9 percent, 74 percent—three-quarters—were black men with white wives. See Ford, *The Race Card*, 314. Thirteen percent of black men who married in 2008 wed a white bride; just 5 percent of black women who married wed a white husband. Among Asian residents of the United States, the gender pattern runs in the opposite direction. Some 40 percent of Asian female newlyweds in 2008 married outside their race, compared with just 20 percent of male newlyweds. Among Hispanic residents of the United States and among white Americans, there are no gender differences in intermarriage rates (Pew Research Center, "Marrying Out," 11–13). Of ironic note, while marriages between black men and white women more commonly lead to divorce than marriages between white men and white women and between black men and black women, marriages between white men and black women lead to divorce less frequently than the other three kinds of unions. See Jenifer L. Bratter and Rosalind B. King, "'But Will It Last?' Marital Instability among Interracial and Same-Race Couples," *Family Relations* (Apr. 2008): 160–71. On the low marriage rate for professional black women, see Nelson, *Black Woman Redefined*, 14. According to Andrew Hacker, looking at data from a decade earlier, about half of black female college graduates aged 35 to 44 were unmarried (Hacker, *Two Nations*, 95).

45. Nitsche and Brueckner, "Opting Out of the Family," 2–3; Banks, *Is Marriage for White People?*, 78–80; Kennedy, *Interracial Intimacies*, 126; Maria P. P. Root, *The Multiracial Experience: Racial Borders as the New Frontier* (Sage, 1996), xv.

46. Margo J. Anderson, *The Census: A Social History* (Yale University Press, 1988), 206; Kim M. Williams, *Mark One or More: Civil Rights in Multiracial America* (The University of Michigan Press, 2006), 18. Writes Kimberly McClain DaCosta: "The practice of self-enumeration lent support to the idea that the person being classified has the right to choose her classification. Moreover, it provided the conditions whereby an individual was obliged to wrestle with the choice of categories on her own, rather than have an outside agent determine that choice for her. In so doing, it fostered the sense

that the purpose of state racial categories was to record the individual's self-identity, something that only the individual could determine" (DaCosta, *Making Multiracials,* 41).

47. The specific instructions read: "Mark one or more races to indicate what this person considers himself/herself to be." "Instructions to Enumerators, 2000 Census," available online at http://www.census.gov/dmd/www/pdf/d61a.pdf, accessed Sept. 30, 2013. "Black," "African American," and "Negro" were synonymous choices offered. The others were "White"; "American Indian or Alaska Native"; "Asian"; and "Some Other Race." According to instructions set out by the Census Bureau, "Some other race" was "intended to capture responses such as Mulatto, Creole, and Mestizo" (see http://www.census.gov/dmd/www/pdf/d61a.pdf, accessed Sept. 30, 2013). On the predominantly middle-class character of the "multiracial movement," see DaCosta, *Making Multiracials,* 119–20. Children of such mixed-race unions formed their own societies on college campuses. Randall Kennedy, *Interracial Intimacies,* 144, provides a representative list of multiracial organizations: MOSAIC (Multiethnics of Southern Arizona in Celebration), A Place for Us (North Little Rock, Arkansas), I-Pride (Interracial Intercultural Pride, Berkeley, California), MASC (Multiracial Americans of Southern California, Los Angeles, California), F.C. (Families of Color) Communiqué (Fort Collins, Colorado), Interracial Family Alliance (Augusta, Georgia), Society for Interracial Families (Troy, Michigan), 4c (Cross Cultural Couples & Children, Plainsboro, New Jersey), the Interracial Club of Buffalo, The Interracial Family Circle of Washington, D.C., and HONEY (Honor Our New Ethnic Youth, Eugene, Oregon). On college campuses: FUSION (Wellesley), Kaleidoscope (University of Virginia), Students of Mixed Heritage and Culture (Amherst), Half 'n' Half (Bryn Mawr), and Mixed Plate (Grinnell). Project RACE was successful in its efforts in a number of states. See Williams, *Mark One or More,* 13, chap. 4.

48. For more on this bill of rights, see Root, *Multiracial Experience,* 7; and Root's website, www.drmariaroot.com/doc/BillOfRights.pdf, accessed July 18, 2013.

49. Kerry Ann Rockquemore and David L. Brunsma, *Beyond Black: Biracial Identity in America,* 2d ed. (Rowman & Littlefield, 2008), 2. See also Reynolds Farley, "Racial Identities in 2000: The Response to the Multiple-Race Response Option," in Joel Perlmann and Mary C. Waters, eds., *The New Race Question: How the Census Counts Multiracial Individuals* (Russell Sage Foundation, 2002), 35–36. Two additional articles in the Perlmann and Waters anthology explore how introducing a "multiracial" category on census forms can complicate enforcement of laws designed to promote civil rights and voting rights: see Joshua R Goldstein and Ann J. Morning, "Back in the Box: The Dilemma of Using Multiple-Race Data for Single-Race Laws," 119–36; and Nathaniel Persily, "The Legal Implications of a Multiracial Census," 161–86. Observes Randall Kennedy: "Long denounced as a method for protecting whites against the taint of Negro blood, the one-drop rule is now embraced by some devotees of black unity as a

way of reinforcing solidarity and discouraging exit by 'blacks' who might otherwise prefer to reinvent themselves racially" (Kennedy, *Sellout*, 14).

50. When the census forms were mailed out, the Congressional Black Caucus mounted a "check the black box" campaign intending to discourage individuals of African descent from claiming multiple racial identities (DaCosta, *Making Multiracials*, 36). DaCosta adds: "Reminding listeners that African Americans were once counted as three fifths of a person, media personalities like Tom Joyner and Tavis Smiley suggested that checking multiple boxes could amount to the same thing" (36). It was, in fact, slaves, and not all people of African ancestry, who were counted as three-fifths of a person in the Constitution for purposes of representation and taxation. It is worth noting that the Leadership Conference on Civil Rights came to endorse the recommendation of the Office of Management and Budget. On the Leadership Conference on Civil Rights endorsing the OMB's recommendation, see Farley, "Racial Identities in 2000," 37. See also Sonya Rastogi et al., *The Black Population: 2010* (2010 Census Briefs, Sept. 2011), 3, available online at http://www.census.gov/prod/cen2010/briefs/c2010br-06.pdf, accessed Dec. 9, 2011. In 2010, a total of 269,421 people identified themselves as "black" and "Native American;" 185,595 as "black" and "Asian"; and 314,571 as "black" and "some other race." In total, then, over 2,800,000 individuals checked black and at least one other box. See Jamie Mihoko Doyle and Grace Kao, "Are Racial Identities of Multiracials Stable? Changing Self-Identification among Single and Multiple Race Individuals," *Social Psychology Quarterly* 70, no. 4 (Dec. 2007): 406; David R. Harris and Jeremiah Joseph Sim, "Who Is Multiracial? Assessing the Complexity of Lived Race," *American Sociological Review* 67, no. 4 (Aug. 2002): 621, 625. See also David R. Harris, "Does It Matter How We Measure? Racial Characteristics and the Classification of Multiracial Youth," in Perlmann and Waters, *The New Race Question*, 77–84.

51. Rockquemore and Brunsma, *Beyond Black*, 99, 41–50, 94–95. Those students who identified exclusively as "black" tended to have dark skin and reported little interaction with whites during their childhood. Representative of the respondents who self-identified as "white" was a young woman, Michelle, with a white mother and black father who grew up in an upper-middle-class home on the East Coast. "She remembers little of her paternal (black) grandparents because they did not play a significant role in her childhood. After moving several times before she was five, Michelle's parents settled in an affluent suburb of Boston, where they were both practicing physicians. She grew up in an all-white neighborhood and attended private elementary and then public high schools that were almost entirely white. Though she did have a close relationship with one black girl and her current best friend is Korean-American, Michelle's friendship networks have been largely white, as have all her boyfriends. She describes her few experiences in all-black environments as 'uncomfortable.' . . . Her logic for determining her racial identification is that she looks white, she is identified

by others as white, she was raised in a white community, she is culturally white, and therefore, she is white. In her mind, and in her social world, having a black parent does not preclude her from claiming a white identity" (41). Kerry Ann Rockquemore and David L. Brunsma found similar sentiments in their survey of 177 students in Detroit, some at a community college, some at a private liberal arts college: see Rockquemore and Brunsma, "Beyond Black? The Reflexivity of Appearances in Racial Identification among Black/White Biracials," in Herring, Keith, and Horton, *Skin Deep*, chap. 6. One of the men whom Rockquemore and Brunsma interviewed for the Detroit study had plastic surgery to solidify his identity as "white." An analysis of 1990 census data by Mary C. Waters found that almost one in three children with a white father and black mother identified as white. The analysis by Waters is included in Fletcher, "Interracial Marriages Eroding Barriers." Kathleen Odell Korgen examines the dating patterns of biracial college students in *From Black to Biracial: Transforming Racial Identity among Americans* (Praeger, 1998), chap. 4.

52. Rockquemore and Brunsma, *Beyond Black*, 89–90. Rockquemore and Brunsma characterize those who self-identify as "biracial" as having a "border identity," a term they borrow from the cultural theorist Gloria Anzaldúa. For some individuals, border status created an "added dimension" to their self-perception. Explained one student: "It is not that just being biracial is like you're two parts [white and black], you know, you have two parts but there is also the one part of being biracial where you sit on the fence. There's a third thing, a unique thing" (Rockquemore and Brunsma, *Beyond Black*, 43). A college senior, the child of an Austrian mother and a black American serviceman, who grew up in Portland, Oregon—a woman who was not part of Rockquemore and Brunsma's study—serves as a useful example of those individuals who reject race as a meaningful form of self-identification: "I was frequently told by friends and acquaintances that society will always label me as a black woman regardless of my mixed background. Sometimes mistaking my desire to claim my European background as wishing to identify with the dominant culture, I was questioned about my allegiance to the black community. In response, I argued that by identifying myself solely as black, I was denying a part of me. . . . Regardless of others' definitions and explanations, I could never quite comprehend the importance of defining myself by race or ethnicity. As a product of a family that did not stress race, it seemed odd to me for such emphasis to be placed upon one's racial background. I was criticized as being too idealistic for stressing the primary importance of regarding people as human rather than as members of a racial group" (Andrew Garrod et al., eds., *Souls Looking Back: Life Stories of Growing Up Black* [Routledge, 1999], 103). Ian Winchester, part Ghanaian, part Scottish-Norwegian, was a junior at the University of Maryland when he was interviewed for an article in the *New York Times*. When he was a boy, he said, his Scottish grandfather would dress him in a kilt. The other side of his family made him wear dashikis. "My family has been pulling me in two directions about what I am. I just want to be a person." See Susan

Saulny, "Black? White? Asian? More Young Americans Choose All of the Above," *New York Times*, Jan. 30, 2011. Even dark-skinned blacks have been known to reject race as a defining element of their self-identity. Yolanda Adams grew up in Baton Rouge, then went on to work in the newspaper business in Atlanta and Dallas. "Though my skin color veers toward the dark end of the spectrum, I have never been Black enough to satisfy some. My mannerisms have been my Achilles' heel since youth. I was often taunted for being 'proper' or 'acting White' because of how I dressed and spoke. My mother can be blamed, or applauded, for making me the anomaly I am. She wouldn't allow split infinitives or Ebonics. She also forbade me to think less of myself because of class (we lived in a shotgun house) or color—and where I grew up, color affected class. In fact, she encouraged me to do just the opposite. For the record, I am not denying that I'm a Black female who hates and suffers from racism. And I'm not saying I want to be White. I simply want to be neither. I can't deny I have dark skin, but I refuse to carry all the baggage that comes with my color. For better or worse, I have decided I don't want to be Black anymore." Yolanda Y. Adams, "Don't Want to Be Black Anymore," *Essence* 30, no. 4 (Aug. 1999): 54. The children of couples composed of a black father and white mother are especially vocal about wanting to be seen as biracial. See Hayward Derrick Horton and Lori Latrice Sykes, "Towards a Critical Demography of Neo-Mulattoes: Structural Change and Diversity within the Black Population," in Herring, Keith, and Horton, *Skin Deep*, 167. A member of the exclusive women's society the Links commented dismissively to Lawrence Otis Graham: "An emphasis on one's black lineage may get diluted by these rich young people who live a more integrated life than the rest of us. And of course some of these new biracial kids and adults don't care about blacks at all. But we'll survive them too" (Graham, *Our Kind of People*, 125).

53. Smith is quoted in Kennedy, *Interracial Intimacies*, 143. In 1997 Tiger Woods famously announced on Oprah Winfrey's television show that he thought of himself as "Cablinasian." As for the woman in the Rockquemore and Brunsma study with Irish ancestry: "Because people saw her as black first, many of her other roles were differentiated by race. She was defined (by others) as the 'black intern,' a 'black feminist,' a 'black student,' and a 'black friend'" (Rockquemore and Brunsma, *Beyond Black*, 44).

54. Obama, *Dreams from My Father*, 99.

55. Recent estimates suggest that roughly 75 percent of Americans with African ancestry also have European ancestry. Frank D. Bean, Jennifer Lee, Jeanne Batalova, and Mark Leach, "Immigration and Fading Color Lines in America," in Reynolds Farley and John Haaga, eds., *The American People: Census 2000* (Russell Sage Foundation, 2005), 323. For the comments by the man from Boston, see John Daniels, *In Freedom's Birthplace: A Study of Boston Negroes* (Arno, 1969), 183. When interviewed by Kimberly DaCosta for her investigation of "multiracial entrepreneurs," Upton conveyed a general discomfort with black people, especially those who are poor and have dark skin. But he also expressed a sense of alienation from light-skinned middle-class men and

women, including the kind of individuals of privilege he had known as a child at Jack and Jill. See DaCosta, *Making Multiracials,* 57–65.

REIMAGINING AMERICA

1. Pew Research Center, "Optimism about Black Progress Declines: Blacks See Growing Values Gap between Poor and Middle Class," Nov. 13, 2007, 4, available online at http://pewsocialtrends.org/files/2010/10/Race-2007.pdf, accessed Dec. 8, 2011.

2. A bare majority in the survey, 53 percent, responded that "it is still appropriate to think of blacks as a single race." Seven percent said they "don't know" and three percent responded "neither/both." For Eugene Robinson's response to the survey's results, see his *Disintegration: The Splintering of Black America* (Doubleday, 2010), 10.

3. Joel Williamson, *New People: Miscegenation and Mulattoes in the United States* (Free Press, 1980), chap. 2; F. James Davis, *Who Is Black? One Nation's Definition,* 10th anniversary ed. (Pennsylvania State University, 2001), chap. 4.

4. The one state where there was a sizeable representation of mixed-race planters was Louisiana, which due to its role in the French and Spanish empires had a distinct pattern of development. See, for example, Lawrence N. Powell, *The Accidental City: Improvising New Orleans* (Harvard University Press, 2012).

5. In the North, which declined to follow the South in restricting voting rights, the arrival of several million Southern migrants meant that black politicians were even able to win election as city councilmen, and, beginning with Oscar de Priest of Chicago in 1928, representatives to Congress.

6. The demographer Reynolds Farley is an example of someone who sees the possible emergence of a post-racial America. See comments by Farley in Michael A. Fletcher, "Interracial Marriages Eroding Barriers," *Washington Post,* Dec. 28, 1998. Other observers have suggested that we are witnessing the reinvention of the privileged men and women of mixed European and African ancestry as a distinct social entity, "a buffer zone" between whites and blacks. See, for example, Margaret L. Hunter, *Race, Gender, and the Politics of Skin Tone* (Routledge, 2005), 116; and Renee C. Romano, *Race Mixing: Black-White Marriage in Postwar America* (Harvard University Press, 2003), 283. That may have been the goal of the "colored aristocracy" of the antebellum era. But it is difficult to think of individuals who today occupy the highest levels of the American power structure as members of a racial "buffer" group.

7. The Pew Research Center findings are described in "Downward Mobility Trend Threatens Black Middle Class," *USA Today,* Apr. 2, 2011. On the vulnerability of a large segment of the middle class, see also Barbara Ehrenreich and Dedrick Muhammad, "The Recession's Racial Divide," *New York Times,* Sept. 12, 2009. The quotation by Williams is in Joel Garreau, *Edge City: Life on the New Frontier* (Anchor, 1992), 167. Research by sociologists Mary Pattillo and Colleen Heflin revealed that over 40 percent of

middle-class blacks have a poor brother or sister compared to just 16 percent of middle-class whites. See Mary Pattillo, *Black on the Block: The Politics of Race and Class in the City* (University of Chicago Press, 2007), 96.

8. Charles W. Mills, "Do Black Men Have a Moral Duty to Marry Black Women?" *Journal of Social Philosophy*, 25th anniversary special issue (1994): 139; Glenn C. Loury, *The Anatomy of Racial Inequality* (Harvard University Press, 2002), 51–52; Dan Bilefsky, "For New Life, Blacks in City Head to South," *New York Times*, June 1, 2011. Reverend Kenney's remarks are in Melissa Victoria Harris-Lacewell, *Barbershops, Bibles and BET: Everyday Talk and Black Political Thought* (Princeton University Press, 2003), 52.

9. A number of observers have called for a "Marshall Plan" for the inner cities. See, for example, Henry Louis Gates, "The Two Nations: The Best of Times, the Worst of Times," *Brookings Review* 16, no. 2 (Spring 1998): 7; Robinson, *Disintegration*, 213. For the comment by Randall Kennedy, see his "My Race Problem—And Ours," *Atlantic Monthly* (May, 1997): 64–65. Kennedy adds: "The fact that race matters, however, does not mean that the salience and consequences of racial distinctions are good or that race must continue to matter in the future." Elsewhere he has written compellingly that race should properly be acknowledged as a matter of personal choice. "Rather than chaining people forever to the racial status into which they were born, we should try to both eradicate the deprivations that have often impelled people to want to pass *and* protect individuals' capacity for racial self-determination, including their ability to revise racial identities." See Kennedy, *Sellout: The Politics of Racial Betrayal* (Vintage, 2008), 185, 80, 178. See also Kennedy, *Interracial Intimacies: Sex, Marriage, Identity, and Adoption* (Pantheon, 2003), 333.

10. Martin Luther King, Jr., *"All Labor Has Dignity,"* ed. Michael K. Honey (Beacon Press, 2011), 43.

11. Ibid. King used almost identical language in other speeches during this period. For example, at the Religious Leaders Conference in Washington, May 1959; at the Golden Anniversary Conference of the National Urban League in New York, Sept. 1960; at the National Press Club in Washington, July 1962. King's later role in organizing the Poor People's Campaign can be understood in terms of these long-held beliefs. But it is worth noting that he grew increasingly radical in the two years before his assassination, criticizing American involvement in the war in Vietnam and openly questioning the morality of capitalism. In an essay published posthumously he wrote: "The black revolution is much more than the struggle for the rights of Negroes. It is forcing America to face all its interrelated flaws—racism, poverty, militarism, and materialism. It is exposing evils that are rooted deeply in the whole structure of our society. It reveals systemic rather than superficial flaws and suggests that radical reconstruction of society itself is the real issue to be faced." Martin Luther King, Jr., *A Testament of Hope: The Essential Writings and Speeches of Martin Luther King, Jr.* (Harper Collins, 1986), 315.

12. "Letter from Thomas Jefferson to James Madison, October 28, 1785," in *The*

Founders' Constitution, 1, chap. 15, doc. 32, available online at http://press-pubs.uchicago .edu/founders/documents/v1ch15s32.html, accessed Dec. 9, 2011.

13. Elizabeth Gudrais, "Unequal America: Causes and Consequences of the Wide— and Growing—Gap between Rich and Poor," *Harvard Magazine* (July–Aug. 2008), available online at http://harvardmagazine.com/2008/07/unequal-america-html, accessed Dec. 9, 2011. In 2009, income inequality reached its highest level since the U.S. Census Bureau began tracking household income in 1967 (see http://economix.blogs.nytimes .com/2010/09/28/income-inequality-reached-high-in-2009, accessed Dec. 9, 2011). For census data on inequality, see http://www.census.gov/hhes/www/income/data/ historical/inequality, accessed Sept. 30, 2013; see also Congressional Budget Office, "Trends in the Distribution of Household Income in the United States between 1979 and 2007" (Oct. 2011), available online at http://www.cbo.gov/ftpdocs/124xx/doc12485/ 10–25-HouseholdIncome.pdf, accessed Dec. 9, 2011. The Gini coefficient, which is an internationally accepted measure of inequality, indicates that the United States has much greater disparity in income than any other industrialized nation—a distribution roughly equivalent to those of Cameroon, Madagascar, Rwanda, Uganda, Ecuador, Mexico, Ivory Coast, Sri Lanka, Nepal, and Serbia. See Max Fisher, "Map: U.S. Ranks Near Bottom on Income Inequality," *The Atlantic*, Sept. 19, 2011, available online at http://www.theatlantic.com/international/archive/2011/09/map-us-ranks-near-bottom -on-income-inequality/245315/, accessed Dec. 9, 2011.

ACKNOWLEDGMENTS

Imagining Black America is the product of more than thirty-five years of conversations with colleagues and friends about race and identity. And of engagement with the creative works of individuals I have never met, even as I have come to think of them as collaborators: professional historians, of course, but also novelists, poets, playwrights, journalists, filmmakers. I hope, then, I will be forgiven for limiting my acknowledgments to just three scholars whose valued and valuable contributions to my thinking extend back over many years. Larry Powell and I have been friends since our days as graduate students together at Yale. Our ongoing dialogue about American history has significantly influenced the interpretation in these pages, and his comments on drafts of my chapters have invariably been incisive and helpful. Beyond that, Larry's books and articles serve as models of how to wrap historical interpretation in engaging, accessible prose. John Ingham was the first historian at the University of Toronto to offer a course on the history of black Americans. We were colleagues for twenty-five years, teaching both graduate and undergraduate courses together. Thanks to John I have a deeper understanding of how the fact of slavery—and the presence of slaves and the descendants of slaves—shaped the experiences of other segments of American society. Rick Halpern arrived at the University of Toronto in 2001. He and I taught together as well. My thinking about the role that class has played in the formation of black identity owes much to our conversations. (My students and I have also benefited from his superb collection of blues recordings.)

I wish to thank Laura Davulis, Ash Lago, and Margaret Otzel of Yale University Press for their hard work in turning my manuscript into a published reality.

And Julie Carlson, my fine copy editor. With patience and good humor, Julie made sure that what I said was actually what I wanted to say.

The University of Toronto has been my institutional home for more than thirty years. I am exceedingly grateful to Donald Ainslie and the fellows at University College for providing me with a comfortable refuge (and an office) on campus in my retirement.

Imagining Black America is dedicated to the hundreds of students who have taken one of two undergraduate seminars I offered during my three decades of teaching at the University of Toronto: "Race Relations in America" and "Voices from Black America." So many of the themes I explore in these pages first came to life in classroom discussions. The book is also dedicated to the memory of Claire Clarke. Claire was born in Barbados in 1913 and came with her family to Canada when she was just eight. She grew up in the vibrant Caribbean community in downtown Toronto, spending happy childhood hours at the Universal Negro Improvement Association. She excelled in school, but gender conventions being what they were in those days, she concentrated on clerical courses, developing exceptional skills in stenography and typing. After graduation, she went looking for a secretarial position. While her resume got her some interviews, she received no job offers. She complained to a man she knew, an employee at city hall. "You won't get a job," he told her, "because the white girls won't work with you." Eventually she did find work: in the garment district, making hats. It would be almost a decade before she finally acquired the kind of clerical position for which she had trained, with the federal government. She remained a government employee for another forty years.

When she retired, Claire entered the University of Toronto, receiving a bachelor of arts degree in 1984, at the age of seventy-one. More than a decade later, she enrolled in my third-year course on the black experience in the United States since the Civil War. The two of us had many stimulating conversations outside the classroom: about her family history, about growing up in Toronto, and, yes, about black life in the United States. She had an aunt in New York, and she fondly reminisced about visiting her as a teenager, and hearing jazz in Harlem. For years after the course ended, we continued to get together from time to time for tea. She passed away in 2009, at the age of ninety-six. My memory of her lingers over these pages.

Finally, to the most important people in my life: my wife, Sandra, my daughters Beatrice and Maya, and my son, Seth. I only wish I could find adequate words to let you know how very much you have enriched my life by sharing my journey through History.

INDEX

Africa, 4, 6–7, 16, 23, 45, 71, 85, 94–95, 183, 189; black Americans' interest in, 54–57, 68, 130–39; emigration to, 51–59, 134; immigration from, 137–41; and independence movements, 130

Africans: black Americans' perception of, 53–58, 130–38; and colonial slavery, 6–9, 12, 15–16, 58

African Studies programs, 131

Afro (hairstyle), 127–30

Afrocentric features, 166, 170, 199

Afrocentrism, 131–35

Alexander, Michelle, 164, 167, 169–70, 199

Alien citizens, 28, 30–32, 46, 76

American Colonization Society (ACS), 50–53

American Dream, 32, 100, 109, 133–34, 158, 161–62, 179, 180, 182

Anderson, Benedict, 5

Anderson, Elijah, 150

Andom, Mary, 138

Anglo-Saxon, 25, 37, 54

Anthony, Sterling, 180

Anti-Drug Abuse Act of 1986, 163–64

Appiah, Kwame Anthony, 177

Asante, Molefi Kete, 131–33

Association of MultiEthnic Americans, 192

Atlanta, 45, 60, 87, 92, 123, 125, 137, 141–44

Bacon's Rebellion, 11–12

Baldwin, James, 76, 94

Ball, Charles, 16

Banks, Ralph Richard, 190

Banneker, Benjamin, 17

Basketball, 178

Battle-Walters, Kimberly, 160

Baxter-Brown, Joe, 157–58

Berlin, Ira, 15, 83

Black(s), black Americans: and American identity, 43–46, 50, 72, 75; and college education, 189–90; and drug use, 163; identity, 134–36, 196–97; and incarceration, 163–66; and intermarriage, 128–29, 187–91, 199; mayors, 123–27; middle class, 140–43, 156–57, 171–86, 190–91, 197–99; migration north, 44–45; military service, 67–73; and poverty, 143, 147–50; relationship to European immigrants, 75–76; and suburbanization 141–42; "victimization" of, 181–82

The Blacker the Berry. See Wallace Thurman

"Black Is Beautiful," 126–27

Black Metropolis, 92

Black nationalism, 57, 61, 75, 118, 120, 127

Black Panther Party, 119–23, 127